Edward IV.

THE

PASTON LETTERS

1422-1509 A.D.

A Reprint of the Edition of 1872-5, which
Contained upwards of Five Hundred
Letters, etc., till then unpublished, to
which are now added others in a
Supplement after the Introduction

EDITED BY

JAMES GAIRDNER

Of the Public Record Office

VOLUME II

EDWARD IV.

1461-1471 A.D.

EDINBURGH: JOHN GRANT

31 GEORGE IV BRIDGE

1910

The Paston Letters.

Edward IV.

384.

A.D. 1461.—John Paston the Youngest to ———.

[From Fenn, i. 226.]

According to Fenn, this letter is in the original "without either date, name, or direction," the contents only proving it to have been written by "one of John Paston's sons." Nevertheless, in a very misleading way, the signature "John Paston" is inserted at the foot of the right hand copy, with a reference to a fac-simile of the signature of John Paston the youngest. There is every appearance, however, that John Paston the youngest really was the writer, and that the date is, as Fenn supposes, just after the accession of Edward IV.

Recomand me to yow, and lete yow wete that notwythstandyng tydinggs come down, as ye know, that pepill shuld not come up tyll thei were sent fore, but to be redy at all tymes; this notwithstandyng, most pepill owt of this cuntre have take wages, seying thei woll goo up to London; but thei have no capteyn, ner rewler assigned be the commissioners to awayte upon, and so thei stragyll abowte be them self, and be lyklynes are not like to come at London half of them. And men that come from London sey, there have not passid Thetford, not passyng CCCC.; and yet the townes and the cuntere that have waged hem shall thynk thei be discharged, and therfore if this Lords above wayte aftyr more pepill in this cuntre, be lyklynes it woll not be easy to get with owt a newe comission and warnyng. And yet it woll be thought ryght straunge of hem that have

waged pepill to wage any more, for every towne hath
waged and sent firth, and are redy to send forth, as
many as thei ded whan the Kyng sent for hem be fore
the feld at Lodlowe;[1] and thei that ar not go, be goyng
in the same forme.

Item, ther was shrewd rewle toward in this cuntre,
for ther was a certeyn person forth wyth after the
jurney at Wakefeld, gadered felaship to have mo[r]dered
John Damme, as is seyd; and also ther is at the
Castell of Rysing, and in other ij. plases, made gret
gaderyng of pepill, and hyryng of harneys, and it is
wele undyrstand they be not to the Kyng ward, but
rather the contrary, and for to robbe. Wherfore my
fadyr is in a dowte, whedir he shall send my brother
up or not, for he wold have his owne men abowte hym,
if nede were here; but notwythstandyng, he wyll send
up Dawbeney, his spere and bowes with hym, as Stapilton and Calthrop or other men of worship of this cuntre
agree to doo. Wherfore demene yow in doyng of yowr
erandes ther aftyr, and if ye shall bryng any masage
from the Lords, take writyng, for Darcorts massage
is not verely beleved be cause he browt no wrytyng.

Item, this cuntre wold fayne take these fals shrewes that
are of an oppynion contrary to the Kyng and his Counsell, if they had no auctorite from the Kyng to do so.

Item, my brother is redy[n] to Yarmowth for to lette
brybers that wold a robbed a ship undyr color of my
Lord of Warwyk, and longe nothyng to hem ward.

385.

A.D. 1461, 4 April.
W. Paston and Th. Playters to John Paston.

[From Fenn, i. 216.]

The date of this letter is sufficiently apparent from the contents.

---

[1] The battle of Mortimer's Cross, near Ludlow, gained by Edward IV.
before he was king, on the 3d February 1461.

To my maister, John Paston, in hast.

PLEASE you to knowe and wete of suche tyd-yngs as my Lady of York hath by a lettre of credens, under the signe manuel of oure Soverayn Lord King Edward, whiche lettre cam un to oure sayd Lady this same day, Esterne Evyn,[1] at xj. clok, and was sene and red be me, William Paston.

Fyrst, oure Soverayn Lord hath wonne the feld,[2] and uppon the Munday[3] next after Palmesunday, he was resseved in to York with gret solempnyte and processyons. And the Mair and Comons of the said cite mad ther menys to have grace be Lord Montagu[4] and Lord Barenars,[5] whiche be for the Kyngs coming in to the said cite desyred hym of grace for the said cite, whiche graunted hem grace. On the Kyngs parte is slayn Lord Fitz Water, and Lord Scrop sore hurt; John Stafford, Horne of Kent ben ded; and Umfrey Stafford, William Hastyngs mad knyghts with other; Blont is knygth, &c.

Un the contrary part is ded Lord Clyfford, Lord Nevyle, Lord Welles, Lord Wyllouby, Antony Lord Scales, Lord Harry, and be supposyng the Erle of Northumberland, Andrew Trollop, with many other gentyll and comons to the nomber of xx.ml. [20,000.]

Item, Kyng Harry, the Qwen, the Prince, Duke of Somerset, Duke of Exeter, Lord Roos, be fledde in to Scotteland, and they be chased and folwed, &c. We send no er [*no sooner*] un to you be cause we had non certynges tyl now; for un to this day London was as sory cite as myght. And because Spordauns had no certeyn tydyngs, we thought ye schuld take them a worthe tyl more certayn.

[1] 4th April.
[2] The battle of Towton, fought on Palm Sunday, the 29th March 1461.
[3] 30th March.
[4] John Nevill, Lord Montague, brother of the Earl of Warwick.
[5] Sir John Bourchier, Lord Berners.

Item, Thorp Waterfeld is yeldyn, as Spordauns can telle you. And Jesu spede you. We pray you that this tydyngs my moder may knowe.

Be your Broder,   W. PASTON.
T. PLAYTERS.

"On a piece of paper pinned to the above letter," says Fenn, "is a list of the names of the noblemen and knights, and the number of soldiers slain at the above battle of Towton, as follow :—"

Comes Northumbriæ.	Millites.
Comes Devon.	Sir Rauff Gray.
Dominus de Beamunde.	Sir Ric. Jeney.
Dominus de Clifford.	Sir Harry Bekingham.
Dominus de Nevyll.	Sir Andrew Trollop.
Dominus de Dacre.	With xxviij.$^{ml.}$ [28,000]
⎰ Dominus Henricus de ⎱ Bokyngham.	nomberd by Harralds.
Dominus de Well[es].	
⎰ Dominus de Scales ⎱ Antony Revers.	
Dominus de Wellugby	
⎰ Dominus de Malley ⎱ Radulfus Bigot Miles.	

386.

A.D. 1461, 18 April.

THOMAS PLAYTERS TO MASTER JOHN PASTON.

[From Fenn, i. 222.]

This letter relates mainly to occurrences just after the battle of Towton in April 1461.

To my maister, John Paston, Esquyer.

PLEASE your Maisterchep to wete, that I have spokyn with Essex, in the matter that ye wete of, and fynd him be his talkyng wel

dysposed, not withstandyng he woll not falle to no
conclusyon to engrose up the mater, tyll the chef
baron[1] be com to London, and that he be mad privy
to the mater, which we loke after this same secund
Saterday[2] after Esterne; and as for Notyngham he is
not yet comyn to London.

Item, as for tydyng, it is noysed and told for trouth
of men of worchip, and other, that the Erle of Wylchyr
is taken, Doctor Morton,[3] and Doctor Makerell, and
be brougth to the kyng at York. Maister William also
spak with a man that sey hem.

Item, sir, I herd of Sir John Borceter and Christofer
Hanson, that Herry the sext is in a place in York
schire is calle Coroumbr; suche a name it hath, or
muche lyke. And there is sege leyde abowte, and
dyvers squyers of the Erle of Northumbrelands, and
gadered them to geder, a v. or vj.ᵐˡ· [*five or six thousand*] men, to byger [*bicker*] with the sege, that in the
mene while Herry the sexte myght have ben stole a
way at a lytyll posterne on the bak syde; at whiche
byker ben slayn iij.ᵐˡ· [3000] men of the North.
Sir Robert of Ocle and Conyrs leyth the sege on
our syde, and thei it is that have do this acte. Sum
say the Qwen, Somerset and the Prince schuld be
there. Item, it is talked now for trouthe, the Erle
of Northumberland is ded. Item, the Erle of Deven-
shire is ded justely.[4] Item, my Lord Chaunceler is to
York. Item, the King and the Lords com not here
before Whitsontyde, as it is sayde. Item, sir, sone
uppon the chef baron comyng I schall send you a
lettre, with Godds grace, who preserve you, and have
you in His blyssed kepyng.   Your,

                              THOMAS PLAYTERS.

At Cokermouthe was the Erle of Wylchire taken,
and these other Doctors. Item, som men talke Lord

---

[1] Peter Arderne.   [2] 18th April in 1461.
[3] Afterwards Cardinal, the Minister of Henry VII.
[4] He was beheaded at York after the battle of Towton.

Wellys, Lord Wyllouby, and Skales ben on lyve.
Item, Sir Robert Veer is slayn in Cornewayll, as it is
tok for trouthe.

387.

A.D. 1461, May.

THOMAS PLAYTERS TO JOHN PASTON.

[From Fenn, iv. 2.]

The reference to the Earl of Wiltshire's head having been set on London
bridge shows this letter to have been written not very long after the battle of
Towton. The exact date is probably about the beginning of May, as it
appears, by the Privy Seal dates in the Record Office, that Edward IV. was
at Middleham on the 6th of that month on his way southwards, having gone
on to Durham and Newcastle after the victory.

*To my rigth reverent and worchipfull John Paston,
Esquyer, or to my maytres his wyf.*

AFTER my most special recommendacion, lyke
your maisterchip wete that the mater for
you and my maistrez, your moder, ayens
Powtrell and Tanfeld hath ben called uppon
as dylygently and as hastely this terme as it mygth be ;
and al way dayes yeven hem by the Court to answer,
and than thei toke smale excepcions, and trifeled
forth the Court, and al wey excused them by cause the
bylle is long, and his councell had no leysur to se it.
And they prayed heryng of the testament of my maister
your fader,[1] and therof made a nother mater, and argued
it to putte hem fro it, be cause they had emparled to
us by fore ; and than Hyllyngworth to dryve it over
this terme, allegged varians be twyx the bille and the
testament that John Damme was named in the testament John Dawme, in whiche cas now the Court must
have sigth of the said testament.   Where fore ye must
send it up the begynnyng of the next terme, or elles we
schall have no sped in the mater.   And therfor, Maistres, if my maister be not cum hom, and ye have not

[1] William Paston, the Judge, who died in 1444.

the sayd testament in your kepyng, that than it plese you to speke un to my maistres, your moder in lawe,[1] for the seyd testament, that I mygth redely have it here, and that it be sealed in a box, and sent to me, and I schall kepe it safe, with Godds grace.

And as for tytyngs, in good feyth we have non, seve the Erle of Wylchir[2] is hed is sette on London Brigge.

Mayster William is reden hom to my Maistrs Ponyngs ; and as for Maister Ponyngs hymself, sche letteth as thow sche wyst not where he were. A gentylman that kam fro York told me my maister was heyl and mery, and rode to mete the Kyng comyng fro Mydlam Castell.

Berwyk[3] is full of Scottys, and we loke be lyklyhod after anoyther batayll now be twyx Skotts and us.

And I pray Jesu have you in His blyssed kepyng.

Your,   THOMAS PLAYTER.

388.

A.D. 1461, 10 May.

JOHN SMYTH TO JOHN PASTON, SENIOR.

[From Paston MSS., B.M.]

This letter was evidently written in the beginning of Edward IV.'s reign ; and as it appears by No. 392 that Paston had already been dispossessed of Caister, not indeed by the Duke of Suffolk, but by the Duke of Norfolk, as early as the 5th June 1461, we may presume that this letter, dated in May, belongs to that year. The margin of the letter is slightly mutilated ; but the words which are lost are obvious, and have been supplied in brackets.

To hys worschepfull mayster, John Paston the Eldest, Esquier.

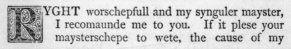

YGHT worschepfull and my synguler mayster, I recomaunde me to you. If it plese your maysterschepe to wete, the cause of my

---

[1] Agnes Paston, the widow of the Judge.
[2] James Butler, Earl of Wiltshire and Ormond.
[3] Henry VI. and his Queen after the battle escaped to Berwick, and from thence retired to Edinburgh.—F.

wryghtyng is thys.   I have understande be comunyng
with othyr credybell men that many and the more
part of the feffeys of the landys late Sir John Fastolf, and also thei that pretende to ben executores
of the seyd Sir John, purpose them to sell to my Lord
of Suffolk, thow he recuver not be tayle, or to othyr
myghty lordys, a gret part of the landys of the seyd
Sir John, to the entent that ye schal not have them ;
upon wech sale thei wole make astate and entre and
put you to your accion, and thow ye recuver in the
lawe, as I am enformyd, ye schall recuver of hard and
but a part, the qwech schuld be dere of the sute.
Qwer it semyth to me, yt wer necessarye to you to se
remedy for thys mater, and eyther putt it in award or
elles that my Lord of Wa[rwick], the qwech is your good
Lord, may meve that the Kyng, or hym sylf, or my Lord
Chawmbyrleyn or sum othyr wytty me[n], may take a
rewle betwexe you and your adversaryes ; for yf ye may
not holde the forseyd landys ther schal growe [great]
losse bothe to the dede and to you, and men schal
putt you in defawte therof ; your frendys schal be
sory.   It is [better to] bere a lyttell losse than a gret
rebuke.   Your mater hangyth longe in the audyens.
Yf ye hadde ther your entent your ad[versaries should]
cese the rather.   I beleve veryly yf ye do your part to
have pees, God of Hys gret grace schal graunte it to
you, the q[wech give] you the speryte of wysdam to
gyde you on to Hys pleser.   Amen.

We desyre to se your maysterschep in Norffolk ;
your pr[esens] there be necessarye.

From Norwych the x. day of May.

                Your clerk,   [JOHN] SMYTH.

389.

A.D. 1461, May.

THOMAS DENYES TO JOHN PASTON.

[From Fenn, iv. 10.]

The writer of this letter speaks of having served with the Earl of Warwick

at the battle of Northampton in July 1460, and again at the second battle
of St. Alban's in February 1461. We know from later letters that he was
murdered in the beginning of July following. As he dates from York, and
speaks of being "here in the King's house," the date would appear to be
about the 10th of May, on which day we find by the dates of the Privy
Seals that Edward IV. was at York.

To my Maister Paston.

RIGHT wurshipfull and myn especiall good
maister, I recomaund me to yow with all my
service, besechyng you hertily, at the reverence of God, to helpe me now in the grettest
extremite that I cam at sith my greet trobil with Ingham.[1] It is not oute of your remembraunce how Twyer
in Norff[olk] vexith me bothe by noise and serchyng
myn house for me, so that theer I can not be in quyete;
and all that, I am verily acerteyned, is by Heydens
crafft. And heer in the Kyngs house annenst Howard,[2]
wher I had hopid to a' relevid myself, I am supplanted
and cast oute from hym by a clamour of all his servaunts at onys, and ne wer oonly that his disposicion
acordyth not to my pouer conceyte, which maketh me
to gif lesse force, be cause I desire not to dele ther
[*where*] bribery is like to be usid, ellis by my trouth this
unhappy unkyndenes wold I trow a' killed me.   I pray
yow, at the reverence of Jesu Criste, to enfourme my
Lord of Warwyk of me.   Parde I haf do hym service;
I was with hym at Northampton, that all men knew;
and now agayn at Seynt Albones, that knowth James
Ratcliff; and ther lost I xx*li.* wurth horse, herneys, and
mony, and was hurte in diverse places.   I pray yow to
gete me his good Lordship, and that I may be toward
hym in Norffolk in his Courts holdyng, or ellis, if ony
thyng he haf to do; and that ye wole gete me a letter
to Twyer to late me to sit in rest.   For now if I made
any felaship agayn Twyer, I can haf no colour now
the Shirref and I be oute, so I must kepe me aparte,
which I am lothe to do, be God, if I myght better do.

---

[1] *See* Nos. 198, 199.
[2] Sir John Howard, who was sheriff of Norfolk this year.

I besech yow to send me your intent by the next
man that come from yow.   I shuld a' come to zow,
but, so help me God, my purs may no ferther.   The
Holy Trinite preserve yow.

Wretyn hastily at York, &c.

Your to his power,

DENYES.

390

A.D. 1461, 31 May.
THE EARL OF OXFORD TO JOHN PASTON.

[Douce MS. 393, f. 85.]

The date of this letter may, with great probability, be attributed to the
year 1461.   It certainly cannot be later, as the writer was executed for high
treason in February 1462.   He was found to have been corresponding with
Margaret of Anjou for the restoration of Henry VI., but the discovery must
have been much later than May 1461.   Sir John Howard, who, for his
services to the House of York, was afterwards made Duke of Norfolk,
appears to have had great influence just after the accession of Edward IV.,
which he used in a very overbearing manner; and we have already seen, by
the last letter, that the Earl of Oxford's servant, Thomas Denyes, was at this
very time suffering much persecution at his hands.

To owre right trusty and welbeloved John Paston.

TH'ERL OF OXENFORD.

RIGHT trusty and welbeloved, we grete yow
well, and pray yow, as oure trust is in yow,
that if ye or any of yowre men here that
Howard purposith hym to make any aray at
owre manor of Wynche, that ye woll lete John Keche,
owre kepere ther of, haue wetyng by tymes, for and
he have warnyng he will kepe it in to the tyme that
we come thedir, with the grace of God, wiche have
yow in His kepyng.   Wretyn in owre manor of
Wyvynho the last day of May.

OXENFORD.

391.

A.D. 1461.—Thomas Playter to John Paston.

[From Fenn, i. 230.]

It is evident from the contents that this letter was written some time before
the coronation of Edward IV.

To my right good maister, John Paston, in all hast.

FTER my most special recommendacion,
please your maisterchip wete, the Kyng,
be cause of the sege a boute Carelylle,
chaunged his day of Coronacion to be upon
the Sunday[1] nexst after Seynt John Baptyste, to the'n-
tent to spede hym northward in all hast; and how
be it, blyssed be God, that he hath now good tydynggs,
that Lord Mountagu hath broken the sege, and slayn
of Scotts vj.ml. [6000] and ij. knyghes, whereof Lord
Cliffords brother is one, yet not wythstandyng he wol be
crowned the sayd Sunday.   And John Jeney enformed
me, and as I have verely lerned sethen, ye ar inbylled
to be made knygth at this Coronacion.[2]   Wheder ye
have understandyng before hand, I wot not; but and
it lyke you to take the worchip uppon you, consyderyng
the comfortable tytynggs afore seyd, and for the glad-
nesse and plesour of al your welwyllers, and to the
pyne and dyscomfort of all your ille wyllers, it were
tyme your gere necessarye on that by halfe were
purveyd fore, and also ye had nede higth you to
London, for as I conceyve the knygthes schuld be
made uppon the Saterday by for the Coronacion ; and
as moche as may be purveyed for you in secrete wyse
wythouten cost I schall by speke for you, if nede
be, ayens your comyng, in trust of the best; neverthelesse, if ye be dysposed, ye had nede send a man by

[1] 28th June.
[2] John Paston was not made knight at the Coronation of Edward IV., but
his eldest son was made knight, probably as a substitute for himself, within
two years after.

fore in all hast, that no thing be to seke. William Calthorp is inbylled, and Yelvertoun is inbylled, whiche caused Markham; because Yelverton loked to have ben chef juge, and Markham thynketh to plese hym thus. And as for the mater ayens Poutrell, we can no farther procede, tyl we have my maister your faders testament. I sent my maistres a letter for it. No more, but I pray Al myghty Jesu have you in His kepyng.

Your,   THOMAS PLAYTER.

392.

A.D. 1461, 5 June.
RICHARD CALLE TO JOHN PASTON.

[From Fenn, iv. 6.]

The date of this letter, like that of the last, is shown by a reference to the approaching Coronation of Edward IV.

To my right reverent worschipfull master, my Master John Paston.

RIGHT reverent and worschipfull master, I lowly recomande me unto your good mastership. Plesith you to witte that I have ben at Framelyngham, and spake Ric Sothwell to hafe hes advice in this mater; wherin he wolde geve me but litell councell, and seide ze were straungely disposed, for ye trusted no man, and had moche langage, weche the berer herof schal enforme your mastership.

And as for the letters, they were delivered my Lorde[1] at the Logge, but I cowde not speke with hese Lordeschip. And suche tyme as they were delyvered Fitz William whas there, weche is now keper of Castre; and what tyme as my Lorde had sene the lettres, he comaunded hym to avoide, and so he did. And

[1] The Duke of Norfolk, who appears by this time to have taken possession of Caister, and appointed a keeper for it.

thanne my Lorde sent for Sothwell. And in the meene tyme my Lorde sent a man to me, and axed me where ye were, and I tolde hem ye were with the Kyng; and so he sent me worde that an answere schulde be made be Sothwel to the King, seyng that ii. or iij. eyers [*heirs*] had ben with my Lorde, and shewed her [*i.e.* their] evidence, and delyvered it to my Lorde, seyng they have had gret wrong, besechyng my Lorde that it myght be reformed. Wherfor he comaunded me that I shulde go hom, for other answer cowde I non have. So I aboude uppon Sothwel to a' know my Lordes answer to the Kyng; weche answere Sothwel tolde me was, that he writeth to the Kyng that certeine points in your lettres be untrew, and that he schal prove suche tyme as he cometh befor the Kyng, besechyng the Kyng to take it to no displesur; for he is advised to kepe it still unto the tyme that he hath spaken with his Highnesse, for he trusteth to God to schewe suche evidence to the Kyng and to the Lords, that he schulde have best right and titill therto; and so he sent a man forthe to the Kyng this day. It were right wele don ye awayted upon hes man comyng, that ye myght knowe the redy entent of my Lordes writyng.

Berthelmew Elysse hathe ben with my Lorde, and made a relesse to my Lord; and Sir Will Chamberleine was ther ij. dayes afore I come thirder, I can thynke for the sam mater. And Thomas Fastolf whas there the same tyme that I was ther; and as I am enformed, they have delyvered my Lorde serteine evidence. Wherfore me semeth it were right wele don, savyng your better advice, to com hom and sele up your evidence, and have hem with you to London, to prove his titill noght. Ther be but ij. or iij. men with in the place, and if ye thynke it best to do it, send word, and I suppose a remedy schal be had.

Also I here no word of Master William, nor of the writts for the Parlament. Also it is tolde here that Tudenham [1] and Heydon have a pardon of the Kyng,

---

[1] Sir Thomas Tuddenham was beheaded in February following.

and that they schal come up to London with the Lady
of Suffolk to the Coronacion.   Also as for the letter
that ye sent to Thomas Wyngfeld, I have it still, for
he is at London.   Some men sey he meved my Lord
for to entre, and some sey Fitz William is in defaute.
So I can see ther is but fewe goode.   Also my master
Sir Thomas Howys schol send a letter to the person
ye wote of, for to deliver you the gere at London the
next week.   My right wourschipfull and reverent master,
Almyghti God preserve you.

Wreten at Norweche, on the morwe after Corpus
Christi Day.

Your pore servant and bedman,

R. C.

393.

A.D. 1461, 19 June.

ROBERT LETHUM TO JOHN PASTON.

[From Paston MSS., B.M.]

As we find by the last letter that John Paston was with the King in the
beginning of June 1461, this may with great probability be attributed to the
same year.

*A tres reverent Sire, John Paston, Esquier, demouraunt
ou lostell le Roy soit d[onne].*

RIGHT worshipfull sir, I recomaund me to you.
And, sir, yesterday I resceived of you a lettre
from oure sovereign lord the Kyng directe to
John Fulman, dyvers othir, and me, by the
quych, for certeyn causes that meved hym, and for the
well and save gard of his person and this his realme,
he desired we chuld fynd men for kepyng of the see.
I said to you that I hade beyn dyvers tymes spoled
and robbed, as ye have herd, and also gretely vexed
and sued to me [*my*] unportab[l]e [charges] ;[1] nevir the
les, to my pouer, with my body and my gode, I chall

[1] Omitted in MS.

be redy to do hym servyce in resistyng his enmyse
and rebelles. Also I said I dwelled uppon the cost
of the see here, and be langage hit were more neces-
sare to with hold men here than take from hit. The
said the Kyng hade wreton to dyvers persones here
quych hade promysed men, queruppon I promysed a
man, quych chall be redy at such tyme I have knowe-
lege quere the shippyng chall be, to waite uppon yow,
or quane the Kyng comaundes. I write to you of my
promyse as ye comaund me, and pray you I may have
a copy of the said lettre. And I pray Godd kepe you.
Wrete at Plumsted on the Fest of Seynt Gervaise and
Prothase.[1]

Your,   ROBT. LETHUM.

394.

A.D. 1461, 21 June.
JAMES GRESHAM TO JOHN PASTON.

[From Fenn, i. 232].

Like Nos. 391 and 392, this letter refers to the approaching Coronation of
Edward IV.

*To my right worshipfull maister, John Paston, at
Heylesdon in Norffolk, in hast.*

FTER due recomendacion hadde; please it
your Maistership to witte, that as for Plaiter
he shall excuse the writte of the parlement,
&c. As touchyng my maister Howard,[2] I cannot yet speke with hym, ne with Moungomerye[3] nether.
But as for the day of Coronacion of the Kyng, it shall
be certeynly the Moneday next after Mydsomer, and
it is told me that ye among other ar named to be
made knyght atte Coronacion, &c.

[1] 19th June.
[2] Sir John Howard.   [3] Sir Thomas Montgomery.

Item, it is seid that the Coronacion do, the Kyng wole in to the north part forthwith; and therfor shall not the parlement holde, but writtes shall goo in to every shire to gyve them, that ar chosyn knyghtes of the shire, day after Michelmesse; this is told me by suyche as arn right credible. Maister Brakle shall preche at Poules on Sunday next comyng as he tolde me, and he tolde me, that for cause Childermesse day[1] fal on the Sunday, the Coronacion shall on the Moneday, &c.

Wretyn in hast at London, the Sunday next tofore Mydsomer,

Your right pouere servant,

JAMES GRESHAM.

395.

A.D. 1461, 26 June.
CLEMENT PASTON TO JOHN PASTON.

[From Paston MSS., B.M.]

Elizabeth Paston, who, as we have seen (No. 322), had been married to Robert Poynings by the beginning of the year 1459, became his widow in 1461, her husband being killed in the second battle of St. Alban's on the 17th February. It would appear by this letter that she was immediately after

---

[1] Childermas, or Holy Innocents' Day, the 28th of December, fell on Sunday in the year 1460. The day of the week on which it fell used to be considered ominous or unlucky during the whole ensuing year. This superstition seems to have continued as late as the beginning of last century, and is alluded to by Addison in the 7th number of the "Spectator." It is not true, however, that Edward's Coronation was put off till Monday. It took place on the Sunday which had been originally appointed for it, but the processions and pageantry were deferred till next day. The following is the account of the matter given in a contemporary chronicle in the Cottonian MS., Vitellius, A. xvi.

"And upon the morn, Sunday, which was St. Peter's Even, and the 28th day of June, he was crowned at Westminster with great solemnity of bishops and other temporal lords. And upon the morn after, the King went crowned again in Westminster Abbey, in the worship of God and St. Peter. And upon the next morn he went also crowned in St. Paul's in the worship of God and St. Paul; and there the angel came down and censed him. At which time was as great a multitude of people in Paul's as ever was seen afore in any days."

dispossessed of her husband's lands by Eleanor, Countess of Northumberland, who was Baroness Poynings in her own right.

To my rythe worchypfull broder, John Paston, be thys delyveryd in haste.

BRODER, I recomawnde me to zow, desyeryng to here of yowre welfare, the qwyche I pray God mayntene. Plesse yow to wette that I have sent my moder a letter for mony for my swster;[1] and if ze wyll agre that I may have xx[ti]*li.* [£20], I xall zeve zow acowmpts ther of, and ze xall be payyd azen of the obligacyon that my moder hathe, or ellys I xall take a swerte of my suster. I wysse obligacion mwste nedes be swyd, and a doseyn accions more in her name, and sche doo well thys terme; and it wyll be doo with in fowertenyut. The Cowntas of Northumberlond[2] and Robarde Fenus[3] ocupie all her lond, and that is a gret myscheffe. I prey zow spe[ke] to my moder her of, and lat me have a awnswer within this sevenyut. Also, broder, Wyndham is come to town, and he seyd to me he wyll goo gett hym a mayster, and me thowte by hym he wold be in the Kynges servise, and he saythe that he wyll have Felbryg azen or Myhelmes, or ther shal be v.[c.] [500] heds broke ther fore. Brodere, I pray zow delyver the mony that I xwld have in to swm prior of swm abbey to swm mayster of swm colage to be delyveryd qwan I can espy ony londe to be porchasyd. I pray zow send me word wyder ze wyll doo thus or no. No more, but owre Lord have zow in Hys kepyng. Wrytyn on Fryday nexst after Seynt John is day.

By zour broder,

CLEMENT PASTON.

---

[1] Elizabeth Paston, now widow of Robert Poynings.
[2] Eleanor, widow of Henry Percy, third Earl, who was slain at Towton in 1461.
[3] Fenys.

396.

A.D. 1461, June.

MARGARET PASTON TO JOHN PASTON.

[From Paston MSS., B.M.]

This letter appears from internal evidence to have been written some time after the second battle of St. Alban's, which was fought in February 1461, and before the murder of Thomas Denys in July following. But to all appearance it was not very long before the latter date. The MS. is mutilated, and a few words are lost in eight consecutive lines.

To my right worchepfull hosbond, John Paston, be this letter deliveryd in hast.

RIGHT worchepfull hosbond, I recommand me to you. Please you to wete that thys day in the mornyng the parson of Snoryng came to Thomas Denys and fechyd hym owt of hys hows, and beryth hym a hand,[1] that he shuld a mad byllys agayns Twyer and hym, and hathe a leed hym ferthe with hem. Hys wyf hathe no knowlege of it. Ferther more the seid parson seythe that the seyd Thomas Denys shuld a take sowdyors owt of hys felachep whan he went to Seynt Albons;[2] that hys a nother of hys compleynts. Item, anothyr of hys compleynts ys, a beryth the seyd Thomas a hand,[1] that he had awey a hors of John Coppyng of Bryslee, and a nother of Kyng of Donham, the wyche hors were stole be the seyd ij. personys. Wher for the seyd Thomas toke hem as a comyshaner and delyveryd hem to the exchetor, Frances Costard, and one of them he bowt of the seyd Fraunces. And the seyd parson hathe a wey the seyd hors, and seyth that he wolle the seyd thevys shuld be recompenst be Thomas Denys. Thys I am enformyd of all thesse maters be hys wyffe, and sche prayythe yow in the reverence of God ye wolle be hyr good maister, and helpe that hyr hosbond may have

[1] *i.e.* accuses him. *See* Vol. i. p. 90, Note.
[2] Thomas Denys was at the second battle of St. Alban's in February 1461, *See* No. 389.

sume remedy be your labor in thys mater, [for she] seythe syn that hyr hosbond ys the Kyngs offycer, that they owt to spar hym the rather. But they that hathe hym take no . . . . . . told me that they hope to have a newe chonge in hast.

Item, Pers that was with my unkyll Barney[1] sent you a l[etter] . . . . . . er desyryng to have your good masterchep, and he woll fyynd sufficient suerte[2] for hym for to com . . . . . . whan som ever ye woll require hym. I' good feyth it ys told me hys leggs ar all . . . . . . [Send] me word, encas the suerte be sufficient, in what sum ye woll have hem bownd for hy . . . . . . te in bayle. Item, it ys told me that ther be many Freynche shyppys of se a geyns Yarmothe, a[nd . . . . . . t]hey woll do harme on the coste. I pray yow hertely that ye woll send me word in hast howe that ye do with my [Lord] of Norffolk, and with your adversaryys. Item, I have do purveyed in thys wareyn xj.ˣˣ· [*eleven score*] rabets and sent up be the berer herof. The blyssyd Trinite have yow in Hys kepyng, and send yow the better of all your adversariis, and good sped in all your maters. Wretyn in hast, the same day that ye departyd hens.

Item, I pray yow that ye wolle remembre my unkyll Barneys mater tochyng the executyng of hys wylle, and how ye wolle that we be demenyd for kepyng of hys yerday, and that it lekyth you to send me word be Mr. John Smy[th.]

397.

A.D. 1461, July.

THOMAS DENYES TO MARGARET PASTON.

[From Fenn, iv., 18].

This letter speaks of the county of Norfolk as being in an unquiet state, and of John Paston as having been elected knight of the shire. It will be seen by

1 John Berney,
2 *See* Letter 362, which it thus appears was written about this time, and not in the preceding year.

No. 392 that writs for an election were expected as early as the 5th of June
in 1461, and as I find that the writer of this letter was murdered on the 4th
of July following, the date is probably about the very beginning of that
month. From what is said at the beginning of the letter about Paston's
absence from home, it was evidently some time after the last, which was
written on the very day of his departure.

*To my right noble and wurshipfull mastresse, my Mas-
tresse Paston, or to William Paston if she be absent.*

RIGHT noble and wurshipfull mastresse, I recomaund me to yow with my pouer servise.
And for so moche as I here no thyng of my
maister your husbonds comyng hastly home,
—and though he cam or come not, it were expedient
that the Kyng were infourmed of the demenyng of the
shire,—therfore I send to yow a testymonyall, which
is made by a greet assent of greet multitude of comons,
to send to the Kyng. I pray you for the good spede
therof that in all hast possible ye like to send it to my
said maister, if he be with the Kyng; ellis fynde the
meane to send it to the Kyng, thogh my maister be
thens; beside forthe that ye vouchsauf to late diligent
labour be made to a sufficient nombir to assele for my
Maister Paston allone, for if bothe holde not, I wolde
oon helde.

I pray yow that it lyke you to send for my Maister
William Paston, and shew hym all thys, and that it
were hastid; for on the adversaire parte Judas slepith
not.

Berney promised to a' sent, but for our Lords love
trust not that; for I se his slouthe and sely labour,
which is no labour. And I wold ful fayn speke with
yow, &c.

My maister your husbond wole peraventure blame
us all, if this mater be not applied; for he may not of
reson do so largely heryn by his myght, be cause he is
elyted, as the Comons myght wisely do with help of
his favour, if it wer wisely wrought. If my Maister
William Paston ride hastly from a x. daies to London,
I wole with hym, if he send me word. The Holy

Trinite preserve yow. Wretyn rudely in hast the Sunday, &c.

Men sey, send a wiseman on thy erand, and sey litell to hym, wherfor I write brefly and litell.

THOMAS DENYES.

398.

A.D. 1461, 3 July.
RICHARD CALL TO MARGARET PASTON.

[From Paston MSS., B.M.]

This letter seems to have been written in 1461, just before Thomas Denys was murdered, in consequence of the occurrences mentioned in No. 396.

To my most reverent and worshipfull mastresse, my Mastresse Margaret Paston, this be delyuered.

PLESITH it your mastresseship that my mastre[1] wolde that ye alowe the berer hereof for hes costs in asmoch as he come hether for that matre, and for non other; but ye must lete Thomas Denys wif be prevy therto, for my mastre wol that she bere the cost, for it is her matre; and that ye make her goode cheere, and if ye wol have her hom to you for a seacon, unto the tyme sche be out of her trouble, my mastre is agreed. And if sche sende to my mastre for any matre, let her sende her owne man upon her owne coste, thowe ye paye the money for a secon, unto the tyme that sche may pay you a yein, mastre holdeth hym content. My right wurshipful mastresse, Almyghti Jesu kepe you. Wreten at London the iij. day of Jul.

Your poore seruaunt and bedman,
RIC. CALL.

On the back of this letter is the following memorandum:—" Memorandum of j. comb whete, whereof was mad iiij.ˣˣ. and x. [*fourscore and ten*] brown lovis and iiij.ˣˣ. and xvj. white lovis, after vj. j.ᵈ. price the . . ."

1 John Paston.

399.

A.D. 1461, 6 July.

WILLIAM LOMNER TO JOHN PASTON.

[From Paston MSS., B.M.]

From the reference to the Coronation, it is quite evident that this letter
must have been written in the first year of King Edward the Fourth.

*To the right worchipfull and my good maister
John Paston.*

RYGHT worchipfull and my good mayster I
recomaunde me to yow. And, sir, yf the Coronacion had be on Relik Sunday,[1] as it was
apoyntyd, I shuld have waytid on yow. And
as for my Lord of Norffolks mene, I told my mastres
your wyfe, here disposission as I coude know, the
wheche I sopose she told yow, as I can espye some of
his meny was grette cause of T. D.[2] deth, &c. Also
ye have knowlych how Fastolff[3] is com yn to my Lord
of Norffolks hous, for ij. causez, as I understande ; on
is to enfors my Lords entre yn Castre be his cleym ; an
other is to helpe his fader yn lawe[4] ayens Felbrigge, &c.
For love of Good take good awayte to your person, for
the word [*world*] is right wilde, and have be sythyn Hey-
donz sauffe gard was proclamyd at Walsyngham ; for
yn good feyth I trow, but if [*i.e.* unless] he be ponysshid
the countre wille rise and doo moche harme, and also
for the comyssyon Sir Miles Stapilton and Calthorp, that
arn among the comunes ought of conseite and reputid
the Kyngs enmez, as the brenger of this bille can telle
yow, to whom I beseche yow to be good mayster, for
he hath doo the Kyng good servyse as ony pore man
of our contre, and yet is he callid traitor be sweche as
he can telle yow, soportid be Roger Bolwer and Aleyn

---

[1] July 12, in 1461.
[2] Thomas Denys.   [3] Thomas Fastolf of Cowhaw.
[4] This would seem to be John Wyndham, but I find no mention of such a
relationship between him and Fastolf.

Roos, Heidonz owyn men [chif constablez].[1]   And it plese yow that John Yve and John Brigge myght have your warentez for cheffe constable, &c., for they ocupye yn Kyng Herris name.   Forther, sire, I am gretly yn your danger and dette for my pension, for it is told me ye have paied, and at your comyng I shalle make amendez with your good maistreship, and suche servyse as lith yn my pore powere is, and shalbe, redy at alle tymez with Godds grace, how have yow yn His kepyng.   Wretyn yn hast at Dallyng, on Sent Thomas Even, &c.

Be your Servaunt,   L.

400.

A.D. 1461, 9 July.

MARGARET PASTON TO JOHN PASTON.

[From Paston MSS., B.M.]

This letter clearly relates to the affairs of Thomas Denys's wife, after the murder of her husband in 1461.   John Paston and William Rokewood were trustees of his lands, and Margaret's cousin, John Berney of Witchingham, it will be seen, wrote more than one letter to them about this time.

To my ryth worchepfull hosbond, John Paston, be thys deliverid in hast.

RIGHT worchepful hosbond, I recommand me to yow.   Please yow to wete that I have spoke with Thomas Denys wyffe, and she recommand hyr to your good masterchep, and she prayeth yow to be her good master, and prayet yow of your good masterchep, that ye wolle geve her your advice howe to be demenid for hyr person and hyr goodes.   For as towchyng hyr owne person, she dare not goo home to hyr owne place, for she is thret if that she myght be take, she shuld be slayne or be put in ferfull place, in shortyng of hyr lyve dayes, and so she standyth in gret hevynes, God her helpe.   Ferther

---
[1] Interlined.

more she is nowe put be her brother in Norwich with
Awbry, and she thynkyth the place is right conver-
saunt of pupyll for hyr to abeyd in, for she kepyth
hyr as close as she may for spyyng. Item, as I went
to Seynt Levenard ward, I spake with Maister John
Salet, and commonyd with hym of hyr, and me thowgt
be hym that he howyth hyr ryght good wylle. And
than I haskyd hym howe she myght be demenyd with
hys[1] goodes and hyr. He cownseld me that she shuld
get hyr a trosty frend, that war a good, trewe, poor man,
that had not moche to lese, and wold be rewlyd after
hyr, and to have a letter of ministracion; and so I told
hyr. Than she seyd she wold have hyr broder advice
therin. Item, she seyth ther be no mor feffes in
hys londes but ye and Rokwood, and she prayeth yow
that it please yow to speke to Rokwood that he make
no relesse but be your advice, as she trostyth to yowr
good masterchep. Item, the last tyme that I spake
with hyr she mad suche a petows mone and seyd that
she wost ner howe to do for mony, and so I lent vjs.
viijd. Item, I sent my cosyn Barney the bylle that
John Pampyng wrot be yowr commanddement to me,
and he hath sent a letter of hys entent to yow and to
Rokwod therof, and also but if it please yow to take
better hed to hys mater than he can do hym self, I
can thynk he shall ellis fare the wors for i' feyth he
standyth daly in gret fere, for the false contrary party
ageyns hym. Item, at the reverence of God, be ware
howe ye ryd or go, for nowgty and evyll desposyd
felacheps. I am put en fere daylyfor myn abydyng here,
and cownsellyd be my moder and be other good frendes,
that I shuld not abeyd here but yf the world wher in mor
quiete than it is. God for hys merci send us a good
world, and send yow helthe in body and sowle, and
good speed in all your maters. Wreten in hast the
Thursday next after Seynt Thomas.

By your, M. P.

[1] i.e. her husband's.

401.

A.D. 1461, 10 July.—JOHN BERNEY TO JOHN PASTON AND WYLLIAM ROKEWODE.

[From Fenn, i. 236.]

To the worshipfull John Paston and Wylliam Roke-wode, Squyeris, and to everych of them.

RIGHT worshipfull cosynes, I recummaund me to yow. And for as mech as I am credybilly informyd how that Sir Myles Stapylton knyght with other yll dysposed persones, defame and falsly noyse me in morderyng of Thomas Denys the Crowner, and how that I intend to make insurexyones contrari unto the law; and that the seyd Stapylton ferthermore noyseth me with gret robries; in whech defamacyones and fals noysyngs the seyd Stapylton, and in that his saying he is fals, that knowith God, &c. And for my playn acquitayll, yf he or any substancyall gentylman wyll say it, and avow it, I say to it contrari, and by lisens of the Kyng to make it good as a gentylman. And in this my playn exskeus, I pray yow to opyn it unto the Lords, that the seyd Stapylton, &c., makyn gret gaderyngs of the Kyngs rebelyones, lying in wayte to morder me. And in that I may make opyn proff. Wretyn in hast the x. day of July anno regni Regis E. iiij. primo. JOHN BERNEYE.

Remembre to take a wryht to chese crowneres in Norffolk.

402.

A.D. 1461, 12 July.
JOHN PASTON TO MARGARET PASTON.

[From Fenn, iv. 20.]

This letter and the next, which is an answer to it, are evidently of the same year as No. 403.

To my cosyn, Margaret Paston.

Recomaund me to yow, letyng yow wete tha the Undershreve doughtyth hym of John Berney; wherfore I pray yow bryng hem to gedyr, and set hem acord, if ye can, so that the seyd Ondershreve be sure that he shall not be hurt be hym, ner of hys cuntrymen. And eyf he woll not, lete hym verely understonde that he shall be compellyd to fynd hym suerte of the pes to agry in thys heed, and that shall nowther be profitabyll, ner worchepful. And lete hym wete that there have be many compleynts of hym be that knavyssh knyght, Sir Miles Stapilton, as I sent yow word before; but he shall come to hys excuse wele inow, so he have a mannys hert, and the seyd Stapylton shall ben ondyrstand as he ys, a fals shrewe. And he and hys wyfe and other have blaveryd here of my kynred in hedermoder;[1] but, be that tyme we have rekned of old dayes and late dayes, myn shall be found more worchepfull thanne hys and hys wyfes, or ellys I woll not for hys gilt gypcer.

Also telle the seyd Berney that the Shreve ys in a dought whedyr he shall make a newe eleccion of knyghts of the shyre, be cause of hym and Grey; where in it were bettyr for hym to have the Shreves good wyll.

Item, me thynkyth for quiete of the cuntre it were most worchepfull that as wele Berney as Grey shuld get a record of all suche that myght spend xl*s.* ayere, that were at the day of eleccon, whech of them that had fewest to geve it up as reson wold. Wretyn at London, on Relyk Sonday.

Item, that ye send abought for sylver acordyng to the old bylle that I sent yow from Lynne.

JOHN PASTON.

---

[1] In hugger-mugger, *i.e.* clandestinely.

403.

A.D. 1461, 15 July.
MARGARET PASTON TO JOHN PASTON.

[From Fenn, iv. 24.]

See preliminary note to preceding letter.

Recomand me to yow. Please yow to wete that I have sent to my cosyn Barney, acordyng to your desyr in the letter that ye deed wright on Relec Sonday to me, wheropon he hathe wreten a letter to yow and anothyr bylle to me, the wyche I send yow. He tolde the masanger that I sent to hym that the Undershereve nedyth not to fer hym nor non of hys; for he seyd, after the aleccion was doo, he spak with hym at the Grey Fryers, and prayyd hym of hys good masterchep, and seyd to hym that he feryd no man of bodely harme, but only Twyer and hys felachep.

Item, Sir John Tatersalle and the baly of Walsynsham and the constabyll hathe take the parson of Snoryng and iiij. of hys men, and sete hem fast in the stokkys on Monday at nyght; and, as it is seyd, they shuld be carryyd up to the Kyng in hast. God defend yt but they be shastysyd as the lawe wolle. Twyer and hys felachep beryth a gret wyght of Thomas Denys dethe in this contry abowght Walsynham ; and it is seyd ther yf John Osberne hade owght hym as good wylle, as he deed befor that he was acqueyntyd with Twyer, he shuld not adyyd [*have died*], for he myght rewlyd al Walsynham as he had lyst, as it ys seyd.

Item, Will Lynys, that was with Master Fastolf, and swyche other as he is with hym, goo fast abowght in the contr, and ber men a hand,[1] prests and others, they be Skotts, and take brybys of hem and let hem goo ageyn. He toke the last wek the parson of Freton, and but for my cosyn Jarnyngham the younger,[2] ther

---

[1] *See* p. 20, Note 1.
[2] John Jerningham, Junior, son of John Jerningham, Senior, of Somerleyton, Suffolk.

wold a led hem forthe with hem ; and he told hem pleynly yf they mad any suche doyngs ther, but [*i.e.,* unless] they had the letter to schewe for hem, they shuld aley on her bodyys. It wer welle do that they wer met with be tymys. It is told me that the seyd Will reportyth of yow as shamfully as he can in dyvers place. Jesu have yow in Hys kepyng. Wreten in hast, the Wednysday after Relec Sonday.

Yf the Undershereve come home, I woll a say to do for hym as ye desyryd me in your letter. As for mony, I have sent abowght, and I can get non but xiij*s.* iiij*d.* syn ye went owght. I wolle do my parte to get mor as hastely as ye may.

By yowr,   M. P.

404.

A.D. 1461, 16 July.
JOHN BERNEY TO JOHN PASTON.

[From Fenn, i. 238.]

To the worshipfull John Paston, and to my cosyn, Wylliam Rokewode, Squyer, with my Lord of Cantyrburi.

RIGHT worshipfull sir, I recummaund me to yow, praying yow hertyli to labour for that the Kyng may wryte unto me, gevyng me thankyng of the good wyll and servyse that I haff doo unto hym, and in beyng with hym a yens his adversaries and rebelyones, as well in the North, as in this cuntre of Norffolk. And in that the Kyng shold please the Comynnes in this cuntre ; for they grudge and sey, how that the Kyng resayvith sych of this cuntre, &c. as haff be his gret eanemyes, and opresseors of the Comynes ; and sych as haff assystyd his Hynes, be not rewardyt ; and it is to be consederyd, or ellys it wyll hurt, as me semyth by reason. And in ayd of this chaungebyll rewle, it wer nessessary to move the good Lords Spiretuall and Temperall, by the whech that myght be reformyd, &c. And in cas that any of myn olde enemyes, Tudynham, Stapylton, and Heydon, with theyr affenyte labur the Kyng and Lords unto my hurt, I am and wylbe redy to come to my souverayn Lord for my exskeus, soo that I may come saff for unlawfull hurt, purveyed by my seyd ennemyes. No more at this tyme, but God preserve yow in gras. Wretyn at Wychyngham the xvj. day in the moneth of July, anno regni Regis E. iiij$^{ti.}$ primo.

JOHN BERNEYE.

Please it yow to move this unto my Lords Cauntyrburi, Ely, Norwych, &c.

405.

A.D. 1461, 17 July.

JOHN BERNEY TO JOHN PASTON.

[From Fenn, iv. 28.]

To the ryght worshipfull John Paston, Squyer, in hast.

SIR, I recomaund me to zow, &c. And as for my playn dysposyssyon towards the Undyrshrewe, I wyll hym no bodyli hurt, nor shal not be hurt by me nor by noo man that I may rewle. But the Comynnes throw all the schyer be movyd agayn hym, for cause of his lyght demeanyng towards them for this elexsyon of knygtts of the shyer for the Parlement. And I suppose yf that he wyll, he may be hastyli easyd as thus :—lat hym make notys unto the seyd Comynnes that this theyr eleccyon shall stande, or ellys lat hym purchas a new wryt, and lat hym make wrytyng unto them what day they shall come, and they to make a new eleccyon acordyng unto the law. And, sir, I pray zow, sey to hym that it is nott his oneste to lye upon too many men, noysyng them rebyliones of Norff[olk], and Berney theyr c . . . No more to zow at this tyme, but I haff sent zow ij. letteris within this viij. dayes. Wretyn the xvij. day of July anno regni Regis E. iiij$^{ti.}$ 1$^{mo.}$

JOHN BERNEY.

406.

A.D. 1461, 18 July.
MARGARET PASTON TO JOHN PASTON.

[From Fenn, iv. 30.]

The date of this letter is certain, as it refers to the murder of Thomas
Denys.

*To my worchepful hosbonde, Jon Pastun, this letter be
delyvered in hast.*

YTH worchepful husbond, I recomawnd me to
yow.   Plesyt yow to wete that I am desyrid
be Sir John Tatersale to wryte to yow for a
comyssion or a noyr in termyner [*oyer and
terminer*] [1] for to be sent down in to this cuntre to sit
uppon the parson of Snoryng, and on soche as was
cause of Thomas Denyssys dethe, and for many and
gret horebyl robryys ; and as for the costs ther of the
cuntre wele pay therfor, for they be sor aferd but [*i.e.* un-
less] the seyd dethe be chastysed, and the seyd robryys,
they ar aferde that mo folks xal be servyd in lyke wyse.

As for the prest and vj. of hese men that be takyn, they
be delyveryt to Twer [*Twyer*], and iiij. be with hem of
the cuntreys cost, for to be sent with to the Kyng; and
yf they be browt up at the reverens of God, do yowr
parte that they schape not, but that they may have the
jugement of the lawe, and as they have deservyd, and
be comytyt to prison, not to departe tyl they be
inqueryd of her forseyd robery be soche a comyssion
that ye can get, that the Keng and the Lords may
hondyrstonde wat rewle they have be of, not hondely
for the moderys and the robbryys, but as wele for the
gret insurrexsin that they were lyke amade within the
shyre.   The preests of Castyr they be streytely take
hede at be Roberd Harmerer and hoder, so that the
seyde prestys may have no thyng out of ther owne, ne
of hodyr menys, but they be rassakyt, and the plase ys

<hr>

[1] *See* Vol i. p. 138, Note 5.

watchyd bothe day and nyth. The prestys thynk ryth longe tyl they tydynggs fro yow. At the reverens of God, be ware hou ye goo and ryde, for that ys told me that ye thret of hem that be nowty felawys that hathe be inclynyng to them, that hathe be your hold adversarys.

The blyssyd Trenyte have yow in hys kepyng. Wretyn in hast, the Saturday nex be fore Sent Margarete. Be yours, M. P.

407.

A.D. 1461, 27 July.—Grant from the Crown.

[From Patent Roll, 1 Edw. IV., Part 3, No. 13.]

Pro Johanne Paston.

REX omnibus ad quos &c. salutem. Cum Nos indebitati sumus Johanni Paston armigero et Thomæ Hows clerico in septingentis marcis legalis monetæ regni nostri Angliæ eisdem Johanni et Thomæ solvendis juxta formam cujusdam billæ manu nostra signatæ cujus tenor sequitur in hæc verba :—

Edward, Kyng of Inglond and of Frauns, Lord of Irlond, recorde and knoweleych that we have receyvyd of John Paston, Squyer, and Thomas Hows, clerk, be the assent of oure trusty and welbelovyd cosyn Thomas Archebysshop of Caunterbury, [and?] Mayster John Stokys, clerk, an nowche of gold with a gret poynted diamaunt set upon a rose enamellid white, and a nowche of gold in facion of a ragged staff with ij. ymages of man and woman garnysshed with a ruby, a dyamaunt and a gret perle, which were leyd to plegge by oure fader, whom Crist assoyle, to Sir John Fastolff, knyght, for CCCC. xxxlvij*li.;* and also an obligacion wherby oure seid fader was bound to the seid Sir John Fastolff in an C. marc; for which we graunt and promitt in

II. D

the word of a kyng to pay to the seid John Paston and
Thomas Hows, clerk, or to her assignez, D.CC. mark of
lawfull money of Englond at days underwritte, that is
to sey ; att the Fest of All Seyntes than next folowyng
after the date of thys bille CC. mark, and other CC.
mark at the Fest of All Seyntis than next folowyng, and
other CC. mark at the Fest of All Seyntes than next
folowyng, and an C. mark at the Fest of All Seyntys
thanne next folowyng.   And also we graunte that the
seid John Paston and Thomas Hows shall have a
signement sufficient to hem aggreabill for the seid payment.   And if it fortune that the same John and
Thomas be unpayd by the seid assignement of any of
the seid paymentis at any of the seid Festis, thanne we
graunt upon notice made to us therof by the same
John or Thomas to pay hem or her assignez that payment so behynd onpaid oute of oure cofirs withoute
delay.   In witnesse werof we have signed this bill with
oure hand the xij. day of Jule the first yere of [our]
reign.

Nos solutionem summæ illius præfatis Johanni et
Thomæ fieri et haberi volentes, ut tenemur, con-
cessimus et per præsentes concedimus eisdem Johanni
Paston et Thomæ Hows septingentas marcas monetæ
prædictæ percipiendas modo et forma subsequentibus,
videlicet, centum marcas inde annuatim percipiendas
de primis denariis provenientibus et crescentibus de
feodi firma civitatis nostræ Norwici et de omnibus aliis
firmis, exitibus, proficuis et reventionibus de eadem
civitate provenientibus per manus majoris, custodis,
vicecomitum, civium seu ballivorum ejusdem civitatis
pro tempore existentium aut aliorum receptorum,
firmariorum seu appruatorum eorundem feodi firmarum,
exituum, proficuorum et reventionum dictæ civitatis pro
tempore existentium, et centum marcas inde annuatim
percipiendas de firmis, redditibus, exitibus, proficuis et
aliis commoditatibus quibuscumque de comitatibus
nostris Norff' et Suff' provenientibus per manus vicecomitum eorumdem comitatuum pro tempore exis-

tentium, quousque septingentæ marcæ eisdem Johanni
Paston et Thomæ Hows plenarie persolutæ fuerint.
In cujus &c. Teste Rege apud Westmonasterium,
xxvij. die Julii. *Per ipsum Regem oretenus.*

408

A.D. 1461, 1 Aug.
JOHN PASTON TO MARGARET PASTON.

[From Paston MSS., B.M.]

This letter is printed from a draft which is partly in John Paston's own
hand. The contents clearly refer to, first, the Norfolk election of 1461, which
it was proposed to confirm by a new meeting of the electors at the shire-
house; and secondly, the necessity of electing a new coroner after the
murder of Thomas Denys. The date is therefore certain.

To my mastres Paston and Richard Calle.

FIRST, that Richard Calle fynde the meane that
a distresse may be taken of such bestes as
occupie the ground at Stratton, and that
cleyme and contynuauns be made of my possession in any wise, and that thei be not suffrid to
occupie withowt thei compoune with me; and that aftir
the distresse taken the undirshreve be spoke with all that
he make no replevyn with out agrement or apoyntement taken, that the right of the lond may be undirstand.

ij. Item, I here sey the peple is disposed to be
at the shire at Norwich on Sen Lauerauns Day for
th'affermyng of that thei have do afore, wherof I hold
me wele content if thei do it of her owne disposicion,
but I woll not be the cause of the labour of hem, ner
bere no cost of hem at this tyme, for be the lawe I am
suer befor, but I am wel a payed it shall be on han
halyday for lettyng of the peples werk. I undirstand
ther shall be labour for a coroner that day, for ther is
labour made to me for my good wyll here, and I wyll
nothyng graunt withowt the under shreves assent, for
he and I thought that Richard Bloumvyle were good

to that occupacion.   Item, ye shall undirstand that
the undirshreve was some what flekeryng whill he was
here, for he informyd the Kyng that the last eleccion
was not peasibill, but the peple was jakkyd and
saletted, and riottously disposid, and put hym in fere
of his lyfe.   Wherefore I gate of hym the writte whech
I send yow herwith, to that entent, thow any fals shrewe
wold labour, he shuld not be sure of the writ, and therfore ye most se that the undirshreve have the writ at
the day, in case the peple be gadered, and thanne lete
th'endentures be made up or er they departe.

iij. Item, that ye remembyr Thomas Denys wyfe that
her husbond had divers billes of extorcion don be Heydon and other, whech that he told me that his seid wyfe
beryid whan the rumour was, so that thei were ny roten.
Bidde her loke hem up and take hem yow.

iiij. Item, as for the seyd distreynyng at Stratton, I
wold that Dawbeney and Thomas Bon shuld knowe the
closes and the ground, that thei myght attende ther
to, that Richard were not lettyd of other occupacions,
and I wold this were do as sone as is possibill, or I
come home.   Notwithstandyng, I trowe I shall come
home or the shire, but I woll nat it be knowe till the
same day, for I will not come there with owt I be sent
fore be the peple to Heylisdonne.   Notwithstandyng,
and the peple were wele avertised at that day, they
shuld be the more redy to shewe the oribyll extorcions
and briberys that hath be do upon hem to the Kyng
at his comyng, desyring hym that he shuld not have
in favor the seyd extorcioners, but compelle hem to
make amendes and sethe [*satisfaction*] to the pore peple.

v. Item, that Berney and Richard Wright geve suche
folkys warnyng as wyll compleyne to be redy with
her billes if thei list to have any remedy.

vj. Item, that the maters ayens Sir Miles Stapilton
may at Aylesham be remembyrd.

vij. Also if ye can be any craft get a copy of the
bille that Sir Miles Stapilton hath of the corte rolles of
Gemyngham, that ye fayle not, but assay and do yowr

devyr, for that shuld preve some men shamefully fals. Master Brakle seyd he shuld a get oon of Freston.   I wold he shuld assay, or ellys peraventure Skypwith, or ellys Master Sloley; for if Stapilton were boren in hande that he shuld be founde fals and ontrewe, and first founder of that mater, he wold bothe shewe the bille and where he had it.[1]

viij. Item, I wold the prestis of Caster were content for Midsomer term.

ix. Item, ther is a whith box with evidens of Stratton, in on of the canvas baggis in the gret cofir, or in the spruse chest.   Ric. Calle knowith it well, and ther is a ded of feffement and a letter of atorne mad of the seyd londs in Stratton to John Damm, W. Lomner, Ric. Calle, and John Russe.   I wold a new dede and letter of atorne were mad owth theroff be the feffees of the same laund to Thome Grene,[2] Thome Playter, the parson of Heylisdon, Jacobo Gloys, klerke,[3] Johanni Pamping, and that the ded bere date nowh, and that it be selid at the next shire; for than I suppose the seyd feffes will be ther if it may not be don er that tyme. I wold have the seyd dedis leyd in a box, both old and new, and left secretly at Ric. Thornis hows at Stratton, that whan I com homwar I mygh fynd it ther, and mak seson [*seisin*] and stat to be take whil I wer ther.   Wret at London on Lammes Day.

409.

A.D. 1461, 23 Aug.—JOHN RUSSE TO JOHN PASTON.

[From Fenn, iv. 42.]

Edward IV. went into the Marches of Wales, as mentioned in this letter, in the autumn of 1461.   He was at Gloucester on the 11th September, and at Ludlow on the 21st, as appears by the dates of his privy seals.   The matter

[1] Between this and the next paragraph is the following sentence crossed out:—" Item, I send yow a writ direct to the Meyer and Shreves of Norwich for to receyve of hem an C. [*hundred*] mark yerly for suche jowellys as the Kyng hath of me."

[2] This name is substituted for three others crossed out, viz. " John Grenefeld, Thomas Playter, Water Wrottisle, Squyer."

[3] Here occurs the name, " Christofere Grenacre," crossed out.

mentioned in the postscript is doubtless Howard's contention with Paston in the Shire-house at Norwich, to which allusion is made in the letter following.

To my right worshypfull and reverent maistyr, John Paston, at Norwich.

RYGHT worshypfull sir, and my right honourable maister, I recomaunde me louly to you. And plese youre maistirshyp to wete that my Maister Clement, youre brothyr, and Plater, wrot a letter to my mayster yore sone [1] yistirday, the tenure of whych was how ye were entretyd there. And as ye desyred me, so I enformyd hem the mater along, for they wist not of it til I told hem; and they wrete the more pleynerly inasmych as a worshypfull man rood the same day, and bare the letter to my seyd maister youre sone.

The Lord Bourgcher is with the Kynge, and my Lord Warwyk still in the North, &c.

Item, sir, thys day cam on John Waynflet from the Kyng streyt weye, and he is of myn aqueyntaunce; and he teld me there was no voyse nor spekyng aboute the Kyng of that mater; and I teld hym all the mater along hou ye were intretyd, whych he wyll put in remembraunce in ony place that he cometh in in Suffolk or Esex as he goth homward, for he owyth no good wil to youre adversary. And the seyd Waynflet teld me that he knowyth for serteyn that the Kyng cometh not to Northefolk til he hathe been upon the Marchys of Walys, and so there is no serteynte of hyse comyng thys many dayez. He teld me he lefte the Kyng with a smal felashyp aboute hym.

And I enqueryd hym of the gyding of my maystyr yore sone, whiche he comendyd gretly, and seyd that he stood well inconseyt, and dayly shuld increse; and he was well in acqueyntaunce and be lovyd with jentilmen aboute the Kyng. But he seyd ther shal no thyng hurte hym but youre streytnesse of mony to hym, for withoute he have mony in hyse purse, so as he may

---

[1] John Paston, the eldest son.

resonably spende among hem, ellys they wyll not sette
by hem ; and there be jentilmen sones of lesse reputacion that hath mony more lyberal x. tymez than he
hath, and soo in that they seyd Waynflet seyd it were
full necessary for you to remembre, &c.

As for tydyngs here bee noon newe, &c.   I truste
I shal brynge you a letter from my mayster your sone,
or thanne I come, for whych I shal rather thanne fayle
abyde on day the lenger.   And Jesu have you, my
right honourable maister, in Hyse mercyfull governaunce, and preserve you from adversyte.   Wretyn at
London, on Seynt Bertylmewys Evyn.

I can speke with noo man but that thynke the
gydyng of youre adversary hath been in many causez
ryght straunce, and as it is soposyd that he shal undyrstonde at the Parlament; but for Gods sake have men
inow aboute yow, for ye undyrstonde is on manerly
dysposecion.

Your bedeman and servaunt,
JOHN RUSSE.

410.

A.D. 1461, 23 Aug.

JOHN PASTON, THE ELDEST SON, TO HIS FATHER.

[From Fenn, iv. 46.]

Allusion is made in this letter, as in the last, to Edward the Fourth's going
into Wales in 1461.   The writer appears to have been with the King, and ex-
pecting to accompany him on the journey.   Edward was at Battle on the
21st August 1461, according to the dates of his privy seals.

*To my rythg reverent and worchypfoll fader, John
Paston, Esquyer, dwellyng in Heylysdon, be thys
letter delyvered in haste.*

OST reverent and worschepfull fadyr, I rekom-
awnd me hertyly, and submytt me lowlely to
your good faderhood, besechyng yow for
cheryte of yowr dayly blyssyng.   I beseche
yow to hold me ascewsyd that I sente to yowe none

erste no wrythgtyng, for I kowd not spede to myn intent the maters that ye sent to me for. I have laboryd dayly my Lord of Essexe, Treserer of Ynglond, to have mevyd the Kyng bothe of the maner [of] Deddham and of the byll copye of the Corte Roll, everye mornyng ore he went to the Kyng, and often tymys inqueryd of hym and he had mevyd the Kyng in these matyers. He answeryd me naye, seyyng it was no tyme, and seyd he wold it war osse fayne spedd os I myselfe, offed tymys de layding me that in trouthe I thowt to have send yowe word that I felyd by hym that he was not wyllyng to meve the Kyng ther in. Neverthe lesse I lawberyd to hym contynually, and prayed Barronners hys man to remembyr hym of it. I told offten tyms to my seyd Lord that I had a man teryyn in town, that I schuld a sente to yow for othyr sundry maters, and he teryid for no thyng but that I mythg send yowe by hym an answer of the seyd matyers; othyr tyms besechyng hym to spede me in theys matyers for thys cawse, that ye schulde thynke no defawte in me for remembryng in the seyd maters.

And nowe of late, I, rememberyng hym of the same mater, inqueryd if he had mevyd the Kyngs Hythgnes therin; and he answeryd me that he hadde felte and mevyd the Kyng ther in, rehersyng the Kyngys answer therin; how that, when he had mevyd the Kyng in the seyd maner of Dedham, besechyng hym to be yowr good Lord ther in, konsyderyng the servyse and trewe part that ye have done, and owthg to hym, and in espesyal the rygth that ye have therto, he seyd he wold be your good Lord therin as he wold be to the porest man in Inglond. He wold hold with yowe in yowr rygth; and as for favor, he wyll nogth be under stand that he schal schewe favor mor to one man then to anothyr, nowgth to on in Inglond.

And as for the bille copyd of the Cort Rolle, when he mevyd to him of it, he smylyd and seyd that suche a bylle ther was, seyyng that ye wold an oppressyd sundreys of yowr contremen of worchypfull men, and the for he kepyd it styll.   Never the lesse he seyd he schuld loke it uppe in haste, and he schuld have it.

Baronners undertoke to me twyes ore thryes that he schuld so a' remembred hys lord and master,[1] that I schuld au had it with inne ij. or iij. dayes.   He is often tyms absent, and therfor I have it nowthg yyt; when I kan gete it, I schall send it yowe, and of the Kyngs mowth, hys name that take it hym.

I scend you home Pekok a geyn.   He is not for me. God send grace that he may do yow good servyse, that be extymacion is not lykelye.   Ye schall have knowleche aftyrward how he hathe demenyd hym her with me.   I wold, savyng yowr dysplesure, that ye were delyvered of hym, for he schalle never do yow profyte ner worchyp.

I suppose ye understand that the monye that I hadde of yowe att Londun maye not indur with me tyll that the Kyng goo in to Walys an kome ageyn, for I under stand it schall be long or he kome ageyn. Wher for I have sent to Londun to myn onkyl Clement to gete an C*s.* of Christofyr Hansom yowr servaunt, and sene [*send*] it me be my seyd servaunt, and myn herneys with it, whyche I lefte at Lundun to make klene.

I beseche yowe not to be dysplesyd with it, for I kowd make non othyr cheysaunce [*arrangement*] but I schuld a boruyed it of a strange man, sum of my felawys, who I suppose schold not lyke yowe, and ye herd of it a nothyr tyme.   I ame in suerte wher as I schall have a nothyr maun in the stede of Pekoke.

My Lord of Estsexe seythe he wyll do as myche for yowe as for any esquyer in Inglond, and Beronners hys man telht me, seyy[n]g, " Yowr fadyr is myche be holdyng to my Lord, for he lovyth hym well."   Bernners mevyd me ons, and seyd that ye must nedys do sum wate for my Lord and hys, and I seyd I wost well that ye wold do for hym that laye in yowre powar. And he seyd that ther was a lytyl mony be twyxe yowe and a jantylman of Estsexe, callyd Dyrward, seyyng

---

[1] Henry Bourchier, Earl of Essex.

that ther is as myche be wern [*between*] my seyd Lord and the seyd jantylman, of the wyche mony he desieryth yowr part.

It is talkyd here how that ye and Howard schuld a' strevyn togueder on the scher daye, and on of Howards men schuld a' strekyn yow twyess with a dagere, and soo ye schuld a ben hurt but for a good dobelet that ye hadde on at that tyme. Blyssyd be God that ye hadde it on. No mor I wryth to yower good faderhod at thys tym, but All myghty God have yowe in Hys kepyng, and sende yowe vyttorye of yowr elmyes [*enemies*], and worschyp in cressyng to yowr lyvys end yn. Wrytyn at Lewys, on Seynt Bertylmwes Eve.

Be yowr servaunt and elder sone,

JOHN PASTON.

411.

A.D. 1461, 25 Aug.
CLEMENT PASTON TO JOHN PASTON.

[From Fenn, iv. 52.]

The references to Howard's conduct, and to John Paston the son being with the King, prove this letter to be of the year 1461. Compare the last paragraph of the letter immediately preceding with the first of this.

To hys rythe reverent and worchypfwll broder, John Paston.

RYTHE reverent and worchypfwll broder, I recomawnde me to yowr good broderhood, desieryng to herre of zour welfar and good prosperite, the gwyche I pray God encresse to His pleswr and zowr herts hesse [*heart's ease*]; certyfyyng zow that I have spok with John Rwsse, and Playter spok with him bothe, on Fryday be for Seynt Barthelmw. He tolde us of Howards gydyng, gwyche mad us rythe sory tyl we herde the conclusion that ze hadde non harme.

Also I understond by W. Pekok that my nevew

hadde knowleche ther of also up on Saterday nexst be for Seynt Barthelmwe, in the Kyngs howse. Not with standyng, up on the same day Playter and I wryte letters on to him, rehersyng al the mater, for cause if ther wer ony questionys mevyd to hym ther of, that he xwlde telle the trowthe, in cas that the qwestions wer mevyd by ony worchypfwll man, and namyd my Lord Bowcher,[1] for my Lord Bowcher was with the Kyng at that tyme.

I fele by W. Pekok that my nevew is not zet verily aqweyntyd in the Kyngs howse, nor with the officers of the Kyngs howse he is not takyn as non of that howse; for the coks [*cooks*] be not charged to serve hym, nor the sewer[2] to gyve hym no dyche, for the sewer wyll not tak no men no dyschys till they be comawndyd by the cownterroller. Also he is not aqweyntyd with no body but with Weks;[3] and Weks ad told hym that he wold bryng hym to the Kyng, but he hathe not zet do soo. Wherfor it were best for hym to tak hys leve and cum hom, till ze hadd spok with swm body to helpe hym forthe, for he is not bold y now to put forthe hym selfe. But than I consyderyd that if he xwld now cum hom, the Kyng wold thyng [*think*] that wan he xwld doo hym ony servie som wer, that than ze wold have hym hom, the qwyche xwld cause hym not to be hadde in favor; and also men wold thynke that he wer put owte of servic. Also W. Pekok tellythe me that his mony is spent, and not ryotesly, but wysly and discretly, for the costs is gretter in the Kyngs howse qwen he rydythe than ze wend it hadde be, as Wyllam Pekok can tell zow; and therof wee must gett hym jCs. at the lest, as by Wyllam Pekoks seyyng, and zet that will be to lytill, and I wot well we kan not get xld. of Christifyr Hanswm. So I xall be fayn to lend it hym of myn owne silver. If I knew verily zour entent

---

[1] Henry, Viscount Bourchier, who had been created Earl of Essex on the 30th June preceding. The writer had forgotten his new dignity.

[2] An officer who had the ordering of the dishes, &c.

[3] John Wykes was an usher of the King's chamber, and a friend and cousin of J. Paston's.—F.

wer that he xwld cum hom, I wold send hym non.
Ther I wyll doo as me thynkithe ze xwld be best plesyd,
and that me thynkythe is to send him the silver.
Ther for I pray zow hastely as ze may send me azen
v. mark, and the remnawnte, I trow, I xall get up on
Christofir Hanswm and Lwket.   I pray zow send me it
as hastely as ze may, for I xall leve my selfe rythe
bare; and I pray zow send me a letter how ze woll
that he xull be demenyd.   Wrytyn on Twsday after
Seynt Barthelmwe, &c.   Christus vos conservet !

CLEMENT PASTON.

412.

A.D. 1461, 28 Aug.
LORD BEAUCHAMP TO SIR THOMAS HOWES.

[From Fenn, iv. 96.]

This letter was probably written in the year 1461, if not in the year preceding.   The disputes about Fastolf's will came before the Spiritual Court in the
year 1465 ; but at the date of this letter they could not have proceeded very far.

To myn welbeloved frende, Sir Thomas Howys, Parson
of Blofeld.

ELBELOVED frende, I grete you well.   And
for as muche as I understonde that William
Wurcester, late the servant unto Sir John
Fastolf, Knyth, whois soule God assoyle, ys
not had in favour ne trust with my right welbeloved
frende, John Paston, nether with you, as he seyth,
namely in such maters and causes as concerneth the
wylle and testament of the said Sir John Fastolf; and
as I am informed the said William purposeth hym to
go into his cuntre, for the whiche cause he hath desired
me to wryte unto you that ye wolde ben a special good
frend unto hym, for his said mastris sake, to have alle
suche things as reason and consciens requireth, and
that ye wolde be meane unto Paston for hym in this
mater to schewe hym the more favour at thys tyme for

this my writyng in doyng of eny truble to hym, trusting
that he wole demeane hym in suche wyse that he shal
have no cause unto hym, but to be his good master, as
he seyth.   And yf ther be eny thing that I can do for
you, I wole be right glad to do it, and that knoweth
Almyghty God, whiche have you in his keping.   Wretin
at Grenewyche, the xxviij^th day of August.

J. BEAUCHAMP.

413.

A.D. 1461, 30 Aug.
LORD HUNGERFORD AND ROBERT WHITYNGHAM TO
MARGARET OF ANJOU.

[From Fenn, i. 246.]

That this letter was written in the year 1461 is sufficiently evident from its
contents. The MS. from which it was printed by Fenn was a copy in the
handwriting of Henry Windsor, and was manifestly the enclosure referred to
in his letter No. 416. It bore the same paper mark as that letter.

A la Reyne D'Engleterre [en] Escote.

ADAM, please it yowr gode God, we have sith
our comyng hider, writen to your Highnes
thryes.   The last we sent by Bruges, to be
sent to you by the first vessell that went into
Scotland ; the oder ij. letters we sent from Depe, the
ton by the Carvell in the whiche we came, and the
oder in a noder vessell.   But, ma dam, all was oon
thyng in substance, of puttyng you in knolege of the
Kyng your uncles[1] deth, whom God assoyll, and
howe we sta[n]de arest [*arrested*], and doo yet; but
on Tuysday next we trust and understande, we shall
up to the Kyng, your cosyn germayn.[2]   His Comys-
saries, at the first of our tarrying, toke all our letters
and writyngs, and bere theym up to the Kyng, levyng
my Lord of Somerset in kepyng atte Castell of Arkes,[3]

[1] Charles VII. of France. He died on the 22d July 1461.
[2] Lewis XI., son of Charles VII.
[3] Arques, in Normandy, south of Dieppe.

and my felowe Whityngham and me, for we had sauff
conduct, in the town of Depe, where we ar yete. But
on Tyysday next we understand, that it pleaseth the
said Kyngs Highnes that we shall come to hys
presence, and ar charged to bring us up, Monsieur de
Cressell, nowe Baillyf of Canse, and Monsieur de la
Mot.

Ma dam, ferth [*fear*] you not, but be of gode comfort, and beware that ye aventure not your person, ne
my Lord the Prynce,[1] by the See, till ye have oder word
from us, in less than your person cannot be sure there as
ye ar, [and] that extreme necessite dryfe you thens; and
for God sake the Kyngs Highnes be advysed the same.
For as we be enformed, Th'erll of March[2] is into
Wales by land, and hath sent his navy thider by see;
and, Ma dame, thynketh verily, we shall not soner be
delyvered, but that we woll come streght to you,
withaut deth take us by the wey, the which we trust
he woll not, till we see the Kyng and you peissible
ayene in your Reame; the which we besech God soon
to see, and to send you that your Highnes desireth.
Writen at Depe the xxx^{ti} dey of August.

Your true Subgettes and Liege men.

HUNGERFORD.
WHITYNGHAM.

At the bottom of the Copy of the Letter is added:—

These ar the names of those men that ar in Scotland
with the Quene. The Kyng Herry is at Kirkhowbre
with iiij. men and a childe.

Quene Margaret is at Edenburgh and hir son.

The Lord Roos and his son.

John Ormond.	Sir Edmund Hampden.
William Taylboys.	Sir Henry Roos.
Sir John Fortescu.	John Courteney.
Sir Thomas Fyndern.	Myrfyn of Kent.

[1] Edward, son of Henry VI.
[2] Edward IV., whom the Lancastrians did not yet recognise as King.

Waynesford of London.	Dauson.
Thomas Thompson of Guynes.	Thomas Burnby.
	Borret of Sussex.
Thomas Brampton of Guynes.	Sir John Welpdalle.
	Mr. Roger Clerk, of London.
John Audeley of Guynes.	John Retford, late Coubitt.
Langheyn of Irland.	Giles Senctlowe.
Thomas Philip of G[i]ppeswich.	John Hawt.

414.

A D. 1461, 6 Sept.

JOHN PAMPYNG TO JOHN PASTON, SENIOR.

[From Paston MSS., B.M.]

In the letter of James Gloys, which follows (No. 415), will be found an allusion to a recent "revel done in Suffolk" by Yelverton and Jenney. That the affair alluded to was the same which is described in this letter, will appear beyond doubt if the reader will refer to Letter 420.

To my right worshipfull master John Paston, the older, Squier.

PLEASE your mastirship to wete that I have be at Cotton, and spoke with Edward Dale, and he told me that Yelverton and Jenney were there on Friday,[1] and a toke distresse of xxvj. or more bullokks of the seid Edwards in the Park, and drofe hem to a town therby; and a neyghbore there undirstandyng the bests were Edward Dalis,[2] and bond hym to pay the ferme, or ellis to bryng in the bests be a day. And whan the seid Edward undirstod the takyng of the seid bests he went to Yelverton and Jenney, and bond hym in an obligacon of x*li.*, to pay hem his ferme at Mighelmes ; whech I told hym was not well do, for I told hym ye had be abill to save hym harmeles. And because of discharge of his neyghbour he seid he myght non other wise do.

[1] Sept. 4.
[2] Apparently the writer has omitted a word or more here.

Nevirthelesse as for mony thei get none of hym redely,
ner of the tenaunts nowthyr, as he can thynk yet.   The
seid Yelverton dyned on Friday at Cotton, and there
chargid the tenaunts thei shuld pay no mony but to
hym, and hath flaterid hem, and seith thei shall be
restorid ayen of such wrongs as thei have had be Sir
Philip Wentworth and other for Master Fastolff; and
because of such tales, your tenaunts owe hym the bettir
will.   And I purposid to have gon to Cotton and
spoke with the tenaunts, and Edward Dale told me
he supposid thei wold be this day at Nakton.   And
because [I desired]¹ to speke with hem as ye
comaundid me, I terid not but rod to Ipwich to my
bed, and there at the Sonne was the seid Yelverton
and Jenney and Thomas Fastolff; and myn ost told
me, that the same aftir none thei had be at Nakton, but
what thei ded there I can not telle, and whan I was
undirstand your man, Hogon, Jenneys man, askyd
suerte of pes of me; and Jenney sent for an officer to
have hed me to prison; and so myn ost undirtoke for
me that nyght.   And this day in the mornyng I wente
to Sen Lauerauns Chirche; and there I spak to hem
and told hem ye merveylid that thei wold take any
distresse or warne any of your tenaunts that thei shuld
pay yow no mony.   And Yelverton seid ye had take
a distresse falsly and ontrewly of hym that ought yow
no mony ner hem nowther.   And he seid he was infeffid as well as ye; and as for that I told hym he
wost odre [*knew the contrary*], and thow he were it was
but your use, and so I told hym that men were infeffid
in his lond, and that he shuld be servid the same
withinne fewe dayes.   And he seid he wost well ye
were not infeffid in his lond, and if ye toke upon yow
to make any trobill in his lond ye shall repente it.
And also he seid that he wold do in like wise in alle
maners that were Sir John Fastolffs in Norfolk as thei
have begonne, and other langage as I shall telle yow.
And so I am with the gayler, with a clogge upon

¹ Omitted in MS.

myn hele for suerte of the pees; wherefore please your mastirship to send me your avise.

Item, John Andrews was with hem at Cotton, and thei have set a man of the seid Andrews to kepe the plase.

Item, Wymondham, Debenham and Tympirle come to Yelverton this day at masse and speke with hym; and I speke to Tymperle in your name that he wold not comforte ner be with hem ayein in this mater; and he seid he undirstod no such thyng, ner it was not his comyng hedir. Wretyn at Ipwych the Sonday next before the Nativite of Owr Lady.

Yowr servaunt,

JOHN PAMPYNG.

The back is covered with some rough memoranda in Richard Calle's hand, of moneys received at different times of year by Richard Charlys, Thomas Howys, William Berton, baker, of Southwark, Ralph Lovel, John Prentyng, Richard Coomber, and John de Dorylot. Some of these payments are made through Dawbeney, John Paston, Junior, and John Paston, Senior (*per manus Johannis Paston Senioris*).

415.

A.D. 1461, 24 Sept.—JAMES GLOYS TO JOHN PASTON.

[From Fenn, iv. 58.]

On the back of this letter, Fenn found the following memorandum in a contemporaneous hand:—" Ric'o Calle p. ord'm b'm[1] pro ij. annis terminatis ad Mic' anno primo regni Regis E. iiij. . . . xxvj*s.* viij*d.*" This shows that the letter itself could not have been written later than 1461, and as there was no " Lord of Gloucester" before that year, it could not have been earlier.

To the right reverent and wurchepfull Sir, and my gode
mayster, John Paston, Esquyer.

RIGHT reverent and wurchepfull sir, I re-comand me to your gode maystershep, prayng you to wete that I was at Blakkes, and spake with his wiffe; and she seth he was not at hame this iij. weks,—he ridith up the

---

[1] What is the meaning of these three words? The first two doubtless are to be read "per ordinationem." But what is "b'm?"

countre to take accompts of balys [*bailiffs*],—and that
this day sevennyght he shuld have satyn in Caystr by
you up on accounts, and fro thens he shuld have redyn
to Lynne, and that he shall be at home un Monday at
nyght next comyng.   Wherfor I have left my heraund
with her.   But she seth that he shall not mown comyn
[*be able to come*] to you, for my Lady[1] have sent for hym
in gret hast, bothyn be a letter and be a tokyn, to
comyn to her as hastly as he may; notwithstandyng
she shall do the herand to hym.

As for Yelverton, I dede a gode fele to enquer of
Yemmys Skynner whan the seid Yelverton shuld go
to London.   He seid not this sevynnyght.   He cowde
not tell what day till he had spokyn with his son.   His
sone shuld come to hym or his master shuld ridyn.
I shall enquer mor at Walsyngham.   And for Godds
love be not to longe fro London, for men seyn ther, as
I have be [told], that my Lord of Glowcetir[2] shuld have
Cayster, and ther is gret noyse of this revell that was
don in Suffolk be Yelverton and Jeney; and your
wele willers thynkyn that if thei myght prevayle in this,
thei wold attempt you in other.   But seas ther pore
and malyce, and preserve you from all evill.   And at
the reverence ot God lete sum interposicion go a twix
you and my mastres your moder or ye go to London,
and all that ye do shall spede the better; for she is
set on gret malyce, and every man that she spekith
with knowith her hert, and it is like to be a fowle
noyse [over] all the countre with aught it be sone sesid.

Also, sir, it is told me that my Lord of Norfolk is
comyn to Framlyngham, and that ye be gretly comendyd in his howshold.   Therfor it wer wele do, me
semyth, that ye spake with hym.   The Holy Trynyte
kepe you.

Wretyn at Norwich, the Thursday next after Sent
Mathewe.   Your pore prest,

JAMES GLOYS.

[1] Alice, Duchess of Suffolk.
[2] Richard, the King's brother, afterwards Richard III.

416.

A.D. 1461, 4 Oct.
HENRY WYNDESORE TO JOHN PASTON.

[From Fenn, i. 240.]

For the date of this letter, compare No. 413.

*To my full worshipfull, speciall gode maister, John
Paston, Squyer, abidyng at Norwich,*

RIGHT worshipfull sir, and some tyme my
moost speciall gode master, I recommaunde
me unto your gode maistership, with all my
pour service, if it may in any wise suffice;
and farthermore, sir, I beseche you, nowe beyng in
your countre, where ye may deily call unto you my
maister Sir Thomas Howys, ones to remembre my
pour mater, and by your discretions to take such a
direction theryn, and so to conclude, as may be to
your discharge and to my furtherance, accordyng to
the will of hym that is passed unto Gode, whose saull
I pray Jesu pardone! for truly, sir, ther was in hym
no faute, but in me onely; yf it be not as I have
remembred your maistership affore thy[s] tyme. For
truly, sir, I der say I shuld have had as speciall and as
gode a maister of you, as any pour man, as I am,
withyn England shuld have hadd of a worshipfull man,
as ye ar, yf ye had never medulled the godes of my
maister F., and as moche ye wold have done, and
labored fore me, in my right, if it hadde byn in the
handes of any oder man than of your self anely. But,
I truste in Gode, at your next comyng to have an
answere, such as I shalbe content with. And yf it
may be so, I am and shalbe your servaunt in that I
can or may, that knoith our Lord Jesu, whom I besech
save and sende you a gode ende in all your maters, to
your pleiser and worship everlastyng. Amen. Writton
at London, iiij^to die Octobris.

As fore tidyngs, the Kyng wolbe at London withyn
iij. deies next comyng; and all the castelles and holdes
in South Wales, and in North Wales, ar gyfen and
yelden up into the Kynges hand. And the Duc of
Excestre[1] and th'erle of Pembrok[2] ar floon and taken
the mounteyns, and dyvers Lordes with gret puissans
ar after them; and the moost part of gentilmen and
men of worship ar comen yn to the Kyng, and have
grace, of all Wales.

The Duc of Somerset, the Lord Hungerford, Robert
Whityngham, and oder iiij. or v. Squyers are comen
into Normandy out of Scotland, and as yette they
stand strete under arest; and as merchauntes that ar
comen late thens sey, they ar like to be demed and
jugged prisoners. My Lord Wenlok, Sir John Cley,
and the Dean of Seynt Severyens, have abiden at
Cales thise iij. wikes, and yette ar there, abidyng a
saufconduit, goyng uppon an ambassate to the Frenshe
Kyng; and Sir Wauter Blount, Tresorer of Cales,
with a grete feleship of souldeours of Cales, and many
oder men of the Marches, have leyn, and yette doo,
at a seege afore the Castell of Hampmes, by side
Cales, and deily make gret werre, either parte toother.

Item, I send unto you a copy of a letter that was
taken uppon the see, made by the Lord Hungerford
and Whytyngham.

Item, we shall have a gret ambassate out of Scotland
in all hast of Lordes.

At your comaundement, and Servaunt,
HENRY WYNDESORE.

417.

A.D. 1461, 11 Oct.
CLEMENT PASTON TO JOHN PASTON.

This letter is reprinted from the *Norfolk Archæology*, vol. iv., p. 26,
where it is edited from a transcript contained in a MS. genealogy of the

---

1 Henry Holland. He married Anne, sister of King Edward IV., but
remained a steady Lancastrian, and was attainted this year in Parliament.
2 Jasper Tudor, half brother of Henry VI.

Paston family drawn up by Sandford, author of the *Genealogical History of England.* The references to Howard's animosity against Paston, and to an approaching Parliament, prove clearly that this letter is of the year 1461.

To his right reverent and worshipfull broder, John Paston, Esquier, be this delivered in great haste.

BROTHER, I recommende me to you.   After all dewe recommendacions, &c.   Sir, it was tolde me by rythe a worshipfull man that loveth you rythe well, and ye him, and ye sall knowe his name hereafter, but put all things out of doubt he is such a man as will not lye : on the xjth day of October the Kinge said, "We have sent two privy sealys to Paston by two yeomen of our chamber, and he disobeyeth them ; but we will send him anoder tomorrowe, and by Gods mercye, and if he come not then he sall dye for it.   We will make all oder men beware by him how they sall disobey our writinge.   A servant of our hath made a complainte of him.   I cannot thinke that he hath informed us all truely, yet not for that, we will not suffer him to disobey our writinge ; but sithen he disobeyeth our writinge, we may beleve the better his gydinge is as we be informed."   And therwith he made a great avowe that if he [*ye*] come not at the third commandement ye xulde dye therefore. This man that told me this is as well learned a man as any is in England ; and the same xj_{th} day of October, he advised me to send a man to yow in all the hast that might be to lett yow have knowlache, and that ye xulde not lett for none excuse, but that ye xulde make the man good cheere and come as hastily ye might to the Kinge, for he understandeth so much that the King will keep his promise.   Notwithstanding, by mine advice, if ye have his letter or the messenger come to you, come to the Kinge wards or ye meet with him, and when ye come ye must be suer of a great excuse. Also if ye doe well, come right stronge, for Howards wife made her bost that if any of her husbands men might come to yow ther yulde goe noe penny for your

life ; and Howard hath with the Kinge a great fellowship.

This letter was written the same day that the Kinge
said these words, and the same day that it was told
me, and that day was the xj^{th} day of October as
abovesaid ; and on the next morning send I forth a
man to yow with this letter, and on the same day send
the Kinge the third privye seale to you. Also he that
tolde me this seid that it were better for yow to come
up than to be fotte out of your house with streingth,
and to abide the Kings judgement therin, for he will
take your contumacy to great displeasure. Also, as
I understand, the Duke of Norffolk hath made a great
complaint of yow to the King, and my Lord of Suffolk[1]
and Howard and Wyngfelde helpe well to every day
and call upon the King against yow. The Kinge is
at this day at Grenewich, and ther will be still till the
Parliament beginne. Some say he will goe to Walsingham, but Mr. Sotyll seid in the aulle in the Temple
that he harde no worde of any such pilgrimage. No
more, &c. Written the xj^{th} day of October at mid-
night.

My nevew John tolde me also that he supposed
ther were out proclamacions against yow, &c. the
same day.

By CLEMENT PASTON,
your broder.

418.

A.D. 1461, 13 Oct.
RICHARD CALLE TO JOHN PASTON.

[From Paston MSS., B.M.]

On comparing this letter with No. 414, no one will doubt that both were
written in the same year.

[1] John de la Pole, son and heir of William, Duke of Suffolk, who was
attainted in 1450, was not restored to the Dukedom till the 23d of March
1463; but being in favour at court, and having married Edward the Fourth's
sister, he seems even at this time to have been popularly called "my Lord of
Suffolk."

To my ryght reverent and wurschipfull maystre, my
mastre John Paston.

PLESITH it your maystreschip to witte that
Mr. John and I, with other mo, have ben at
Cotton on Friday[1] last passed, and there
Jenney had do warned the corte there to be
the same Friday, and he was at Eye at the cescions
the Thorsday before; and on the Friday in the
mornynge he was comyng to Cotton to hoolde the
corte there. And it fortuned we had entred the place
or he come; and he herd therof and turned bac a yein
to Oxon[2] to my Lorde of Norwiche, and there dyned
with hym. And my Lorde sent Mr. John Colleman to
Cotton Halle to speke with you; and at hes comyng he
undrestode ye were not there, and if ye had, my Lorde
desired you to come and spoken with hym, and that
my Lorde desired to put your matre in a trety; in so
moche that Mr. John Colleman tolde to my master,
John Paston, that diverse of your elmees [*enemies*] had
labored to my Lorde to have a trety if he cowde brynge
it aboute, &c. And as for the tenaunts they wolde not
come at the place on to the tyme that I sent for hem,
for they sey pleynly they woll not have a do with hem;
and so the corte whas holden in your name, and the
tenaunts ryght weele plesed ther of, excepte Thurn-
berne and Agas, and as for any socour, they have there
ryght noone at all. And so Mr. John whas ther Friday
all day and Saterday tyll none; and than he toke hes
horse with xxx. men with hym and rode to Jeney place,
and toke there xxxvj. heede of nete, and brought hem
in to Norfolk; and so whas I left still at Cotton with
xij. men with me, be cauce they reporte and we abode
there ij. dayes we schulde be pult out be the heeds.
And so we a mode [? *abode*] there v. dayes and kepte
the place, and I walked aboute all the lordeschippes
and spake with all the fermours and tennaunts that
longen to the maner to undrestande her disposessyon

and to receyve money of hem; and I fynde [them]
ryght weele disposed to you.   And be cauce the corte
whas warned in ther name and not in youre, therfore
they purvey no money; but they have promysed me
to pay no money to no man but to you, so that ye woll
safe hem harmeles; and I told hem ye wold safe hem
harmeles.   They have apoynted with me to make redy
her money withinne a fornyght aftre Halowemesse, &c.
I have receyved of the tenaunts that I undrestod out
[owed] you werst wyll viij. marc, &c.   And as for Edward
Dalys money it is redy, so that your maistreschip woll
se that he be not hurt be hes obligacion.   Ferthermore,
plesit your maistreschip to sende worde if they entre
into the maner ayein, how we schall be rwled and gidyd;
for the tenaunts fere hem they wol entre whan we be
gon, and than wol they distreyne the tenaunts, for they
sey there that my Lorde of Cauntyrbury and other Lords
woll relese to hem, notwithstandyng that I have enformed hem other wice; wherfore, savyng your better
advice, me semethe it were ryght weele doo that ye had
a letter of my Lorde of Cauntirbury, and other to the
tenaunts of Cotton that it is her wyll and entent that
ye schulde have the rwle and gouernaunce, and receyve
the money of that maner, and other that were Sir John
Fastolff, on whom God have mercy, for I dought not
and suche a lettre came downe to the tenaunts there
schulde no man sey nay to it.   Besechyng your
maystreschyp to have an answere of how we schall be
gided and rwled, &c.   Item, to sende worde howe we
schall doo with the geere that wee toke out at the
Wyght Freris, wether it schall be sent to you or
nought.   And Jesu preserve you.   Wreten at Norwiche
upon Sein Edwards Day.

By your servaunt and bedman,
RIC. CALLE.

Endorsed in a hand nearly contemporaneous: "Latter' circa anno (sic)
E. 4tt iij. vel iiijo."

419.

A.D. 1461, Oct.
WILLIAM NAUNTON TO JOHN PASTON, SENIOR.

[From Fenn, iii. 414.]

This letter corresponds so closely with the next in what is said about the occupants of Cotton Hall, that it is clear they were both written about the same time.

To my Master Paston, the elder, be thys letter delyveryd in hast.

RYGHT wurchypful sir, I recommend me to zour good masterchyp. The cause qwy I wryth I let zour have knowlech of the mene that be in Cotton Halle, how they be strangely dysposyd ageyns zow; for, as I here say, they make revell there. They melt led and brek down zour bregg, and make that no man go in to [the] place but on a ledder, and make them as strong as they kan a geyns zow be the supportacion of Jeney and Debenham, and hys sone; for they seye ther that Jeney hath sold the lyflod on to Debynham, and that hys son the knyth shall dwell ther, and ther forr they have warnyd a cort ageyns Munday, and now they ar a vysed to kepyt on Saturday be forr Munday. Qwat they mene therby I wot never, but as for the felechyp in the place that ys there now, and have be here al thys weke, there ys no man of substans, as we here, and there have be but vij. or viij. al thys wyke; but there wyll be a gret felechyp thys nyth or to morwe up on Saturday, for than they wyl kepe the cort. And as for Edward Dale, he dar not abyde wyl at hem [*home?*], they thret hym so, be cause he wyl send them no vytaly. And as for me self, Edward Dale dar not let me wyll [*well*] be there for takyng in suspecyon. And jas for the tenaunts, they be wel dysposyd except j. or ij., so that ze wyl support them in hast, for they may nowt kepe

of ther katel of the ground long; and specyally they
desyr to have zowr owne presens, and they wold be of
gret cownfort. No mor I wryth to zour, but the
Holy Gost have zour in kepyng. Wretyn on the
Fryday after my departyng.

Be your Servaunt,

WYLLYAM NANTON.

420.

A.D. 1461, Oct.
RICHARD CALLE TO JOHN PASTON, JUNIOR.

[From Paston MSS., B.M.]

This letter was written in a year in which the morrow of All Souls' Day
(*i.e.*, the 3d November) fell on Tuesday. The Dominical letter of the year
must therefore be D. This was the case in 1461, and no other year will suit
a letter addressed to John Paston, Junior. For if we go back there is no
earlier year in which D. was the Dominical letter till we come to 1450, when
John Paston, Junior, was only ten years old; and if we go forward the next
is 1467, which was after John Paston, the father's death.

*To the right worschipfull sir and maistre, John Paston,
jun., esquyer.*

RYGHT worschipfull sir, I recomaunde me unto
your mastreschip, certifiyng you that Jenney
and Yelverton hathe certified up in to the
Kynges Benche inssurrecions [and] congrega-
cions a yenste me; wherupon they have sente to the
scheryff a writte chargyng hym in peyne of C*li.* to brynge
me in to the Kyngs Benche the morwe after Sein
Marteyn. And this daye the seide Jenney hathe sent
doune to the scheryff an other writte called an *habeas
corpus* retornable *crastino Animarum*, weche schalbe on
Twesday next comyng be cauce they were in dought
and in greete feere that I schulde have ben aquytte of
the inditement of fellony now at this gayle delyverye.
And also my maistre hathe sente an other writte for
me retornable at the seid *crastino Animarum*. And

so I am like to ride to London warde to morwe. And
the scheryff wold make me to fynde suerte that I
schulde appere in the Kyngs Benche the seid daye;
and yet, that notwithstandyng, he wolde send me with
strengthe of men as a presoner; and if any thynge
schall cauce me that I goo not up to London, it
schalbe be cauce I woll fynde no suerte; for in cas he
wold have suffred me to have gon up be my selfe at
myn owne coste, I wolde have founde hym suertee.
And so at the makyng of this bille we were not fully
condesended hough we schulde doo. My mastre is
in goode hele, blissed be Godd, and dothe and schall
doo ryght weele in alle hes maters. Ther is an on-
gracious felaschip of hem and a fals. They have sent
for Fitzraff and Schipdam, be a citacion for the proffe
of the testement, and alle is but for to delay it; yet it
were weele done ye rode over to Fitzraff and felte hes
disposicion how he woll be disposed, and in like wice
with Schipdam, for I have spoken with hem of that
matre, in cas that any citacion come doun for hem,
how they wolde be disposed, and I have founde the
too straunchely disposed. God send us a good scheryf
thys yere, and thanne we schalle do weele inough, be
the grace of God.

And, sir, your man tolde me that ye desired to
knowe the demenyng at Cotton of the tenaunts and
other. I lete you wete the moste parte of alle the
tenaunts have bene here with me for to see me, and
they have tolde me all the demenyng as it is undre-
wrete. Furst, as for the money that they receyved
there it drwe upon a xxiiij^{ti} *li.* and more silver, for
the tenaunts myght not cheese but they moste nedes
paye, for they distreyned on my Lords of Suffolk fee,
my Lords of Norwich fee, and on all men grounde, so
that they myght not have her catell in reste, weche
cauced hem to paye her money. I knowe weele i
nough who payed and wo paied not. All the grete
fermours have payed. And as for the kepyng of the
place ther be therin iiij. men, and on of Debenham

men, called Sokelyng, and hes wyff, and on Mannyng,
a tenaunt, a fals knave ; and they have enforced them
as stronke as they kan, and they have broken doune
the brigge and have leide a planke over, in cas that
ye go theder ye may not come at Dale is howce in no
waie, for he have had meche trouble for my mastre
and for me ; but and ye wolde gete my Lords meane
and pulle the knaves out be the heede, it were weele
done.   I purpose me to com hom warde that same
wey.   Item, I lete you witte that the gayle delyverye
holdeth not this daye, and alle is doone be cauce of
mee, Jenney wolde not lete the clerke of peas come
hether this daye for feere that I schulde have been
aquytte of the felonye, for in trouthe and tho it had
holden, I had founde the meane for to have ben
quytte, for I whas through with the scheryff and panel
made aftyr myn avice ; but though the gayle delyver
had holden, I cowde not have ben delyverd, becauce
of thes writtes that be come downe.   Item, the
scheryff hathe a grete losse that this daye holdethe
not, for ther schulde have ben quytte xl. men this
daye.   Item, the scheryff tolde me that my maistre
tolde hym that I whas assent to my takyng at Scoolys,
weche was to me ryght greete hevynes and discom-
forture nough in my trouble.   And God knoweth it
was never my wylle ner myn entent, as I mot be saved
at the dredful day of Dome; for ther is no man so sore
hurte as I am be the takyng, bothe in losse, and also
in reprefe of myn owne persoune and of my frends,
withoute that my mastre be my good maistre, as I
truste he wolle be, or elles I am disseyved.   He hathe
my trewe servyce and shal have whylle that I leve,
what so ever his mastreschip do to me, but I can
thynke he hathe be enformed be myn elmyes [*enemies*]
that wold make hym disp[l]esed with me, and to be myn
evy [*heavy*] mastre, but dissimulacion dothe muche
harme, &c.   I reporte me, &c.   No more to you at this
tyme, but Jesu kepe you, and send you as much fortune
and grace as I wolde ye had, &c.   I beseche [you] to be

my goode mastre as ye have be, for I never deserved
nor wol deserve the contrary.

> Your servaunt, RIC. CALLE,
> presoner.

421.

A.D. 1461, 2 Nov.
MARGARET PASTON TO JOHN PASTON.

[From Fenn, iv. 232.]

This letter is ascribed by Fenn to the year 1465, in consequence of the
allusion to John Paston's imprisonment in the Fleet. But there were more
occasions than one on which he was confined there. Fenn himself knew of
two. Paston was committed to the Fleet, as we know from William
Worcester, on Saturday, the 3d November 1464. He was also confined there
in August and September 1465, and may very possibly have been released by
the beginning of November. But I am inclined to think this letter refers to
an imprisonment prior to either of these. For, in the first place, the news of
it seems only to have been recent. It had become general subject of conver-
sation at Norwich, "on Saturday last," whereas in 1465 it must have been
known two months earlier. Secondly, Sir William Chamberlain, whose influence Sir Thomas Howes hopes will be of service, must have died in the
spring of 1462. According to Blomefield (Hist. of Norfolk, i. 321), his will
was dated the 3d March 1461 (which would be in the modern computation
1462), and was proved on the 21st April 1462. It may be presumed, therefore, that on receiving the letter from his brother Clement (No. 417), written
on the 11th October 1461, John Paston hastened up to London and was immediately thrown into prison. By this letter, however, we find that he was
soon afterwards released, and his great enemy Howard sent to prison in his
stead.

*A Lettre to J. Paston, Armig., from his wife, shewing
his imprisonment in the Fleete.*[1]

RYTH worchepfull husbond, I recomand me to
yow. Plesyt yow to wet that I receyvyd
yowyr lettyr that ye sent me by John Holme
on Wednysday last past, and also I receyvyd
a nothyr lettyr on Fryday at nyt, that ye sent me by
Nycolas Newmanys man, of the whyche lettyrs I thanc
yow; for I schold ellys a' thowt that it had be wers
with yow than it hathe be, or schal be, by the grace of
Almyty God. And yet I kowd not be mery, sethyn I

[1] There is no direction to the letter, but the words above inserted are written in an ancient hand upon the back of it.—F.

had the last lettyr tyll thys day that the Meyir sent to
me, and sent me werd that he had knowlege for very
trowthe that ye wer delyveryd owt of the Flet, and that
Howard was comytyd toward for dyvers gret compleynts
that wer mad to the Kyng of hym.   It was talkyd in
Norwyche and in dyvers othyr plasys in the contre on
Saterday last past, that ye wer comytyd to Flet, and in
good feyth, as I herd sey, the pepyle was ryth sory
ther of, bothe of Norwyche and in the contre.   Ye
ar ryth myche bownde to thank God, and all tho that
love yow, that ye have so gret love of the pepyll as ye
have.   Ye ar myche behold to the Meyir[1] and to
Gylberd,[2] and to dyvers othyr of the aldyrmen, for
feythfully they owe yow good wyll to ther porys.

I have spoke with Syr Thomas Howys for swyche
thyngys as ye wrot to me for, and he promysyd me
that he schold labour it aftyr yowyr intent as fast as
he kowd; and in good feyth, as my brodyr and Playter
kan tell yow, as be hys seying to us, he is and wole be
feythfull to yow.   And as for Wylliam Wyrcestyr, he
hathe be set so up on the hone, what by the parson
and by othyr, as my brodyr and Playter schall telle yow,
that they hope he wole do well i now.   The parson
seyd ryth well and pleynly to hym.   The parson tolde
me that he had spook with Syr Wylliam Chambyrleyn,[3]
and with hys wyfe, and he thynkyth that they wole do
well i now aftyr yowyr intent, so that they be plesantly
intretyd.   The parson tolde me that he wyst well
that Syr Wylliam Chambyrleyn cowd do more ese in
swyche matyers as ye wrot of, towchyng my Lord of
Bedford,[4] than ony man kowd do that leveyth at thys
day.   Also he tolde me that he felt by hem that they
wold owe yow ryth good wyll, so that ye wold owe

---

[1] William Norwich was Mayor of Norwich in 1461.
[2] John Gilbert was Mayor in 1459 and in 1464.   He died in 1472.
[3] Sir William Chamberlain of Gedding, Suffolk, a Knight of the Garter,
who had served under the Regent Bedford in the French wars.   He married
Anne, daughter and heir of Sir Robert de Herling, who, though she long
survived him, and had two husbands after him, the second of whom was
John, Lord Scrope of Bolton, was buried by her own desire beside her first
husband, in the chancel of Herling Church.
[4] John, Duke of Bedford, Regent of France, died at Paris in 1435.—F.

hem good wyll.   The parson hopyth verily to make
yow acordyd when he comyth to London.

Item, my brodyr and Playter wer with Calthorp[1]
to inquer of the mater that ye wrot to me of.   What
answer he gave hem, they schall tell yow.   I sent the
Parson of Heylysdon[2] to Gurnay[3] to spek to hym of
the same mater, and he seyth feythefully ther was no
swyche thyng desyiryd of hym, and thow it had be
desyiryd, he wold nowthyr a' seyd nor done a yens
yow.   He seyd he had ever fownde you lovyng and
feythfull to hym, and so he seyd he wold be to yow to
hys power, and desyiryng me that I wold not thynk
hym the contrary.   As for John Gros, he is at Slole;
ther for he myth not be spok with.

I pray yow that ye wole send me word whedyr ye
wole that I schall remeve frome hens, for it begynyth
to wax a cold abydyng her.   Syr Thomas Howys and
John Rus schall make an end of all thyngys aftyr
yowyr intent, as myche as they can do ther in this wek,
and he purposyth to come forward to yow on the
Monday next aftyr Seynt Leonardys Day.

My brodyr and Playter schold a be with yow er
thys tym, but that they wold a byd tyl thys day wer
past, be cause of the schyer.   I spok to my brodyr
Wylliam as ye bad me, and he told me, so God hym
help. that he hyryd ij. horse ij. dayis be for that ye
redyn, that he myth a' ryde forthe with yow ; and be
cause that ye spak not to hym to ryde with yow, he
seyd that he wend[4] ye wold[5] have had hym with yow.

Thomas Fastolfys modyr was her on the next day
aftyr ye wer redyn, to have spoke with yow for hyr
sone.   Sche[6] prayith yow, at the reverens of God,

---

[1] *Query.* If Sir William Calthorpe, Knight, High Sheriff of Norfolk, &c., in
1464. and died very old in 1494.—F.

[2] Thomas Hert was instituted to the Rectory of Hellesdon in 1448.—F.

[3] Thomas Gurney of Norwich, Esq., died in 1471.—F.

[4] "Woud" in Fenn in the original text, but this is evidently a misprint.
The right hand copy reads "wend," *i.e.* weened or thought, and the note
immediately following shows that this was the reading intended.

[5] The word "not" seems here to have been omitted in the original letter.—F.

[6] The word "He" occurs in the text before "Sche," but is evidently a
mistake.

that ye wole be hys good mastyr, and to help hym in
hys ryth, that he may have hom hys lyvelod owt of ther
handys that have had it in hys nownage. Sche seyth
that they wold mak hym a yer yonger than he is, but
sche seyth that he is more thane xxj., and upon that
sche dare take an othe.

And the Blyssyd Trynyte have yow in Hys kepyng,
and send yow good sped in all yowyr matyrs, and
send the vyctary of all yowyr enmyis.

Wretyn in hast, on Sowlemas Daye.[1]

       By yowyrs,   M. P.

422.

A.D. 1461, 20 Nov.
MARGARET PASTON TO JOHN PASTON.

[From Paston MSS., B.M.]

This letter seems to have been written in 1461, the year of John Paston's
great dispute with Howard.

*To my ryth worchepfull [hus]bond, John Paston, be thys
delyveryd in hast.*

RYTH worchepfull husbond, I recomand me to
yow. Plesyt yow to wet that I receyvyd
yowyr lettyr that ye sent by the gold smyth,
as thys day in the mornyng. As for Syr
Thomas, he sent me word he schold to yow ward as on
Twysday last past; if he fayle ony thyng that ye sent
word he schold bryng with hym, it is not for no lak of
remembrans, for I sent to hym thryis or fowyr tymys
ther for, and that he schold hast hym ther in. As for
Rychard Call, he was not at home thys fortnyth. When
he comyth I schall do yowir erendys to hym; and as
for all yowyr odyr erendys I schall do hem as well as
I can. I sent yow a byll yestyrday by old Taverham,

---

[1] All-Souls', otherwise Soulmas Day, 2d of November.—F.

and a byll of Jone Gaynys mater, the whyche bylle I
pray yow may be delyveryd to Thomas Playter.   I
spak to hym of the same mater or he yed hens, and I
pray yow, if it plese yow, to geve hym yowyr avyse what
ye thynk is best to do ther in.   Sche seyth sche is ryth
sory, and if hyr old mastyr demene hym not well to
yow sche prayith yow that ye wole be hyr good mastyr,
and I that sche fare never the werse for hys defawtys.
And also I pray yow that ye wele be John Lysterys
good mastyr in hys mater.   He spak to Playter ther
of, and Playter seyd he hopyd to fynd a mene aftyr
that he had spook with yow, that schold ese hym ther
in.   I thank yow hertly for yowyr lettyr, for it was to
me gret comfort to her fro yow.   God knowyth my
modyr and I thowt ryth longe tyll we herd tydyngys
fro yow.   And the blyssyd Trinite have yow in Hys
kepyng.   Wretyn in hast on Seynt Edmundys Day
the Kyng.   By yowyr M. P.

The pepyll was nevyr bettyr dysposyd to yow than
they be at thys owyr.   The byll that Howard hathe
mad a yens yow and odyr hathe set the pepyll in thys
contre a rore.   God yeve grace it be no werse than it
is yet.

423.

Year uncertain.

ROGER TAVERHAM TO JOHN PASTON.

[From Fenn, iv. 252.]

This letter and the next are placed here merely for convenience.   The two
are evidently some years apart in point of date, and nothing is quite clear
about the date of either, except that the latter must have been written in the
reign of Edward IV., and of course before the death of John Paston in 1466.
This, which is several years earlier than the other, was almost certainly
written in the reign of Henry VI.   The writer was probably the "old
Taverham" mentioned by Margaret Paston in the last letter.

To my reverent and most be trusted maister, John Paston, Esquyer, duelling in the Inner Temple, be this delyvered.

RYGHT reverent and most be trusted maister, I recommaunde me in the most lowly wise un to your good and prevyd maysterchep, and desiring many days to here of your welfare, whiche I be seche God encrese un to his plesauns and un to the prosperite and welfare of your person, and of all youres. And I be seche you of the good con-tynuaunce of your maysterchep at diverses tymes befor this writing shewed un to me; and, sir, ther is non man a lvye that I trust more to than I doo un to you, and I am your bedman, and so shall remayn be the grace of God all the days of myn liff. And, sir, I suppose I shall never see you no more, nor non of myn frendes, whiche is to me the grettest lamentacion that myght come un to myn herte; for, sir, by the grace of God, I shall go to Rome and in to oder holy places, to spende myn dayes of this present liff in the servise of God. For I hadde lever liffe in gret tribulacion in the service of God in this present liff, than for to folowe the wretchednesse of this worlde.

And, syr, of on thing I be seche specially your good maysterchep that ye wolle shew your good maistershep un to my fader in tyme of his nede, and that ye wolle recomaunde me in the most lowly wise with all reverence un to his good faderhode, be sechyng hym that he wole yeff me every day, during the dayes of his liff, his paternall blissing. And I have marvayle san that I have writen so many letters un to hym be for this tyme, that I hadde never non letter ageyn, whiche is to me the grettest lamentacion that ever come to my hert; and nowe knowing that I shall never see hym more, nor you, nor non other of my frendes, marvayle ye not thow sorowe is imprended in myn hert.

But, reverent maister, myn singuler trust remayneth

nowe in your person, for, sir, and it please you, I most
nedes write un to your good maisterchep, in the whiche
my most trust remayneth. For, syr, and it please
you, as for myn inheritaunce and other things whiche
shulde come to me after the deth of my fader, whoes
liff God preserve to his long plesauns, knowing that I
shall never com ther, I hadde lever that by your good
a vise that ye wolde take it unto you, for I hadde
lever that ye hadde it rather than any person in the
worlde during my liff, with all the profites ther of; and
if that ye wole make as good evidences for you in that
partye as ye can, and I shall a seale hem. And as
you semeth best, and in the most secret wise, rewle
you in this mater.

And, sir, I be seche you to recomaunde me in the
most lowly wise to myn reverent Maister Willam
Lumnour, seyeng hym that I am and shall be his perpetuall bedman, and as ye thenk best, ye may telle
hym of all these maters. And, syr, I be seche you to
recomaunde me with all reverence un to my masteras
your wiff, and to all other maysters and frendes ther.
And, sir, that ye wolle thank the bringer of this letter,
whiche hathe ben in my gret tribulacion my good
frende; and, sir, whan ye speke with my fader, recomaunde me un to hym with all reverence, and sey
un to hym I shall send hym a letter in all hast
possible.

And, syr, as for this mater, demene you as ye wolle,
and I shall doo your plesauns as moche as in me is.
And, reverent maister, remitte me summe letter by the
bringer her of of all thes maters, for he duellith with
my Lorde, and he is ryght moche be trusted, for I
knowe wele he wole yef a tendaunce un to you for to
have summe letter from you; for, syr, it shall not be
longe or that I go to Rome, by the grace of God.
And as sone as I have a letter from you at this tyme,
I shall send you a noder ageyn.

No more at this tyme, but the Holy Trinite have
you in His blissed keping. Wreten at Sarum, the

Monday aftyr Mydsomer Day. And lete these maters
be kept secrete by your best a vise.

> Be youre poure servaunt,
> ROGER TAVERHAM.

424.

A.D. 1461 ?—ROGER TAVERHAM TO JOHN PASTON.

[From Fenn, iv. 258.]

The mention of Lord Wenlock in this letter proves that it cannot be earlier
than 1461; but if the writer be, as we have surmised, the "old Taverham"
mentioned by Margaret Paston in No. 422, it is most probably of that year.

*To my right wourshipful maister, John Paston,
Esquyer, be this letter delyvered.*

RIGHT wourshipful maister, I recommaunde
me un to your maistership, and I thank your
maistership that hit pleased your maistership
to sende me wourde a yen of my letter that
I sende you by the brynger herof. Sir, as I am enfourmed, ye sent me wourde how that my fader was
dede long tyme passed, and also ye desired to knowe
my titylle of ryght. Sir, I am very heyre, by the
disceas of my fader, to a place called Keswyk, in
Taverham, with all the apportenauncez, and that
comyth by enherytaunce and discente to me, for I am
the helder and heyr; and though my Lorde Cromwell[1]
hath taken Thomas Taverham, my yonger brother, as
warde for the same enheritaunce, that maketh no mater
to me, in so moche I am helder brother. Wher for I
beseche you to sende me a letter of attournay made
to you in my name in the strengest wise that ye can,
for to entre in to the same lyvelode, and I shall asseal
that, and than I shall do my service and feaute to the
seid Lorde Cromwell in all thing as by the tenure of
the same lyvelode of olde tyme aught to be done.
And herin I kno well the King shal cause my Lorde

---

[1] Humphrey Bourchier, Lord Cromwell, so created in 1461.

Cromwel to do me bothe lawe and right; and also my Lorde Chaunceler, with oder Lordes diverse, shall do the same. And, sir, I beseche your maistership to do and to take possession in the saide place with the apportenaunce in short tyme, for losyng of the rent this yer passed.

And, sir, as for the place of Attylbrigge that my moder in lawe now duellith in, sir, your maistershep shal right not [*naught*] attempte ther now in; for my Lorde of Warwik[1] hath seen how the same place was yeven me by testament by Sir Roger Dallyng after the disease of my fader, whiche is redy to be shewed. And therupon my Lorde of Warwik hath comaunded certeyn gentil-men to entre in the same place, and your maistership hadde be moved ther in or this, but for cause that ye love wel Lumpnour,[2] and that my moder in lawe is his sister; but I knowe wel hit woul cost CCC*li.*, but that she shal be dispossedded of that place in short tyme. And, maister, how ye woul be rewled in the seid place of Keswyk, I be seche you to sende me wourde, as my sengler trust is in you; for and ye woulde not take possession in the saide place, my Lorde Wenlok[3] woulde have that ful fayne, for all the contray knowith while that while I leve, I am heyr and non other. And therfor I beseche you in all hast sende me wourde by the bryngger herof in hast, quia mora trahit periculum. And, sir, I would come speke with you. I am seke, and may not goo; but telle the bryngger heroff all your entent. For my liff duryng I hadde lever that ye hadde that place for j*d.* than a nother man, thow he woulde yeff me meche mony, for your maistership ther shewed to me in my yong age. And God kepe you, &c.

Your chapeleyn,   ROGER TAVERHAM.

---

[1] Richard Neville, Earl of Warwick.
[2] William Lumner, of Mannington, in Norfolk.—F.
[3] John Wenlock was created Baron Wenlock in 1461 by Edward IV.; but he afterwards left the York party, and joined that of Lancaster. He was cleft down with a battle-axe by the Duke of Somerset for not coming up in time at the battle of Tewkesbury in 1471, whereby that battle was lost.—F.

425.

A.D. 1461, 20 Nov.—ABSTRACT.

[From Paston MSS., B.M.]

RICHARD CALLE TO JOHŃ PASTON.

Since I left you I have received at Cotton £4 : 2s., with which I have made purchases of linen shirts, &c. for you. Shall have more money before Christmas. Debenham, Jenney, nor none of his men "come not there sen' that I was there." A letter of attorney is made for Nakton in your name to Sir John Heveningham, and a rental and fermal sent him. We kept a court this week at Calcotte but could get little money, not so much as I paid my Lady of Suffolk's officers. Farmers will not occupy there till appointment be made between Paston and Debenham ; nor Risynge till he hear from Paston. Can get no day for Mautby. They will not give a noble, nor even 6 shillings, for a cow. Dey occupies your lands there till you come home. Risynge would take them and the closes at Castre if he is not to have Calcotte. The prests shall be paid as soon as we get money, I hope this week. Wheat 12d. a comb, barley 8d., malt 9d. and 10d. No good price for malt, "saving, as we understand, it is good Flanders." John Russe and Robert Glover are sending a ship with corn over, and we have ventured with them 100 comb malt. You should make some bargain with your beer brewers. Can get no money from Aleynes, farmer of Gresham, since ye rode, but 40s. Has laid in sufficient beef for Paston's household till "Fastegang" (Lent). Sir Thomas Howys advises my mistress not to send Edmund Paston to Cambridge or elsewhere till after Christmas. Please ask Clement, your brother, to get a writ against Geoffrey Clerk of West Somerton for the 20s. that Belys gave him to pay Clement. Remember the letter I sent you last week.

Caister, St. Edmund's Day.

[From what is here said of the levying of rents at Cotton, and from the mention of Debenham and Jenney in connection with it, we may presume this letter was written in 1461. With this supposition agrees the reference to John Paston's brother, Clement, who, as we see by No. 417, was in London in October.]

426.

A.D. 1461, 1 Dec.—AGNES PASTON TO JOHN PASTON.

[From Paston MSS., B.M.]

The year in which this letter was written is determined by the mention of John Northale as Sheriff of Norwich.

To John Paston, at London, be this delyverd in hast.

I grete you welle, and lete you wete that this day Berth' Elys of Paston come to Norwych to me, and shewet me a rentall for the terme of Scynt Mich., the yer of Kyng H. vj. xxxix°; and in the ende of the seyd rentall, of Waryn Kynges hand is wretyn "Agnes Paston vij*d. ob.* [7½*d.*]   Item, the same Agnes for v. acre lond xx*d.*"   Item, Aleyn Bayfeld askyth the same rent for the yer last past at Mich.   Item, I have knowlech be a trew man that whan Sharpe the reseyvor was at Gemyngham last, Waryn Herman was dyvers dayes with hym, and put hym in mynde that the mercyment for makynge of the walle chuld be askyd ageyn and be distreynyd ther for.   Item, I sent you be Doctor Aleyns man the restew [*residue*] of Waryn Herman, and seche names as Cullynge and Sammys putt in of her owyn fre wylle befor John Northales, shereve of Norwyche,[1] under her selis.   God be with you and send you His blyssyng and myn. Wretyn at Norwych the Tuisday next after Seynt Andrew.

Item, the seyd Berth' Elis seyth that the seyd reseyver wold not alowe the rent in Trunche nor the mercyments for my sute to the curt.   Gonnor wold suffyr no man to answer for me.

Be your moder, AGNES PASTON.

427.

A.D. 1461, 12 Dec.

SIR JOHN HEVENYNGHAM TO JOHN PASTON, SENIOR.

[From Paston MSS., B.M.]

This letter is evidently of the same year as No. 425.   The contents, more-over, seem to show that the date cannot be far distant from that of Richard Calle's letter of the 1st of February following.

To myn ryght worchipffull cosyn, John Paston the elder, Esquyer, be this letter delivered in hast.

Ryght worchipffull cosyn, I recomaunde me to you in as hertely wyse I can, desyryng ever to here off your welffare, whiche I beseche our Lord Jesu to preserve to your hertes pleaser, &c.   Sir, ye sent me a letter of atorney to reseyve and to ocupye in your name the maner called Burnevyles in Nakton. Sir, as for that ocupacion, I can litil skylle en, ne I wel not take up on me non suche ocupacionis ; wherffor I beseche you holde me excused, for it is no werd [*world*] for me to take suche ocupacionis.   I have as moche as I may to gader myn ownne lyfflode, and truli, cosyn, I can not gader that well.   And therffor, cosyn, I pray you take it to non displeaser.   Sir, that

[1] He was Sheriff of Norwich in the 1st year of Edward IV.

I may worchepfulli doo for you, ye shal fynde me redy be the
grace of Jesu, whom I hertely beseche to have you in Hise
mersyfull kepyng.   Wretyn at Hevenyngham on Seynt Lucye
Even.   Be your cosyn,

JOHN HEVENYNGHAM, knyght.

428.

A.D. 1461(?), Dec.—ANONYMOUS TO JOHN PASTON.

[From Fenn, iv. 64.]

The date of this letter is a little uncertain, but it seems to have been
written at the beginning of the dispute between Paston and Yelverton about
Fastolf's will, and the year 1461 appears to me on the whole most probable.

RYGHT worchefull master, I recommend me on
to yow, &c.   The cause of my wrytyng is
this; I was at Blofeld on Sent Andruys Day[1]
wyt the person,[2] and he understode non
noder but that I cam to se is master chepe, for it was
hese cheve day,[3] and that I mevyd in to hym of the
lond in Sochewerk, how I hard sey qwan I was in Soche-
folk that Geney mad hys avaunt that he had zon [*given*]
zow and hym a choppe of xx. pownd of lond.   And in
contynent he telde me al the mater beter than I cowde
telle hym, and as I cowde understond in hym be my
sympyl wyt, that he was of knoleche of alle the mater;
for he seyd that Yelverton cam don fro the benche,
and plete the mater, and for cause ye wer to laches,
and cam not in tyme, the mater yede a mys.   And so
I understode be hym that he is dysposyd to excuse
Yelverton in al materys rather than yow; but never de
les make good cher to the person, as thow ye understode that he wer your frend, tyl tyme ye have your in
tente.   But be warr and trost hym not, but make yow
so strong in lorchepe and in the lawe, that ye reeke
not meche qwder he be good or bad, &c.

Item, ye be meche be held on to Tomas Grene and
Edmund Wydewel, broder to Heu à Fen, for thei

[1] 30th November.   [2] Thomas Howes.
[3] The day of his *chief* or patron saint.   Blofield Church is dedicated to St.
Andrew.

reporte meche worchepe of your master chepe in al
maters, and that cause the substans of the towne to
howe yow servese, and be wel dysposyd on to yow
masterchepe, and that understonde I hevery day.
And yf that plese yow, qwan we partyt at Norwyche
in yowr plase, ye seyd on to me ye wold som qat do
be my sympyl a wyse; and this is myn a wyse that in
ony wyse ye make Heu à Fen and Tomas Grene on your
consel, yf ye can fyne in yow herte.   For I dare sey,
as I her and understonde, that thei how yow ryth
good well and servyse, for a man may her be the halfe
qwat the hole menyth, and therfor for Godds lowe
remember yow wel in this mater; for and it stode on
myn lyfe, I wold do as I awyse yow, &c.

   Item, for howr Lords love, goo tharow with Wyll
Weseter, and also plese Chrewys as ye thynke in yow
hert best for to do; for it is a comon proverbe, "A man
must sumtyme set a candel befor the Devyle;" and
therfor thow it be not alder most mede and profytabyl,
yet of ij. harmys the leste is to be take.

   Item, ye xul oonderstonde that the parson telde me
that dey wer somuned to cum for the probat of the
testement at Convercyon of Sent Powle;[1] and therfor
I wolde avyse yow in ony wyse that ye xuld understond the mater wysely her ye com hom, for I sopose
that Yelverton and he is confydett and acorde to
geder.

   Item, qwan I was at Blofeld with the parson, ther
cam Robert Fyrass to hym, seyyng that he is compeld
be the Kyngs Commycyoners to have harnes after is
degre, and that the parson sent hym to my mastras
that che xuld delyver hym harnes, and I understond
che wylle not tylle ye com hom.   But ye xul understond it is an halmes dede to do hym good, understondyng is nesessyte and nede that he stond in, and
also understondyng that he was kynnyes man to my
master, and it is a comon proverbe, "A man xuld kepe
fro the blynde and gevyt to is kyn;" and hevery man

[1] Jan. 25.

wyl sey wel ther of, the mor cause he is a gentylman,
and of is kyne, and in gret penur.   And therfor, for
the love of God, remembyr seche maters.

No mor at this tyme, but God have yow in Hys
kepyng, bothe body and sowle, and sqede yow in yowr
maters as wel as wel as I wolde ye xulde do.

429.

A.D. 1461(?), [3] Dec.
MARGARET PASTON TO JOHN PASTON.

[From Fenn, iv. 106.]

Except that it seems to be of the reign of Edward IV., the date of this
letter is about as uncertain as that of the last ; but as they are both written
about the same time of year, and both recommend John Paston to use the
counsel of Hugh Fenn, it is highly probable that they are of the same year.
Perhaps the last letter may have been written by the vicar mentioned in
this.

To my right wurchepfull husband, John Paston.

RIGHT wurchepfull husbond, I recomaund me
to you.   Please it you to wete that myn
awnte is dissesid, whos sowle God assoyll.
And if it please you to send word how ye
wull that we do for the lifflode that she had at Walcote,
wheder ye wull that any body take possession thir in
your name or not.   And if it like you to have with you
my cosyn William her sone, I trow ye shuld fynde
hym a necessary man to take hede to yowr howshold,
and to bye all maner of stuffe nedefull therto, and to
se to the rewle and gode gidyn therof.   It hath be
told me be for that he can gode skill of such thyngs ;
and if ye wull that I send for hym and speke with
hym ther of, I shall do as ye send me word, for in
feyth it is tyme to crone your old officers for diverse
thyngs wher of I have know parte be Dawbeney, and
more I shall telle you whan ye come hame.

Also it is thought be my cosyn Elizabeth Clere, and
the viker[1] and other that be your frends, that it is

---

[1] The vicar of Paston? Robert Williamson was vicar of Paston at this time.

right necessary for you to have Hew of Fen to be your
frende in your maters; for he is callid right feythfull
and trosty to his frends that trost hym, and it is
reported her he may do myche with the Kyng and the
Lords, and it is seid that he may do myche with hem
that be your adversaryes: and therfor, Godds sake,
if ye may have his gode wille, forsake it not. Also it
is thought the more lerned men that ye have of your
owyn contre of your councell, the more wurchepful it
is to you.

Also if ye be at home this Cristmes, it wer wele do
ye shuld do purvey a garnyssh or tweyn of powter
vesshell, ij. basanes, and ij. hewers, and xij. candle-
stikes, for ye have to few of any of thes to serve this
place. I am a ferd to purvey mych stuffe in this
place till we be suerrer therof. The Blissid Trinyte
have you in His blissid kepyng.

Wretyn the Thursday next after Sent Andrew.

Be yowr   M. P.

430.

A.D. 1461, Dec.

THOMAS PLAYTER TO JOHN PASTON.

[From Paston MSS., B.M.]

The mention of Tuddenham and Heyden in this letter proves that it cannot
be of later date than the year 1461, as the former was executed in February
1462. At the same time the reference to John Paston, Junior, could not be
much earlier, and the message from the King to the people of Norfolk certainly could not have come from Henry VI. only a year or two before. The
date must therefore be 1461 precisely. Further it will appear by the correspondence of this letter with No. 134 that the editor was mistaken in attri-
buting that letter to the year 1450. It also must be of the year 1461, and its
date proves this letter to have been written in December.

To John Paston, the older, in hast, and if he be not at Lon-
don, than to be delyvered to Clement Paston in hast.

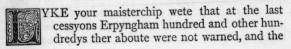YKE your maisterchip wete that at the last
cessyons Erpyngham hundred and other hun-
dredys ther aboute were not warned, and the

schreff excused hym be cause he cowde not knowe
who was officer there. Item, Yelverton lete the
pepoll understand that the Kyng wold have his
lawes kept, and that he was dysplesed with the maner
of ther gaderyng, and that he wold have it amendyd;
for he conceyveth that the hole body of the shire is
well dysposed and that the ille dysposed pepoll is but
of a corner of the hole shire; and yet that ther mys-
doyng growyth not of ther owyn dysposysyon but of
the abbettement and steryng of sum ille dysposed
persones whiche is understand and knowe to the Kynges
hygthnesse. Item, he lete hem wete that the Kyng
had commandyd hym to sey if ther were any man,
pore or ryche, that had cause to complayne of any
person that he schuld put up his bylle to the
shref and hym, and they schuld set a reule be twyx
hem; and if he wold not abyde ther reule they
schuld delyver the sayd bylle of compleynt to the
Kynges hignesse, and he schuld set the rewle and
suche dyreccion that the party compleynaunt or
defendaunt schuld be punysshed for his dysobey-
sauns of the said rewle if the case requyred; and also
more over, if ther were ony person that put up ony
suche bylle, and it mygth apere to them by ther examinacion or other wyse fals or untrewe, or elles be
cause of malyce, that than suche compleynaunts schuld
sharpely be punysshed. And than whan he had sayd
this and moche more, in dyscoragyng to the pepoll to
put bylles, as after my conseyt, he reported hym to the
schref ther present, that the Kyng thus comanded hem
thus to sey, desyreng the said schref if ony thyng of the
Kyngs comaunded were be hynd unspoken by hym
self that he wold remembre and helpe forthe to telle
it. And than the schref said, lyke as he rehersed the
Kyng comanded, and more over that the Kyng named
ij. men, by name Tudenham and Haydon, and if ony
man wold put bylles a yens them, he said in feythfull
wyse he wold help hem, and ferther the mater to the
Kyng higthnesse. And for his demenyng ther every

man thougth hym rigth wel dysposed; but Yelverton
had for yeten to expresse the names of Tudham and
Haydon.

Item, the schref desyred the jentylmen to go with
[him] to Felbryg Halle, and specially he requyred
Mr. John P., the younger; but he cowde no pepoll
gete, and so he cam not there. Item, there was a
bylle set up on the shirehous dore, and the content
ther of was but of the favour to you ward, Barney,
Knyvet and Felbrygge, and of the hatered of
other; it was but of sum lewde dysposed person it
semeth. Item, sir, at the last shire was moche pepoll
and ille governed for they wold not be rewled be no
body, they had almost a slayne the underschref, for
they told hym wryttes of eleccion was sent doun and
he kept it on syde to be gyle hem, and to make hem
labour ayen, and ther for he that kepyth it is to blame,
me thynketh. Item, sir, please you to telle Mr.
Clement, we have goten a reles of al maner accions
and appelles of Margret Clerk, made to Gymmyngham,
on of the pryncypalles, and that he woll inquyre
wheder it be suffycyant for alle, and send me word,
and weder it dyvers fro trespas and dette, wher
damages is to be recovered, for in this appell is no
damages to be recovered, but only an execucion,
whiche non of them may be contributory to other
execucion as is in other cases. Nevertheles, I hope it
be suffician for all, for sche is in the cas to have the
lyf in stede of damages.

Your THOMAS PL.

431.

NOTE.

As mentioned in the preliminary note to last No., Letter 134
has been erroneously attributed to the year 1450, and ought to be
placed here as of the year 1461. The same is the case with
Letter 135, which must be read in connection with the former.
In restoring these letters to their true date, we must observe that
the sheriff therein mentioned must be not John Jermyn, but Sir

Thomas Montgomery, who was sheriff of Norfolk from Michaelmas 1461 to 1463. This explains the remark in the former letter
"As for a knight there was none in the King's house that might
worse 'a be forbore than the sheriff might at that time." Also in
No. 135 it must be noted that "Master Berney" is not Philip
Berney, as the editor had supposed, but John Berney of Witchingham. John Paston and John Berney had been elected knights
of the shire for Norfolk in the preceding summer, and in consequence of the efforts of Sir John Howard, who was sheriff at that
time, to set aside the election, they were both summoned up to
London, and the case was heard before the King (*See* No. 417).
Their long detention in the capital it seems gave rise to appre-
hensions that it would be decided against them, and even on the
28th of December there was a riot in the shire-house at Norwich,
from the suspicion entertained that the under-sheriff had a writ
for a new election.

Letter 136 was placed after No. 135, not as being of the same
year, but as referring to the same subject. Its precise date is
uncertain and immaterial, but it, too, probably belongs to the reign
of Edward IV., as the farm at Boyton seems to have been part
of the lands of Sir John Fastolf, and only came to John Paston
after his death.

432.

A.D. 1461 ?—Anonymous to Margaret Paston.

[From Fenn, iv. 104.]

This letter appears to have been addressed to Margaret Paston at a period
when her husband was a man of some influence, and perhaps the year 1461 is
not far from the true date. It is not unlikely to have been written about the
same time as No. 430, which also refers to a meeting at the shire or county
court.

To my right worchepfull Mastres Paston.

Recomawnde me to your good mastreschep,
besechyng yow in the weye of charyte, and
as I maye be your bedeman and servaunt,
that ye wyll lete me have wetyng hoghe I
maye be rewelyd ageyns the next schyer. It is seyd
that ther xal be mych more pepyll than was the last;
and also if I be in my Ladys place, or in ony other in
the town, I xall be takyn owte. Also, mastres, that
my Maystyr Radclyffs xal take all my catell and all

other pore good that I have, and so but I maye have
helpe of my mayster and of yow, I am but lost.   Also
my servaunt Maryot wyll go fro my wyfe to my ryght
gret hurte.   Wherfore, mastres, I besech your help in
all thes, and I xal content the costs as ye xall be
plesyd, be the grace of God, hoo ever preserve
yow, &c.

Also, mastres, I can not be with owte your contynuall
help, but I must selle or lete to ferme all that I have.

Mastres, my Lady sent to Cawnbrygg for a doctour
of fesyk.   If ye wyll ony thyng with hym, he xal abyde
this daye and to morwe.   He is ryght a konnyng man
and gentyll.

433.

A.D. 1461–6.

ELIZABETH MUNDEFORD TO JOHN PASTON.

[From Fenn, iv. 108.]

The date of this letter must lie between the years 1461 and 1466. The
writer's husband, who is spoken of as dead, was put to death in June 1460,
and John Paston, the person addressed, died in May 1466.

*To my right worchipfull sir, and my right good neveu,
John Paston, Squyer, be this lettre delyvered, &c.*

RIGHT worchipfull sir, and my right good
neveu, I recomand me un to you with all
myn herte.   Plece it you to undyrstande the
grete nessessyte of my wrytyng to you is this,
that ther was made an exchaunge be the graunsyre of
my hosbonds Mundeford, un hose sowle God have
mercy, of the maner of Gressenale with the aunsetrys
of Rows for the maner of Estlexham, the qwych is
parte of my juntor, and my grauntfadyr Mundeford
recoweryd the said maner of Estlexham be assyze[1] a
geyne the aunsetrys of Rows, and so madyt clere; and

[1] Assize is a writ directed to the sheriff of the county for recovery of the
possession of things immoveable, whereof yourself or ancestors have been
dispossessed.—F.

nowe have Edmund Rows[1] claymyt the seyd maner
of Estlexham be the verteu of a tayle [*an entail*], and
hathe takyn possesseon, and made a feffement to my
Lord of Warewyke,[2] and Water Gorge,[3] and to Curde.[4]
And un Fryday be for Seynt Walentyne is Day Water
Gorge and Curde enteryd and toke possessyon for my
seyd Lord of Warewyke, and so bothe the forseyd
manerys were ontayled, and at the tyme of the
exchaunge made, the tayles and evydens of bothe for
seyd manerys were delyvered un to the partyes inde-
ferently be the avyse of men lernyd. Qwerfor I
beshech you that it plese you to take the grete labor
upon you to informe my Lordys good Lordchep of the
trowthe in the forme a bowyn wreten, and that it plese
you to undyrstand qwedyr that my Lord wyll a byde
be the feffment made to hym or not; and that it shall
plese my Lord that I may have right as lawe requeryt,
for I trust to God be soche tyme as my Lord shall be
informyd of the trowthe be you, that hese Lordchip
wyll not supportt the forseyd Rows a geyne my right.
And if I hadde very undyrstandyng that my Lord
would take no parte in the mater a bowe seyd, I would
trust to Godds mersy, and to you, and other of my
good fryndes, to have possession a geyne in right hasty
tyme, beshechyng you to pardon me of my symple
wrytyng, for hadde no leyser. Right worchipfull and
my right good neveu, I beshech the Blyssed Trenyte
have you in Hese gracyous kepyng.

Wreten at Norwych in gret hast, the Tewysday aftyr
Seynt Walentyne is Day.

Youre ouyn,   ELIZABETH MUNDEFORD.[5]

[1] Edmund Rous was second son of Henry Rous, Esq. of Dennington, in
Suffolk, the ancestor of the present Earl of Stradbroke.
[2] Richard Neville, Earl of Warwick.
[3] Walter Gorges, Esq., married Mary, the daughter and heir of Sir William Oldhall, and was at this time Lord of the Manor of Oldhall, in Great
Fransham. He died in 1466. His son and heir, Sir Edmund Gorges, afterwards married a daughter of Sir John Howard, Knight, the first Duke of
Norfolk of that family.—F.
[4] John Curde was Lord of the Manor of Curde's Hall, in Fransham.—F.
[5] Elizabeth Mundeford was the widow of Osbert Mundeford, Esq. of Hock-
wold, in Norfolk, and was daughter of John Berney, Esq., by which means
she was aunt to J. Paston.—F.

434.

A.D. 1460-4.

SIR ROBERT WILLIAMSON TO AGNES PASTON.

[From Fenn, iii. 48.]

The writer of this letter was Vicar of Paston from 1460 to 1464, and as he dates from Bromholm, which is in the immediate neighbourhood of Paston, we may presume that it was written during the time he held that benefice.

To my right reverent mastras, Agnes Paston, be this lettre delyveryd in haste.

RYGH wurchepful mastres, I recomaund me un to yow, thankyng yow of the gret chere that ze made me the last tyme that I was with zow. Mastres, in alle zour godys and ocu-pacyons that lyth in my simpil power to do in wurd, wil and dede, I have do my dylygens and my power therto, so I be savyd be fore God, and have owyn to your person ryght herty love; for the qwych I am ryght ille aqwyt, and it be as I understande yt; for it is do me to wete that I am swid with mor of my paryshchons for a reskuse makyng up on the offycers of the shrewys [*sheriff*], and I take God to record that it is wrongfully do on to us. And the gret fray that the [*they*] mad in the tyme of masse it ravyched my witts and mad me ful hevyly dysposyd. I pray Jesu gef hem grace to repent hem therof that the [*they*] that caused it may stand out of perel of soule.

Maystras, at the reverens of God, and as evyr I may do servyce that may be plesyng on to yow, send me justyly wurd be the brynger of this bylle ho ze wil that I be gydyd; for it is told me that if I be take I may no other remedy havyn but streyth to prison. For the whiche I have sold away xx*s*. wurth of stuffe; and the reswd [*residue*] of my stuff, I have put it in swier hande, for trwly I wil not abyde the joparte of the swth,—I have levir to go as far as my fet may ber me. Nevir the less as ze komand me to do, so it be not to my

'I.   G

gret hurt, I wil fulfille it.   Nomor to zow at this tyme,
but God send yow that grace that ze may kome to
His blyss.

　　Wreten at Bromholm in gret haste,
　　　　　　　　　Be your
　　　　　　　　　　　　Sir ROBERT WILLYAMSON.

435.

A.D. 1462, 7 Jan.
MARGARET PASTON TO JOHN PASTON.

[From Paston MSS., B.M.]

The contents of this letter clearly show that it was written in January 1462,
nine days after the misplaced letter No. 134. Compare Note, No. 431.

*To my ryth worchepfull husbond, John Paston, be thys
delyveryd in hast.*

RYTH worchepfull husbond, I recomand me to
yow.   Plesyt yow to wet that I sent yow a
lettyr by my cosyn Barneys man of Wychyngham wyche was wretyn on Seynt Thomas
Day in Crystmas,[1] and I had no tydyngys nor lettyr
of yow sene the wek befor Crystmas; wher of I mervayle
sore.   I fere me it is not well with yow be cawse ye
came not home or sent er thys tyme.   I hopyd verily
ye schold have ben at home by Twelthe at the ferthest.
I pray yow hertly that ye wole wychesave to send me
word how ye do as hastly as ye may, for my hert schall
nevyr be in ese tyll I have tydyngys fro yow.   Pepyll
of this contre begynyth to wax wyld, and it is seyd her
that my Lord of Clarans and the Dwek of Suthfolk and
serteyn jwgys with hem schold come downe and syt
on syche pepyll as be noysyd ryotous in thys contre.
And also it is seyd here, that there is retornyd a newe
rescwe up on that that was do at the scher.   I suppose
swyche talkynge comyth of false schrewys that wold
mak a rwmor in this contre.   The pepyll seyth here

　　　　　　　　　　　[1] *See* No. 134.

that they had levyr go up hole to the Kynge and compleyne of siche false screwys as they have be wrongyd
by a fore, than they schold be compleynyd of with owt
cause and be hangyd at ther owne dorys. In good feyth
men fere sore here of a comone rysyng but if [*i.e.* unless]
a bettyr remedy may be had to a pese the pepyll in hast,
and that ther be sent swyche downe to tak a rewyll as
the pepyll hathe a fantsy in, that wole be indeferent.
They love not in no wyse the Dwke of Sowthfolk nor
hys modyr. They sey that all the tretourys and ex-
torsyonerys of thys contre be meynteynyd by them and
by syche as they get to them with her goodys, to that
intent to meynten suche extorsyon style as hathe be do
by suche as hathe had the rewyll undyr them be fore
tyme. Men wene, and the Dwke of Sowthfolk come ther
scholl be a schrewd reuell but if [*unless*] ther come odyr
that be bettyr belovyd than he is here. The pepyll feryth
hem myche the more to be hurt, because that ye and
my cosyn Barney come not home; they sey they wot
welle it is not well with yow and if it be not well with
yow, they sey they wot well, they that wole do yow
wronge wole sone do them wronge, and that makyth
them all most mad. God for Hys holy mersy geve
grace that ther may be set a good rewyll and a sad in
this contre in hast, for I herd nevyr sey of so myche
robry and manslawter in thys contre as is now within
a lytyll tyme. And as for gadyryng of mony, I sey
nevyr a werse seson, for Rychard Calle seyth he can
get but lytyll in substans of that is owyng, nowthyr of
yowyr lyvelod nor of Fastolfys th'eyr. And John
Paston seyth, they that may pay best they pay werst;
they fare as thow they hopyd to have a newe werd
[*world*]. And the blyssyd Trinite have yow in Hys
kepyng and send us good tydyngys of yow.

    Yelverton is a good thredbare frend for yow and for
odyr in thys contre, as it is told me.

    Wretyn in hast on the Thorsday nex aftyr Twelthe.

        By yowyr

                MARGARET PASTON.

436.

A.D. 1462, 27 Jan.
MARGARET PASTON TO JOHN PASTON.

[From Paston MSS., B.M.]

This letter relates to the prisoner Piers mentioned in Nos. 361, 362, and
363. He seems to have been delivered by a general pardon issued at the
commencement of the reign of Edward IV. The letter bears no address. It
is endorsed, but in a much later hand:—" A lettre to J. Paston, Ar., from
his wife."

RYTH worchepfull husbond, I recomand me to
yow. Plesyt yow to wet that Perse was
delyveryd owt [of] preson by the generall
pardon that the Kynge hathe grantyd, whyche
was opynly proclamyd in the Gyld Hall. A none as
he was delyveryd he cam hedyr to me, God wote in an
evyll plyte, and he desyiryd me wepyng that I wold be
hys good mastres and to be mene to yow to be hys
good mastyr, and swore sore that he was nevyr defawty
in that ye have thowte hym defawty in. He seyd
that if ther wer ony coyne in the cofyr that was at
Wylliam Tavernerys it was ther withowt hys knowlage,
for hys mastyr wold nevyr lat hym se what was in that
cofyr, and he told me that the keyis wer sent to Thomas
Holler[1] by mastyr John Smyth. What Holler leyd in
or took owte he wot not as he sweryth. He offyrd me
to be rewlyd as ye and I wold have hym, and if I wold
comand hym, to go ageyn to preson, whedyr I wold
to the Castyll or to the Gyld Hall, he wold obey my
comandment. And seth that he came of hys owne
fre wyll withowt ony comandment of ony man or
desyir, I seyd I wold not send hym ageyn to preson,
so that he wold abyde yowyr rewyll when ye came
home. And so he is here with me and schall be tyll ye
send me word how ye wole that I do with hym.

[1] He was John Berney's executor.

Where fore, I pray yow that ye wole lete me have know-lage in hast how ye wole that I do with hym.

Item, I have spok with John Dame and Playter for the lettyr testymonyall, and John Dame hathe pro-mysyd to get it, and Playter schall bryng it to yow to London. Item, I have purveyd yow of a man that schall be here in Barsamys sted and ye wole, the wyche can bettyr cherysch yowyr wood, bothe in fellyng and fensyng there of than Barsam can; and he schall mak yow as many hyrdyllys as ye nede for yowyr fold, of yowyr owne wood at Drayton, and schall tak as lytyll to hys wagys as Barsam dothe; and he is holdyn a trew man. Item, Playter schall tell yow of a woman that compleynyd to the Dwk of Sowthefolk of yow, and the sey[d] Playter schall tell yow of the demenyng and answeryng of the scheryfe for yow, and also of the demenyng of the seyd Dwke, and of othir materys the wyche wer to longe mater to put in wryttyn. The pepyll of that kontre be ryth glad that the day yed [*went*] with yow on Monday as it ded. Ye wer nevyr so welcome in to Norfolk as ye schall be when ye come home, I trowe. And the blyssyd Trynyte have yow in Hys kepyng. Wretyn in hast on Wednysday next aftyr Seynt Augnet the Fyrst.

By yowyr M. P.

Item, Ric. Calle told me that he hathe sent you ; answer of all erands that ye wold shuld be do to Sir Thomas Howes. Sir Thomas Howes cam nowther to me nor sent syn that he cam home from London.

Will Worceter was at me in Cristemes at Heylysdon, and he told [me] that he spake with you dyvers tymys at London the last terme; and he told me that he hopyd that ye wolle be hys good master, and seyd he hopyd ye shuld have non other cause but for to be hys god maister. I hope and so do my moder and my cosyn Clere, that he wolle do well inowe, so that he be fayre fare with Dawbeney and Playter. Avise me to lete

Peers go at large and to take a promys of hym to com
to me a mong unto your comyng hom, and in the
mene while his demenyng may be knowyn and espyed
in mo thyngs.

437.

John Dowbigging to John Paston.

[From Paston MSS., B.M.]

This letter is evidently earlier in date than the last, and may perhaps have
been written at the close of the year 1460, but as it refers to the same prisoner
as the preceding No. we place it here for convenience. It is printed in the
fifth volume of Fenn's edition as a letter of Henry VII.'s time owing to a
misreading of the address, which might easily convey the impression that it
was directed to " Sir John Paston."

To the ryght reverent and worship sir, John Paston,
sum tyme Lord of Gresham, and now fermour therof,
as hit is seide.

PERYS of Legh come to Lynne opon Cristyn-
messe Even in the fresshest wise, and there he
dyned so as was; bot when my Lorde of
Oxenforde herde hereof he with his feliship
and suche as I and other your presoneres come rydyng
unto Lynne, and even unto the Bysshop gaole where
the seid Perys dyned with other of his feliship.   My
Lorde pulled hym oute of the seid gaole and made to
kest hym opon an horse, and tyed an halter by his
arme, and so ledde hym furth like hym selff.   And
even furthwith the seid Bysshop, the Mair, and other
their feliship mette with my seide Lorde and your
presoneres, and also the seide Perys tyed by an halter,
the Bysshop havyng thies wordes unto my Lorde with
his pillion[1] in his handes, "My Lordes, this is a presoner,
ye may knowe by his tepet and staff.   What will ye
do with hym?"   Therto my Lorde seide, "He is my
presoner nowe."   Wherto the Bysshop seid, "Where

[1] The hat worn by a Doctor of Divinity.

is youre warraunt or commission therto?" My Lorde
seide, " I have warraunt sufficiaunt to me." And
thus they departed, the Mair and all the cominaltie of
Lynne kepyng theire silence. Bot when we weren
goon, and Perys of Legh fast in Rysyng Castell, then
the yates of Lynne, by the Bysshop comaundement
weren fast sperred [*shut*] and keped with men of armes.
And then the Bysshop and his squyers rebuked the
Mair of Lynne and seid that he hade shamed both hym
and his toun for ever, with muche other langage, &c.

The Bysshop shulde have keped his Cristenmesse
at Gaywode, bot yet he come not oute of Lynne. In
faith, my Lorde dyd quyte hym als curageousely as ever
I wist man do. The Bysshop come to the toun with
lx. persones the same tyme, and made to sper the yates
after hym, bot when we mette, ther bode not with hym
over xij. persones atte the most, with his serjaunt of
armes; whiche serjaunt was fayn to lay doun his mase;
and so atte the same yates we come in we went oute,
and no blode drawen, God be thanked.

Yf ye will any thyng atte I may do, send me worde;
hit shall be doon to my power, &c. Comaunde me
to my maistresse your wyff, &c. And yf ye dar
joperdie your suyrtie of C. marc I shall come and se
you. And elles have me excused, for, &c.

> From youre oune,
>
> JOHN DOUEBIGGYNG.

438.

A.D. 1462, 1 Feb.
RICHARD CALLE TO JOHN PASTON.

[From Paston MSS., B.M.]

The manor of Burneviles in Nacton, near Ipswich, was part of the lands
of Sir John Fastolf which Paston inherited by his will; but his claim was
disputed by Jenney, one of the executors. As Jenney is here said to have
complained that his fee was two years in arrear, we may presume that it was
little over two years since Fastolf's death when this letter was written. For
further evidences of date compare No. 427. It may also be observed that we

find undoubted evidence that John Paston was residing in the Inner Temple six weeks later (*See* No. 442), whereas in the preceding year he was in Norfolk, where his brother Clement wrote to him news from London (No. 367).

To the ryght reverent and my mooste worschipful master, my Master John Paston, in the Inneer Tempyll.

Plesith it your maistership to witte that I have been at Burne-wyll in Nacton to receyve the rentes and fermys of the tenauntes. And I undrestande be them, and be Robert Goordon that Mastre Jenney whas there and helde a coorte on the Mondaye next aftre Tlwelthe, and warned the tenauntes that they schulde pay no money to no man onto the tyme they had worde from hym, seyng that he whas on of the feffeys of the same maner, and that he whas feed with Sir John Fastolff, of weche fee he was be hynde for ij. yere ; wherfore he desired the tenauntes that they schulde not be redy in payement onto the tyme they had word from hym, but that he myght be payed of his seide fee, lyke as the wylle of the deede was. Wherfore I can gete no money of them unto the tyme they have knowleche how it stond be twyx your maistership and Mr. Jenney ; for withoute Jenney write to hem or come hom ward that wey, and have the tenauntes to-gether and lete hem witte that ye ought to have the rentes and fermes of the seid maner, I can not see that ye be like to have but litell money there, withoute ye woll do distreyne throuout all the lordeschip. I have sette dayes to purvey her [*their*] money ayenst the first weke of cleene Lenton, and than they schul have an answere who shal receyve it. Wherfore that it please your maistership to remembre to speke to Mastre Jenney. The blissed Trinite preserve you and kepe you from all advercyte. Wreten at Yebbyshep [1] the furst daye of Februare.

Your pore servaunt and bedman,
R. CALLE.

Item, the maner of Stratton shuld paye of rente xxvj*s.* viij*d.*, weche the fermour seythe my mastresse Brandon is acorded with you. He is be hynde for certeine yeres, &c.

439.

A.D. 1462, 9 Feb.—JOHN PASTON TO ——————.

[From Paston MSS., B.M.]

The MS. is a rough draft signed by John Paston the eldest, and corrected in his hand. It seems to have been written on the cover of a letter addressed to himself ; for on the back is this direction in another hand :—" To my most reverent and worchepfull maister, John Paston the eldest, Esquier, be this deliveryd in hast."

_____

[1] Ipswich ?

We have inserted this letter in the year 1462, as this was the first year after Fastolf's death, when John Paston appears to have been residing in London in the beginning of February. The only other possible years are 1463, 1465, and 1466.

RIGHT trusty and welbeloved, I grete yow hartily well, and will ye wite that where hit is so, that Sir John Fastolf, whom God assoyle, with other, was sum tyme by Sir Herry Inglose enfeffed of trust of his maner offe Pyke-wurthe in Rutlande, the which made his wille, proved, that the seid maner sholde by solde by Robert Inglose and Edmunde Wychingham his executours, to whom the seid Sir John hath relesed, as his dute was to do; now it is so that for John Browne[1] ther is shewed a dede under seall of armes berynge date byfore his reles made to the Duke of Norffoke, Henry Inglose and other, contrarie to the wille of the seid Sir Herry and the trust of the feoffement that the seid Sir John Fastolff was enfeffed inne. And a letter of Attorney under the same seale of armes to yow, to deliver seison acordynge to the same feffement, to the gret disclaundre of the seid Sir John and all his, yef this be true. Wherfore I preie yow hertili that ye feith-fully and truly rescribe to me in all the hast ye may what ye knowe in this mater such as ye wull stonde by with outen glose, and how ye can imagine that this crafte shulde be practised, and specially whether ye yourself delivered seison in Rutlond or noo. And this and what incedentes ye knowe, I preie yow by wrytinge certefie me in all hast, that I may be the more ripe to answer to this, to the wurship of the seid Sir John, that was your maister, so that thorowh your defaute your seid maisters soule ther for lie not in perell, but this disclaundre may be eesed and cesed as reson requireth, to the wurship of hym and all that longe to hym. And this I pray yow faile not offe as I truste yow. Wret at Londo[n] the ix. day of Februar.

Yowr frend, JON PASTON.

[1] This name is substituted for "Herry Inglose," struck out.

440.

A.D. 1462, [Feb.]
SIR THOMAS HOWES TO JOHN PASTON.

[From Fenn, iv. 68.]

For evidence of the date of this letter, Fenn quotes the following **extracts** from the Institution Books in the Registry of the Bishop of Norwich :—
    " Draiton
    "Reg. xi. 124.   29 January 1460-1. Johannes Bullock ad præsentationem Joh'is Paston arm. et Tho. Howys capellani.
    "Reg. xi. 131. 15 March 1461-2. Joh'es Flourdew ad præsentationem eorundem."
    It thus appears that the living was resigned by John Bullock in 1461-2, and on the 15th March John Flourdew was presented to it, not the person here recommended by Howes.

To the ryght wurshipfull sir and meyster, myn Mayster John Paston, Squier.

RYGHT worshipfull sire and mayster, I recomaunde me to yow. And please yow that
the chirche of Drayton is or shal be resyngned
in hast in to the Bysshopys hands by Sir
John Bullok, desyryng yow hertly that ye lyke I may
have the presentacion of the next avoydaunce for a
newew of myn, callyd Sir Reynold Spendlove, whiche
I truste youre maystership wold agree to make in
youre name and myn as was last, &c.   And, sir, please
yow also that I have hadde diverse communicacions
with Worcestr sethe Crystmesse,[1] and I fele by hym
otterly that he wole not appoynt in other fourme than
to have the londs of Feyrechildes and other londes in
Drayton to the sume of x. marc of yow proprely, by syde
that that he desyreth of myn mayster, whom God
assoyle, whiche mater I remytte to your noble discrecion.

And as for answere of the bylles that I have, I have
ben so sekelew sethe Crystmasse that I myght not
yette don hem, but I shal in alle hast, wher inne ye
may excuse yow by me if ye please tyl the next terme,

1 This word is indicated by Fenn as indistinct in the MS.

at whiche tyme alle shal be aunswered, be Godds grace, who preserve yow and send yow th' accomplyshement of youre desyres, &c.

Item, sere, please youre maystership hit was leten me wete in ryght secrete wyse that a pyssaunce is redy to aryve in thre parties of this londe, by the meane of Kyng Herry and the Quene that wes, and by the Dewk Somercete and others, of vi.ˣˣ· m.ˡ [120,000] men; and here dey, if wynde and weder hadde servyd theym, shuld a' ben here sone upon Candelmasse; at Trente to London werdes thei shuld a' ben by Candelmasse or sone after, one parte of theym, and another parte comyng from Walys, and the thredde fro Yernessey and Garnesseye. Wher fore it is weel don ye enforme myn Lord Warwyk, that he may speke to the Kyng that good provy[s]ion be hadde for withstandyng there malicyous purpose and evyl wylle, whiche God graunt we may our come theym; and so we shuld, I dought not, if we were alle on [one]. There ben many mede-lers, and they ben best cheryshed, whyche wold hurt moche if these come to, as God diffende, &c.

T. Howys.

441.

A.D. 1462, March.
Margaret Paston to John Paston.

[From Fenn, ii. 288.]

It appears by the dates of the Privy Seal writs that Edward IV. was at Cambridge on the 2d and 3d March 1462, and this is probably the visit alluded to, although we do not find that the King went on to Sandwich afterwards.

To my ryth worchepfull husbond, John Paston, be this delyveryd in hast.

PLESYTH yow to wete that John Wellys and hys brodyr told me thys nyth that the Kyng lay at Cambryge as yestyrsnyth to Sand-

wyche ward, for ther is gret dyvysyen be twyx the
Lordys and the schypmen ther, that causyth hym to
goo thedyr to se a remedye therfor.

I thank God that John Paston yed non erst [*went
no earlier*] forthe, for I trust to God all schall be do
er he comyth. And it is told me that Syr John
Howard is lek to lese hys hed.

If it plese yow to send to the seyd Wellys, he schall
send yow mor tydyngys than I may wryt at thys tyme.
God have yow in Hys kepyng.

Wretyn in hast at Thetford, at xj. of the clok in the
nyth, the same day I departyd fro yow.

I thank Pampyng of hys good wyll, and them that
wer cause of changyng of my hors, for they ded me a
bettyr torne than I wend they had do, and I schall
aquyt them anothyr day, and I maye.

　　　　　By yor　　　　　　　　　　M. P.

442.

A.D. 1462, 13 March.
JOHN PASTON, THE ELDER, TO HIS FATHER.

[From Fenn, iv. 126.]

It appears by the dates of the Privy Seal writs that Edward the Fourth was
at Stamford, from the 9th to the 17th March in the second year of his reign,
i.e. in 1462. This letter belongs therefore to that year.

*To myn ryth reverent and worschypfull fader, John
Paston, beyng in the Inder Temple.*

RYGHT reverent and wyrshypfull fader, I recomand me un to you, be sychyng you of your
blessyng and gode faderhode. Pleasyt it
you to understond the grete expens that I
have dayly travelyng with the Kyng, as the berour
here of can enfourme you; and howe long that I am
lyke to tary here in thys country or I may speke with
you a gayn, and howe I am chargyd to have myn hors

and harnys redy, and in hasty wyse, besykyng you to consyder theys causes, and so to remembr me that I may have suche thynges as I may do my mayster servys with and pleasur, trusting in God it schall be to your wyrshyp and to myn and vayll [*avail*]. In especiall I besyche you, that I may be sur where to have mony somwhat be fore Estern, other of you, or by myn uncle Clement, when nede ys. Of othir causes the berour hereof can enfourme you. No more to you at thys tyme, but God have you in Hys kepyng.

Wryten at Stamford, the xiij. day of March.

Be yowr sone and servant,

JOHN PASTON, THE OLDER.

443.

A.D. 1462, March.—REPORT OF FRENCH PRISONERS.

[From Fenn, i. 250.]

This letter evidently refers to the state of matters in the beginning of the year 1462, when Henry VI. and Margaret of Anjou were in Scotland, and when the Earl of Oxford had just been beheaded for conspiring against Edward IV. The date of Oxford's execution was the 20th of February. This confession of the Frenchmen is dated in the third week of Lent, that is to say, between the 14th and the 20th of March.

Memorandum. This is the confessyon of xvj. Frenshe-men with the Mastyr, takyn at Sheryngam, the iij. wek of Lent.

RIGHT worshipfull sir, I recomaund me to you, and lete you wytte, that I have be at Shiryng-ham, and examyned the Frenshmen to the nombre of xvj. with the maister. And thei telle that the Duke of Somerset is in to Scotland ; and thei sey the Lord Hungyrforthe was on Monday last passed afore Sheryngham in to Scotland ward, in a kervyle [*carvel*] of Depe, no gret power with hym, ne with the seid Duk neyther. And thei sey that the Duk of Burgoyn[1] is poysened, and not like to recovere. And

1 Philip the Good,

as for powers to be gadered ayenst our weelfare ; thei
sey, there shulde come in to Seyne CC. gret forstages[1]
owt of Spayne, from the Kyng there ;[2] and CCC.
shippes from the Duk of Bretayne[3] with the navy of
Fraunce, but thei be not yet assembled, ne vitayll there
purveyd, as thei sey, ne men. And the Kyng of
Fraunce[4] is in to Spayne on pilgrymage with fewe
hors as thei sey; what the purpose is thei can not telle
certeyn, &c. In hast at Norwich.

The Kyng of Frauns hath comitted the rewle of
Bordews on to the marchaunds of the toun, and the
browd[5] tha[t] be therin to be at ther wages; and like
as Caleys is a Stapole of wolle here in England, so is
that made staple of wyne.

John Fermer, presoner, seyth, on [_one_] John Gylys,
a clerk that was with the Erle of Oxforthe, wych was
some tym in Kyng Herrys hows, was a prevy secretary
with the Erle of Oxforthe ; and if any wrytyng wer
made by the seyd Erle, the seyd Gylys knew ther of in
this gret matyeres.

444.

A.D. 1462, 24 March.
JAMES GRESHAM TO JOHN PASTON.

[From Fenn, iv. 76.]

It does not appear that Edward IV. ever did spend an Easter at Bury,
as here projected. He was, however, at Cambridge in the beginning of
March 1462; from which he proceeded to Peterborough, Stamford, Newark,
and Lincoln, and at Easter (18th April) he seems to have been at Leicester.

To my right singler maister, J. Paston, Squyer, in hast, &c.

FTER due recomendacion, please it your
maistership to wyte Maister Yelverton, justice,
seid in the Sessions that the Kyng shulde

---

[1] Large ships with forestages or forecastles.
[2] Henry IV., King of Castile.
[3] Francis II., the last Duke.   [4] Lewis XI.
[5] This word, says Fenn, is imperfect in the original.

kepe his Estern at Bury, and from thens come
unto this cuntre and se suyche riottes as have be in
this cuntre punyshed in suche fourme as happely
summe shulde hange by the nekke.   And he tolde
what thank he had of the Kyng at Cambrigg for cause
he declarid so well the charge of extorcions doon by
Shirefs and other officers, &c., for the whiche declara-
cion the Kyng tooke hym by the hand, and seid he
cowde hym grett thanke, and prayed hym so to do in
this cuntre, &c.

In hast, at Norwich, the Wednesseday next tofore
th'Annunciacion, &c.

Your povere,   J. GRESHAM.

445.

A.D. 1462, 25 March.

JOHN WYKES TO JOHN PASTON.

[From Fenn, i. 252.]

As this letter relates to the arrest of a confederate of the Earl of Oxford
and his son, who were executed in February 1462, for conspiring against
Edward IV., the date must be referred to that year.

*To my right trusti and welbelovid frend, John Paston,
Esquier.*

RIGHT worshipfull, and myn enterly welbelovyd
frend, I recomaund me un to you, hertely
thankyng you of your gret present of fisch,
and of the felyshipp that my cosyn your
sonne shewid unto me att Norwiche, purposyng be the
grace of God to deserve it un to you in tyme to come,
in such place as I may do for you.

Desiryng you specyally, wher as a tenaunt of myne
of Lavenham, called John Fermour, is sesid and
arestid with in the towne of Yermowth, be cause he
dwellid with the Erle of Oxonfords son, and purposid
to have passid the see withou[t] lycence, and stondyth

out of the conceyte of much peple, I wold desyre you, that ye wold wryte to the Baylyffs of Yermouth to delyver the seid John Fermor to my servaunt John Brenerigg, brynger of this, with an officer of the seid Towne, to be caried unto the Kyngs Castell of Rysing at my cost; ther to be examynid of certeyne Artycules, which I may not disclose, til I have spoke with the Kyngs Highnes: praying you to wryte to the seid Bayliffs, that I shall be her suffisant discharge ayenst the Kynge. Desyryng yow to geve credence to the brynger herof, as my verray trust is in yow.

Wretyn at Lavenham, the xxv^{th.} day of Marche.

> Your trew and feithfull frend, havyng no blame for my gode wylle.   JOHN WYKES,

Ussher of the Kyngs Chambre.

446.

A.D. 1462, April?
JOHN RUSSE TO JOHN PASTON.

[From Fenn, iv. 112.]

This letter must have been written before the 14th of April 1462, on which day the Earl of Worcester was appointed Treasurer of the Exchequer. (Patent Roll, 2 Edw. IV. p. 1. m. 19).

To the right reverent and worshipfull sir, and my right honourable maystyr, John Paston.

RIGHT worshipfull sir, and my right honourable maistir, I recomaunde me to you in my most humble wise. And plese it youre good maistirshyp to wete that it is seyd here that my Lord Worcestre is lyk to be Tresorer, with whom I truste ye stonde right wel in conseit, with whiche God contynwe. Wherfor I beseke youre maistirshipp that if my seid Lord have the seid office, that it lyke you to desyre the nomynacion of on of the officez, eythyr of the countroller or serchorship of Jernemuth, for a servaunt of yowrez, and I shuld so gyde me in the office as I truste shuld be most profit to my seyd Lord. And if youre maistirshyp lyked to gete graunt thereof, that than it plesyd you to lycense on of youre servaunts to take out the patent of the seyd office; and if it cost v. or vj. or viij. marke, I shal trewly contente it ageyn; and yeerly as longe as I myght have the officez, or any of hem, I shal geve my maister youre sone v. marke toward an haukeney.

It shuld be to me right a good mean to stondyn as well in the trust as in the conseyt amongs marchaunts, with whom and with alle men I calle myself a servaunt of yourez, and soo wil do, if it plese you, which boldyth me the more to calle upon youre right wurshipful maistyrshyp in this mater, where in I beseke you to forgeve me my boldneyse in thys behalve. And if I knew that my Lord shuld have the office in sertayn, than I wold wayte upon youre good maystyrshyp there to opteyne the patent, if it plesyd youre good maystirship to gete me the graunt, &c.

No more on to you, my right honourable maister, at thys tyme, but Jesu I beseke sende you a good conclucyon in all yore maters, and graunt you ever youre herts desyre.

Yore contynwal servaunt and bedeman,

JOHN RUSSE.

447.

A.D. 1462, 4 May.—W. C. TO JOHN PASTON.

[From Paston MSS., B.M.]

The manor of Weeting, in Norfolk, came to John Vere, 12th Earl of Oxford, by his marriage with Elizabeth, daughter and heir of John Howard, Esquire, son and heir of Sir John Howard, Knight. This Earl was beheaded in February 1462, for treason against Edward IV., and the present letter seems to have been written 'n May following.

*To myn ryght worshipfull and ryght singler good mayster, myn
Mayster John Paston.*

Myn ryght worshipfull mayster, I recomaunde me to yow in
myn ryght homble wyse. And please your maystershyp that I
have ben at Wetyng and there hald the court and lete on Hok-
monday[1] as hit hath bene of olde tyme accostomed; and the
tenauntes have attorned and bene full gladde that myn lady
shuld rejoyse hit and kepe here possession. The priour of Brom-
hill that was fermoure his terme is expired, and wole sewe to myn
lady and hir councell to have a newe terme; but lete myn lady
be ware, for, as I here seyn, he bydeth but a tyme that he myght
gete a summe of money to geders of myn ladyes lyflode, and to
gone ther with[2] a love of his sojornyng as yette in Hokehold.
She hath bene dreven fro town to town for his sake. Hit is wele
done ye advertyse myn lady, if she be in that cas that she hath
governaunce of hir owen londes, that she do no thyng to that
lyflode ner non other in Norffolk, with ought advyse of theym
that have vysyted and overseen theym; for there hath bene
straunge rewle, bothe in woodsales and sale of londes helde at
wylle for fre rent, as ye shal knowe here after. Thoresby, a man
that was generall attorney for myn Lord Oxenford that was, told
me that the Kynge hadde made Keche generall receyvoure by
priveseale of alle londes that were the Erle of Oxenford and
Dame Elyzabet, ecept tho that Howard hadde entered and Lan-
ham and an other graunted to Wykes, and certeyn lyflode in
Kent that was assigned to the tresorer of howshold of the Kynges
hows; and she shuld have be Keches hande v.ᶜ [500] mark, ij.ᶜ and
l. [250] mark to bene payed at this Estern and the remulant at
Mihelmasse. And of the remulant the Kyng shuld be answered.
Ye shal sone understande how it is; and if hit be so, hit [is][3] but
foly to laboure any ferther. I wold fayn knowe, for the courtes
for the half yere wold bene holde for nede. And our Lord be
with youre maystership and sende yow th'accomplyshement of
youre noble desyres. Wreten hastely at Norwyche, the iiijᵗᵉ
day of May.

Youre servaunt to his power,

W. C.

And whan ye comon with myn ryght worshipfull lady I
beseche yow remembre myn pore maters in whiche is greet
concyens, &c.

---

[1] Hock Monday was a fortnight after Easter Monday. In 1462 it fell on
the 3d May, the day before this letter was written.
[2] *With* repeated in MS.   [3] Omitted in MS.

448.

A.D. 1462, 18 May.
MARGARET PASTON TO JOHN PASTON.

[From Paston MSS., B.M.]

This letter is evidently not far removed in date from No. 422, in which "Joan Gayne's matter" is also mentioned. The year, however, cannot be 1461, as William Paston was in London that year as early as the 4th April. It seems also from this letter that John Paston had recently left home, which could not have been the case in 1461 if No. 388 be of that year. We have therefore little doubt that the true date is 1462, and that the substance of the letter relates to proceedings taken by the widow of Thomas Denys against her husband's murderers.

To my ryght wurschipful maister, John Paston.

I recomaunde me unto you. Plesith it you to witte that I have spoken with Furbuschour and other of the matre that ye spake to me off, and they have promysed me to be as feythefull in it as it where for hem selfe. Also I have spoken with my modre and seide to here as ye desired me to doo, and sche seide sche knewe the massache weele inowe before be other persones in like wice as ye comaunded hem to sey to her; and sche seide she wode fayne that ye dede weele what so ever ye sey and fille forthe in other talkyng. Me semethe che is displesed that ye came not to her or than ye roode foorthe. I schall telle you more whan that ye come home. Thomas Denys wyff whas at me, and desired me that I schulde sende to you and desire you that che myght have knowleche from you how ye woll that sche schall doo with her matre; sche seithe her brother and other of her frendes thynke that she schulde up to London and calle uppon her matre there, but she seithe pleynly sche woll nought doo therin withoute your advice. It whas toolde me that Bacon and Gonnor whas here to speke with me for the matre that Bacon spake to you of, and at that tyme I whas at Norweche and I herde no more of hem sethen. And as for my brother

William, he is not purposed to come to London tyll
aftre Pentecost; but my brother Clement is purposed
to come forward on Monday or on Twesday next
comyng at the ferthest. No more at this tyme but the
blissed Trinite preserve you. Wreten the xviij. day of
May.   Your MARGARET PASTON.

I prey yow that ye woll wete safe to remembre
Johane Gayne matre, and that ye woll take John
Paston that he remember you of it, for Dawbeney and
Pampyng woll sone for gete it.

449.

A.D. 1462, May.
JOHN PASTON, JUNIOR, TO HIS FATHER.

[From Fenn, iv. 100.]

On the 29th May 1462 a commission was granted to Sir John Howard and
Sir Thomas Walgrave to arrest the ships, the *Mary Talbot* and the *Mary
Thomson*, both of Lynn, and other vessels in Norfolk, Suffolk, and Essex,
for a fleet which the King was fitting out (*see* Patent Roll, 2 Edw. IV.,
p. 1, m. 14, *in dorso*). Sir Thomas Walgrave may perhaps have been the
person designated in this letter as the Master of Carbrooke. At all events,
the date is clearly about this time.

To my ryght wurschipfull fadre, John Paston.

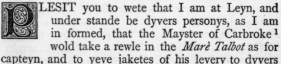PLESIT you to wete that I am at Leyn, and
under stande be dyvers personys, as I am
in formed, that the Mayster of Carbroke [1]
wold take a rewle in the *Marè Talbot* as for
capteyn, and to yeve jaketes of his levery to dyvers
personis qwych be waged be oder men, and nouth be
hym, beyng in the said shep. Qwerfor in as moch as
I have but few sowdeors in myn levery her, to stren-
keth me in that qwych is the Kynges commandement,
I kepe with me yowr too men, Dawbenney and Calle,
qwich I purpose shall seyle with me to Yermeth; for

[1] At Carbrooke, in Norfolk, was a commandry formerly belonging to the
Knights Templars, which, like most of the possessions of the order, when it
was suppressed in Edward II.'s time, was given to the Knights of St. John.

I have purveyed harneyse for hem.   And ye shall well
understande, be the grace of God, that the said
Mayster of Carbroke shall have non rewle in the
sheppes, as I had purposid he shuld have had, because
of his besynesse, and for this is on of the specyall
causes I kepe yowr said men with me, besechyng you
ye takyt to non dysplesur of ther taryng with me.
Nat withstandyng, ther herden [1] at Wyggenalle shall be
don this day be the grace of God, Whoo have you in
kepyng.

Wreten at Leynn, the morow after my departyng
from you.

Item, as far such tydynges as be here, Th. shall in
forme you.   JOHN PASTON.

450.

A.D. 1462, 6 June.—ABSTRACT.

[From MS. Phillipps, 9735, No. 354].

Inventory of household stuff remaining at Castre, 6 June 2
Edward IV., viz., of robes, jewels, arras, &c.

451.

NOTE.

Among some MSS., which seem formerly to have belonged to
the Paston Collection in the Bodleian Library at Oxford, is one
endorsed—" A Pedigree showing how the manor of Caister was
divided," tracing its descent from earlier owners to Sir John
Fastolf.

452.

A.D. 1462, 3 July.—J. DAUBENEY TO JOHN PASTON.

[From Fenn, iv. 138].

The date of this letter is shown by an entry on the Patent Roll, 2 Edward
IV., p. 1, m. 7, *in dorso.*   On the 27th June 1462, a commission was given to

[1] I do not understand the meaning of the word "herden."—F.

Gilbert Debenham, Jun., Esquire, Walter Alderiche, master of the *George* of Yarmouth, and John Childe, to arrest for the King's service a ship called *The Barge of Yarmouth, alias The George*, with victuals, masters, and mariners for the same.

To my most reverent and worchepfull maister, John Paston, dwellyng at Heylysdon, be this delyveryd.

Ih's.

MOST reverent and worchepfull master, I recommaund me onto your god masterchep. Please you to have knowlage, on the Fryday at afternoon next after Seynt Peter, there was at the taveran in London old Debnam and young Debnam, Thomas Edmonds, and I; and ther the seyd Thomas Edmonds fell in communicacion with old Debnam, and seyd that my Lord Tresorer [1] had put hym to a gret charge for the vetelyng of *Mary Talbot*,[2] seyyng to old Debnam that he hard sey that he had a C. bulloks to selle, the wyche the seyd Edmonds wolle bey so that they may a cord of the price. Than the seyd old Debnam answerd ageyn, and seyd he wold, so that he myght have good payment, or elles the seyd Edmonds to be bound in abligacion to pay hym at suche dayys as they myght a cord. And noon upon thys same langwage, yong Debnam spake to hys fader, "Sir, I pray you that ye wolle take avisment of this mater tille to morowe, for I trost to your good faderhod that ye wolle late me have a serteyn of your bullocks for the vetelyng of the *Barge of Yermothe*, and I shall fynd you sufficiant suerte for the payment therof for Edmonds. I wolle that ye knowe I have be ther, and spoke with the owner and with the maister of the seyd barge, and they knowyn myn oppoyntment."

Than the seyd Edmonds answered to yong Debnam, and told hym that the sety of Norwic and Yermothe hathe grauntyd, and send wrytyng to the Kynge and

---

[1] John Tiptoft, Earl of Worcester. He was beheaded in October 1470.—F.
[2] *See* Preliminary Note to No. 449.

to the Lords that they wolle manne and veteylle the
seyd barge of her owne cost fro the tym of hyr goyng
owt tylle hyr comyng home; and thus the seyd
Edmonds told hym that my Lord Tresorer and all the
Lords that be at London thynk they do ryght well her
devyer, and be worthey moche thanke of the Kyng.
"Well," quod yong Debnam, "I had in commaundment for to have the rewle of the seyd barge, and I
wolle be at Yermothe as thys day iiij. dayys, and man
hyr and bryng hyr downne to the Gylys of Hulle, for
that ys my chype."

Also he seyd mor, with out that he myght have the
seyd barge, he wolle note goo to see but hym self and
hys xxiiij. men. And thus, yf please your maisterchep,
he departyd from the taveran; and at hys departyng,
he told the seyd Thomas Edmonds, "Thys ys Paston
labor." Than the seyd Edmonds answerd hym ageyn,
and seyd playnly he was to blame for to reporte so of
your masterchep, for he knoythe veryly he seyd on
trewly of you and of my master your son bothe, and
ther on he wold take a hothe. And so, yf it please
your good masterchep, late the cety of Norwic and
Yermothe have knowlage of hys gret crakyng and
bost, and let hym of hys purpose by the autorite that
they have.

Item, my master your son wolle have to hys jakets
murry[1] and tany [*tawny*], and that it please yow sum
of my felachep may spek to on of the drapers for to
ordeyn yt ageyns hys comyng hom, for I trowe it shall
be thys day sevenyght ar he comithe home.

Item, sir, if please you, Skrowpe hathe sent to you
to London be Byngham for the mony that ye knowe
of, zit I spake not with hym; but I shall telle hym
that I suppose ye shall be here in the last end of the
terme, and I shall send your masterchep word what
answer I have of hym.

Item, sir, if pleese suche tydyngs as I her of, I send
you word. My Lord of Warwek hathe be in Skotlond,

---

[1] Dark red or purple and yellowish colour.--F.

an take a castell of the Skoots; and upon thys ther came the Quene of Skoots [1] with other Lords of her contre, as ye shall her the namys, in basetry [*embassy*] to my seyd Lord of Werwek, and a trews is take betwyx thys and Seynt Bertylmew Day in Auguste. Thes is the last tydyngs that I knowe. No mor to your god masterchep at this tyme, but Jesu have [you] in kepyng.

Wretyn on the Saturday next after Seynt Peter.

By your por servaunt,

J. DAUBENEY.

453.

A.D. 1462.
RICHARD CALLE TO JOHN PASTON, JUNIOR.

[From Fenn, iv. 144.]

This and the next letter were evidently written not very long after the last.

To my maistre, John Paston the yonger, be this delyvered.

SERE, I have receyved your lettre, wherin I undrestand that my maistre desired that my maistre your brother myght have the gidyng and governaunce of the *Barge of Yermouthe*. As to that, and men of Yermouthe had knowen my maistre entend a fornyght a goo, he had ben swer of it, but nough it is so that Debenham hathe a comyscion of the Kyng expressed oonly for that schip named in hes comyscion; and he hathe ben here at Yermouthe, and spoken with the balyffs and with the owners of the seide schip, and takyn suche a direccion that they may graunted it ne man but hym. And moreover he hathe endented with the owners of the schip what daye it schulbe redy as well vetaylled as manned; and also he hathe brought downe letters

[1] Mary, daughter of Arnold, Duke of Gelders, and mother to James III., King of Scotland.

from my Lord Tresorer to all priours and gentlemen in this contre to helpe hym and assiste hym to vetayle and manne the seide schip, and hes men is here dayle, and gothe abought and gathereth whete, malt, money, and what so ever any man woll geve, &c.

The blissed Trinyte preserve you. Wreten at Castre, the Friday next aftre I receyved your lettre.

Item, is talked here that my maistre your brother and Debenham were at words at London, and that Debenham shuld have streken hym, had nought Howard a' beene, &c., wherof I am ryght sory, &c. Neverthelesse I trust to God all schul be weell.

Your servuant,   Ric. Calle.

454.

Richard Calle to John Paston.

[From Fenn, iii. 430.]

To my maistre, John Paston.

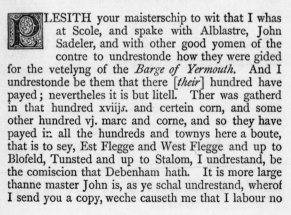

PLESITH your maisterschip to wit that I whas at Scole, and spake with Alblastre, John Sadeler, and with other good yomen of the contre to undrestonde how they were gided for the vetelyng of the *Barge of Yermouth.* And I undrestonde be them that there [*their*] hundred have payed; nevertheles it is but litell. Ther was gatherd in that hundred xviij*s.* and certein corn, and some other hundred vj. marc and corne, and so they have payed in all the hundreds and townys here a boute, that is to sey, Est Flegge and West Flegge and up to Blofeld, Tunsted and up to Stalom, I undrestand, be the comiscion that Debenham hath. It is more large thanne master John is, as ye schal undrestand, wherof I send you a copy, weche causeth me that I labour no ferther therin.   Notwithstandyng your maisterschip schal have knowleche what every hundred geve, and Yermeth bothe.

Wreten at Wynterton, the morwe aftre I departed from your maisterschip.

> Your poore bedman,
>
> Ric. Calle.

455.

A.D. 1462 ? [5 July].—Abstract.

[From Paston MSS., B.M.]

Richard Calle to John Paston.

Cannot inform him how much malt he has at Castre, "for the malters have not moten all up yet,"—probably 400 quarters new and 160 comb old malt of Castre and Mauteby, of which 40 quarters will be spent in the household by Hallowmas.   At Yarmouth it is now 2s. 2d. a bushel—it was 2s. 6d.   But London is a better market.   Thinks the price will fall here, as the fields are reasonably fair in Flegge, and so up to Norwich.   The carriage from Yarmouth to London will be 6d. per quarter, "and I understand j. quartre of Yermothe mette makethe at London but vij. busschell."

Norwich, Monday after St. Peter's Day.

[As John Paston does not seem to have been in undisturbed possession of Caister before 1462, and we have evidence of Richard Calle having been there in that year about the time of year when this letter was written, we may with great probability refer it to that year.]

456.

A.D. 1462 (?) 15 July.
John Russe to John Paston.

[From Fenn, iv. 120].

The precise year in which this letter was written is a little uncertain, but from the date and contents it would appear that Russe was now in possession of the office, which, in No. 446, he had asked Paston to procure for him ; so that it cannot be earlier than 1462.

To the right worshypful my right honourabyl mayster,
John Paston.

IGHT worshipfull sir, and my right honourabill maister, I recomaund me to you in my most humble wyse, and please your maistirship to wete that her is on Thomas Chapman, an evyl disposyd man al wey ayens you, as I have informyd youre maistirship many tymes, and now he hathe labouryd to my Lord Tresorer to subplante me, and brought down wryghting from the Kyng and my Lord Tresorer; but or hise wryting cam, Wydwell fond the meanys, be the supportacion of Maistir Feen, that we had a discharge for hym out of the Chauncery; wherfor the seyd Chapman proposyth to be at London in all haste, and to avertise the Kyng and my Lord Tresorer ageyn me to the grettest hurt he can imagyne. Wherfor I beseke youre maystirship, consedryng is evyl disposecion to yow, and also the rather at my pore instaunce, that ye lyke that my Lord Tresorer myght undyrstonde that the seyd Chapman is of no reputacion, but evyl disposyd to brybory of straungers, and be colour of hise office of supervisor of the searche shal gretly hurte the port. The seyd Chapman supportors is Blakeney, clerk of the sygnet, and Avery Cornburght, yoman of the Kynges chaumbre. He hathe here of Avereyes xxiiij. tune wyn, whereof at the long wey he shal make the seyd Averey a lewd rekenyng. The seyd Chapman lovyth not you, nor no man to yow wards, &c.

Sir, I prey God brynge you onys to regne amongs youre cuntre men in love, and to be dred. The lenger ye contynwe there the more hurt growyth to you. Men sey ye will neyther folwe the avyse of youre owyn kynred, nor of youre counsell, but contynwe your owyn wylfullnesse, whiche, but grace be, shal be youre distrucion. It is my part to enfourme youre maistirshyp as the comown voyse is, God betir it, and graunt yow onys herts ease; for it is half a deth

to me to here the generall voyse of the pepyll, whiche
dayli encreassyth, &c.

Sir, I beseke youre maistirshyp to remember my
maystresse for the lytil sylvir, whiche for serteyn
thyngs delyverid to youre use is dewe to me. I have
nede of it now. I have bought salt and other thyngs,
whiche hathe brought me out of myche sylvir. I wold
trust, and I nedyd to borwe xx*li.*, your maistirshyp
wold ease me for a tyme, but thys that I desyre is
myn owyn dute. And Jesu graunt yow ever yowr
herts desyre to youre worshyp and profyt, and preserve
yow my right honourabyll maister from all adversyte.

Wretyn at Jernemuthe, the xv. day of July. Here
is a kervyl [*carvel*] of Cane in Normandy, and he
takyth Duchemen, and raunsumyth hem grevously.

Yore servaunt and bedman,

JOHN RUSSE.

457.

A.D. 1462, July.
WILLIAM PASTON TO JOHN PASTON.

[From Paston MSS., B.M.]

The reference to the death of Christopher Hanson proves this letter to have
been written in July 1462, as the precise date of his death is given in Letter
459.

To myn wurchipfull broder, Jon Paston.

RYTHTHE wurchipfull broder, I recomand [me]
to zow. Lekit it zow to wethe [*wit*], Jon of Dam
is come to towne, and purposit hym to tary
here a day ar ij. ar longar, I can thynk, and
he be desyryd. Were fore I pray zow, and as I have
afore this tyme desiryd zow the same, that suche
materis as hathe be comunyd now lathe be twyx myn
moder, zow and hym, may take some good conclucyon

be twyx owre selff here at hom. And in myn consayt,
savyng zow better avyse, it were so most convenyent
and wurchipfull for us all, and comforthe to all owre
fryndis. And for this ententhe I wold tary here the
lengar; for I wold be as glad as any man a lyve that
suche an ende mythe be take be twix us that iche off
us all schuld inyoy the wylleffar off odyr, qweche I
trust with zowr good help schall be rythe wyll, and I
dowthe nat myn mastyr Markam wyll be will plesyd
thus.

I have tydynges from London, and a monge odyr
tydynges I have knowlage that Cirstofre Hanson is
passid to God on Saterday last past, at ij. of clok after
mydnythe. It is good to take hede there to, &c.

Item, I sent to zow to have had zowre avyse qwat
menys were best to make for the mater towchyng the
Lord Scrop, qwere in I had an answer, but me thowthe
it was not to the poynthe. I sopose, and I purposyd
to make the labore that ze sent me word I schuld do
towchyng me, I can thynk I schuld sone be answerid,
meche sonar than he. I must send some answer to hym,
were in I wold have zowr consayll; for he desirid the
same, and I wold not he schold thynk that he were
forgotyn be us.

Be zowr pore broder,

WILLIAM PASTON.

I can thynk and he were here he wold be a feythfull frynd to zow; but and so were that ze thowthe
that it were for to labore for any oder man, me thynkit
it were for zow to remembre myn nevew. That were
somewat lykly, and there to wold I be glad to help
and lene to the toder. For as for me, I know so
moche that sche will none have but iff he have, ar
be leke to have, meche more lond than I have; and
iff I knewe the contrary, it schuld nat be left for the
labore, but I wold not be in a folis paradyce, and ze
be myn good brodir. I trust thow to do rythe will,
&c.

458.

A.D. 1462, July.
THOMAS PLAYTER TO JOHN PASTON.

[From Fenn, iv. 124.]

This letter, like the last, is dated by the letter following.

To my rigth good maister, John Paston the oldest, beyng at Heylesdon, besyde Norwiche, in hast.

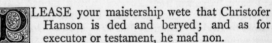PLEASE your maistership wete that Christofer Hanson is ded and beryed; and as for executor or testament, he mad non.

As for tydyngs, the Erles of Warrewyk, of Essex, Lord Wenlok, Bysshop of Dereham, and other go in to Scotland of inbassat. And as for the sege of Kaleys, we here no mor ther of, blyssed be God, ho have you in His kepyng.

Item, as for Christofers papers that longeth to your tenants, I have goten of William Worcester; and as for all the remnaunt of Christofer good, William Worcester hath the reule as hym semeth most convenient.

Your,   THOMS PLAYTER.

459.

A.D. 1462, July.
PLAYTER TO JOHN PASTON.

[From Fenn, i. 270].

This letter seems to have been penned immediately after the last was sent off.

To my maister, John Paston, at Heylesdon.

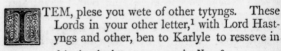TEM, plese you wete of other tytyngs. These Lords in your other letter,[1] with Lord Hastyngs and other, ben to Karlyle to resseve in

¹ *i.e.* the other letter to you—meaning No. 458.

the Qwen of Scotts ;[1] and uppon this appoyntement,
Erle Duglas [2] is comaunded to come thens, and as a
sorwefull and a sore rebuked man lyth in the Abbey of
Seynt Albons ; and by the said appoyntement schall
not be reputed, nor taken, but as an Englyssheman,
and if he come in the daunger of Scotts, they to sle
hym.

Item, Kyng Harry and his Aderents in Scotland
schall be delyvered ; and Lord Dakres of the Northe
is wonne and yelden, and the seid Lord, Sir Richard
Tunstall, and on Byllyngham in the said Castell ben
taken and heded.

Item, the Qwen and Prince ben in Fraunce and ha
mad moche weyes and gret peple to com to Scotland
and ther trust to have socour, and thens to com in to
Inglond : what schall falle I can not sey, but I herd
that these appoyntements were take by the yong Lords
of Scotland, but not by the old.

Your,

PLAITER.

Christofer dyed on the Satarday next be for Seynt
Margret,[3] Anno . E. ij^{do.}

460.

A.D. 1462, September.
JOHN RUSSE TO JOHN PASTON.

[From Fenn, i. 260.]

This letter must have been written in the year 1462 before the Duke of
Somerset was received into favour.   Proclamations similar to those mentioned
in this letter were issued on the 6th March 1461 and the 11th May 1464 ; but
neither of these can be the case referred to.   The coming of the King to
London must have been in the beginning of September 1462.   He was in
London on the 14th of that month, and had been at Fotheringay on the 1st,
as the dates of privy seals inform us.

---

[1] Mary of Gueldres, widow of James II.
[2] James, Earl of Douglas, who had been banished from Scotland, but was
made by Edward IV. a Knight of the Garter.
[3] St. Margaret's Day was the 20th July.   The Saturday before it in 1462
was the 17th.

*To my right honorabil and worshypfull maister, my
Maister Paston.*

PLEASE it youre worshipfull maistyrshyp to
wete, that it is informyd me thys day
scretly, that there is dyrected out a com-
myssion to mayster Yelwyrton and maister
Jenney, which shall tomorwyr syttyn be vertu of the
same at Seynt Oleffes;[1] and the substaunce of jentilmen and yemen of Lodyngland be assygned to be
afore the seyd commesyoners; and it is supposed it is
for my maisters londs, for as the seyd persone informyd me, the seyd comesyoners have been at Cotton,
and there entred, and holdyn a court. I can not informe youre maystyrship that it is thus in serteyn, but
thus it was told me, and desyryd me to kepe it secret;
but be cause I conseyve it is ageyn your maistyrship,
it is my part to geve you relacion thereof.

I sende you a letter which cometh from Worcestyr[2]
to my maister youre brothyr. I wold ye undyrstod the
intente of it, for as for Worcester, I knowe well he is
not good. Sum men ar besy to make werre, for p'[3] the
absentyng of my maister, the parson comyth not of
hyse owyn mocyon, but I wold youre maistyrship
knewe be whom it is mevyd. I herd you never calle
hym false pryst, be my trouth, nor other language that
is rehersyd hym, but Gode sende a good accord, for of
varyaunce comyth gret hurt of tyn tyme, and I beseche
Jesu sende youre maistyrship youre herts desyre, and
amende hem that wold the contrary.

Sir, yesterevyn a man came from London, and he
seyth, the Kyng cam to London on Satyrday, and
there dede make a proclamacion that all men that
were be twyx lx. and xvj. shuld be redy to wayte upon
hym whan so ever they were callyd; and it is seyd,
that my Lord Warwyk had sent to the Kyng, and

---

[1] St. Olave's, in Suffolk.   [2] William Worcester.
[3] p'.—So in Fenn's left hand copy. The word seems to have been ambiguous in the original MS., and is rendered "*by*" (in italics) in the modern
version.

informyd hyse Hyghnesse that the Lord Summyrset
had wretyn to hym to come to grace; but of the fleet
of shyppis there is no tydings in serteyn at London on
Monday last past.

Youre bedman and servaunt,
JOHN RUSSE.

461.

A.D. 1462?
JOHN PASTON TO THE LORD CHANCELLOR.

[From Paston MSS., B.M.]

This is a draft bill in Chancery prepared by John Paston with a view to
the commencement of a suit against Yelverton and Jenney for their entry
into the manor of Cotton and other lands of Sir John Fastolf in Suffolk. The
document may have been drawn up in the latter part of the year 1461 ; but
from the contents of the preceding letter it is not unlikely to have been a
year later. Two copies of this document exist, with the very same corrections and interlineations in both.

SHEWYTH and lowly compleynith on to
your good Lordship John Paston, the older,
Squier, that where Sir John Fastolf, Knyght,
cosyn to your seid besecher, was seasid of
diveris maners, londs, and tenements in Norfolk,
Suffolk, and Norwich, the xxvij. yere of Kyng Herre
that was, and therof infeffid diveris persones to execute
and performe his will, and mad his will in especiall
that a college of vij. monks shuld be stabilisshed,
founded, and indewed withinne a plase late be the
seid Sir John edified at Caster be the see in Norfolk,
and certeyn livelode to be immortesid[1] therto, to prey
for his sowle, his faders and moders, in forme and
maner as in his will mad at that tyme more pleynly
specifyth ; whech will and feffment continued till the
xxxv. yere of the seid late Kyng.   And aftir, upon divers
communicacions had be divers personis with the seid
Sir John Fastolff, and upon divers consideracions mevid
to hym, the seid Sir John Fastolff conceyvid that such

---

[1] Amortized, or granted in mortmain.

be monkys hym there to be indewed shuld not be of
power to susteyne and kepe the seid plase edified, or
the lond that shuld be immortesid ther to, acordyng to
his seid entent and will; wherfore, and for good will
that the seid Sir John Fastolff had to the proferryng
of your seid besecher mevyd hym to have the seid
plase and certeyn of his livelode of gretter valew than
the charge of the seid college schuld drawe, and to
found the seid college and to bere the reparacion and
defens therof.   Upon whech mocion the seid Sir John
Fastolff and your seid besecher apoynted be word
withowt writyng at that tyme mad that your seid
besecher shuld, aftir the decese of the seid Sir John
Fastolff, have the seid plase in Caster, and all the
maners that were the seid Sir John Fastolffs or any
other to his use in Norfolk, Suffolk, and Norwich, up
trust that the same John Paston shuld founde there a
college of vij. monkes or prestes havyng a certeyn
pension for her sustentacion payid clerly in mony
withowt any charge, cost, reparacion, or joperde of
defens of the seid plase or of any other livelode to be
bore be the seyd collegians, and more over to paye a
certeyn somme of mony of the revenews of the seid
maners, londes and tenementes to be disposid yerly be
certeyn yeres for the sowle of the seid Sir John Fastolff till
the summe of v.$^{ml.}$ [5000] mark were so disposed.   Upon
wech apoyntement it was acordyd be thwyx the seid Sir
John and your seid besecher, for as moch as your seid
besecher had non astate in the seid maners and londes
and tenementes, that for his more suerte, and upon
trust that the seid Sir John had to your seid besecher
in this behalfe that a newe feffement shuld be mad of
the seid plase and of the maner of Caster, and all the
seid maners, londs and tenements to your seid besecher, and divers other personys to the use of the
seid Sir [1] John, terme of his lif, and aftir his decese to
the use of your seid besecher.   And moreover, for as
moch as your seid besecher was in dowte whedir God

---

[1] " Sir."—This word is omitted in the first copy.

wold send hym tyme of life to execute the seid apoyntement, intendyng that th'effect of the old purpose of the
seid Sir John Fastolff schuld not be all voyded, thow it
so fortuned your seid besecher cowd not performe the
seid apoyntement, mevid the seid Sir John Fastolff
that, not withstandyng the seid apoyntement, that he
aftir the seid feffement mad shuld make his will for the
seid college, to be mad in all maner wise as thow the
seid Sir John Fastolff and your seid besecher shuld not
make [1] the seid apoyntement; and that aftir that, the
seid apoyntement to be ingrosid and made so that
the seid college shuld hold be the same apoyntement
of your seid besecher, and ellis this seid will of the seid
Sir John Fastolff to stand in effect for executyng of his
seid purpose.   And sone aftir this comunicacion and
apoyntement the seid feffement was mad acordynge,
and season deliverid to your seid besecher at the seid
plase edified in Caster, as well as at the seid maners,
londs, and tenements, the seid Sir John Fastolff beyng
present at delivery of season mad to your seid besecher
of the seid plase and maner of Caster, where the seid
Sir John, more largely expressyng the seid will and
entent, deliverid your seid besecher possession with
his owne hands, declaryng to notabill personys there
the same feffement to be made to the use of the seid
Sir John as for terme of his lif only, and aftir his decese
to the use of your seid besecher and his heyrs; and
divers tymes in divers yeres aftir declared his entent in
like wise to divers personys.   And aftir, be gret deliberacion and oft communicacion of the seid mater,
the seid Sir John Fastolff and your seid besecher
comenauntyd [2] and apoynted be writyng thoroughly
for the seid mater so that your seid besecher shuld
have the seid plase and all the seid maners, londs, and
tenements in Norfolk, Suffolk, and Norwich, to hym
and to his heyrs; and that he shuld found a college of
vij. monkes or prestes withinne the seid plase perpetually

---

[1] "Shuld not make."—These words are interlined in place of the word
"left," which is erased.   [2] So spelt in both copies.

as is before seid, and to pay iiij.$^{ml.}$ [4000] mark to be disposed in certeyn yers for the sowle of the seid Sir John Fastolff; the whech apoyntement declarid and red before the seid Sir John Fastolff, be good deliberacion was be the seid Sir John fully concludid, agreyd and stabilisshid for his last will in that behalve.

And also the seid comenauntes and apoyntementes eftsonis callid to remembraunce be the seid Sir John Fastolff, the same Sir John, for certeyn consideracions movyng hym, be his word, withowt writyng, dischargid your seid besecher of the seid somme of iiij.$^{ml.}$ mark, desiryng hym so to ordeyne that ich of the seid monkes or prestes shull yerly have as the prestes of the chauntry of Heylesdon had, and that vij. pore men shull also be founde yerly in the seid plase inperpetuite to pray for the sowles above sayd.

[And aftir, that is to sey the Satirday, Sonday, and Monday next before the decese of the seid Sir John, the same Sir John, remembryng divers maters and intents in his mynd necessary for the wele of his sowle, wheche were not expressid in the seid will and apoyntement, nowther in his testament, and that he wold have one will mad and wrete conteynyng the seid apoyntements, as well as the seid other maters not declarid in his intent and will acordyng, comaundid to have it so ingrosid and wrete.][1]   And where your seid besecher hath don his part acordyng to the will and apoyntements of the seid Sir John, as well in fyndyng of the seid prestes and pore men as in all other thyngs that to hym belongyth to do in that behalfe ; and, this not with standyng, William Yelverton, Knyght, and William Jenney, whech be infeffid joyntly with your seid besecher in divers of the seid maners, londs and tenements, have[2] mad a sympill entre in all the seid maners in Suffolk, and chargid the baylifs, fermors, and tenaunts of all the seid maners to pay hem the profitez and revenews of the same maners, londs, and tene-

---

1 The clause between brackets is cancelled in the first copy.
2 This word is interlined in the second copy only.

ments; and thus, contrary to th'entent of the seid feffement, and contrary to the will of the seid Sir John
Fastolff, thei trobill and lette your seid besecher to take
the profitez of the seid maners, londs, and tenements;
of whech your seid besecher hath no remedy at the
comen lawe. Wherfore please your good and gracious
Lordship to direct severall writts of subpena to the seid
William and William, chargyng hem severally upon a
peyne convenient to appere before your Lordship in the
Chauncery at a certeyn day be your Lordship to be
limityd, to answer to these premisses, and to do as right
and consiens requirith. And your seid besecher shall
pray God for yow.

*The following article is added in the first copy with many
corrections :—*

And aftir, late before the discese of the seid Sir John Fastolff,
he wold and ordeynid that on wryting shuld be mad of the
fundacion of the seid college aftir the forme of the seid apoyntement mad with your seid besecher, and of diverses othir articles
conteynid in his seid former willes, not conserning the seyd colegge
and also of divers maters wheche he remembrid necessary for the
wele of his sowle, that were nevir expressid in writyng before,
joyntly to geder expressyng his hole and inter and last will and
intent in all.

462.

A.D. 1462.—JOHN RUSSE TO JOHN PASTON.

[From Fenn, i. 262.]

This letter was evidently written not very long after No. 460. The fleet
mentioned here and in that letter is that referred to in the preliminary note
to No. 449.

*To my right honourabyl and worshypfull maister, my
Maister John Paston.*

LESE your worshypfull maistership to wette,
here is a ship of Hith, wyche seith that John
Cole cam from the west cost on Wednysday
last past; and he seyth that the fleet of
shippis of this londe met with lx. seile of Spanyards,

Brettenys, and Frenshemen, and there tok of hem l. [50],
wherof xij. shyppys were as gret as the *Grace de Dewe;*
and there is slayn on thys partyes the Lords Clynton[1]
and Dakyr,[2] and many jentilmen juve (?)[3] and othyr,
the nombre of iiij.ᵐˡ [4000]; and the seid Spanyards were
purposyd with marchaundise in to Flaundres.   My
Lord of Warwyks shyp, the *Mary Grace* and the *Trenyte,*
hadde the grettest hurt, for they wer formost.   God
send grace, thys be trew.   On Thursday last past at
London was no tydings in serteyn where the flet was,
nor what they had doon, and therfore I fere the tydings
the more.

Item, sir, as for tydings at London, ther were
arystyd be the tresorer xl. seyles lyeng in Temse,
wherof many smale shyppis; and it is seyd it is to carye
men to Caleyse in all haste, for feer of the Kyng of
Fraunce for a sege.   And it was told me secretly there
were CC. in Caleyse sworn contrary to the Kyngs well,
and for defaute of there wages; and that Qwen Marget was redy at Boleyn with myche sylver to paye the
soudyers, in cas they wold geve here entresse.   Many
men be gretly aferd of thys mater, and so the tresorer
hath mych to do for thys cause.

Item, sir, as for tydings out of Ireland, ther wer
many men at London at the feyre of the contres next
them of Ireland, and they sey thys iij. wyks came there
neythyr shyp nor boot out of Irelond to bryng no
tydings; and so it semyth there is myche to doo there
be the Erle of Pembrook.[4]   And it is seyd that the
Kyng shuld be at London as on Satyrday or Sonday
last past, and men deme that he wold to Caleyse hym
selfe; for the soudyors are so wyld there, that they
wyll not lette in ony man but the Kynge or my Lord
Warwyk.

---

[1] John, Lord Clinton. The rumour was false, as he was summoned to
Parliament in 1463. Nicolas supposes he died about ᴠ465.
[2] Richard Fynes, Lord Dacre of the South, who was Lord Clinton's father-
in-law. He did not really die till 1484.
[3] This word, Fenn says, is doubtful in the original MS.
[4] Jasper Tudor, Earl of Pembroke, half-brother to Henry VI.

Othyr tydings the were come to London, but they were not publyshyd; but John Wellys shal abyde a day the lenger to know what they are.

No mere un to you, my right honourable maister, at thys tyme, but Jesu send yow youre herts desyre, and amende hem that wold the contrary.

Your bedman and conty[n]wal servaunt,

JOHN RUSSE.

463.

A.D. 1462, 1 Nov.
JOHN PASTON, JUNIOR, TO HIS FATHER.

[From Fenn, i. 266.]

In the month of October 1462, as we learn from William Worcester, Margaret of Anjou came out of France, whither she had fled in spring, with a force of 2000 men, landed on the coast of Northumberland, and laid siege to Bamborough, which she took and placed in the keeping of the Duke of Somerset.

To my ryth reverent and worchepfull fadyr, John Paston, be thys delyveryd in hast.

RYTH reverent and worchepfull fadyr, I recomand me on to yow, beseechyng yow lowly of your blyssyng. Plesyt you to have knowlage that my Lord[1] is purposyd to send for my Lady, and is lyke to kepe his Crystmas here in Walys, for the Kyng hathe desyered hym to do the same. Wherfor I beseche yow that [ye][2] wole wychesave to send me sume mony by the berer herof; for, in good feythe, as it is not on knowyng to yow that I had but ij. noblys in my purse, whyche that Rychard Call took me by your comandement, when I departyd from yow owt of Norwyche. The berer herof schuld bye me a gowne with pert of the mony, if it plese yow to delyver hym as myche mony as he may bye it with;

---

[1] The Duke of Norfolk.   [2] Omitted in original.

for I have but on gowne at Framyngham and an other
here, and that is my levere gowne, and we must were
hem every day for the mor part, and one gowne withowt change wyll sone be done.

As for tydyngs, my Lord of Warwyk yed forward in
to Scotland as on Saterday [1] last past with xx.ᵐˡ·
[20,000] men; and Syr Wylliam Tunstale is tak with
the garyson of Bamborowth, and is lyke to be hedyd,
and by the menys of Sir Rychard Tunstale [2] is owne
brodyr.

As sone as I here any more tydyngys, I schall send
hem yow by the grace of God, who have yow in Hys
kepyng.   Wretyn in hast, at the Castle of the Holte,[3]
upon Halowmas Daye.

Your sone and lowly servaunt,
J. PASTON, Junior.

464.

A.D. 1462, 11 Dec.
JOHN PASTON THE YOUNGEST TO JOHN PASTON THE
ELDER.

[From Fenn, i. 272.]

The sieges mentioned in this letter took place, according to Warkworth, in
December of the *first* year of Edward IV, *i.e.*, 1461; but according to
William Worcester in 1462. The dates of the Privy Seal writs prove that the
atter is right, and that Edward IV. was at Durham in December 1462.

*To my ryth worchepful brodyr John Paston, the elder,
sone of John Paston, Esquyer, be thys delyveryd in
hast.*

RYTH worchepfull brodedyr, I recomaunde me
to yow.   Plesyt yow to wet, that as thys day
we had tydyngs here, that the Scottys wyll
come in to Inglend with in vij. days aftyr the

---

[1] 30th October.
[2] Sir Richard Tunstal was on Queen Margaret's side, while his brother
William, it seems, was on that of King Edward.
[3] In Denbighshire.

wrytyng of thys lettyr, for to rescue these iij. castellys,
Alnewyk, Donsamborowe[1] and Bameborowe, whyche
castellys wer besegyd, as on yesterdaye.   And at the
sege of Allnewyk lythe my Lord of Kent and the
Lord Scalys; and at Donsameborow castyll lythe the
Erle of Wyrcetyr [and] Syr Rafe Grey; and at the
castyll of Bameborow lythe the Lord Montagwe and
Lord Ogyll, and othyr dyvers Lordys and gentylmen
that I knowe not; and ther is to hem owt of Newe
Castyll ordynans inowe, bothe for the segys and for
the feld, in cas that ther be ony feld takyn, as I trow
there shall none be not yet, for the Scottys kepe no
promes.   My Lord of Warwyk lythe at the castyll of
Warcorthe, but iij. myle owt of Alnewyk, and he
rydyth dayly to all thes castelys for to overse the
segys; and if they want vataylys, or any othyr thyng,
he is redy to pervey it for them to hys power.   The
Kyng comandyd my Lord of Norfolk[2] for to condyth
vetaylys and the ordynans owt of New Castyll on to
Warcorthe Castyll, to my Lord of Warwyk; and so my
Lord of Norfolk comandyd Syr John Howard, Syr
William Peche, Syr Robert Chamberlyen, Rafe Ascheton
and me, Calthorp and Gorge, and othyr, for to go
forthe with the vytalys and ordynans on to my Lord
of Warwyk; and so we wer with my Lord of Warwyk
with the ordynans and vytalys yesterdaye.   The Kyng
lythe at Durham, and my Lord of Norfolk at New
Castyll.   We have pepyll inow here.   In cas we abyd
here, I pray you purvey that I may have here more
mony by Crystmas Evyn at the ferthest, for I may get
leve for to send non of my wagyd men home ageyn;
ne man can get no leve for to go home but if they
stell a wey, and if they myth be knowe, they schuld be
scharply ponyschyd.   Mak as merry as ye can, for
ther is no joperte toward not yet.   And ther be any
joperte, I schall sone send yow word, by the grase of

---

[1] Dunstanborough.
[2] John Mowbray, who succeeded his father in the Dukedom of Norfolk in
1461.   He was at this time only eighteen years of age.

God.   I wot well ye have more tydyngys then we have here, but thes be true tydyngs.

Yelverton and Jeney ar lek for to be gretly ponyschyd, for because they came not hedyr to the Kyng.   They ar morkyn [*marked*] well inowe, and so is John Bylyngforthe and Thomas Playter; wherefor I am ryth sory.   I pray yow let them have wetyng therof, that they may purvey their excuse in hast, so that the Kyng may have knowlage why that they come not to hym in ther one personys; let them come or send ther excuse to me in wrytyng, and I schall purvey that the Kyng schall have knowlage of ther excuse; for I am well aqueyntyd with my Lord Hastyngys, and my Lord Dakarys,[1] whyche be now gretest abowt the Kyngys person; and also I am well aqueyntyd with the yonger Mortymere, Fererys, Hawte, Harpor, Crowmer, and Bosewell, of the Kyngys howse.

I pray yow let my grandam[2] and my cosyn Clere[3] have knowlage how that I desyryd you to let hem have knowlage of the tydyngys in thys letyr, for I promysyd for to send them tydyngs.

I pray yow let my modyr[4] have cnowelage how that I, and my felawscep, and your servauntys ar, at the wrytyng of this lettyr, in good hell, blesyd be God.

I pray yow let my fadyr have knowlage of thys lettyr, and of the todyr lettyr that I sent to my modyr by Felbryggys man; and how that I pray bothe hym and my modyr lowly of her blyssyngys.

I pray yow that ye wole send me some lettyr how ye do, and of your tydyngys with yow; for I thynk longe that I here no word fro my modyr and yow.

I pray yow that thys bill may recomand me to my systyr Margery, and to my mastres Jone Gayne, and to all gode mastyrys and felawys within Castyr.   I sent no lettyr to my fadyr, never syn I departyd fro yow, for I kowd get no man to London, and never sythe.

See p. 118, Note 2.   [2] Agnes Paston.
[3] Elizabeth, widow of Robert Clere of Ormesby.   [4] Margaret Paston.

I pray yow in cas ye spake with my cosyn Margaret
Clere, recomande me to hyr; and Almythy God have
yow in Hys kepyng.

Wretyn at Newcastyll on Saterday next aftyr the
Consepsion of owyr Lady.

Your,   JOHN PASTON, the
                             Yongest.

I pray yow let Rychard Call se thys lettyr.

465.

A.D. 1463, 19 Jan.

MARGARET PASTON TO JOHN PASTON.

[From Fenn, iv. 150.]

This letter refers to a coming election of knights of the shire, which seems
to be for the Parliament which met on the 29th April 1463. No other general
election of Edward IV.'s time will suit the date, and it is quite certain that it
was written during Edward's reign.

*To my right worchepful hosbond, John Paston, be this
letter deliveryd in hast.*

RIGHT worchepfull hosbond, I recommand me
to you. Please you to wete that I received a
letter frome you on the Sonday[1] next after
Twelfthe day, weche was sent be a prest of
Seynt Gregorys paryche of Norwic; and wher as ye
mervaylyd I sent you no wrytynggs of suche letters as
ye sent me be for, I sent you a answer of the substauns
of suche maters as ye have wretyn of me be for (be
Playter), the weche he told me a sent hem to you to
London. And as towchyng the erands that ye sent
to me for to do to Richard Calle, I have do as ye
command me to do, and callyd upon hym therfor,
bothe be for your wrytyng and sithyn; he thar have
non excuse for defaute of leyser, for he hathe be but

[1] January 9.

ryght litill her syn ye departyd hens. He is owght
at this tyme, and whan that he comythe home I shall
make hym make yow a cler bylle of the receyt of your
lyvelod, and Fastolf bothe; and I shale send yow a
cler bylle of my receyts, and also of my payments
owght thereof ageyn; and as for suche erands that shuld
be do to Sir Thomas Howys, I have shewyd Richard
Calle your wrytyng, and told hym your entent, as for
suche thyngs as ye wold he shuld sey to hym on hys
none heed. Also I have do your erands to my moder
and to my cosyn Cler[1] after your wrytyng. Item, I
have spoke to John Adam and to Playter of your
entent of the last bylle that ye sent me, and they sey
they wolle do after your entent as moche as they may,
and ye shall have a answer therof in hast.

Item, Sir Robert Coniors dinid with me this day,
and shuyd me a letter that came frome the Kyng to
hym, desyryng hym that he shuld a wayt upon hys
welle be lovyd broder the Duke of Suffolk, at Norwiche,
on Monday next comyng, for to be at the alection of
knyghts of the chyer [shire]; and he told me that every
jentylman of Norffolk and Suffolk that arne of any
repetacion hathe wrytyng from the Kyng in lyke wyse
as he had. I felle hym be his seyyng that he ys right
welle disposyd to you ward; he seythe ther shall no
man make hym to be a geyns you in no mater. Skypwith shall telle you suche tydyngs as bethe in this
contre, and of Thomas Gornay and of his man; hym
self is clerk convicte, and hys man is hangyn; ye shall
here her after what they and oder wer purposyd to a
do to her master.

I thank you hertely of your wrytyng to me be for
that John Paston came home, for God knowith I
thowght right longe tyle I hard frome you; I shalle
send word in wrytyng of suche tydings as we have her
on Monday in hast. Daubeney deseyryht to wet what
tyme that it please you that he shuld come ageyn to you.

My moder and many other folkys makyth moche of

[1] Elizabeth, widow of Robert Clere of Ormesby.

your son John, the elder, and right glad of hys comyng hom, and lekyth reght welle hys demenyng. Heydon[1] son hathe bor owght the syyd stowtly her this Critstemes, and whan that he rydyth, he hathe iiij. or v. men with hym in a clothyng; but he hathe but lytyl fafor in this contre but yf [*unless*] it be of the Bischop[2] and of the Prior of Norwic.[3] The seyd prior hathe grauntyd hym the stewerdchep that hys feder had . . . . he hathe it under the Covent Seals, and Spylman,[4] his tutor, to lerne hym howe he shuld be demenyd . . . . it is seyd abowght Bakynstorp that Herry Heydon shuld a seyd that it wer welle do that men of the . . . . . . shuld make redy her [*their*] bald batts[5] and her clot shon[6] and go feche hom her knygts of chyer [*shire*] . . . . Barney; and it is promysyd hym that he shall be met with be cause of hys langage . . . . us a good world and a pesybyll. I shall purvey for all thyngs that ye have sent to me for, so that I ween ye shal be pleasyd. The blyssyd Trinite have you in Hys kepyng. Wretyn in hast, the Wednysday next . . . . Seynt Agnet. Your,

M. P.

466.

A.D. 1463, Jan.—EXTRACT.
THOMAS PLAYTER TO JOHN PASTON.

The following extracts are quoted by Fenn from a letter now lost, in reference to what is said in the last letter about Thomas Gurney and his man.

[1] This must be Henry, son of John Heydon, Esq., Recorder of Norwich.—F.
[2] Walter Lyhert, Bishop from 1445 to 1472.—F.
[3] John Molet or Mowth, Prior from 1453 to 1471.—F.
[4] Henry Spilman, afterwards Recorder of Norwich; he was the founder of the Spilmans of Narborough, by marrying Ela, daughter and heir of William de Narborough.—F.
[5] *Bald batts* seem to mean here ball bats, or bats to play at ball with.—F.
[6] *Clot shoen*, clouted shoes—shoes shod with thin plates of iron.—F.

Please your maistership wete, that as for my Lord of Norwich cosyns deth, Thomas Gurneys man hath confessed that he slewe hym by commaundment of his maister, and confessed over that the same dager he slewe hym with, he kest it in a sege [*a jakes*] whiche is founden and taken up al to-bowyd [*bent together*], for he cowde not breke it, and in prison is bothe he and his maister.

. . . .

Also on Thursday next after Cristemasse was a man slayn, by whom no man woot, nor what he is that was slayn no man knowe, his face is so mangled.

467.

A.D. 1463, [Feb.]
RICHARD CALLE TO JOHN PASTON.

[From Paston MSS., B.M.]

As the writ, of which a copy is subjoined to this letter, is dated on the 31st January in the 2d year of Edward IV. (1463), the letter itself must have been written in February.

To my ryght reverent and wurschip[full] mayster, my Mayster John Paston in the Ynner Temple at London.

PLESITH your goode maystrechip to witte that ther comen doune to the undrescheryff of Norwiche, a writte to a tache Mr. John P. the yongere, wherof I sende you a copy closed herin, but they woll not a reeste hym within Norwich; but I undrestande ther is comen an other writte to the undrescheryff of Norfolk bothe for hym and me, and for all thoo that ben indyghted. Wherfore I purpose me to ride to Hoonyng to the scheryff thys day, to undrestande how he is disposed, and to desire hym to shewe favour to your pore tenaunts; and as I feele hym disposed I schall send your maystreship answer.

And as for tidyngs here in this contre, we have noon but that ther be many Frenchemen upon the see and do moche answer upon the coosts. Mr Yelver[ton] knew of the comyng up of the *teste* within ij. dayes after they were goon, &c. My ryght reverent and wur-

schipful maystre, the blissed Trinite preserve and kepe
and ferther you in all your maters.

Sir William Wyllugby whas at Risynge Castell, and
yesterday he come home a yenne. On Tentale hathe
entred in to a parte of Felbregge lyvelod, and a corte
holden, and the tenaunts retorned. Item, as for the
cort that Deben[ham] schuld holde at Calcot we here
not of it.

> Your pore servaunt and
> bedman, R. C.

Rex vi[ce]comitibus Norwici, salutem. Præcepimus vobis quod
capiatis Johannem Paston juniorem, nuper de Norwico, armi-
gerum, si inventus fuerit in balliva vestra, et eum salvo custo-
diatis, ita quod habeatis corpus ejus coram nobis a die Paschæ
in unum mensem ubicunque tunc fuerimus in Anglia, ad respondendum nobis de quibusdam feloniis et transgressionibus unde in
comitatu nostro Suffolchiæ indictatus est. Et si prædictus
Johannes in balliva vestra inveniri non poterit, tunc ad duos
comitatus in balliva vestra citra terminum prædictum proximo
tenendos juxta formam statuti in hujusmodi casu provisi pro-
clamari faciatis quod idem Johannes sit coram nobis ad præfatum
terminum ad respondendum nobis de premissis. Et habeatis ibi
hoc breve. Teste Johanne Markham apud Westmonasterium,
xxxjᵒ die Januarii, anno regni nostri secundo.

> CROXTON.

Rotulo xxvjᵒ R. Per contr' Anno secundo Regis Ed. iiijti r. xiij. Irrotu-
latur coram Rege de recordo, termino Hillarii anno secundo Regis Ed. iiijti,
prout patet in rotulo infrascripto.[1]

468.

About A.D. 1463.—ABSTRACT.

[From Paston MSS., B.M.]

[JOHN PASTON] TO JOHN PAMPYNG, RICHARD CALLE, AND
WILLIAM WYKES.

Remember my instructions about bills and actions against
Debenham by my tenants at Calcot. Make a "remembrance
apart" of the ground on which every trespass has been commit-

---

[1] This note is to imply that the writ is enrolled among what are called the
Records on the Coram Rege Roll of Hilary term, 2 Edw. IV., rot. 26, a
former writ against John Paston, jun., being enrolled in the Controlment
Roll, 2 Edw. IV., rot. 13.

ted, whether it be in my lands or in those of my tenants, and whether the land was holden of me by Calcote Hall fee, or Freton Hall fee, lest Debenham justify [on the plea that] he took them elsewhere. As my tenants at Cotton have been compelled to pay much money to Jenney and Debenham against their wills, I would, as I have told John Paston the younger, that he should ride to Cotton with Richard Calle and such friendship as he can get, and demand my duties, except from those who had been compelled to pay the others. The latter to take actions next term against Debenham. Will respite them for this once all they have paid, till it may be recovered by law; that is, provided they ask it: otherwise, will politicly put them in jeopardy of losing their farms. Desires Calle to make a roll of the tenants and when he comes to Cotton enter therein how much cattle has been distrained from each.

It appears by the last letter that a writ was issued, evidently at the suit of Debenham, against John Paston, Junior, and the other agents of his father in Suffolk. From the present paper it would seem that John Paston also instituted a prosecution on behalf of his tenants against Debenham. We shall find by later letters that these suits were going on in 1463, and were not terminated in the beginning of the following year. The MS. from which the above abstract has been made is a draft with a heading in John Paston's hand. On the back are notes of the Statutes of Westminster and of Richard II. touching *scandalum magnatum, &c.*

469.

A.D. 1463, 19 March.
RALPH LAMPET'S TESTIMONY.

[Tanner MS. 106, f. 35 b.]

O all tho to whom this present wrytyng shall come, Rauff Lampet, Squier, sendyth gretyng in our Lord. And forasmoch as it is meritory to bere witnesse of trought, and that I knowe and herd the disposicion and will of Ser John Fastolff, knyght, aftir the forme folowyng, and am requered to sey the trought, I record and testifie, and bere witnesse that Ser John Fastolff, knyght, abought the tyme of hervest was v. yere, that was the yere of our Lord M^{l}cccclvij., at Caster, fast by Mekyll Yarmouth, in the Shire of Norffolk, in presens of divers persones that tyme callid to by the seid Ser John, ded make estat and feffement and livery of seison of the maner of Caster aforeseid, and other maners, londs, and tenements in Norffolk to John Paston, Squier, and other. And at that livery of season thereof delivered, as well by the hands of the seid Ser John as be other, the seid Ser John Fastolff by his owne mouth declared his will and entent of that feffement and livery of season, mad to the use of the seid Ser John as for duryng his life only, and aftir his decese to the use of the seid John Paston and his heyrs. And also the seid Ser John seid and declared, that the seid John Paston was best frend, and helper, and supporter to the seid Ser John, and that it was his will that the seid John Paston shuld have and inherite the same maners, londs, and tenements, and other, aftir his decese, and ther to dwelle and abide, and kepe how-sold, seying that he knew well that the disposicion of the seid Paston was to do good in the contry, and be non oppressor of the pore pepill. And the seid Ser John desired me, and Daune William Bokenham, that tyme Prior of Yarmouth, beynge presente, to record as he had seid to us. And this I record and witnesse for trought be the feyght that I owe to God and all Seynts. In witnesse wherof to this my writyng I have set to my seall and signe manuell the xix. day of March, the third yer of the reigne of Kyng Edward the Fourth.   R. LAMPET.

470.

Date uncertain.—ABSTRACT.

[From Paston MSS., B.M.]

RAFF LAMPET TO HIS COUSIN DAUBENEY.

Reminds him that he spoke to him at Redham, in the church, about certain lands 'which John of Berney bought of me,' and for which there is still owing to him 13s. 4d., and a rent of 6d. four years in arrear. Begs him to speak to Master Paston to get him the money.

We place this letter immediately after another document signed by Ralph Lampet, the exact date being uncertain and immaterial. It is probably, however, about this period, as it may be surmised to be after the death of John Berney.

471.

A.D. 1463, 6 April.—ABSTRACT.

[From MS. Phillipps, 9735, No. 280.]

Testimony of Sir Roger Chamberlain, witnessed by Reginald
Tylneye, prior of Ixworth, and Sir John Rose [a brother of the
house], that he was with the Duke of Norfolk in September
before Sir John Fastolf died, when my Lord urged Fastolf to sell
him the reversion of Caister, or (as he wished to give it to the
Abbey of St. Benet's) to exchange it for a manor of my Lord's in
South Walsham, which lay more convenient for the Abbey.   Sir
John, however, begged him not to press it, as he had appointed
with his cousin, John Paston, to have Caister and all his other
livelode in Norfolk and Suffolk in order to endow a college of
seven priests and seven poor men.   My Lord said, many thought
Sir John would make Paston his heir; to which he replied that
there was no man living that he would like better to be his heir,
and begged my Lord to be his good lord if it so fortuned, which
the Duke promised to do.   Has heard the Duke since often
acknowledge that Sir John had declared plainly he would make
Paston his heir.   Not having his own seal present, has sealed
this with that of the prior of Ixworth, and requested him to put
his seal to it besides.   Ixworth, 6 April 1463.

472.

A.D. 1463, 6 May.
MARGARET PASTON TO JOHN PASTON.

[From Fenn, iv. 188.]

Our reason for believing this letter to have been written in the year 1463,
will be seen in a footnote.

To my rytz wurchepfull mayster, Jon Paston, in hast.

RYT wurschipfull hosbond, I recommand me to
zou, desyring hertyly to her of zour wellfar,
praying zou to wete, that I [have] spoken with
Strawngs wyf of the matter that ze spoken to
me of; and sche seyth pleynly to me, be her feyth, that
sche knew never non seche ne never herd of non
scheche, and told to me in lyk wyse as sche had seyd

to Jamys Gloys. And sche seyd to me if sche kowd inquier of any other that sche thinght xuld have knowleche of any seche, sche xuld wetyn of hem, and letyn me have knowleche therof; and if ze soppose that any other be in this contre that ye thync xuld have knowleche of this forseyd mater, yf ye wyll send me word ther of, I xall do my part ther in.

Also I have ben att Sweyngsthorp and spoken with Kokett, and he seyth that he woll don lyche as ye bad me that I xuld sey to hym for to don. And I have spokyn with the sexteyn, and seyd to hym as ye bad me that I xuld don, and he axid me ryt feythfully hw ye sped in zour materys.

I teld hym that ze haddyn fayr be hests, and I seyd I hopyd that ze xuld don rytz well therin; and he seyd that he supposyd that D.[1] wold don for zou; but he seyd he was no hasty laborer in non mater. He seyd be hys feyth he wost qher a man was that laboryd to hym for amater ryth along tym, and alwey he be hestyd that he wold labor itt effectualy, but qhyll he sewyd to hym that he kowd never have remedy of his mater; and than qhan he thowth that he xuld no remedy have to sew to hym, he spak with Fynys,[2] that is now Speker of the Parlment, and prayid hym that he wold don for hym in hys mater, and zaf hym areward; and withinne ryth short tym after his mater was sped. And the seyd sexteyn[3] and other folkys that ben yowr ryth wele willers have kownselyd me that I xuld kownsell

---

[1] Possibly John Damme.

[2] This looks like a mistake, for no Speaker of the name of Fynes is met with during this period. The expression, however, suggests that the letter was written about the beginning of a new Parliament, which could only have been that which met on the 29th April 1463. On the following day the Commons elected John Say as their Speaker, who, I am almost inclined to think, may have been a brother or near relation of William Fenys, Lord Say, the trusty friend of Edward IV. who accompanied him into exile when he fled from his kingdom in 1470, for it was not uncommon in those days to use a family title as a surname. I find no mention, however, of a John Fenys of the Say family in Dugdale.

[3] The Sacrist or Sexton of the Priory of Norwich, was the officer who had the care of Sacra, or Holy Things, as the Church Plate, Copes, &c.; he was likewise Secretary, Auditor, and Chancellor of the Convent, and had a Sub-sacrist or Deputy to perform the servile parts of his office. In 1444 Brother Richard de Walsham was appointed Sacrist.—F.

zou to maken other menys than ye have made to other folks, that wold spede your materys better than they have don thatt ye have spoken to therof be for this tym.   Sondery folks have seyd to me that they thynk veryly, but if [*unless*] ye have my Lord of Suffolks[1] godelorchyp, qhyll the werd [*world*] is as itt is, ye kan never leven in pese with owth ye have his godelordschep; therfor I pray that with all myn herth, that ye wyll don yowr part to have his godelordschep and his love in ese of all the materis that ye have to don, and in esyng of myn hert also ; for be my trowth I am afferd ellys bothen of these materys the qhyche ye have in hand now, and of other that ben not don to yett, but if he wyl don for zou and be your godelord.   I pray yow hertylye send me werd how ze don, and how ye speden in zour materys ; and I pray you as for seche thyngs as Jamys hath a byll of, that I may have hem as hastyly as ze may ; and that ze wyll vowchesave to bey apese of blak bukram for to lyn with a gown for me, I xuld bey me amurrey gown to gon in this somer, and leyn in the koler the satyn that ze zeve me for an hodde ; and I kan gettyn non gode bokeram in this town to lyn it with.   The Holy Trinyte have yow in His kepyng, and send zou helth and good spede in all yowr maters.

Wretyn att Norwyche, on ye Fryday nexst after Crowchemesse Day.[2]

Yours,   M. P.

473.

A.D. 1463, July.

[JAMES GRESHAM] TO JOHN PASTON.

[From Paston MSS., B.M.]

This letter seems to be in James Gresham's handwriting.   It is evident that it was written shortly after Midsummer.   Rather more than a year and a day had elapsed since a murder committed on the morrow of St. Peter's Day (*i.e.* on the 30th June), and it is mentioned that Convocation was to sit some little time after Relic Sunday, which always falls in the middle of July.

1 John de la Pole, Duke of Suffolk.—F.
2 Crouchmas Day, or the Invention of the Cross, was on the 3d of May.—F.

Further, the King is said to be at Northampton, which he was in July 1463, and no other year appears to suit.

To mygth rigth good and speciall maister, John Paston, dwellyng at Heylesdon be syde Norwich.

RIGTH reverent, &c.   Please your maisterchip wete that I resseived your letter whiche ye sent by Crome, and as for the examinacion of, &c. that I wrot to you of in my former letter to be taken on the Munday or on Tewysday, &c. this was the cause.   Ye yaff me informacion at my last departyng fro you that the murdre was don uppon the day nexst after Seynt Petre.   And for doute lesse ye had be ougth at the comyng of my seid letter, and for dowte that I supposed that my maistres, your wyf, had not be remembred of the day, it caused me, accordyng to your informacion, to wryte the uttermost day for her remembrans.   Neverthelesse, if ye certifie that ye toke the examinacion with in the yere and day, and sette the day in certayn, your certificat is sufficiant in lawe and shall bynd any of the parties to sey the contrary.   And also the writte is that ye schuld certefie *sine dilatione*, and no day expresly yoven you whan to certifie it; wherfor ye may kepe uncertefiet tyl the nexst terme. And so do sir, for it schal do no hurt; but if ony questions or jangelyng schuld be mad when the examinacion was, let a sufficiant day with inne the yere be noysed, and if the *teste* be to schort we schal fynd the mene it schal be amendyd by hym that wrot it.   For after the informacion that I had of Crome the Sunday was the uttermest day, and therefor it was happy that sche was examined thenne.   And where that ye wold I schuld tak the advise of Maister Markham, &c., if all thyng were laufull, and elles not, it is full hard to my self to determine the certaynte of every circumstans of the mater, and it is not gretely to be comuned of with other, nor to comune of casez lyke; for whan the mater schuld come in revelysshon it wold cause prevy titlers and flaterers ougth of suche

questions to ymagyn, and contryve mater of distour-
bans. Wherfor uppon the certeynte of myn deter-
minacion I brak the mater to Master Markham, which
called to hym Master Byngham, and so thei ij. meved
Y.[1]; and after that mocion he kept not his owyn
councell but brak to every man of it. Hou be it he
was sore mevyd with it, I wote it well, and glad to take
avyse and comfort of other personez than of Masters
Markham and Byngham. Al circumstans were to
long to wryte, but I hope to speke with you be tymes
i nougth or ye schall nede to certefye, &c. And, sir,
in conclucion, Masters Markham and Byngham thynk
it sufficiant i nougth to take his promys and his othe with
ougth obligacion that he schal mak amends if profe here
after can be mad uppon hym. And to this Maister
Markham prayed you to agre by the same token ye
mevyd hym to sette an ende be twyx you and my masters
your brethern. Neverthelesse if ye thynk this wey not
sufficiant, ye may lete sum other handele the mater
at hom to hym if that ye hope to gete good pref in the
mater, for with ougth evydent proffe the mater schall
be but noysefull to you, and cause men to thynk that
it growyth of your ille wyll to hym ward, &c.; for he
noyseth and seyth, because of ille wyll ye have caused
a mad woman to take apell a yens hym.

Item, sir, as for Leukenore he is not at London, but
peraventure I schal make hym to be meved in the
mater here after.

Item, I dede your erand to my maister your son.

Item, as for John Say,[2] he recomendyth hym to
you, bothe for your billes and for your labour, and
prayeth you if ony land that lyth for the priour ease
mygth be aspyed, that ye wold help to gete it hym
and send hym word; and as for the morteysyng   .
. . . . . and at his cost and labour.

Item, as for tydyngs, the Kyng and the counsell is

---

[1] Yelverton.
[2] Probably the Speaker of the Parliament of 1463, whom Margaret Paston
named Fynes in Letter 472. *See* page 131, Note 2.

at Northampton,[1] and the Convocacion schall be .
. . . . after Relyk Sunday. And
ther be ij. marchaunts come fro Caleys, and they
mygth no leve have to com[e] . . . .
. schuld bere the Kyng certeyn lettres and juste
tytyngs that sege is comyng to Caleys. And trew[s]
. . . . [ou]re Lady Day, as I herd
sey.

Item, it is talked that Duchemen and Englysshe-
men ben at contraversie with in . . . .

474.

A.D. 1463.—JAMES GRESHAM TO MARGARET PASTON.

[From Fenn, iv. 130.]

John Paston's eldest son appears to have been knighted in the course of the
year 1463. The earliest notice which I find of him as knight is in a writ
dated 11th July, 3 Edward IV., entered on the Coram Rege Roll of Trinity
term, 3 Edward IV. This letter is not unlikely to have been written about
that time, as it appears by a subsequent letter (No. 478) that Sir John Paston
remained for some time at home in Norfolk, when the friends of the family
thought he ought to be abroad in the world.

*To my right wurshepfull mastres, my Mastres Margret
Paston, at Caster.*

PLEASE it your good mastresship to wete that
a *fieri facias* is come out of the Exchequir
for Hue Fen to the Shireff of Norffolk to make
levy of CC. mark of the propir goods and
catels of my masters, as executor of Sir John Fastolf;
of whech *fieri facias* we sent my master word, whech
sent us word ayen by Berney that we shuld lete the
Shiref undirstand that my master nevir toke upon hym
as executor, and so for that cause that writte was no
warant to take my masters goods; and also that my
master mad a dede of gift of all his goods and catels
to Master Prewet and Clement Paston and other, so that
my master hath no goods whereof he shuld make levy
of the forseid summe; and if the Shireff wold not take

1 According to the dates of the Privy Seals the King was at Northampton
from the 8th to the 28th July 1463; also on the 2d May 1464.

this for non answere, that thanne my master wold he shuld be lettid in Master Prowetts and Clement Pastons name. Nevirthelesse we spak with the Shireff this day, and lete hym undirstand the causes aforeseid, and he agreid, so that he myght have suerte to safe hym harmeles, to mak such retorne as my master or his counsell coud devise. And because my master wrote by Berney that he wold not fynd the Shireff no suerte, we wold not apoynt with hym in that wyse; and so we toke avyse of Thomas Grene, and by cause the Undir-Shireff shall be on Monday at Hygham, by Bastewyk brygg, and he and we thought that it was best that Master Prowet shuld mete with the Shireff there, and require and charge hym that by colour of the foreseid *fieri facias* that he make no levy of any goods and catels of the seid Prowetts and Clement Pastons ayens the seid John Pastons, letyng hym vete that such goods as the seid Paston had, be now the seid Prowetts and Clement Pastons by vertu of a dede of gift mad to hem almost ij. yere agoo; and if the Shireff woll be besy aftir that to take any catell, that he be lettid in Master Prowetts name and Clement Pastons by Daubeney and other; whech besines of the Shireff shall be on Tuisday or Wednesday, and as we understand at Heylesdon. Wherfor ye must send thedir Daubeney with Pecok, and the may gete hym here more felasep by the avise of Master Sir John Paston.   JAMES GRESHAM.

475.

A.D. 1463, 15 Aug.—ABSTRACT.

[From Add. Charter 14,514, B.M., D. Turner's Coll.]

Deed poll whereby Elizabeth, widow of John Vere, Earl of Oxford, Lady of the manor of Knapton, Norfolk, grants to Agnes, widow of William Paston, the right of removing obstructions in two water-courses belonging to the mill called Wodmyll in Bacton; the first of which water-courses flows out of Knapton Fen, and the second from the mill of the Abbot of St. Benet's of Holme.

Stratford of the Bowe, 15th Aug. 1463, 3 Edward IV.
Fine Seal.

476.

A.D. 1463, 31 Aug.
THE DUKE OF NORFOLK TO JOHN PASTON, SENIOR.

[From Fenn, iv. 250.]

John Mowbray, Duke of Norfolk, the writer of this letter, succeeded his father in the dukedom in November 1461, being at the time only seventeen years of age. A year afterwards, in November 1462, we find him living at his castle of Holt in Denbighshire, where he proposed to spend Christmas (*See* No. 463), but before that season came, he was sent for by the King to serve against the Scots (No. 464). I am inclined to think this letter was written in the August of 1463; for although the Duke was again living at Holt in March following, it seems probable that he would have visited his chief family seat at Framlingham in the meanwhile. John Paston, the youngest, who was attached to his household, was certainly at home with his family in the latter part of this year (See No. 486).

To oure right trusty and entierly welbelovid servaunt,
John Paston th'elder.

THE DUC OF NORFF.

RIGHT trusty and entierly welbelovid servaunt, we grete you hertily well, and specially praying you that ye will be with us at Framlyngham on Sonday next comyng, that we may comon with you there, and have youre sadde advise in suche matiers as concernyth gretly to oure weel, whiche shall be mynestred unto you at youre comyng. Prayng you that ye fayle not herof, as our speciall trust is in you. And our Lord preserve you in His keping.

Written at Framlyngham the xxxj. day of August.
NORFF.

477.

A.D. 1463, 4 Sept.
THE ABBOT OF LANGLEY TO SIR JOHN PASTON.

[From Fenn, iv. 146.]

The date of this letter is clear, from the statement it contains as to the length of time which has elapsed since the decease of Sir John Fastolf.

To the ryght worcheppful Sere John Paston, Knyght, be this delyvered.

RYGHT worchepful ser, and tendyrly belovyd in our Lord God, I comend me to you, sendyng you knowyng that I dede your erand to my brother, the persoon of Blofeeld, on Wednysdaye was sevenyght, after the undyrstandyng that I had of you and from you be this brynger; whech man I felte ryght wele and favorabelye dysposyd to you ward, and more favorable wole be than to ony other jentylman levand, the wylle of the dede performyd, and his conscyens savyd; and more thinges seyd favorably for yow which I entytelyd in a scrowe to a' certyfyed to your servaunt Calle, yf he had come, as ye sent me woord he sculd ado, and xuld, as ye behestyd me, abrowte me our ferme for Heylesdon, which not don, causeth me to wryte, prayng your jantylnesse that I send no more therfore, for it is unpayed for the zeer afore the Halwemesse that my Mayster Fastolf deyed, and for the same zer that he deyed in, and sythen for ij. zer, and v*s*. unpayed of a zer, and come Myhelmesse nexte xal be another zer unpayed. Thus is iiij. zer unpayed and v*s*., and at Myhelmesse next xal be v. zer and v*s*.

This thus kepte from Holy Chirche that is Holy Chirchez good, may not be withoute grete parelle of soule; wher the parelle is God knoweth, I pray God amend it, and geve hem grace that have his goods so to dyspose them, that thei and the dede both may be oute of parelle. And the Trynyte have you in His mercyful kepyng. Wretyn at Langle, on Soneday, at evyn late, next after Seynt Johne Daye Decollacion.[1]

Be your welewylland,
ABBOT OF LANGELEYE.

---

[1] The Decollation of St. John the Baptist was observed on the 29th August.

478.

A.D. 1463 (?)
R. C. V. C. to John Paston the Eldest.

[From Fenn, iv. 128.]

In the preceding letter Sir John Paston seems to have been at home; in Letter 480, we find that he had left home without leave. It is very probable therefore that the present letter was written in the interval between them; seeing that the writer complains of Sir John being kept at home.

To my worcheppefull master, Master Paston the heldest.

RYTH worchepfull master, I recommend me on to zowr masterchepe. And of on mater at reverens of God take hede, for in trowth I her meche talkyng therof, and that is both in Norffolk, Suffolk, and Norwyche, among halle men of worchepe, as welle that love zow as oder, and that is of my master, your son, Syr Jon, causse he is so at home, and no noderwyse set for. Summe sey that ze and he both stond howth of the Kyngs good gras, and summe sey that ze kepe hym at home for negard chepe, and wyll no thyng ware [*spend*] up on hym; and so heche man sey is avyse as it plese hem to talke. And I have hanqwerryd [*inquired*], and seyd the most cause is inparty for cause ze har so meche howte, that he is the rather at home for the save gard of the costs. But at the referens of God, excheuyng of common langage, se that he may worchepfull be set for, heyder in the Kyngs servyse, or in maryache; for as towchyng the Lady Chaberlen[1] that mater is don, for I spake with the

---

[1] This Lady Chamberlayne was Anne, daughter and sole heir of Sir Robert Herling, Knight, by Jane, daughter and heir of John Gonvile, Esq. She married to her first husband, Sir William Chamberlayne, Knight of the Garter, a renowned and valiant soldier, who died in 1462. She was at this time his widow, and inherited from her father a very considerable fortune.

She afterwards married Sir Robert Wingfield, and after his decease she became the wife of John, Lord Scroop of Bolton.

By the name of Lady Scroop she founded and endowed a Fellowship in the College of Gonville and Caius at Cambridge, originally founded by an ancestor of her Ladyship's.

She was born in 1426, and was alive in 1502.

At the time this letter was writing she must have been nearly forty years old, when Sir John Paston could not have been much above twenty.—F.

parson therof, and I hard be hym that that mater wyll not pre [*proceed?*]

No more, but God spede zow as well in all maters, as I wold ze xuld do, I be seche zow that this leter be kept secrete.

Be zow[r] bede man,

R. C. V. C.

479.

A.D. 1463, 13 Nov.
MARGARET PASTON TO JOHN PASTON.

[From Fenn, iv. 88.]

I have found no letters of Margaret Paston dated from Caister before the year 1463 : but I am inclined to think that this and the letter following both belong to that year. The latter, being addressed to Sir John Paston, at least cannot be earlier, and my reasons for believing it to be of that very year will be seen in the note prefixed to it. It is just possible that this letter may be of a different date, but considering that both were written in November, and both of them certainly between the 12th and the 19th, and that in both Margaret Paston not only dates from Caister, but speaks of Daubeney as being with her, the presumption, I think, is pretty strong that they are of the same year.

To my ryght worchipfull hosbond, John Paston, be thys letter delyveryd in hast.

RIHT worchepfull husbond, I recommand me to you. Please you to wete that I was at Norwic this wek to purvey suche thyngs as nedythe me ageyns thys wynter; and I was at my modder, and wille I was ther, ther cam in on Wrothe, a kynnysman of Elysabet Clers, and he sey your dowter, and preysyd hyr to my moder, and seyd that she was a goodly yong woman; and my moder prayd hym for to gett for hyr on good mariage yf he knewe any; and he seyd he knewe on shuld be of a CCC. mark be yer, the wyche is Sir John Cley son, that is Chamberleyn with my Lady of York,[1] and he

---

[1] Cecily, Duchess of York, widow of Richard Plantagenet, Duke of York, and mother of Edward IV. She died in an advanced age, at her Castle of Berkhamstead, in May 1495, and was buried near her husband, in the Choir of the Collegiate Church of Fotheringhay, in Northamptonshire.—F.

ys of age of xviij. yer old.　Zyf ye thynk it be for to be
spok of, my moder thynkyth that it shuld be get for
lesse mony nowe in thys world than it shnld be her
after, owthyr that j. [*one*], or sum other good mariage.

Item, I spake with Master John Estgate for Peke-
rynes mater after your entent of the mater of the letter
that ye sent home, and he seyd to me he shuld write
to yow howe he had don ther in ; and so he sent you
a letter, the wyche was sent you be John Wodows[1]
man with other letters.

As for answer [of] other mater, Daubeney tellythe me
he wret to you.　I be seche Alle myghty God have
you in Hys kepyng.　Wretyn at Caster, the Sonday
next after Seynt Marteyne.

Be your　　　　　　　　M. PASTON.

480.

A.D. 1463, 15 Nov.
MARGARET PASTON TO SIR JOHN PASTON.

[From Fenn, iv. 168.]

As Sir John Paston was knighted in the year 1463, and his father died in
May 1466, the date of this letter must lie between the years 1463 and 1465.
I think the first of these years is probably the true date.　Sir John Paston, it
seems, had left home without letting his mother know of his intention.
Whither had he gone?　Not to London, because he addressed a letter to his
father there ; besides he had passed by Lynn.　One would naturally suppose,
therefore, that he had gone to wait upon the King, at a time when Edward
was at a distance from the capital.　And in this view we are confirmed by the
passage in which Margaret desires her son to speak with Wykes, who,
as we know by Letter 445, was an usher of the King's Chamber.　Now
Edward IV. was in Yorkshire, staying, for the most part, at Pomfret, during
October and November 1463, while about the same time of year in 1464 he
was at Reading, and in 1465 at Greenwich.　Sir John would naturally have
passed through Lynn on his road to the North.

*To my welbelovyd son, Sir John Paston, bc this deliveryd
in hast.*

---

[1] John Wodehouse, Esq. of Kimberley, son of the renowned John Wodehouse, Esq., who gained so much honour at the battle of Agincourt ; he died
in 1465, and lies buried in Kimberley Chancel.—F

GRET yow welle, and send yow Godds blissyng and myn, latyng yow wet that I have receyved a letter from you, the wyche ye deliveryd to Master Roger at Lynne, wherby I conseyve thar ye thynke ye ded not well that ye departyd hens withowt my knowlage. Wherfor I late yow wett I was ryght evyll payed with yow. Your fader thowght, and thynkyth yet, that I was asentyd to your departyng, and that hathe causyd me to have gret hevinesse. I hope he wolle be your good fader hereafter, yf ye demene you welle, and do as ye owe to do to hym; and I charge you upon my blyssyng that in any thyng towchyng your fader that shuld be hys worchep, profyte, or avayle, that ye do your devoyr and dylygent labor to the fortherans therin, as ye wulle have my good wille, and that shall cause your fader to be better fader to you.

It was told me ye sent hym a letter to London. What the entent therof was I wot not, but thowge he take it but lyghtly, I wold ye shuld not spar to write to hym ageyn as lowly as ye cane, besechyng hym to be your good fader; and send hym suche tydyngs as be in the contre thir ye bethe in, and that ye war [*beware*] of your expence bettyr and ye have be befor thys tyme, and be your owne purse berer, I trowe ye shall fyndyt most profytable to you.

I wold ye shuld send me word howghe ye doo, and howghe ye have schevyfte for yourself syn ye departyd hens, be som trosty man, and that your fader have no knowlage therof. I durste not late hym knowe of the laste letter that ye wrot to me, be cause he was so sor dyspleasyd with me at that tyme.

Item, I wold ye shuld speke with Wekis, and knowe hys dysposysion to Jane Walsham. She hathe seyd, syn he departyd hens, but [*unless*] she myght have hym, she wold never maryd, hyr hert ys sor set on hym; she told me that he seyd to hyr that ther was no woman in the world he lovyd so welle. I wold not he shuld jape hyr, for she menythe good feythe; and yf he wolle not have hyr, late me wete in hast, and I shall purvey for hyr in othyr wysse.

As for your harneys and ger that ye left here, it ys in Daubeneys kepyng; it was never remevyd syn your departyng, be cause that he had not the keyes. I trowe it shall apeyer [*get injured*], but if it be take hed hate [*unless it be taken heed at*, or *to*] be tymys. Your fader knowythe not wher it is.

I sent your grey hors to Ruston to the ferror, and he seythe he shull never be nowght to rood, nowthyr ryght good to plowe nor to carte; he seyth he was splayyd, and hys shulder rent from the body. I wot not what to do with hym.

Your grandam wold fayne here sum tydyngs from yow. It wer welle do that ye sent a letter to hyr howe ye do, as astely as ye may. And God have you in Hys kepyng, and make yow a good man, and zyf yow grace to do as well as I wold ye shuld do.

Wretyn at Caster, ye Tewisday next befor Seynt Edmund the Kynge.

Your moder,

M. PASTON.

I wold ye shuld make mech of the parson [of] Fylby, the berer herof, and make hym good cher yf ye may.

481.

A.D. 1463, 10 Dec.—ABSTRACT.

[From Paston MSS., B.M.]

Indenture, 10th Dec. 3 Edward IV., between Robert Wodlark, Provost of the College of St. Mary and St. Nicholas, Cambridge, and John Paston, Esq., witnessing a loan by Paston to the college of 100 marks till the octaves of St. Hilary, 1464, [*i.e.* 1464-5] upon certain plate.[1]

Note below in a different hand:—"Memorandum quod Mr. Alexander Lye erit apud Norwicum in die Martis pro[ximo] post diem Carniprivii."

[1] The plate specified in this document is the same as that contained in the *second* list in No. 487, at p. 154.

482.

A.D. 1464, 26 Jan.
JAMES GRESHAM TO JOHN PASTON.

[From Fenn, iv. 156.]

The date of this letter is abundantly evident, first from the circumstance that the 26th of January (the morrow of St. Paul) was a Thursday, and secondly, from the mention of the King's going into Gloucestershire. In January 1464, Edward IV. was at Northampton, and on the 9th of February he was at Gloucester.

To my right worshipfull mayster, John Paston, at Castre, in Norfolk.

AFTER due recomendacion hadde, please it your maistership to wytte that this day the plee by twene Ogan and yow was sore argued in the Kynggs Bench by your counsell, in lettyng of the jugement, and to morwe have they day to argue ageyn. And for lak of copies of the plee, I am fayn to sewe for newe copies therof for your counsell. Your counsell hopeth to do weel therin. These argued for yow, Maisters Grenefeld,[1] Catesby,[2] Pygot,[3] Notyngham,[4] and Starky,[5] &c. And yesterday was the matier by twene Debenham and yow called by Geney[6] for an answer. I have spoken onto Catesby, and delyvered hym your enfromacion, and to be advysed, and to commune with Maister Grenefeld, &c. The two Chefe Juges[7] and Maister Lyttleton[8] arn

---

[1] John Greenfield. He and the two next named were made serjeants-at-aw in November 1463.

[2] John Catesby. He was appointed Judge of the Common Pleas in 1481.

[3] Richard Pygot.

[4] William Nottingham. He was appointed Chief Baron of the Exchequer in 1479.

[5] Humphrey Starkey. He was made a serjeant in 1478.

[6] William Jenney was made a serjeant in 1463, and a Justice of the King's Bench in 1481.

[7] John Markham, Chief Justice of the King's Bench, and Robert Danby, Chief Justice of the Common Pleas, both appointed in 1461.

[8] Thomas Lyttleton, the famous lawyer, was created a serjeant in 1453, and appointed a Judge of the Common Pleas in 1466. He died in 1481, aged 79, as Fenn here tells us in a footnote; but Foss, in his Lives of the Judges, says nothing of his age.

awaytyng up on the Kyng, for the Kyng is purposed in to Gloucestreshire, &c.

It is seid that my Lord Chaunceller [1] shull be here on Saterday or on Moneday next comyng, as the maisteres of the Chauncerye sayn. I write to yow this by cause ye seid to me if ye wyst that my Lord Chaunceller shuld be here, thanne wolde ye come hidder, and ell[es] wolde ye not come here this terme.

As touchyng Rysyng, he hath his day, Utas [2] Purificationis, but I have that weye that his presence is recondet for al this terme.

Maister Clement [3] tellyth me that Wysseter hath put excepcion on to your wyttenesseres, [4] &c.

It is seid that the Kyng wold ride Sussex, Kent, Essex, Suffolk, and Norffolk, and so to the Parlement, for he hath sent for alle his feed men to awayte up on hym in their best aray in al hast.

Wretyn at London, the Thursday in the morwe after Seynt Poule.

> Your owen poure man,
>
> JAMS GRESHAM.

483.

A.D. 1464, 28 Jan.

HENRY BERRY TO JOHN PASTON.

[From Fenn, i. 278.]

By the mention of Sir John Paston it is evident that this letter was written after 1463, but of course the date cannot be later than 1466, in which year John aston the father died, to whom this letter is addressed. It appears also to have been written shortly after the death of James Sevenoke, Abbot of St. Augustine's, Canterbury, which Fenn, I know not on what authority, says occurred in 1463. Even the new edition of Dugdale does not give the date; but Fenn's date is in all probability right.

[1] George Neville, now Bishop of Exeter, but soon after the writing of this letter translated to York.

[2] The Utas or Octave of a feast is the seventh day after it.

[3] Clement Paston, brother to John Paston.

[4] This relates to the disputes concerning Sir John Fastolf's will.

*To my Rygth worsschipful cosyn, John Paston, Squyer,
be this Letter delyveryd, &c.*

RYGHT worsschypfull and reverent cosyn, I
recomaunde me on to you wyth al myn hert,
as your feythful kynnesman and oratour,
desyrynge to here of the goode prosperite
and welfare of your worsschipfull modyr my Lady and
cosyn, wyth your wyff, Sir John Paston, your brethern
Wylliam and Clement, with all your sonys and
doughters, to whom I beseche you hertely that I may
be recomaundyd. God of His hyghe mercy preserve
you all un to Hys mercy and grace, and save you from
all adversite.

Worsschipfull cosyn, my speciall writynge and
hertys desire afore rehersyd, nature naturaly so me
compellyth,

> Watt thou I be putt fer ought of conceyte and syght,
> I have you all in remembrance both day and nyght;

besechynge you, gentyll cosyn, to tender my writynge.
I take God to my wyttnesse, I wold as fayn do that
myght be un to your honor, worsschippe, and profit as
any herthly man can thynke.

Worfor now late deyde the Abbot of our Monastery,
and lefte us in grete ded [*debt*]; the brynger heroff is
my speciall frende: the holdyst brother in our place
never hard nor saw our chirche in that mysere that is
now; we have cast the perellys amongys us, and there
is nowne other helpe, butt every brother that hath any
worsschipfull kynne or frendys, every man to do his
part to the well fare, socour, and releve of our monas-
teri; therfor, worsschipfull cosyn, I, a brother of that
worsschipfull monastery, wer inne begoon the feyth of
all thys lond, mekely besechyth you in the reverence
of Allmygty God to render help, and socour us in our
grete necessite; for in London lyth to wedde many
ryche jowells of ouris, with other grete detts, wych my
brother wyll enforme you of.

Plesyth your goodnesse, for Godys sake, and all the Seyntts of evyn, and att my sympyll request, to have compassion upon us, ye havynge dooe swerte [*due surety*] both in obligacions and pleggs; in the reverens of All myghti God, do your allmesse and charite; hitt schall cause you to be prayed for, and all your kynne as long as the chirche stantt; and be this menys, I trust to All myghty God, to se my cosyn William, or Clement, to be stward of our londys, and so to have an intresse in Kentt, to the worsschippe of God and you all, wych ever have you in His kepynge.   Amen.

Writyn at Caunterbiry in hast the xxviij^{ti} day of Januare.

Also I beseche you, schew the brynger of this letter sum humanite and worsschipe, that when he comyth home, he may reporte as he fyndeth.

[1] [This is the cause every wele thi putt my kynne in my berd, seyinge, I am come of lordys, knygtes, and ladys. I wold they wer in your daunger a m^{l.} merke, that they mygte know you, &c.]

Be your cosyn and bedman,
HENRY BERRY.

484.

A.D. 1464, 27 Feb.
RICHARD CALLE TO JOHN PASTON.

[From Fenn, iv. 72.]

This letter and the next both mention assizes at Thetford. The latter, which is dated on Wednesday, the last (29th) day of February, and which was certainly written in the year 1464, mention them as being held on that very day. The present letter, dated on the second Monday in Lent, says they are *to be* held on Wednesday following. Now the second Monday in Lent 1464 fell on the 27th of February, that is to say just two days before that particular Wednesday on which we know that the assizes really were held. This alone seems almost sufficient evidence of the date of the letter. As for the King's going up to London, it appears by the dates of the Privy Seals that on the 9th February he was at Gloucester, on the 16th and 17th at Kimbolton; and it is stated in the next letter that he was at Waltham on the 27th, which shows that he really was moving towards the capital. This was **not**

---

[1] This last paragraph is crossed out in the original MS.

the case in 1462, the year to which Fenn assigns the letter; nor do I know his authority for stating that there was a Burgundian Embassy in the beginning of that year.

To my mooste reverent and wurchipfull mastre, my Mastre John Paston, be this delyverd.

PLESITH it your goode mastreschip to undrestande that I have receyved a byll of John Boteler, weche speketh of your heygh at Heylesdn, and of your barly in other places, but I undrestand not what ye wold I schulde do therin; nevertheles I schal do make it redy. And as for your heygh I schull tell you whan I come hume; and as for money at Heylesdon I can non gete, and at Sueynesthorp I have take iiij. marc.

Item, as for tidyngs the Sescions schal be at Thetford on Wednesday next comyng, where I undrestande Mr. Berney wol be with moche people, be cauce ther is come to hym a Prevy Seale that he schuld be with the Kyng within vj. dayes that the Prevy Seale whas delyverd hym, weche he can not doo, for the vj. day is to morwe. Ther is on comen to Felbrigge, to William Yelverton on other, and to Robert Rough an other, and non of them wol goo to the Kyng; and the Undrescherif tolde me that ther is comen a comyscion doun to hes maistre, that in cas they come not up to the Kyng be ther Prevy Seales, that than he rere the contre and take hem and bryng hem to the Kyng wher so ever he be.

Item, Jamys Gresham tellethe me the same, and as for tidyngs fro London we here non, but that John Colman telleth me that if Berney or Robert Rough come up they are like to die.

Ther be come to London Embasetors from the Duke of Burgundy, weche cauced the Kyng to spede hym the rather to London.

Item, as for any newe assises at Thetford ther is non but that hathe hanged this v. yere, as the Scherif tellethe me.

I whas purposed to be at home this nyght tell I had your bille, weche cauceth me to ride on to Drayton for divers thyngs, &c.   Almyghty Jesu preserve you.

Wreten at Norwiche, the ij. Munday of clene Lente.

Your pore beedeman and servaunt,

RIC. CALLE.

485.

A.D. 1464, 29 Feb.
JOHN PAMPYNGE TO JOHN PASTON, SENIOR.

[From Fenn, iv. 158.]

The circumstance of the last day of February falling on a Wednesday, fixes the date of this letter to the year 1464.   There is no evidence in the dates of Privy Seals that the King was at Waltham in the end of February, or that he had previously visited Cambridgeshire, in any year during the period when this letter must have been written ; but it is quite possible that he was at Waltham on the 27th February 1464, and if so, that he had passed through Cambridgeshire on his way from Kimbolton, where he had been on the 17th.

To my right worshipfull master, John Paston, the elder, Squier.

LEASE your mastership to wete that the Assise holde this day at Thetford ; and as for any newe Assise, that ye spak of, ther is non, ner non other savyng on for a man a bought Brunham.

I spak with Herward, and I askyd hym if ther was any gret day at Bury, and he seid ther was but a small day, and as for any assises ther wer non but old ; and he told me that Debenham and the Undershireff were falle ought.   Debenham bare the Shireff on hand[1] that he had do indited an hundred men son he cam in to his office, and the Shireff told hym that the Kyngs bokkes apperid whedir it was so or nought ; and he told Debenham that he coud indite an hundred at on tyme whan ye wer indited, and named yow the cause of ther brekyng.

[1] *i.e.*, accused him. *See* Vol. I. p. 90.

Ther was a man kyllid now late in Suffolk, and he that ded it was on of Debenhams men; and Herward told me that the Shireff seid to hym he wold do Debenham a shrewd turne and he coud.

Item, it was told me at Norwich that Master Berney shuld have be here with a gret felaship, and it is not so, ner no man heryth of hys comyng, ner her is but litell pepill nowther, ther wer not so few this iij. yer, as men say.

Item, Herward askyd me where John Gayn was, and I askyd why, and he seid ther is a *capias* ought ayens hym upon the condempnaceon,[1] and the Shireff hath it, he bad me geve hym warnyng; it is retarnabill xv. Pasch.[2]

Item, thei sey here that the Kyng was on Monday at Waltham.

Item, Nicholas Colman hath brought home your fardell; it is at Norwich.

Item, ther be no more Juges here but Sir Pers Ardeyn.[3]

Wretyn at Thetford, the Wednesday the last day of Februar.

Item, Wymondham[4] is here, and was at the shirehows this day, and the Kyngs livery abaught his nekke, and ther stood be the Juge, whill a lettir of the Kyngs was red. The effect was, as it was told me, that the Kyng will that justice be had, and that all risers ayens the pees, and oppressers of the pepill, be chasteised, letyng hem weet[5] that he was late in Cambrigge Shire, and there such as had offendid askyd grace, whech thei had, savyng such as wer rewlers, whom he woll somwhat

---

1 Query, as to this word, it being not perfect in the original?—F.

2 Quindena Paschæ, the fifteenth day after Easter.

3 Sir Peter Ardern, Knight, was appointed Chief Baron of the Exchequer, and also a Justice of the Common Pleas in 1448 ; but in 1462 a new Chief Baron was appointed, and Ardern retained only the judgeship in the Common Pleas. He died in 1467.

4 John Wymondham, Esq., the purchaser of Felbrigg ; he died there in 1475, and was buried in the Augustine Friars at Norwich.—F.

5 The word "weet" is omitted in Fenn's original text, but occurs in the modern copy.

bee punyshid, purposyng to be in this contry abought Estern, &c.

Your servaunt, &c.

JOHN PAMPYNGE.

486.

A.D. 1464, 1 March.
JOHN PASTON THE YOUNGEST TO JOHN PASTON, HIS FATHER.

[From Fenn, i. 284.]

"The Duke of Somerset's going" here referred to cannot well be his flight to Scotland in 1462 (*See* No. 443), though the time of year at which this letter is dated would agree very well with that supposition; for it appears by Letter 442 that John Paston, the father, was at that time residing in the Temple and not at Caister; nor indeed have we distinct evidence of his being at the latter place before 1464. Moreover, in the beginning of 1463, Somerset had just made his peace with King Edward and been received into favour, but early in 1464 he rebelled again. There can be little doubt, therefore, that this year is the true date.

To my rygte reverent and worchepfull fadyr, John Paston, dwellyng in Castyr, be thys delyveryd.

RYTH reverent and worchepfull fadyr, I recomand me on to yow, besechyng yow lowly of your blyssyng, desyryng to here of yowyr wellfar and prosperyte, the whyche I pray God preserve on to Hys plesans, and to yowyr hertys desyir; besechyng yow to have me excusyd that ye had no wrytyng fro me syth that I departyd frome yow; for so God me helpe, I send yow a lettyr to London anon aftyr Kandylmas, by a man of my Lordys; and he forgat to delyver yt to yow, and so he browt to me the lettyr ayen; and sythe that tyme I kowd get no messenger tyll now.

As for tydyngs, syche as we have here I send yow. My Lord and my Lady[1] ar in good hele, blyssyd be God, and my Lord hathe gret labore and cost here in

---

[1] John Mowbray, Duke of Norfolk, and Elizabeth, his wife.

Walys for to take dyvers gentyllmen here whyche wer
consentyng and helpyng on to the Duke of Somersettys
goyng; and they were apelyd of othyr se[r]teyn poyntys
of treson, and thys mater.   And bycause the Kyng
sent my Lord woord to keep thys contre, is cause that
my Lord terythe here thus longe.   And now the Kyng
hathe geve my Lord power, whedyr he wole do exe-
cusyon upon thes gentyllmen, or pardon hem, whedyr
that hym lyst; and as fertheforthe as I kan undyrstand yet, they shall have grase.   And as sone as thes
men be come in, my Lord is perposyd to come to
London, whyche I supose schall be within thys fortnyght.   The menys namys that be apechyd ar thes,
John Hanmer, and Wylliam hys sone, Roger Pulyston,
and Edward of Madok; these be men of worchepe that
schall come in.

The Comenys in Lancasher and Chescher wer up
to the nombyr of a x. m[l.] [10,000] or more, but now
they be downe ayen; and one or ij. of hem was hedyd
in Chestyr as on Saterday last past.

Thomas Danyell[1] is here in Chesscher, but I wot
not in what plase, he hathe sent iij. or iiij. letyrys to
Syr John Howard, syne my Lord come hedyr.

And othyr tydynggs her we none here, but that I
supose ye have herd before; I supose veryly that it
schall be so nye Esterne[2] er ever my Lord come to
London, that I schal not move [q. mowe? i.e., be able]
come home to yow before Estern; wherfor I besech
yow, that ye wole wyche save [vouchsafe] that one of
your men may send a byll to myne oncyll Clement,
or to som othyr man, who that ye wole, in youyr
name, that they may delyver me the mony that I am
behynd of this quarter syn Crystmas, and for the next
quarter, in parte of that some that it plesid yow to

<hr>

[1] This gentleman had a reversionary grant of the constableship of Rising
Castle in 1448, 27 H. VI. He married Margaret, daughter of Sir Robert
Howard, and sister of Sir John, afterwards Duke of Norfolk. He is said to
have been attainted in the 1 E. IV., but fully restored both in blood and pos-
sessions in the 14th of the same King. He was esquire of the body to
Henry VI.—F.

[2] In 1464 Easter Day fell on the 1st of April.

grant me by yer; for by my trowthe, the felawchep
have not so myche mony as we wend to have had be
ryth myche; for my Lord hath had gret costs syn he
came hedyr.   Wherfore I besech yow, that I may
have this mony at Estern, for I have borowyd mony
that I must paye ayen after Estern: and I pray to
Allmyty God have yow in kepyng.

Wretyn in the Castyll of the Holte, in Walys, the
fyrst day of Marche.

Your sone and lowly servant,
JOHN PASTON, the yongest.

487.

A.D. 1464, 11 April.—ABSTRACT.

[From Paston MSS., B.M.]

Copy of an indenture bearing date 11th April, 4 Edward IV.,
witnessing the delivery to Richard Calle, servant of John Paston,
Esquire, by John, prior of the monastery of Holy Trinity, Norwich, by virtue of the King's writ, of a red box containing
seventeen bundles of evidences, with £40 of silver in groats, and
80 nobles of gold, in a bag, and other valuables.

An inventory of the articles referred to in the foregoing indenture is contained in a separate paper mutilated in the right hand margin, which we give
verbatim as follows:—

This is the parcell be endenture received by Richard Calle of
. . . . day of Aprile the forthe yere
. . . . . . as it apperit by the copye that the seyde
Richard sendeth me by John Threcher.

Unam cistam rubeam cum xvij. bundellis evidenciarum in
eadem cista contentis.
Quadraginta libras argenti in grossis et iiij[xx] nobil.
Duo turribula[1] argenti et deaurata.
Unam pixidem argenti et deauratam
Unum osculatorium cum imagine Sancti Jacobi et . . . . .
Unum cruett argenti et deauratum.   I left no cruet
Unum crismatorium rotundum.   Md.[2]   in the cofer.[2]
Unum calicem argenti et deauratum.   )   I left non
Unum alium calicem cum imagine Sanctæ Trinitatis. ∫   soch in the
                                                                                          cofer but
                                                                                          chalis of
                                                                                          gold.[2]

[1] Thuribula, censers, from *thus.*
[2] These marginal notes are in John Paston's hand.

This is the copy of a bille drawin in Englyche that I sent home [of all] manner of suche stuff as was in myne coffre in the abb[ey] . . . . . . by a letter sent with the same bylle that he chowlde take hede that . . . yf he fonde aney more, well be it, as it aperit in the seyd lett[er] . . . woulle be lokyd [*locked*] uppe.

Thes to chalis after the unc' xx.s. ar worth xliij. *li.*[2]

Unum calicem de auro playne ponderis duas li[bras].

Unum alium calicem de auro cum scriptura "Cal[icem salutaris accipiam,"[1] ponderis xix. unc'].

This is worth xiij. li. xv. s.[2]

Unam tabulam de auro cum imagine Sancti J[acobi positam cum lapidis pretiosis,] ponderis xiij. unc' et iij. quarteria.

Thes be worth, after xxx. d. the unch xxviij. li. xiij s. ix. d.[2]

Unum par turribulorum argenti et deaurat' cum scriptura, viz., in prima parte "Dat' est eis," &c.; et in secunda parte "Ascendit fumus," pond' xiij. lb. et [x. unc'].

Unam pixidem argenti pro sacramento deaurat' cum cruce [in summitate ac chased cum] liliis, pond' v. lb. et iij. unc' di'.

Unam ampullam argenti deaurat' pond' i. lb.[3]

[4] All this was put in a paner togyddre and . . . . for to berit in to the coffre.

Item, xl. mark in noblis and xl. li. in gro[tis].

Item, evydens.

488.

A.D. 1464, April–Nov.—ABSTRACT.

[From MS. Phillipps, 9309.]

DEPOSITIONS TOUCHING SIR J. FASTOLF'S WILL.

These depositions, of which we shall only attempt to give some of the principal points, were produced in the Spiritual Court by Sir William Yelverton and William Worcester in opposition to the claim of John Paston and Thomas Howes to be Sir John Fastolf's executors. The examinations were taken at intervals during the years 1464, 1465, and 1466, and the suit was not terminated when John Paston died. The MS. volume here referred to contains three distinct bundles of these depositions bound up in a wrong order. A volume containing similar matter among the Paston MSS. in the British Museum, will be found entered in the year 1465.

"Primum testes reprobatorii producti per Yelverton, contra testes Paston principaliter productos &c.

"Facta fuit sequens examinatio testium subscriptorum secrete et singillatim, videlicet, Domini Johannis Davy capellani vicesimo octavo die mensis Aprilis, Thomæ Upton quinto, Johannis Bockyng duodecimo, Nicholai Newman xvj[to] diebus mensis Maii; Johannis Loer, Willelmi Eton quarto, Roberti Lynne quinto, diebus mensis Junii; Bartholomei Elys tercio, magistri Roberti Wylly sexto, Johannis Marshall, Johannis Davy tercio-

---

[1] Psalm cxv. [cxvi.] 13.   [2] *See* Note 2 on last page.

[3] The plate in this list is the same as that described in No. 481, by which the words lost in this MS. have been supplied.

[4] Added in John Paston's hand.

decimo et Willelmi Lyne ultimo, diebus mensis Julii; Anno
Domini millesimo quadringentesimo sexagesimo quarto, Indictione
duodecima, pontificatus Sanctissimi in Christo patris et domini
nostri, domini Pii Divina prudencia Papæ Secundi anno sexto, In
Domo Thesaurarii ecclesiæ Cathedralis Sancti Pauli, London,
infra parochiam Sancti Gregorii civitatis London situat', per
venerabilem virum magistrum Johannem Druell, utriusque juris
doctorem, examinatorem et commissarium ad infra scripta
specialiter deputatum. In præsentia mei Nicholai Parker notarii
auctoritate Apostolica, publici scribæ in hac parte de et super
exceptionibus infra scriptis, per partem domini Willelmi Yelverton et Willelmi Worceter productorum."

1. John Davy chaplain, staying at the University of Cambridge,
liberæ conditionis, 30 years old and more, examined *super exceptionibus infrascriptis* of which the tenors are quoted, viz., on the
part of Yelverton and Worceter against John Russe, Robert
Cutteler clk., Master Clement Felmyngham, Rob. Boteler,
Ralph Lampet, Brother Will. Bokyngham, and Master Robert
Popy, witnesses on the opposite side, whose testimony is dis-
credited "eo quod parte sua non præsenti juraverunt et super
non juratis deposuerunt, ac in depositionibus suis fuerint et sint
varii, contrarii, singulares negativam asserentes, causas dictorum
suorum minime reddentes, unumque et eundem præmeditatum
sermonem proferentes, a testatore non vocati aut rogati perhibere
testimonium, nec sufficienter probantes in hac parte, prout ex
inspectione depositionum suarum liquere poterit intuenti."
Further, John Russe was illiterate, and did not understand Latin
when he made his deposition, and he contradicted the other
witnesses on his own side : viz., to the 9th interrogatory he said, Sir
J. Fastolf's will was not written before his death, which Clement
Felmyngham and Robt. Cutteler in their reply to the 3d said
it was. Moreover he expected advantage to himself from his
testimony, and was discharged by Howys of £300 that he owed
Fastolf. He had also secretly abstracted certain muniments and
charters of the testator, which were in the custody of Will. Worceter, in the house of John Tovy, at Castir, Norwich dioc., in Nov.
1459. Moreover he was *supravisor et locator* of the testator's
lands called Akethorpe, yearly value 9 marks, appointed by
Paston or Howys, who promised to sell them to him much under
value for his testimony. Further, his statement that he was
present *in quadam bassa camera* at Caister between 8 and 9
a.m. on the Saturday before Sir J. Fastolf's death, was a
perjury, for he was really all that time in other places a long
way off. His declaration that he was no servant or tenant of
those who brought him forward was untrue : he had hired a
house of Howys in the town of Yarmouth, value 40s. a year.
He was inconsistent in his testimony about the hour Sir J.
declared his will. He also pretended never to have seen Fastolf's

will before his death, although he wrote the said pretended will with his own hand with the date at the head, which at the beginning of this suit he caused to be cut off from the writing and hidden.

Also the said Rob. Cutteler chaplain, when he made his deposition, was "levis opinionis, malæ conscientiæ et de mensa Joh'is Paston ac tenens ipsius, prout ad primum interrogatorium examinationis suæ primæ et secundæ respondebat." Also he was perjured; because in April 1457 in par. of Holy Trin., Castir, he beat and maimed one Jo. Flemyng, and boasted of it (*ac sic factum nomine suo ratum habuit*), but being taken before Sir J. Fastolf, justice of the peace, he swore he had not done so.—Proofs that he was not disinterested.

Exceptions to Rob. Popy: He was a tenant of Paston's, &c. &c.

Davy says John Rus was at Yarmouth on the Saturday in question, as he usually was on Saturdays, to buy victuals for Fastolf's house, &c. (Proof declared insufficient in the margin). Sir J. Fastolf was so ill, that, as Davy had heard he was unable to speak from 22d Oct. "Quæ quidem infirmitas vocabatur judicio medicorum, *sincope*, quæ ipsum vexabat singulis horis et ipsum deduxit ad extasim de scientia istius jurati, qui continue conversabatur cum eo usque ad ipsius mortem."

2. Thos. Upton, one of the clerks of the King's kitchen, *literatus*, "liberæ conditionis," forty years old and over; 2d. witness.

Mentions that W. Worceter gave Jo. Rus a casket to keep containing certain documents, which Rus delivered to Howys after Fastolf's death. Was clerk of the kitchen to Fastolf when Rus used to go on Saturday to Yarmouth, &c.

9 May. Jo. Bokkyng produced by Jo. Naseby, proctor of Yelverton and Worceter, before Master Tho. Wynterton, LL.D., auditor of Thomas Archbishop of Canterbury, at his house in the parish of St. Martin, in presence of Robert Kent, proctor of John Paston.—Examination committed to John Druell, LL.D. who on the 12th May examines him secretly in the house of the treasurer of St. Paul's.

"Dicit quod Johannes Tovy quædam munimenta et evidencias[1] in certis bagis et pixidibus contenta quæ Willelmus Worceter eidem Johanni Tovy liberavit custodienda." Rus was and is Howys' tenant for the house he lives in. After Fastolf's death Upton delivered to Clement Felmyngham a signet or gold ring, "ad signandum sigilla dicti domini Johannis Fastolf," in a little bag, which was to be returned "post signacionem hujusmodi," but afterwards he said he had lost it. Touchyng brother W. Bukyngham, it was publicly noised at Yarmouth that Robert Brown, a chaplain of that town, had killed one Seman Burton, that Bukyngham knowingly received him, and that by his advice

---

[1] There is no verb in the MS., to govern *munimenta et evidencias.*

he fled. To the last exception he says he believes Fastolf did
not release Paston from the payment of the said 4000 marks,
"quia iste juratus non intellixit in tota vita sua tantam liberalita-
tem in dicto domino Johanne Fastolf." Fastolf had such difficulty in breathing for five or six days before his death that he
could hardly speak.

Interrogatories proposed on the part of Paston and Howys, and
administered to witnesses.

" In primis, interrogetur quilibet testis hujusmodi cujus sit conditionis et an sit famulus, ¹ serviens aut tenens partis eum pro-
ducentis, et cui parti magis favet partium prædictarum." Secondly,
whether he be in the pay of any one.   There are six interrogatories
in all, and they are numbered.

Then follow answers of some one whose name does not appear,
to each of these six interrogatories ; and other answers by—

1. Nich. Newman, Usher of the Chamber to Lady Catherine,
Duchess of Norfolk.

2. John Loer, servant of the Abbot of Langley.

3. Will. Eton.

4. Rob. Lynne of Bucklande.

5. Barth. Elys of Yarmouth, " literatus liberæ conditionis,"
fifty years old and more (proves Rus's absence, but his testimony
is declared in the margin to be improbable, and not to agree
with Davy's.)

6 *July.* Naseby produces Rob. Wylly on the part of Yelverton
and Worcester.   Examined on the 9th.—Says he was required by
Paston and Howys to see Fastolf's will, and " ad impediendum
[*impendendum*] consilium suum:"—that on a Sunday in the
summer after Fastolf's death, John Paston showed him, at
Fastolf's house in Southwark, Sir John's will written on paper,
in presence of Clement Felmyngham and John Bracley, and
asked his opinion if it was valid.   Thought it insufficient to
overthrow any previous will.   A clause mentioning Tudenham
and Heydon as executors was cancelled by this deponent's
advice, " eo quod erat contra caritatem."

13 *July at Bow Church.* Naseby produces John Marshall and
John Davy, whose examinations follow.

19 *Oct.* 1464. Druell examines Hen. Wenstall at the treasurer's
house of St. Paul's.

15 *Nov.* 1464. Druell examines Rob. Hert.

1 *Dec.* Naseby produces Rob. Fyztrauf, whose production
Kent opposes ; who tries to prove Rus's absence (insufficiently,
as remarked in the margin), because he was constantly with
Fastolf, except half an hour that morning, and held the basin

---

¹ The text is continued here at another part of the volume, the leaves being
misplaced.

while Henry Barbour lathered the beard (*lavit barbam*) of the said Sir John Fastolf.

"Responsiones personaliter factæ per dominum Thomam Howys unum executorum domini Joh'is Fastolf, ultimo die mensis Aprilis Aº Dⁿⁱ 1464," &c., "coram Ven. viro Mag'ro Thoma Wynterbourne, LL.D.," &c., "in camera ejusdem infra manerium Revᵐˡ patris apud Lamehith, Winton dioc' situat', in præsenncia mei Nicholai Parker," &c.

Howys says he did not see Coteler or Rus in Fastolf's chamber that Saturday before he went to dinner. On Saturday and Sunday before his death Fastolf spoke so low he could hardly be heard by any one, and Howys heard him only by putting his ear close to his mouth. Fastolf's mind was clear.

489.

A.D. 1464, 12 May.—ABSTRACT.

[From MS. in Bodleian Library.]

Power of attorney by Roger Fidyon, clerk, and William Bondys to Richard Lynstede, John Holme, and John Brikkes, to enter and take possession of the manor of Hornynghall, in Castre, by Yarmouth, with appurtenances in Castre, Maudeby, Ormesby, Filby, and Scroudeby, or elsewhere in the hundred of East Flegge, Norfolk, which the said Roger and William have of the gift of Edmund Clere ; and thereafter to deliver seisin therein to Agnes Paston, William Paston, Elizabeth, Countess of Oxford, John Veer, Earl of Oxford, John Scroop, Knight, Lord Scroop, Sir William Yelverton, Elizabeth Cleere; William Jennay, John Grenefeld, John Catesby, Serjeants-at-Law ; John Hastynges, John Clopton, John Calthorp, Hugh Fen, Thomas Cornewaleys, Thomas Howes, clerk, Roger Marchall of London, Henry Spilman, William Lomnour, Bartholomew Whyte, William Whyte, John Applyerd, James Arblaster, William Wurcetyr, and Richard Maryot, according to a charter granted to them by the said Roger and William.

Castre, 12th May, 4 Edward IV.

490.

A.D. 1464, 8 June.
MARGARET PASTON TO JOHN PASTON.

[From Fenn, iv. 176.]

The commission to Lord Scales and Sir John Howard mentioned in **this**

letter seems to have reference to a proclamation dated the 11th May 1464, by
which all men between the ages of sixty and sixteen were ordered to attend
the King.   The date is confirmed by the reference in the postscript to the
death of " Rous of Suffolk," for Reginald Rous of Denington died in 1464.
(See Weever's *Funeral Monuments*, p. 782.)

To myn ryght worshypful hosbond, John Paston, be thys
delyveryd in haste.

RYGHT worshypful hosbond, rekomaund me on
to you.   Pleasyth you to wete that I sent
yesterday Loveday to Norwyche to speke
wyth the Vykyr of Derham[1] for the mater
betwen Master Constantyn and hym; and he seyth
that as for that mater, Master Constantyn sewyd hym
for feyth and trowth brekyng, and he sewed Master
Constantyn in the Temporall Curte uppon an obligacion of x*li*.; and ther was made appoyntment be twen
hem by the advyce of bothe ther Conceylis, be for
Master Robert Popy, that eche of hem shuld relece
othyr, and so they dede, and the sewtys wer wyth-
drawyn on bothe partyes, and iche of hem aquyt-
auncyd othyr; and as for any copy of the plee, he
had never non, ner he ner Master John Estegate, that
was hys atornay, remembryth nat that it was regestryd;
and Master John Estegate seythe, if it schuld be
scergyd in the regester it wold take a fortenyght werk,
and yit peraventur never be the nerer.

Syr Thomas Howes hathe ben ryght besy thys weke
at Bloofeld, in wrytyng and lokyng uppe of ger, and
John Russe hathe ben with hym ther the moste parte
of alle thys weke, and thys day was Robert Lynne
ther with hym; what they have do I wote nat, but I
schal wete if I may.

It was told me that Syr Thomas desyryd of John
Russe to make hym a new inventory of Syr John
Fastolffs goods.   John Russe myght not be spoke with

[1] Constantine Dalby was instituted to the Vicarage of East Dereham in
1451, and was succeeded in 1458 by Robert Sheringham.

yit, for the letter that he shuld a wretyn, whych ye sente me word of.

Item, it is tolde that the Dwke of Suffolk[1] is kome home, and owthyr he is ded, or ellys ryght seke, and not lyke to eskape; and Syr John Howard is kome hom; and it is seyd that the Lord Skalys[2] and he have a comyssyon to enquer whye they of this contre that were sent for kame not hastylar uppe afftyr they wer sent for.   It is reportyd that the Kyng is gretly dyspleasyd ther with.   At the reverence of God, arme yowr selve as myghtyly as ye kan ageyn yowr enmyes, for I know verrayly that they wyl do ageyn yow as myghtyly as they kan with all ther power.

It is told me that Syr Thomas shal kom uppe in haste, and othyr, suche as he kan make for hys partye.

Also for Goddys sake be war what medesyns ye take of any fysissyans of London; I schal never trust to hem be cause of your fadr and myn onkyl, whoys sowlys God assoyle.

The blissyd Trynyte have yow in Hys kepyng, and sende yow helthe and good spede in all yowr materis. Wretyn in haste, on the Fryday next befor Sceynt Bernabye.

By yowrs,   M. P.

Alle the jentylmen of thys contre that went uppe to the Kyng ar contrmaundyd, and ar com home ageyn. It is told me that Rowse of Suffolk[3] is ded.   If John Gayn myght have any releese of his sone, if it myght do hym ese, it wer a good torne for hym.

---

[1] John De la Pole, Duke of Suffolk.
[2] Anthony Widville was created Lord Scales in 1461.—F.
[3] Reginald Rous, Esq. of Denington, in Suffolk, died in 1464.   He was the ancestor of the present Earl of Stradbroke.

491.

A.D. 1464, 28 June.
RICHARD CALLE TO JOHN PASTON.

[From Paston MSS., B.M.]

This letter refers to the suit brought by Jenney against Paston in 1464, in which, as will be seen hereafter, Paston failed to appear at four successive county courts held at Ipswich, and was at last outlawed in Michaelmas term. See No. 494.

To my ryght wurschipfull my mastre, John Paston, be this delyverd in haste.

PLESITH it youre goode maisterchippe to witte that I have be with my Mastre Calthorppe for the matre ye wrote to hym fore, wherin I have founde hym ryght weele disposed and favorabley; nevertheles he tolde me that William Jenney hath bene hes goode frende and have ben of hes councell this ij. yere in all hes matres towchyng the lawe, but he seide lever he hadde lose the lesser frende than the greete frende, and so he hathe graunted favour accordyng to youre desire, and wrote a lettre to the undrescheryff of Norfolk that he schuld take suerte sufficient to save hym harmeles, and that done to write a letter to the undrescheryff of Suffolk and lete hym witte that he hath taken suerte that ye schall appere in the *crastino Animarum* upon the exigents returnable, or elles to bryng a *super sedias* [1] lauful before that daye, chargyng hym that he do sece [*cause to cease*] the callyng of the writts, and to retorne that ye appered the furst day. Weche suerte is taken, and a letter wreten to the undrescheryff of Suffolk acordynge herto.

Item, as for Sir Thomas Howes, he lythe most at Norwiche. I can thynke he come not up to London tyll Michelmes.

Item, I rode over to Techewelle whan that I whas at Mastre Calthorppes for to have money of the fermours,

---

[1] *Super seaus.* So spelt in MS.

and Yelverton and Sir Thomas hathe sent to hem that they schol pay to you no more money, for that they had payed to you they schulde payed [*pay it*] ayene to them; and so I gane [*can*] gete no money of hem. Wherfore I went for to distreyne hem; and so they seide that I myght not distreyne hem, for I come before the daye, for her [*their*] day is at Midsomer. Neverthles I wold not lette, for that Simond Miller and other promysed to Mr. William Cotyng and to me that I schuld have the money aftre Midsomer, so that I brought with me a quetaunce of suche money as ye have receyved of hem, or elles a generall quetaunce; and the tone I purposed to do in haste be the advice of the seide Mastre W. Cotynge. For, and I torned, I can thynke it schuld hurte. I am purposed to lete it in youre name to other folks or to them ayen, and suerte founde to you, &c. And Almyghty God preserve and kepe you. Wreten at Norwiche on Sen Petres Even.

Your pore servaunt and
bedman, RIC. CALLE.

492.

A.D. 1464.—JOHN PASTON TO EDWARD IV.

[From MSS. in the Bodleian Library.]

This, and the alternative petition which follows, seem to have been drawn up in the year 1464, as one or other of them must have been the subject of the agreement of the 10th September in that year (No. 493). The two are printed from two parchment MSS. in the Bodleian Library. There is also, among the Paston MSS. in the British Museum, a third copy, fair written on parchment like the other two, of which the text corresponds in the beginning to the second petition, and in the latter part to the first.

To the Kyng, our Liege Lord.

BESECHYTH lowly your humble servaunt, John Paston the older, squier, that it please youre good grace, for such a fyne as your highnes hath apoynted your seid besecher to content yow, wherof ye be put in suerte, to graunt

on to your seid besecher your gratious lettirs patentes
of licence to found, stabilissh, and endewe in the gret
mancion of Caster in Flegge in Norffolk, that late was
John Fastolffs, knyght, cosyn to your seid besecher,
a college of vij. prestes, wherof one to be master, and
of vij. porefolk, to pray for your noble astate and for
the soule of the seid John Fastolff and such other as
he was behold to inperpetuite, aftir ordinauns by your
seid besecher in that behalff to be made; and to
inmortese, geve and graunt to the seid prestes and to
ther successours, for the sustentacion of hem and of
the seid porefolk CXX. mark of annuite and rent
charge, or annuites and rentes charge, yerly goyng out
of the maners callid Redhams, Vaux, and Bosomes,
in Caster forseid, Begviles in Wynterton, Reppis in
Bastewyk, Spencers in Heryngby, Loundhall in Saxthorp, Heylesdon, Drayton, Heynesford, Guton in
Brandeston, Beyton, Techewell, and of the thrid part
of the maner of Runham with th'apportenauns in the
shire of Norffolk, and of the maners of Hemnales in
Cotton, Burneviles in Nakton, Akthorp in Leystoft,
Calcotes, Havelound, Spitlyngges, with th'apportenauns
in the shire of Suffolk, and out of any part of the seid
maners, with a clause of distresse for defaut of payment of the seid rente, and vj. acres of lond in the
seid towne of Caster, and the avowsons of the chirches
of the same town, and the fourth part of the seid
mancion, or any part therof for the habitacion of the
seid prestes and porefolk, to be reparid at the costs of
your seid besecher, and his heires or assignes for evir.
And also by your seid lettirs patentes to graunt the
same prestes to be one body incorperate and to have
succession perpetuall, and a comon seall, and to be
persones abill to plede and to be impletid, and to
purchase and alienyn all maner londes, goodes and
catell, by the name of the master and his brethyrn of
the college of Sen John Baptist of Castre aforeseid.
And also by your seid lettirs patentes to licence the
seid prestes to take and reseyve, and to hold to them

and to ther successours the seid annuite, rent charge, vj. acres of lond, avousons, and the seid ————[1] part of the seid mancion, for evir. And to geve your Chaunceler of Inglond for the tyme beyng, comaunde-ment, power, and auctorite that where as in this peti-sion is not comprehendid the certeynte of termes, maters, clauses, and other circumstaunces convenient and requisite after forme of lawe for licens of the seid fundacion, that your seid Chaunceler, that notwith-standyng, do make your seid lettirs patentes in forme of lawe effectuall and sufficient in that behalf after the very entent aforeseid, not excedyng the valew and somme before specifyd, without any fyne or fee other thanne is afore specifyd to be payd for the seid lettirs patentes, licens, or grauntes, by your seid besecher or by the seid prestes; and thei shall pray hertly to God for yow.

Endorsed in a later hand:—Supplicatio Jo. Paston [pro] fundacione Collegii apud Caistor [secundum] formam testamenti Jo. Fastolf, mil.

II.

To the Kyng, our Sovereyn Lord.

Please it yowr highnes to graunte unto yowr humble servant John Paston the older, Squier, yowr gracious lettres patents of licence to fownde, stabelysh, and endewe in the gret mancion of Castre be Mekyll Yermowth in Norffolk, that late was John Fastolffs, knyght, cosyn to yowr seyd besecher, a colage of vij. prystes wheroff on to be master, and vij. pourmen, to praye for your noble astate, and for the sowle of the said Fastolff and suche othir as he was be holde to inperpetuite, and to inmortese and gyve to the seyd prystes, and to ther successours for the sustentacion of hem, and of the seyd pourmen C. marke of annunite and rent charge, yerly goyng owt of all maneres, londes, and tenementz that were the seyd Fastolffs within the Shyres of Norffolk and Suffolk, and vj. acres of londe in the sayd town of Castre, and the iiij. parte of the sayd mancion for the habitacion of the sayd prystes and pourmen, to be repared at the costes of your seyd besecher and hys heyres and assignes for ever, as suerly and lawfully as your seyd besecher can devise. And also be your letters patentz to

1 A blank on an erasure.

graunt the same prystes to be one bodie incorperate, and to have succession perpetuall, and a comon seall, and to be persones abyll to plede and be impletid, and to purchase and alienyn all maner londs, tenements, godes, and catell, be the name of the master and hys brethyrn of the collage of Saynt John Baptiste of Castre aforsayd. And also be your letters patentz to licence the sayd prystes to take and receyve, and to holde to theym and to ther successours the sayd annaunite, rente charge, vj. acres of lond, avowsons, and the seyd iiij. parte of the said mancion for ever, with owte eny ffyne or fe to be payde for the sayd lettres patentz, licens or grauntes be your sayd besecher, or be the said pristes. And thei shall pray hertly to God for you.

Endorsed in a later hand:—Peticio Joh'is Paston Arm' ad Regem pro collegio in Caister.

493.

A.D. 1464, 10 Sept.
FOUNDATION OF CAISTER COLLEGE.

[From Fenn, iv. 182.]

Apunctuament' Regis pro fundacione Collegij apud Caistre, &c.

THE Kyng, for the soume of CCC. mark ot lawfull mony of Inglond, or of silver plate to the valew therof, grauntith to John Paston the older, Squier, to have licens, lawfully mad, to make and found a College of vij. prests and vij. pore folk at Caster, in Flegge in Norffolk, for the soule of Sir John Falstolf, Knyght; thei to be indued with certeyn rent, and otherwise aftir the intent and effect as is specifijd in a bille therof, signed by the Kyng; and that he shall showe his good grase, favour, and assistence to have the said fundacon inacted and auctorised in the parlement next holden, and discharge the seid John Paston and the seid prests of any other fyne or fee to be mad in the Chauncerie for the seid fundacion; and that the Kyng shall signe and graunt warants for seid licens, and shewe his good grace and favour in the expedision therof, what tyme he be sued to therfore by the seid John Paston.

Also, the Kyng grauntith to be good and favorabill Lord to the seid John Paston, and inespeciall in all thyngs touchyng the execucion of the will of the seid Sir John Fastolf, and also to be good and favorabill Lord to the seid John Paston, in supportyng and helpyng hym, in that the Kyngs Highnesse may law-fulle do, in such maters as are in debate athwyx the seid John Paston and William Yelverton, or William Jenney, or any other, concernyng the londs and tene-ments, goods or cattell, that were the seid Sir John Fastolfs. Also the Kyng grauntith to help and support the seid John Paston to opteyne and have to the use of the seid Sir John Fastolf such goods as were the seid Fastolfs deseitfully aloyned out of the possession and knowlech of the seid John Paston ; and that the Kyng shall graunt the seid John Paston such lawfull wrytynggs and lettirs from the Kyng, directed to such persones as shall be behovefull for the same, what tyme the seid John Paston suyth to the Kyngs High-nesse therfore.

Also where Yelverton, or Jenney, or any Justise of the Peas of the Shire of Suffolk hath recorded any riot, trespas, or offenses to be do ayens the Kyngs peas, by the seid John Paston, his servaunts, or tenaunts, or frends ; or where any inditement or presentment is found ayens them, or any of them, before any of the seid Justises, for any such riot, offenses, trespas, or for any other mater remaynyng of record in the Kyngs Benche, or in any other plase, the Kyng grauntith to the seid John Paston, and all other persones named in the seid records or inditements, or in any of hem, and to alle her boroughs [*sureties*] and plegges, and to ich of hem that woll sue it, a pardon of all riotes, trespas, offenses, felonys, forfetures doon ayens the Kyngs peas, and of fynes therefore dempt [*adjudged*], or to be dempt, and of all other thyngs generally, treason except, and that the Kyng shall signe warants lawfull of the seid

pardons, what tyme his Highnesse be requerid by the
seid John Paston or his attornys.

And also that his Highnesse shall do inquere and
examinacion be mad whedir the seid record of the seid
Justises and presentments, and other informacions or
compleynts mad ayens the seid John Paston, were do
trewly and lawfully or nought; and if it be found that
thei were do otherwise thanne trought, lawe, or consiens woll, thanne the Kyng grauntyth to cause the
doers therof to recompense the seid John Paston and
the seid other persones, as far as lawe and good consiens woll in that behalf.

And that if it fortune any compleynt to be mad
ayens the seid John Paston, by any persone in tyme
comyng, to the Kyng, that he shall take no displeasir
to the seid John Paston till the tyme he come to his
answer, and be found in defaut.

And that the Kyng shall receyve an *Cli.* of the seid
CCC. mark, what tyme he send for it, and the remnaunt
as sone as the seid fundacion take effect; and also that
his Highnesse shall gete the assent of the reverent
fader in God, the Archebisshop of Caunterbury, in such
apoyntments as is mad athwyx the Kyng and the seid
John Paston, of such goods as were the seid Sir John
Fastolfs, for the delivere therof; and that if the seid
John Paston refuse the administracion of the goods
and catell that were the seid Sir John Fastolfs, sufferyng
other to take it opon hem, the Kyng, at the instauns
of the seid John Paston, grauntith to be good and
favorabill Lord to such other as the coors of the lawe,
and assent of the seid John Paston, shall take the seid
administracion in execucion of the seid Fastolfs will,
touchyng the administracion of the goods and catell
forseid, acordyng to the same wyll; and that the Kyng
shall not cleyme nor desire any of the londs or tenements, goods or catell, that were the seid Sir John
Fastolf, ayens the seid John Paston, or any other
executor, adminïstror, or feffe of the seid Sir John
Fastolf, nor support or favour any other persone in

cleymyng any of the seid londs or tenements, goods
or catell, ayens any the seid administers, executores,
or feffes.

And the Kyng grauntith that where as this bille is
not sufficiently mad in clauses and termes accordyng to
th'ententtherof, that his Highnessewolltakeandexecute
the very entent therof, notwithstandyng the insufficiens
of any such termes and clauses in thes bille.   Wretyn
at Marleburgh, the Monday next after the Nativite of
oure Lady, the fourthe yere of the reigne of the Kyng.

494.

A.D. 1464, 20 Nov.—ABSTRACTS.

[From Paston MSS., B.M.]

OUTLAWRY OF JOHN PASTON.

The following writs and copies of writs stood originally on a file in the order
in which they are here noticed.

I. Edward IV. to the Prior of Norwich.—Orders him to
deliver to the bearer all goods in his hands belonging to John
Paston, Esq., who is outlawed.   Reading, 20 Nov.

II. Writ to Edmund Clyre, Escheator of Norfolk, touching the
above outlawry.—John Paston is here called "the elder."   Dated
20 Nov.

III. *Supersedeas* addressed to the Escheator of Cos. Cambridge
and Hunts to stay confiscation of the goods of John Paston, who
has been outlawed, first for trespass agaihst William Jenney, and
secondly for trespass against William Hogan ; of which he was
convicted in Suffolk on Monday, 10 Sept., 4 Edw. IV.   Both
cases are removed by writs of error into the King's Bench.—
Teste J. Markham apud Westin., 28 Nov., 4 Edw. IV.

IV. Copy of *supersedeas* on the exigent issued at Jenney's suit
to the Sheriff of Suffolk.—Teste J. Markham apud Sekbrok, 24
Aug., 4 Edw. IV.   With the return on the writ of exigent,
notifying Paston's non-appearance when proclaimed at the county
courts held at Ipswich on Monday 21 May, Monday 18 June,
Monday 16 July and Monday 13 Aug., 4 Edw. IV.   The *super-*

sedeas was delivered to the sheriff by Richard Calle in Paston's name on the 29 Aug.

V. Edward IV. to Sir John Markham, Chief Justice of the King's Bench.—Commands him to make *supersedeas* upon the exigents. For, as the King understands, Jenney obtained a judgment against Paston for £23 : 10s., and William Hogan by the support of Jenney took another action, and obtained a judgment of £16 : 13 : 4 "against conscience and law, as we be informed." If Paston has delivered to the sheriff any writs of error to send the actions to our court of parliament, he is to comply, according to the usual course in such cases.—Fotheringay, 3 Aug.

VI. Edward IV. to Thomas Croxton, Clerk of the Crown.— Commanding him to search the records and see that the processes of outlawry against John Paston have been well and sufficiently made out.—Reading, 3 Oct.

Memorandum subjoined, "that William Jenney's counsel hath openly vaunted in Westminster Hall that the King hath sent another letter to the sheriff, commanding him to certify John Paston outlawed."

*** V. and VI. are copies on the same paper.

495.

A.D. 1464, 27 Nov.—Note.

A letter, which must at one time have belonged to the Paston collection, is noticed by Blomefield in his account of the Priors of Norwich, (Hist. of Norfolk, iii. 604), as follows :—

"John Molet, doctor of the decrees, late sub-prior, was confirmed prior by the Bishop, Jan. 29. 1453. He was a favorite of John Paston, as appears by an original letter" (*penes me*, says the author in a footnote), "of Sir Walter Blount's then Treasurer of England, dated at London, 27 Nov., 1464, when the said John was outlawed; in which the treasurer tells him that the King is advertised that he is entrusted with 7 or 8,000 marks of the said John's, all which the King is intituled to, and therefore if it be in his hands, or within his monastery, he commands him not to part with anything, but keep all for the King's use. But however, it was so managed, that Paston's son got it out of the priory, without the prior's knowledge, as was pretended."

496.

A.D. 1464? 3 Dec.
ANONYMOUS TO JOHN PASTON.

[From Fenn, iii. 418.]

It is difficult to assign with confidence either a date or a meaning to this strangely worded epistle. The signature itself is a mystery. The order of the Temple of Sion is unknown to archæologists, and the place from which the letter is dated cannot be identified. From the peculiar device used as a signature, resembling what in heraldry represents a fountain, Fenn threw out a suggestion that Fountaine was the writer's name, remarking that a family of that name resided at Salle, in Norfolk, and might have been related to Paston as the writer claimed to be. But there seems to be an air of irony about the whole communication which forbids us to construe any of its statements seriously ; nor do we find the slightest allusion to this letter or its contents in all the rest of the correspondence. For my part, I am inclined to think it was a mocking letter addressed to John Paston by one of the prisoners in the Fleet, where Paston had himself been confined in 1464. His imprisonment on that occasion was probably of short duration, but I cannot tell the precise date of his release. He was committed to the Fleet, as we are informed by William Worcester (Itinerary, p. 366), on Saturday the 3d November. If I am right in my conjecture about this letter, he had, perhaps, been already liberated ; but some of his late fellow-prisoners, probably members of the Inner or Middle Temple like himself, who had formed themselves into a fancy "Order of the Temple of Sion," amused themselves by speculating on the probability that he was not yet quite clear of the toils of the law, and that he would be obliged to come back and spend Christmas in gaol, among the jolly companions whom he had recently deserted. I may remark that the name of Thomas Babington occurs in Dugdale's *Origines Juridiciales*. p. 163, as having been elected a reader in the Inner Temple in 22 Hen. VII., when he seems to have been an old man ; for, owing to his sight failing, he was excused from reading, and John Port, who was afterwards Attorney General, and later still, Justice of the King's Bench, read in his place.

To my ryght worshipfull maister and brother, John Paston, this letter be taken.

RYGHT worshipfull and reverend mayster and brother, with alle my service I recommaunde me on to yow. Please hit onto your grete wysedom to have yn your descrete remem-brauns the streite Ordre on which we ben professid, and on which ze er bownden to kepe your residens, and specially on this tyme of Crystmas amonggis your confrerys of this holy Ordre, the Temple of Syon ; for ynlesse than ze kepe dewly the poynts of your holy Religion, owr Maister Thomas Babyngton, maister and soverayn of owr Order of th'assent of his brythryn ben avysed to awarde azenste yow ryght

sharp and hasty proces to do calle yow to do your
obcervauns, and to obeye the poynts of your Religion,
which wer on to me grete hevynesse. Wherfore I, as
he that hath most grettest cause, and ys most bownden
on to your grete gentylnesse, and also whom nature
and kynde most specially byfore every of alle owr
breth[r]yn bynden me to owe and wilne yow goode
wylle and trewe hert, consyderyng the grete tyme of
penawns that ze havyn ben yn fro sone upon Mighel-
mas hederto, that ys to say, yn relevyng and susten-
awns of your evyn Crysten,[1] and also yn the charytable
and meritory dede of almyssdoyng, that ys to say yn
plenteous and liberall zeftis, which ys more precyusseur
than goolde er sylver, which hath nat be at alle tymys
to your grete ease, neyther hertis plesauns, but rathei
to your grete desese and yntollerable peyne. And
wher Godds lawe and manys lawe acorden that hit
shall nat be lawful to non erthely man to be so lyberall
and plenteous of that that God sendith hym, that he
sholde so despose hit so that he sholde nowgch have
to lyve by ; and forasmych as I have perfite knowlich
of your freell [*frail*[2]] and naturall disposiseon so set
on to theym that ben nedy and hunggery that of your
selfe ze have no myght, neyther power to absteyne and
rewle yourself, but also long as God sendith and
zevyth yow whereof to dispose and help your evyn
Crysten ze most nedis despose hit forth a monggus
your evyn Cristen, I conseile yow that yn also hasty
and goodely tyme as ze kan to come on to your holy
brytheryn that ben of that devowt and clos conversa-
cion, to th'entent that ze myght ben advertysid and
lernyd by theym the goode rewle and messur that ze
owght and sholde have yn the despociscion and
delyng of your almys.

And also, sethnys ze haven chosen zow a place yn
this seson of Avent, yn which ze have had a resonable

---

[1] *i.e.*, Your fellow-Christians.
[2] Fenn interprets this word *free will*, which I cannot think to be the meaning intended.

leysour and space to do your penauns yn, which drawith
fast to a ende; which hath been a convenyent place as
for the ceson of the yer; and now hit drawith fast on
to Cristmas, on which tyme every trewe Crysten man
sholde be mery, jocunde, and glad.   And sethnys ther
is no place which by lyklyhod of reason ze shulde
fynde yn your hert to be so gladde and yocunde yn
as ze sholde be yn the place of your profession a
mounggis your holy brytheryn; yn which place yn
this ceson of the yer hit ys a custumyd to be alle
maner of desport, lyke as hit is nat unknowe to your
wisse descrescion; wherfore, as my symple reason
ledith me your grete descrescion sholde rewle you that
ze sholde approche nygh the plase of your holy
relegion yn also hasty tyme as ze code er myght, of
of whos comyng alle your saide bretheryn wolde be
glade and fayn, and yn especiall I, your servaunt and
brother, lyke as I am most syngguler bownden to
th'encresse of your prosperite and welfar, which I
shall ever desir with Godds mersy, which have yow
undir His blessid and favorable proteccion.   Wrytten
yn the Temple of Syon, iij^d. day of December, yn
grete hast.

By your Servaunt and brother,

497.

A.D. 1465, 7 Feb.
JOHN WYKES TO MARGARET PASTON.

[From Fenn, iv. 134.]

This letter must be later than the year 1463, as Sir John Paston does not
appear to have been knighted so early as February in that year.   But as John
Faston, the father, was at Caister and not at London in the early part of the

year 1464, it cannot be that year. Neither can we assign it to 1466, the last year of John Paston's life, as it appears by a letter written on the 17th February in that year, that although John Paston was in London, his son Sir John could not have been there for some time before. We are therefore shut up to the year 1465 as the only possible date for this letter.

Unto my maystres, Margageret Paston, be thys letter delyveryd in hast, &c.

RYGHT wyrshypfull maystres, I recomaund me un to your gode maystresshyp. Please it you to wyte that my mayster your hosbond, my maystres youre moder, my mayster Sir John, Mr. Wyllyam, Mr. Clement, and all ther men, wer in gode helth whon thys letter was wryten, thankyd be Jesu, and also ther maters be in a gode wey, for my Lord Chaunseler ys ther syngeler gode Lord in thys mater at thys tyme; and that it provyth so . . . he was yesterday in the Escheker, and ther he had a foren hym alle the Juges, all the Barons of the Escheker, and all the Shurgents, and ther argued wher that the Barons of the Escheker shold award any such Comyssyon or not, and uppon that the seyd Comyssyon shull be broght uppon Fryday unto the Chaunsery, and ther to be provyd, wher it be lafull or not, &c.

Item, and yf it please it you to gyve Daveney[1] knowlych that ther ys jugement gyven uppon the condempnacion a yenst Hall,[2] that he claymed for hys bond man, and the jugement ys gyven a yenst Daveney, Ric. Call, and Thomas Bon, and ther ys comen owte proces for to take ther bodys thys same day, and if thay or any of them be taken thay shull never gon oute of prison on to the tyme that they have satesfyed the party of viijˣˣ marc, and ther for lete

[1] So in Fenn, but the name ought certain.y to be Daubeney, perhaps spelt Dabeney.

[2] Robert Hall. I find that he brought an action in Trinity term, 3 Edward IV., against John Daubeney of Norwich, gentleman, and Thomas Boon and Richard Call of Norwich, yeomen, for having, in conjunction with William Daubeney of Sharyngton, Norfolk, Esq., unlawfully imprisoned him at Norwich for three hours on the 20th February, 39 Hen. VI. (1461), until he gave them a bond of £100 for his ransom.

them be ware. And the Holy Trinyte have you in Hys kypyng. Wryten at London, uppon Thursday next after the Purificacion of our Lady, &c.

By your Servaunt,

JOHN WYKS.

498.

A.D. 1465, 31 March.

WILLIAM WORCESTER TO ————

[From Paston MSS., B.M.]

In this letter reference is made to a "testament" drawn up by Sir John Fastolf eight years previously. This, however, cannot be his last will, as that would carry the date to a year after John Paston's death, who seems to be here spoken of as living. The settlement referred to is doubtless the testamentary declaration of 1457 mentioned in No. 469.

PLEASE your maistershyp to wete that aftyr recomendacion that I sende Thomas More to myne oncle the parson[1] wyth certeyn credence to hafe aunsuer uppon by hym for myn acquytaille another day, yff onye thyng falle sinistrely only yn theyr deffaut, as God defend, not be my wille, for I hafe as feythfulle demesned me seth I rode to London thys terme, and hedertoo as anye maner creatur yn reson coude desyre me; and hafe demened me at London accordyng to the message sent me by the baylly of Drayton, and I vele but littille that my gode wille ys allowed.[2] I hafe also, seth I came to Norwiche, enformed hym whate proffyt ease and avaylle I may help stand hem both yn my maister godes and yn hys lyvelode; yff he or hys frendys set littlle by it, I may nat do wyth all. And the blessed Trinite be with yow, because ye wolle the wellfare off my maister, whoos soule God hafe pytie on and bryng hym owte of peyn, as the wellfare of the parties it meovyth me wryte to yow the rathyr. I enformyd

[1] Sir Thomas Howes.
[2] i.e., Little credit is given me for my good will

yow for trouth, and as I wille prefe, that I was the
principall doer and cause that both Maister Paston
and myne oncle came fyrst yn the testament viij. yeer
goon, to a gode entent; and yff they wold wyrke
ayenst me to minussh my power, theyr disposicion woll
be construed ferther than they wille it were, and they
not so avaylled as they weene yn all thynges.   The
blessed Trinete be wyth yow.   Wryt on Passyon
Sonday.

Your W. WYRCESTRE.

Memorandum to Thomas More that because ye
myzt foryete myne erand to Maister Bernay, I pray
you rede hym my bille, and that he wille take it to a
gode entent; for how so evyr I wryte I meene well,
and so shall.

499.

A.D. 1465, 8 April.

MARGARET PASTON TO JOHN PASTON.

[From Paston MSS., B.M.]

The claims laid by the Duke of Suffolk to Drayton and Hellesden occupy
a prominent place in this correspondence during the year 1465, and I do not
find them alluded to in any letter of an earlier date.   Moreover, the purchase
by virtue of which the Duke laid claim to the latter manor, which is reported
here as a secret, is mentioned again as a piece of news in a letter undoubtedly
written on the 10th May 1465.   There can be little doubt therefore that this
letter is of the same year.   The apostle, or set of marginal notes appended,
is in the handwriting of John Paston.

*To my ryght worchepfull hosbond, Jon Paston, be this
deliveryd in hast.*

RIGHT worchepfull hosbond, I recomand me
to you.   Please you to wet that I send you a
copy of the deed that Jon Edmonds of
Taveram sent to me, be the menys of Dor-
let.   He told Dorlet that he had suche a deed as he

Carte
Drayton.

supposyd, that wold don ease in prevyng of the tytyll
that the Duk of Suffolk cleymythe in Drayton; for the
same deed that he sent me, the seale of armys is lyke
onto the copy that I send you, and noo thyng leke
to the Duk of Suffolks aunscesters.

Item, the seyd Edmond seythe, yf he may fynd any
other thyng that may do yow ease in that mater he
wolle do hys part therin.

Item, Jon Russe sent me word that Barker and
Herry Porter told hym in councell that the Duk of
Suffolk hathe bowght one Brytyeff ryghte, the wyche
Heylisdon,
Brythyeve,
Barker,
Porter.
makythe a cleyme on to Heylysdon, and the seyd Duke
is proposyd to entere within shorte tyme after Esterne,
for in so moche the seyd Russe felle be the seyd
Barber and Porter that all the feffees wolle make a
relees on to the Duk and helpe hym that they can in
to her power, for to have hys good lorchep.

Item, yf it please you, me thynkythe it war ryght
Bracium.
nessessary that ye send word howe that ye wolle your
old malte be purveyed for; for and any hote weder
come affter that it hathe leyne this wynter season, it
shall be but lost but yf [*unless*] it be sold be tymys, for as
for the pryse [*price*] here, it is sore falle. I have sold a
C. comb of malt that came fro Guton, to Jamys
Golbeter, clenefyed, and strek met, and non inmet, (?)
for ijs. ijd., the comb, and to be payed at Mydsomer
and Lammes.

Item, ther be dyvers of your tenantrys at Mauteby
Sirpi pro
repara-
sione de
Mautby.
that had gret ned for to be reparyd, at [? but] the tenaunts
be so por that they ar not a power to repare hem;
wherfor yf leke you, I wold that the marche that Bryge
had myght be kept in yourowne hand this yer, that the
tenaunts myght have ruschis to repare with her howsys.
And also ther is wynfall wod at the maner that is of
noo gret valewe, that myght helpe hem with toward the
reparacion, yf it leke you to late hem have it that
hathe most need therof. I have spoke with Borges that
Burgoys,
Mareshs,
Mauteby.
he shuld heyne [*raise*] the price of the mershe, or ellis I
told hym that he shuld no lenger have it, for ye myght

[have]¹ other fermors therto that wold geve therfor as it was late befor, and yf he wold geve therfor as moche as another man wold, ye wold that he shuld have it befor any other man; and he seyd he shuld geve me answer be a fortenyght after Esterne. I can get non other fermor therto yet.

Item, I understand be Jon Pampyng that ye wolle not that your sone be take in to your hows, nor holpe be you, tylle suche tyme of yere as he was put owt therof, the wiche shall be abowght Seynt Thomas messe.² For Gods sake, sir, a pety on hym; remembre yow it hathe bed a long season syn he had owt of yow to helpe hym with, and he hathe obeyed hym to yow and wolle do at all tymis, and wolle do that he can or may to have your good faderood. And at the reverence of God be ye hys good fader, and have a faderly hert to hym; and I hope he shall ever knowe hymselff the better here after, and be the more ware to exchewe suche thyngs as shuld dysplease you, and for to take hed at that shuld please you. Pecoke shalle telle you be mothe of more thyngs than I may write to you at this tyme. The blyssyd Trinite have you in Hys kepyng. Wretyn at Caster in hast, the Monday next after Palme Sonday.   Your M. P.

Pro recuperatione Johannis Paston.

500.

A.D. 1465, 3 May.
MARGARET PASTON TO JOHN PASTON.

[From Paston MSS., B.M.]

Holy Rood Day, on which this letter is dated, commonly means the 14th of September (feast of the Exaltation of the Holy Cross). Here I suspect it is the 3d May (Invention of the Holy Cross), as the contents of the letter suit that date in the year 1465. It will be seen that Margaret Paston dates from Caister, and proposes next week to be at Hellesden. Her next letter, dated the 10th May, is from Hellesden, and shows that she carried out the intention here expressed of sending men to collect money at Drayton, and had left her eldest

---

¹ Omitted in MS.

² This might be the translation of St. Thomas the Martyr, 7th July, or St. Thomas Apostle's Day, 21st December; but most probably it means the day of St. Thomas à Becket, 29th December.

son at Caister to keep the place. There is also a close agreement between that letter and this, in what is said about the demeanour of the tenants and Mr. Phiiip's conduct. The apostyle of this letter, as of the preceding, is in the hand of John Paston, very ill written, and occasionally ambiguous.

To my ryght wyrshypfull husband, John Paston, be thys delyveryd in hast.

RYGHT wyrshipful husbond, I recomaunde me unto you. Pleasyd you to wyte that I have spokyn thys wyke with dyvers of youre ten-naunts of Drayton and put hem in comfort that all shalbe well hereafter by the grace of God; and I fyle well by hem that they wylbe ryght glad to have ayen there olde mayster, and so wold they all except j. or ij. that be fals shrewys. And thys next wyke I purpose on Wensday or Thursday to be at Haylesdon, and to a byde ther a wyke or ij., and send oure men aboute to gedere money at Drayton and Haylesdon ; and yf ye wyll I woll do kepe a corte at Drayton or I com thens. I pray yow send me word how ye wyll that I doo there in. I recevyd ij. letters from you of Nicholl Tolman yesterday, werin ye desyre that we shuld purvey for your malte and barley; and soo shall we doo as well as we cann, and send you word howe that we may doo therewith in hast.

Item, yesterday Master Phylyp[1] toke Dorlets hors up-pon Drayton lond as they went to the plowe for the hole yere ferm; and as it ys told me the tenaunts of Drayton tolde hym that he dyde hym wrong to make hym pay for the hole yere, for non of the tenaunts had payd hym but for the di' [*half*] yere and he say thohg they had not payd but for the di' yere, Paston shuld pay for the other di' yere, and for moo yers also yf he lyvyd. But I trow to gyte Dorlet ayen hys hors or els Mr Phylyp ys lyke to be unhorssyd óns, and we lyve all. Your son[2] shall com hom to moryn, as I trowe, and as he demenyth hym hyr after I shall lete you have knowlych; and I pray you thynk not in me

Marginal notes:
Drayton tenaunts bony, preter ij.

Malt, barly.

Dorlat et verba M.P.

J. P., sen.

---

[1] Philip Lipgate, the Duke of Suffolk's bailiff.   [2] Sir John Paston.

that I wyll supporte hym ne favour hym in no lewdnesse,
for I wyl not.   As I fynd hym hereafter, soo I wyll
lete you have knowlych.   I have put your evydens
that com owte of the abbay [1] in a seck and enseylyd
hem under Ric. Call ys seall that he shal not say but Rotuli
they eryn as he left hem; but as for the place where prioris (?)
they ern kypt he hath no knowlych . . . . . .
. . . .   As for the gentylwoman that ye wrote
to me for yn youre lettere, I . . . .
. . . .   there, yf it lykyd all folks as well as it
shold doo me, I trow . . . . a bowte
yf her frends were as well a gryed therto, and as they
. . . . parte, yf ye wyll that it be
movyd of more hereafter I wyll . . . .
wyll make a newe parson, at Drayton.   Also it ys sayd
that . . . . there, by cause it hath
stond so long voyd; yet and any sh. . . . . . .
had lever that he com in by the Byshop then by a
. . . . doo therein yf ye wyll send
hom any presentacion selyd . . . .
we shall a say to gyte som gode priste and sette hym
. . . . Wryten in haste at Caster on
Holy Rode Day &c.
  As . . . . doo therein as well as I
cann.   I have gyte a replevyn . . . .
CC shype, and yf they may not be hadde ayen, then
he grau[nteth] . . . . We fynd hym Data
ryght gode in that we desyre of him for you, and ther- obliga-
fore yf it lyke you I wold he were th . . . . . . cione (?)
                                                   pro ovibus

501.

A.D. 1465, 6 May.
JOHN RUSSE TO JOHN PASTON.

[From Paston MSS., B.M.]

As this letter refers to the Duke of Suffolk's claim to the manor of Drayton, the date must be 1465. The original MS. is mutilated to some extent in
both margins.

[1] *See* No. 487.

To the right worshypfull sir, my right honourabyll
maister, John Paston, at London.

RIGHT worshipfull sir and my right honorabyll
maister, I recomaund me to you in the most
humble wise. And please youre maistir ship
to wete that my maistresse hathe dyverse
tymes spokyn to me to helpe to purvey a merchaunt
for sum of youre malt; but in good feyth I can gete no
man that wyll geve at the most more than xxij*d*. for a
quarter, for soo men selle dayli at the moste, and sumtyme xx*d*. a combe. My maistresse is right hevy therfor, but I can not remedy it; if ony good marchaunt
were there, after my sympil conseyt it were good to
take hym, for the yeer passith faste and the [feldes][1]
be right plesaunt to wards, &c. Sir, at the reverence
of Jesu, laboure the meanys to have peas; for be my
trowth the contynwaunce [of this] trobill shall short the
dayez of my maistresse, and it shall cause you to gret
losse, for serteyn she is in gre[t hevi]nesse as it apperith at . . . . ll covertly
she consederith the gret decay of youre lyflode, the
gret detts that hange in detours hands and h . . .
. . . . [she speaket]h not thus
to me, but I conceyfe this is cause of here gret hevynesse ; me semyth of ij. hurts the leste is mos[t] .
. . . . well the
dayli contynewyng maleyse of youre insessiabyll
enemyes, how they contryve and seke occacions to
. . . . . . informyd, more wyll doo every
foot of grownd withinne fewe dayez, and rather to
geve it awey for nowght tha[n] . . . . . . it.
Where as they many tymes have meovyd a trety and
never it taketh to noo conclucion, and as they have
seyd in youre d . . . . . . Sir, after my sympyll conseyt it were well doon to agree to a trety, and
be that ye shuld knowe ther desyre and the uttir . .
. . . . . the lond were dubyll the valwe that it

[1] The tops of the letters f. l. d. visible.

is. Worsestyr shewyth hem presedents what every
maner cost at the fyrst byeng, and ther . . . .
. . . rekne the bargeyne shuld avayle you foure
tymes mor than it shall; and in thys they be gretly
blyndyd ; my maister the parson hathe . . . .
to rellesse in serteyn londs whiche he refus[eth to]
doo, but I conseyve, and ye drawe not to a conclucion thys terme that he wyll be as redy to rellesse
. . . . men, truste ye thys for serteyn; and soo
he [told] me serteynly. He hathe be meovyd to re-
voke Maister Roberd Kente and to take the avoket
or proctor [that] Maister Yelwirton hathe. What it
myght hurtyn if he soo dede I knowe not, but they
have made gret labour to hym therfor. He gaf me a
gret reb[uke] . . . . the bill that was put in
ayens Elyse Davy and otheris, to whiche I answeryd
hym as me thowght and soo in maner made my peas, &c.
Maister . . . . was here and in presence of men
of the most substance in Jeremuth he be havyd hym
to you wards in full goodly termys, soo God helpe
. . . . and after my conseyt he wyll not be redy
to relesse in ony of the londs. A man of hyse teld me
secretly that Maister Yelwyrton and otheres blamyd hym
and seyd . . . . to hym be cause he was so redy
be hym self to agree to trete and make hyse peas with
yow, neyther he seyd to me to trete nor the contrary
nor had but langwage to me as he had to othyr. I
askyd my maister the parson if he undyrstod that
Maister Yelwyrton yaf ony favour to my Lord of Suffolk
in Drayton, and he seyd he supposyd Maister Yelwyrton
was not cler of that mater, but Mayster Jenney was in
nowyse pleasyd with all, &c. Sir as for the wytnesse that
were desyred to be redy whan nede requirith in thys
mater, R. Calle can avertise youre maistirshyp.   Sir, at
the reverence of Jesu consedre how many yeers it is
past that my good lord and maister deseasyd and how
lytill is doon for . . . . of the grete substaunce
that he hade it is hevy to remembre; ye sey the defaute is not in yow after your conseyt, but I can here

no . . . . in that of youre openyon, for thys I
knowe for serteyn and it had pleasyd you to have endyd
be the meanys of trety, ye had ma[de] . . . peas to
the gret well of the dede with the forthe part of the mony
that hathe be spent, and as men sey only of very wylful-
[nesse of your] owyn person.   For the mercy of God
remembre the onstabylnesse of thys wold hou it is not
a menut space in comparyson to ever . . . .
. . . leve wylfullnesse whyche men sey ye occupye
to excessifly.   Blyssyd be God ye had a fayre day laste
whiche is noysyd cost yow . . . . to iiij. lords,
but a newe mater anewe cost and many smale growe
to a gret summe, and summe mater on recurabyll, for men
seyd . . . . is lyk to stonden in a perplextif if
ye take not a conclucion in haste, and if it were doo it
were hard to have recovery ; but as my [maister] the
parson seyd, thys terme they wyll prove if ye wyll
agree to trete, and if ye refuse they all wyll do the
uttirmest.   I conseyve well [your] maistirshyp hathe a
conseyt that if a man of good will meove yow or remembre you to trete, that that man, what soo ever he
be, shuld be meovyd be youre adversaryez to meove
you in that mater, and soo in that it hertyth you gretly
that they shuld seke to you for peas.   Be my trowth,
sir, there was nor is no man, savyng onys, as I teld you,
Maister Jenney spake to me, that ever I knewe wold
seke or feythefully desyre to have peas with yow,
savyng because of the exspence of the good so onpro-
fitably in the lawe, and that is the prynsypal cause of
meovyng of ther peas, &c.   I wold well God helpe me soo
it grevyth me to here that ye stonde in no favour with
jentylmen nor in no gret awe with the comowns.   Ye
truste the jury of Suffolk ; remembre what promyse
Daubeney hade of the jury and what it avaylid ; it is a
dethe to m[e] to remembre in what prosperite and
in what degre ye myght stonde in Norfolk and Suffolk
and ye had peas and were in herts ease, and what
worshyp my maisters your sones and my maistresse
youre douters myght have be proferryd to if ye had be in

reste.   A day lost in idyll can never be recoveryd, &c.
Sir, I beseke youre maistershyp for yeve me that I wryte
thus boldly and homly to you; me thynkyth my hert
. . . .   not be in ease but if I soo doo, for ther was,
nor never shal be, no mater that ever was soo ner
myn herte, that knowy[th God,] whom I beseke for
Hese infenyt mercy preserve you and my maistresse
and all youres from all adversyte and graunt yow
. . . .   herts desyre.   Wretyn at Jernemuthe the
vj. day of May.

Youre contynw[al bedesman]
and servaunt, JOHN [RUSSE].

502.

A.D. 1465, 10 May.
MARGARET PASTON TO JOHN PASTON.

[From Paston MSS., B.M.]

The date of this letter is rendered certain by the mention of Thomas Ellis,
as having been elected Mayor of Norwich.   He was so elected for the second
time in 1465.   He had been Mayor before in 1460-1, and was again after this
in 1474-5; but neither of these latter dates will suit the other contents of this
letter.   Like some others of this year, this letter is apostyled by John Paston.

To my mayster, John Paston the oldest be thys delyveryd
in hast.

RYGHT wyrshypfull husbond I recomaund me
unto you.   Pleysed you to wyte that on Wensday last passyd Dabeney, Naunton, Wykes
and John Love werr at Drayton for to speke
with your tenaunts ther to put hem in comfort and for
to aske money of hem also.   And Pyrs Waryn, other-   Distr'
wyse callyd Pyrs at Sloth, whych ys a flykeryng felowe Petr'.
and a besy with Mr Phylyp and the Bayly of Cosshay,   Warin.
he had a plowe goyng in your lond in Drayton, and
ther your seyd servaunts at that tyme toke hys plowe
ware, that ys to say ij. marys, and broght hem to
Heylysdon, and ther they be yet.   And on the next

mornyng after Mr Phylyp and the Baylly of Cosshay
com to Haylysdon with a grete nomber of pepell, that
ys to say viij.ˣˣ· men and mor in harnysse, and ther
toke from the persons plowe ij. hors, pris iiij. marc
and ij. hors of Thomas Stermyns plowe, pris xls.,

Distr'
Sturmyn
et rectoris
de Heylis-
don.

saying to hem that ther was taken a playnt ayenst
hem in the hunderd by the seyd Pyrs for takyng of
the forseyd plowarre at Drayton, and but they wold
be bond to com to Drayton on Tewysday next comyng to awnswer to such maters as shalbe sayd to them
ther they shold not have ther bests ayen; whych they
refusyd to do on to the tyme that they had an awnswer
from you; and so they led the bestes forth to Drayton,
and from Drayton forth to Cosshay.   And the same
after none folwyng the parson of Haylesdon send hys
man to Drayton with Stermyn for to speke with Mr
Phylyp to know a way yf they shuld have ayen ther
cattell or not; and Master Phylyp awnsweryd them yf
that they wold bryng home ther destresse ayen that
was taken of Pyrs Waryn, that then he wold delyver
hem thers, or els not; and he lete hem playnly wyte

Crak.

that yf ye or any of your servaunts toke any dystresse
in Drayton that were but the valew of an hen, they
wold com to Haylesdon and take ther the valew of
an ox therefore; and yf thay cannot take the valew
therof there, that then they wyll do breke your
tenaunts howsys in Haylesdon, and take as moch as
they cowd fynd therein; and yf they be lettyd therof,
wych shall never lye in your power for to do, for the
Duck of Suffolk ys abyll to kepe dayly in hys hows
more men then Dabeney hadde herys on hys hede, yf
hym lyst; and as for Dabeney he ys a lewde felowe,
and so he shalbe servyd herafter, and I wold he were
here.   And therfore yf ye take uppon you to lette
them so for to do, that then they wold goo in to any
lyflode that ye had in Norfolk or Suffolk, and to take
a destresse in lykewysse as they wold do at Haylysdon.
And other awnswerr cowde they non gyte, and so they
departyd.   Ric. Calle axid the parson and Stermyn yf

they wold take an accyon for ther catell, and the parson[1] seyd he was agyd and syklow, and he wold not
be trobelyd herafter; he sayd he had lever lose hys
catell, for he wyst well yf he dyde so he shold be
endytyd, and so vexid with hem that he shold never
have rest by hem. As for Stermyn, he sayd at that
tyme he durst not take no sute ayenst hem nother;
but after that Ric. was rydyn, I spake with hym, and
he sayd he wold be rulyd as ye wold have hym, and I
fond hym ryght herty and wel dysposyd in that mater;
and he is bownde to you an obligacyon of x*li*. sengyll
with outen condycyon that he shall abyde by such
accyons as shalbe takyn by your advyse in hys name;
wherfore I have send you a tytelyng therof in a byll
closyd herin. I axyd Thomas Gryne avyse when
they had take the dystresse hyre, and he avysyd me
that herre destresse shold be delyveryd a yen to
them so that we myzt have ayen ours; and me thoght
it was non awnswer after myn entent, and wold
not therof but axyd avyse of Skypwith what hym
thoght that were best to doo there in, and most wyrshypfull. He seyd by hys avyse that I shold send to you
in al the hast that I cowde, and that ye shuld fynde
a mene therfore above, by the avyse of youre lernyd
counsell to have a wrytte from above for to delyver yt
of lesse then the undershyrff werre other wysse dysposyd to you then we fynde hym, for it symyth that he
ys made of the other party. And as for the replevyn
for the CC. shype ys not yet servyd. Skypwyth
thynkyth that ye myzt have a wrytte both for the
shype and the destresse now taken at Haylysdon, I
pray you that ye wyll send word in hast how [ye] woll that
we doo in thys maters. Skypwith went with me to
the Byshop of Norwych, and I lyte hym have knowlych of the ryotous and evyll dysposicyon of Master
Phylyp, desyryng hys Lordshyp that he wold see a

Accio rectoris et Sturmyn.

Replevin

---

[1] Thomas Hert, perhaps a relation of the Bishop of Norwich, was presented
to the rectory of Hellesden by Sir John Fastolf in 1448, but how long he
held it is uncertain, as the list of rectors is very defective, and the next name
that appears on it is George Gardiner in 1579.

Episcopus
Norwic'.

mene tha[t] a correccyon myzt be hadde, in as
moch as he was chef Justic of the Peas and hys
ordynare, and inasmoch as he was a prest[1] and under
hys correccyon that he shold have understondyng of
hys dysposicyon; and I made Dabeney to tell hym
all the mater howt it was; and he seyd he wold send
for hym and speke with hym. And he told me of
dyvers thyngs of the demenyng of hym, wherby I
understode he lykyd not by hys dysposicyon nor
demenyng in thys mater nor in no nothyr; for it symyd
he had provyd hym what he ys in other maters.

Episcopus
Norwic'.

My lord seyd to me that he wold ryght fayn that ye
had a gode conclusyon in your maters, and seyd by
hys trouth, that he ought you ryght gode wyll, and
wold ryght fayn that ye wer com home, and seyd to
me that it shold be a grete confort to your frends and
neghbors, and that your presens shold do more amongs
hem, than a C. of your men shold do in your absens,
and more, your enmys wold ferr to do ayens you yf
ye myght be at home, and steryng amonges hem, and
seyd full playnly in meny other thyngs it were to long
to wryte at thys tyme, as Skypwith shall tell you when

Skipwith.

he comyzt to you. I pray you thanke Skypwith of
hys gode wyll, for he was ryght well wyllyd to go with
me and yeve me hys avyse, me thynkyth he ys ryzt
well wyllyd to you.

Per'
Heyl'd.[2]

Item, I pray you send hastely word how that ye
wyll that we be gydyd with thys place, for as it ys
told me, it ys lyke to stond in as grete jupardy in hast
as othere don. On Thursday al day there were kept
in Draton logge in to lx. persons, and yet as it ys
told me, ther be within dayly and nyztly in to a xvj.
or xx. persons.

Elys.

Item, it ys told me that Thomas Elys of Norwych,
whych nowe ys chosyn Mayer, seyd at Drayton that
yf my Lord of Suffolk nede a C. men he wold purvey

---

1 Philip Lepeyate was presented to the rectory of Salle in Norfolk, in 1460,
by Thomas Brewse, Esq., afterwards father-in-law of John Paston, the youngest.
2 *i.e.* Periculum Heylesdon.

hym therof, and yf any men of the town wold go to
Paston he wold do lay hem faste in prison. I wold
youre men mygh have a *supersedias*[1] owte of the chaun-
cere, and be owte of the danger of there men here;
and I pray you let not Wyll Naunton be foryete therin.
Ric. Calle and other can tell you of hys demenyng;
and I pray you that ye be not dysplesyd for his abydyng with me, for in gode feth he hath ben a grete
comfort to me syn ye departyd hens, as I wyll lete you
wyte hereafter. I pray you yf hys brother com to
you for a relesse of hys londe, lette him non have on to
the tyme that ye see hys faderes wyll, the whych I
wote wher it ys, and that it like you to desyre hym to
be gode brother to him.

Item, I have left John Paston the older at Caster,
to kype the place there, as Ric. can tell you; for I
had lever, and it pleasyd you, to be captensse here
then at Caster; yet I was nothyng purposyd to abyde
here when [I] come from home but for a day or ij.,
but I shall abyde here tyll I here tydyngs from you.

Item, it ys told me that the Duck of Suffolk hath
boght or shal by in hast the ryzt that on Bryghtylhed
hath in Haylesdon &c.

Item, as for the evydens that Watkyn Shypdam
hadd, he delivered to hys wyffe a box enselyd with hys
owyn seall by hys lyffe for to be delyveryd to you,
whych box she delyveryd to Ric. Call under the same
seall after hys dessesse. Ric. can tell you of the gydyng of the cofere with other boks that were at Shypdams
And as for all your other evydens ye ther not feer as
for the syzt of hem, for ther hath nor shall no man
sen hem tyll ye com hom. I can not fynd that ye
send to me fore to have oute of the rolle.

Item, I here no word of Colte of New Castell, nor
of no nother from you that shold have your malte, but
I have spoken to the Viker, John Rus and Robert
Boteler, to help for to sell your malte, and as we can
do therein, we shall send you word. The Provest of

Super-sedeas.

Naunton.

J. Paston at Castre.
M. P. at Heylisdon.

Brightled.

Evidens.
Pekering.

Evidens.
Norwic'

Colt.
Malt.

---

[1] So in MS.

Præpositus **Cambrygge** ys com into thys contry and Dabeney
de
[Cantab].¹ shall receve of hym that lóngyth to you on Monday
or Tewysday, and he shall have hys delyveryd accordyng to your wrytyng.

Mater.   Item, my moder told me that she thynkyth ryght
Clere. strange that she may not have the profects of Clyre ys
place in peasabyll wyse for you, she seyt it ys hers
and she hath payd most therfore yet, and she sayth
she wyll have the profects therof, or ells she wyll make
more folk to speke therof.   She seyth she knowyt
not what ryght ne titell that ye have therin but yf ye
luste to trobell with herre, and that shold be no wyrshep
to you ; and she sayth she wylbe ther thys somer and
repayre the housyng ther.   In gode feyth I hyre moch
langage of the demenyng betwene you and herre.   I
wold ryght fayn, and so wold many moo of youre
frendes, that it were otherwyse bytwene you then it ys,
and yf it were I hope ye shold have the beter spyde
in all other maters.   I pray God be your gode spyde in
all your maters, and yef yow grace to have a gode
conclusyon of hem in haste for thys ys to wyry a lyffe
to a byde for you and all youre.   Wryten in haste at
Haylysdon the x. day of May.

The cause that I send to you this hastely ys to have
an awnswer in haste from you.

                                    Your M. P.

503.

A.D. 1465, 13 May.
MARGARET PASTON TO JOHN PASTON.

[From Fenn, iv. 164.]

There can be little doubt this letter was written in the year 1465, when
Margaret was troubled by Mr. Philip Lipyate and the Duke of Suffolk's
bailiff of Cossey.   It may be observed also that Margaret here dates from
Hellesden, and speaks of having been recently at Caister.   Compare Nos.
500 and 502.   Further, the name of John Jenney is found on the Commission
of the Peace for Norfolk, dated the 1st April 1465 (Patent, 5 Edward IV., p.

¹ This word is left blank by Paston.

1, m. 32). but it is not on the commission issued on the 20th February following (*ib.*, m. 27); so that John Paston seems to have acted on his wife's suggestion and been successful in getting him removed.

To my ryght wyrshypfull mayster, John Paston the oldest, be this delyveryd in haste.

 Recomaund me, &c.

Yf it pleasyd you, I wold ryght fayn that John Jenney werre putte oute of the Comyssyon of the Peas, and that my brother Wyll. Lumner wer set yn hys stede, for me thynkyth it wer ryght necessere that ther were such a man in that county that oght you gode wyll, and I knowe verely he owyth you ryght gode wyll; he was with me at Caster but late. Yf ther be made any labour for Doctour Alyn to be Justice of the Peas, I pray you for Gods sake let it be lettyd yf ye may, for he wyll take to moch upon hym yf he werr. I wold not that he wer remembyrd of your parte but yf [*unless*] he be spokyn of of other parts: he ys ryght grete with Master Phylyp Lypzate and the Baylyf of Coshay.

Yf it please yow to wyte that Wyks dyde a reste one Wyll. Dylmyn of Norwych, as Pampyng can enforme you of, for sertyn harnys wych he delyveryd hym at New Castell for to cary to Yarmoth by water, and ther to delyver it to hym ayen; whych harnys he kypt styll, and may not be delyveryd; and now ther ys com down an *habeas corpus* for hym, and most appyr at the Comyn Place [*Common Pleas*] on Fryday next comyng. Wherfor yf it pleased you that ther mygth be taken an accyon in Wyks name of trespas under such forme as ther may be a *capias* a wardyd a yenst hys comyng; for after that he was arestyd he dyde Daubeney to be arestyd for mayntenyng; and as for the harnys Wyks delyveryd it to hym the x. day of Januar, the ij. yer of Kyng E.[1] in Pylgryme strete, at New Castell: Inprimis, a peyr brygandyrs, a salet, a boresper, a bawe, xviij. arwys,

---

[1] A.D. 1463. This was at the time the King was in the north, when Alnwick Castle surrendered to him.

ij. payr polronds [*shoulder pieces*], a standard of mayle,
a payr slyvys of plate, to the valew of v. marc.   And
at the reverens of God, slowth not your maters nowe,
and make any end of hem, other purvey you to make
hym or to marre hem in haste, for thys ys to orybyll
a coste and trobell that ye have and have had, for to
endur any whyle, and it ys grete hevenys to your
frends and welwyllers, and grete joy and comfort to
your ennemyes.   My Lord of Norwych seyd to me
that he wold noth abyde the sorow and trobell that ye
have abyden, to wyn all Sir John Fastolf ys gode.
And God be your spede in all yor maters.   Wryten
at Haylesdon the xiij. day of May.

I thynk ryght long to hyr tydyngs tyll I have tydyngs
from you.   Your   M. P.

504.

A.D. 1465, 20 May.

MARGARET PASTON TO JOHN PASTON.

[From Fenn, iv. 200.]

A comparison of this letter with No. 502 will leave no doubt that they were
both written in the same year.

*To my ryght wyrshypfull husbond, John Paston, by thys
delyvery[d] in hast.*

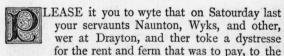

PLEASE it you to wyte that on Satourday last
your servaunts Naunton, Wyks, and other,
wer at Drayton, and ther toke a dystresse
for the rent and ferm that was to pay, to the
nomber of lxxvij. nete, and so broght them hom to
Hayllesdon, and put them in the Pynfold, and so kept
hem styll ther from the seyd Satour day mornyng un to
Monday[1] at iij. at clok at after non.   Fyrst on the same

1 This was the day the letter was written.

Satour day the tenants folwyd uppon, and desyryd to
have ther catell ayen; and I awunsweryd hem, yf they
wold do pay such dewts as they oght for to pay to
you, that then they shold have ther catell delyveryd
ayen; or els yf they wer not a power to pay redy
money, that then they to fynd suffycyant suerty to pay
the money at such a day as they mygh agrye with me,
and therto to be bonden to you by obligacyon; and
that they seyd they durst not for to take uppon hem
for to be bonden, and as for money they had non for
to pay at that tyme, and therfor I kept stylle the
bestys.

Harleston was at Norwych, and send for the tenants
the seyd Satour day at after non, and ther, by the
menys of the Bayllyf of Coshay, put the tenants in
such feer, sayng that yf they wold pay such dewts, or
els for to be bonden to pay, that then they wold put
hem owte of such londs as they huld bondly of the
Lordshyp, and so to dystrayn hem and trobell hem,
that they shuld be wery of ther part; and that put
hem [in] such feer that they drust nother pay nor be
bonden.

And on the same day at evyn-song time Harleston
com to me to Haylesdon, desyryng me that I wold
delyver a yen the seyd dystresse; and as for such
dystressys as they had taken here of your tenants shold
be delyveryd a yen in lyke forme; and I seyd I wold
not delyver hem soo, and I told hem that I wold
delyver hem as ys wryten a fore and other wyse not,
and other wyse I wold not delyver hem but by the
form of lawe. And other comynycacyon was had by
twene us at that tyme of dyvers maters whych wer to
long to wryte at thys tyme, but ye shall have knowlych
therof in hast.

And on Monday next after at ix. at clok ther com
Pynchemor to Haylesdon with a replevyn,[1] whych
was made in Harleston ys name as Understewerd of the

---

[1] This is a writ for restitution of cattle that have been distrained or
impounded. It was commonly granted by the sheriff on security being given
that the party would bring the matter to an issue at law.

Duche[*Duchy*],sayng that the bests were taken upon the
Duche Fee, wherfor he desyryd me to mak hym levery
of the seyd bests so taken ; and I seyd I wold not
delyver hem on to the tyme that I had examenyd the
tenants of the trough[truth]. And so I send theder Wyks
with Pynchemor to understond what they wold say ;
and the tenants seyd that ther was taken non uppon the
Duche at ther knowlych, save only Pyrs Warryn the
yonger.   And Paynter seyd that ther catell was taken
uppon the Duche, whych they connot prove by non
record, save only by ther awyn sayng ; and so we wold
not a bey that replevyn, and so they departyd.   And at
iij. at clock at after non Pynchemor come to Haylysdon
a yen with ij. men, whych broght with hem a replevyn
from the Shyryff, whos namys be John Whytherley
and Robert Ranson, whych requyryd me by the same
replevyn to make them delyvery of the seyd bestys
taken at Drayton ; and so I, syyng the Shyryffs
replevyn and under hys seale, bade my men delyver
hem, and soo they wer delyveryd.

And as for all other maters that ye have wretyn to
[me] of, I wyll spede me to send you a awnswer as
hastely as I may, for I may no leysor have to wryte no
more to you thys tyme.   The blyssyd Trynyte have you
in His kepyng.   Wryten at Haylesdon, the xx. day of
May.   By yours,   M. P.

505.

A.D. 1465, 27 May.

MARGARET PASTON TO JOHN PASTON.

[From Fenn, iv. 206.]

What is said here about the tenants of Hellesden and Drayton, and about
Master Philip Lipyate, leaves no doubt that this letter was written in 1465.
It contains, moreover, a distinct reference to Letter 503.

*To my ryght wyrshypfull husbond, John Paston, l*₁
thys delyveryd in haste.

RYGHT wyrshypfull husbonde, I recomaunde me to you. Please it you to wyte that I have send to Master John Smyth and to Master Stephyn to have a vyse for the church of Drayton ; and they send me word that ther moste be had a comyssion from the Byshop to calle in the person Flowredew,[1] and that most be proclaymyd in the church of Drayton iij. tymes by a Deen,[2] and after that yff he appyre not with in vj. monthys after the fyrst proclamacion, that then he for to be depryvyd, and the patron to present whom he luste, and ells your presentacyon ys not sufficyant. And I have so purveyd that a comyssyon ys hadde, and shal be servyd as hastely as it may be.

As for John Rysyng, I have sent to hym to wyte the cause that he ys not broght up to London, and he sayth that he callyd uppon the Shyrff that he myght be had up for [to] com to hys awnswer, and the Shyrff told hym that he wold not bryng hym up at hys owyn coste ; and John Andres seyd that he wold not have hym up, and so he ys styll in prison at Ipswych ; and so shall he be but yf ye canne fynde the beter mene for to have hym oute.   I have sent to hym xiij^s. iiij^d. to help hym sylf ther with ; he payth for hys borde wykely xx^d.   And Hopton and Smyth be ther styll allso, and they have money ynogh, wher som ever that they have it.   Rysyng dymeth that they have confort of the other party ; and I send you a copy of the warant that they wer a restyd by, &c.

I spake not with my moder syn Rychard Calle broght me the letter from you tochyng her mater, for I myght have no lesor.   When I speke with her at leysure I wyll remember her in that mater, acordyng to your wrytyng.   And as for your tenants of Drayton, as I canne understond by hem, they be ryght gode

---

[1] John Flowerdew was instituted to the Rectory of Drayton on the 15th of March 1461, on the presentation of John Paston, Esq., and Thomas Howes, Clerk.—F.

[2] This means the Rural Dean, who had a district of ten churches in the country, wherein he exercised a jurisdiction of great advantage to ecclesiastical discipline, and the sentences of superior Ecclesiastical Courts were to be executed by him.—F.

and trew hertyd to you to ther powers, and full fayn wold that ye had it a yen in peasse, for they had as leffe al most be tenants to the Devell as to the Duke, except Wyll. Herne, Pers at Sloth, and on Knott of the same towne, for they be not gode.

All your tenants at Haylesdon and Drayton, except thes iij., be ryght glad that we err ther a mongs hem, and so be many other of our olde nebers and frends; and but yf [*unless*] ye com hom by Wensday or Thursday[1] in Wytson wyke, I purpose me to ssee you in secrete wyse by Trynyte Sonday,[2] but yf [*unless*] ye send to me contrary comaundement er that tyme; and I pray you send me yeur avyse how ye wyll that we doo a yenst the next shyr, whych shulbe the Monday next after Trynyte Sonday, as for callyng uppon the replevyn that the bests of Drayton wer delyveryd by.

Item, Richard Calle told me that ye desyryd to have Master Phylyp ys name, and hys name ys Phylyp Lypzeate, and I send you a letter[3] by Henre Wylton ys man, wherin I wrote Master Phylyp ys name; and in the same letter I wrote to you for Wyll. Lumnor. I pray you send me word yf ye have it. And the Blysshyd Trynyte have you in Hys kypyng. Wryten the Monday next after Assencyon Day.[4]

By yours,   M. P.

506.

A.D. 1465, 11 June.
MARGARET PASTON TO JOHN PASTON.

[From Paston MSS.]

This letter, in which it is anticipated that the Duke of Suffolk will obtain possession, first of Drayton, and then of Hellesden, is evidently a little later in date than Nos. 499 and 502, and can only be of the year 1465.

[1] 5th or 6th of June.   [2] 9th of June.
[3] No. 503.   [4] 23d of May.

*To my ryght wyrshypfull husbond, John Paston, be thys
letter delyveryd.*

RYGHT wyrshypfull husband, I recomaunde me
unto you. Please it you to wyte that I recevyd
letters from you on Wensday laste passyd, the
were wryten the Monday next before, wherof
I thanke you of the letter that ye send to me.   I wolde
fayn doo well yf I cowde, and as I canne I wol doo to
youre pleasure and profet; and in such thyngs as I cannot skyle of, I wyll take a vyse of such as I know that
be youre frendes and doo as well as I canne.   Wher as
ye wrote to me that Lydham told you that I told hym
that the Ducks men werre not so besy as they had be
by fore, no more thay were not at that tyme, but sythen
thay have be bysyer.   What confort that thay have I
canne not have no knowlych as yet, but I suppose and
all your felshyp were gode, thay shold not have so grete
confort as they have, or ells they wold not be so besy
as thay have be.   Grete bost they make that the Duck
shold have Drayton in peas, and after thys Haylesdon,
and that with in short tyme ; thay er moch the bolder,
I suppose, by cause that ye be wher as ye be.   At the
reverens of God, yf ye may by any wyrshypfull or
resonabell mene, com oute therof as sone as ye may
and come home amonges your frends and tennaunts,
and that shold be to hem the grettyst confort that thay
myzt have and the contrary to your enmys.

It ys sayd here that the Duck of Suffolk shall com to
Coshay in haste and logge ther for a season ; I fyle well by
your tenaunts that yf ye were peaseabyly possessyd and
your cort holden in peaseabyll wyse, and that they myzt
be in pease a yenst the other many, than they wold take
accyons a yenste hem for such wrongs as have be don to
hem, and ells they say that they ther not [*dare not*] take it
uppon hem, for they dwelle so ney to the other many that
thay knowe well thay shold never be in ease yf thay
dyde soo whyle that thay dele amonges hem. On Thursday
last John Doket, the Bayly ys son y lawe, and Thomas

Ponte, with other, erly in the mornyng, an owre by fore
the sonne rose, com to your fold, and drove away the
flock at Drayton, both Colyet and other, in to Coshay
fee, or ever that the shipherd myght have knowlych
therof and then he fowlyd one and desyryd to have hem
a yen, and thay wold not suffer hym to have them no
more but the Colyet and ther were c. and j. of yours
and tho had thay forth with hem to Coshay, and the
same day we had a replevyn for the cc. shype and
replevyn for the hors that wer taken at Haylesdon, and
how that thay were obbeyd Ric. Call shall enforme
you, and of other maters also, the whych I may not
wryte to you of at thys tyme.

Item, I have spoke with [John] Strange of the mater
that ye wrote to me of, and in gode feyth I[1] fynd hym,
as me symyth, ryght well disposyd to you wards; and he
hath, acordyng to your desyre, spoken with Yelverton
yesterday to fyle his dysposicion in that mater, and
Yelverton, as it symyth by hym, roght not gretely thogh
the mater brake, so that he myght have any resonabell
colour to breke, he ys so callyd uppon by Wayte and
other of the Duck of Suffolk ys counsell that he ote
[wot] not where to hold hym, and he ys put in so gret
confort, as I am enformyd, to receve money for the lond,
and that temptyth hym ryght sore; for with money he wold
fayn be in handelyng, as ye know he hath nede therof.
He told John Straunge that it ys informyd hym that
ye have up an enquest to depreve ther wytnesse and
ther with ys he sore movyd . . . .
that yf any thyngs be don in temporall maters other in
spyryt[uall] . . . . . .   maters tochyng executors or feoffeys or wyttnes tyll the day of . . .
. . .   trety be passyd, he wyll not abyde no trety
therin, but do as . . . .   thynkyth
best for to do therein. I told John Straunge that I
kn[ew] . . . .   thogh it were soo that
shold passe any such enquest it shol n . . . . .
. . . . .   of them in provyng of her trothys, the

---

[1] The MS. has "in" instead of "I," evidently by mistake.

whych shold be no hurt . . . . for
John Straunge desyryd me that I shuld send to you in
al haste that . . . . any such folks
that thay shold not doo in the mater till the day of .
. . . . may have knowlych howe he and
other wold doo in such maters as sh . . . . .
. . he wold be loth that he shold have any colour to
breke for any thyng . . . . and Yelverton sayth it shall not breke thorf his defaute yf ye wyll
n[ot] . . . . be ryght glad to have
your gode wyll and to goo thorgh in all maner mate[rs]
. . . . eschewyng of wastfull expens
of the dede ys godes and that the godes myzt be dyspendyd
to the welle of the dede. Straunge desyryd to knowe
what appoyntements he desyryth to have in the trety,
and he sayd he wold not let that be understond tyll the
tyme of trety cam. Me symyth, save your beter avyse,
it were wel do that thay that be com up for you myzt
be kypt in som secryte place and not do [*naught done?*]
in the mater tyll the tyme of the trety were passyd.
The cost there of shall not be grete to that it myzt hurte
yf the trety were broken by that meane and then ye
may have hem nyer; and yf ye thynk it be to doo ye
may have hem to go to ther mater after the seyd tyme,
for of ij. hurtes the grettyst ys best to be eschewyd.

Item, as for youre houshold at Caster, savyng your
beter avyse, me thynkyth that v. or vj. of your folkes,
such as ye wyll assyngne, were [enough to ?][1] kype the
place, and they for to go to bord with the prustes, and
ye not to kype no houshold ther yet; and that ye shall
fynd more profettabyll than for to doo as we do nogh;
for ther expens, as I understond, have not be moch
the lesse by fore Wytsontyde than it shold be thogh I
had be at home by cause of resortyng of pepell theder;
and yf the houshold were broke thay myzt have a gode
excuse in that, whosome ever come. Ric. Call shall enforme you of thys maters, and mo other, more playnly
than I may do wryte at thys tyme. It is necessary that

<hr>

[1] Paper decayed.

possessyon be kypt hyre yett tyll ye be more ferther forth
in other maters. The Blessyd Trynyte have you [in] Hys
kypyng, and send you gode spyde in all your maters,
and send you grace to have a gode conclusyon in hem
in haste. Wryten on the Tewysday nex before Corpus
Christi.

By your faynt houswyff at thys tyme,
M. P.

507.

A.D. 1465, 15 June.

RICHARD CALLE TO SIR JOHN PASTON.

[From Paston MSS., B.M.]

This letter seems to have reference to the depositions touching Sir John
Fastolf's will in the suit brought by Sir William Yelverton and William Worcester against John Paston and Thomas Howes. Robert Popy seems to have
been examined in the spring of 1464 (See No. 488); but the suit was still
going on in 1465, and in a letter of Margaret Paston's of the 24th June following, Richard Calle is mentioned as having recently left her and gone to
her husband in London.

*To my ryght reverent and worschippfull master, Sir
John Paston, Knyght.*

PLESITH it your gode masterschip to wete that
as for the examynacion of Master Robert
Popy, his examinacion was wreten in a longe
bille of parchemyn accordyng to the deposicion in the Spirituall Coorte. And Master Robert
come in to the Chauncery, and was sworne that all
that was wreten in the seide bille was trewe, and so
delyverd the same bille to the Mastre of the Rolles;
and he bare it forthe with hym in his hande, for it was
delyverd hym at the risyng of the Coorte. Tounesende
was by and I bothe, &c. And as for delyveryng of
money to Dawbeney, I do that I may do, and more
thenne I may weele doo, for I have put my selfe in
gret daunger for that I have borwyd, &c. Almyghty

God spede you in all your maters, &c.   Wreten the Saterday next after Corpus Christi Daye.

Your servaunt R. C.

508.

A.D. 1465, 18 June.

JOHN RYSYNG TO JOHN PASTON.

[From Paston MSS., B.M.]

The imprisonment of John Rysing is referred to in Margaret Paston's letter of the 27th May 1465 (No. 505), and in another of the 24th June following (No. 510). There can be no doubt this letter is of the same year.

Onto my ryght reverent and worchipfull maister, John Paston, Esquyer, be this letter delyvered.

RYGHT reverent and worchipfull sir, I reco-mende me onto your good maisterchip in the moste lowly wise that I can or may, letyng your masterchippe understonde howe that John Smyth, of Freton, and John Hopton, of Freton, and I were attached and led onto Gippeswich, and there putte into the Kynges pryson by cawse of the fyn which was sessed upon the forsaid John Smyth, John Hopton, and me, as your maisterchippe knowith well. And as for John Smyth and John Hopton, they had labored the meanes onto Master Jenney, that they were delyvered owt of pryson or than the massenger come ageyn to theym which they sent onto yow; and I remayne stille in pryson, and I can not knowe but that they labour the meanes to make me to paye the money for theym. And so I can not se non other meane but that I shall ly stille in pryson, and been ondo for ever withoute your good masterchippe shewed to me at this tyme; for as I am enformed that Jenney hath promysed theym that I shall paye the fyne for theym, and also alle the costes that haith be spent ther

upon, and shall be spent, for thei say that I am sufficient to bere the hole daunger. And my keper yafe me
licence to goon home, and thei had hevyed the peple
that dwelle ther, and that gretly, and said playnly how
that ye myght not beere the dawnger a geyns Jenney
for your self; therfor the seiden that ye myght not
helpe them owt of dawnger when thatte ye myght not
helpe your self. Wherfor I pray your masterchippe to
lete me have word in as hasty tyme as ye may, to
knowe whether that I shall abyde her stylle or not,
and if I myght do yow any good at London, I pray
your mastershippe that ye will sende for me, and I
will come up to yow. And if ther be non other remedy
but that the money most nedys be paid, I pray your
masterchippe that ye will make such purveyaunce
therfor that it may be to myn delyveraunce at the
reverence of God, and in the weye of charite as myn
hole truste is in your masterchippe, for I can not seke
to no man, nor will not but only to yow. Wherfor
I pray yow that ye will tenderly understond this letter,
as I may pray for yow onto God, who have yow in H'.
kepyng. Wretyn at Gippeswich the xviij. day of Junc.

These ar the names of theym that have parte of my
catell, Gilbert Nicoll, of Sprowton, William Merssh and
John Woode of Gippeswich, bocher.

By your man and feithfull
servant, JOHN RYSYNG.

509.

A.D. 1465, June.—ABSTRACT.

[From MS. Phillipps, 9309].

Examinations taken at the house of the treasurer of St. Paul's
Cathedral, London, of the following witnesses in the matter Sir
John Fastolf's will, viz.:—of Thomas Torald and Robert Lawe on
the 18th; of William Waterman on the 19th; of John Osbern
and John Heydon on the 20th; of William Pykeryng, John
Symmys and John Shawe on the 21st days of June 1465.

510.

A.D. 1465, 24 June.
MARGARET PASTON TO JOHN PASTON.

[From Paston MSS., B.M.]

As this letter refers to Paston's disputes with the Duke of Suffolk and his officers, the date must be 1465.

To my ryght wyrshipfull husband, John Paston, be thys delyveryd in hast.

RYGHT wyrshypfull hosbond, I recomaund me to you. Please it you to wyte that the same Wensday that Ric. Call departyd hens I send Ric. Charlys to speke with the undershryf, requyryng hym that he shold serve the replevyn for the shype and hors that were take, &c.; and the shyrf sayd playnly that he wol not, nor derst not serve it, not thogh I wold yeve hym xx *li.* to serve it. And Ric. Charlys axhyd the cause why, and he sayd, for he wold not have to doo with that felshyp, and so it ys yet un-servyd. I suppose that Ric. Calle hath told you what revell ther was by the Bayllyf of Coshay and his felaw uppon your men that shold have servyd the replevyn.

Item, the same Wensday that Ric. Call rode from hens the were endytyd v. of men by the enquest of Fourhoo hunder, as Crome can enforme you, and on Fryday last paste John Paston, the yonger, Wykes and Thomas Honewerth were endytyd at Dyram, by what menys the berour herof Crome shall [en]forme you. I send theder Ric. Charlys, John Seve, and iij. or iiij. other gode felows, for to have don other folks as gode atorne; but it wold not be, for the Juge ys soo parcyall with the other party that I trowe ther shalbe sped no maters before hym for you, nor for non of yours tyl it be otherwyse by twene you than it ys. Crome shall tell you of hys demenyng at the last sessyons at Dyrham. I send you a copy of both the endytements. Your son John Paston the yonger, I hope shal be with you thys

wyke and enforme you of mo thyngys, and howe myn
hors and hys sadell and harnys ys prysoner at Coshaye
Halle and have ben ever syn Wensday last.

Item, I recevyd a letter from you on Satorday last,
whych was wryten on Monday next before and I have
sent to Sir Thomas Howys the same day for such
maters as ye wrote to me of, and he sent me word that
Wyllyam Worceter had a boke of remembraunce of
recaytys that hath be recevyd by Sir John Fastolf or
any of hys sythen the iiij.ᵗᵉ· yere Kyng Harry, both of
hys owyn lyflode or of any other mannys that he had
to doo wyth all.   He sayd, yf ye wold send to Wyll.
Worceter to loke therfore he sayd he wyst well he wold
lete you have knowlych yf any such thyng may be
founde, and also he sayd that he wold send to the seyd
Wyll. to serche therfore, and as for such bokys as he
hath hyre at hom he wol doo loke yf any remembraunce
canne be founde therof, and ye shall have knowlych
ther of, as he hath promysyd, by Satourday next comyng.
And as for the woman that made the clayme that ye
wrote of he ys wellwyllyd that she shold be seyn to in
the way of almys.   And as I here say, it symyth by
hym that in any thyng that he canne doo tochyng the
savacyon of the dedys gode,[1] other in lyflode, other in
other godys, he sayth that he wyll doo.   I canne not
have no knowlych that Haydon mellyth in the mater
of Drayton ; yf he do oght therin, he doyth it closely,
as he ys wont to doo, and wayshyth hys hondys ther
of as Pylate dyde.   It shalnot be long to or that I send
to yow ; of such tythynges as we have I shall lete
you have knowlych ther of.   I fynd Crome ryght wel-
wyllyng to you in such thyngys as lyth in hym for to
do.   I pray you lete hym be thankynd therfor, and
that shall cause hym to be the beter wyllyd ; he hath
not be rewardyd as yet but by Ric. Call, as he canne
tell you.   The Blyssyd Trynyte have you in His
kepyng and send you gode spyde in all your maters.
Wryten in hast on Mydsomer day.

[1] *i.e.*, The dead man's goods.

As for Rysyng, but yf [*unless*] ye purvey for hym he
canne no helpe have at home.

By yours, M. P.

511.

A.D. 1465, 6 July?
Margaret Paston to Sir John Paston.

[From Paston MSS., B.M.]

This letter is not addressed on the back, nor is the handwriting that of
Margaret Paston, but from the subscription it would appear to have been
written by her to one of her sons; and as John Paston the younger is
mentioned in the body of the letter, the person addressed was evidently
his elder brother. The letter seems to have been written shortly before the
Duke of Suffolk's attempt on Hellesden mentioned in the next No., probably
on the Saturday preceding it.

 GRETE yow wele, letyng yow wetyn that I am
informyd for certeyn the Duc of Suffolk
reysyth grete pepyl bothe in Norffolk and
Suffolk to comyn doune with hym to putte
us to a rebeuc and thei may; querfor I wold in ony
wyse that ze make yow as strong as ze can wyth inne
[*in the*] place, for I and other moo suppose that zyff
they fynd zow not here they wyl seke yow there ze
arn. I wold John Paston the zonger schuld ryde
azyn to my Lady of Norffolk and be wyth hyr stylle tyl
we haff other tydyngs, and ther may he do sum good,
after that he heryth tydyngs, in goyng forth to hys
fadyr or in to sum other place quere we may hafe
remedy; for yt [is] told me that there ar come to
Cossay onward more than ij. hundred, and ther ys
comyng, as yt ys seyd, more than a thowsand. I wold
that ze sende hyder Lytyl John that I mygth sende
hym abowte on myn errandys. Sende me worde how
that ze doo by summe of the tenantes that be not
knowyn.

Item, byd Richard Calle send me word in a bylle,
of how many materys that he hath sent myn husbond
an answere of, the quych he sendt hom in divers

letters for to be sped here and of the fermours of
Tychwelle.

Item, zyf Sir Jamys Gloys may come to Norwych to
Adam Talyours hows I wold he come on Munday by-
tymys, and I schal sende to hym thyder.   God kepe
yow alle.   Wretyn in hast on Satyrday.

By your Modyr.

Item, yt ys told me that zong Heydon reysyth mych
pepyl in the sokyn and in other place.

Item, I wold ze schuld do Rychard Calle hye hym of
makeng of alle the acountes and, zyf nede, lete hym
gete help and kepe Thomas Hunnworth stille wyth
yow, and be war of Pykyng [*Pickering?*]

512.

A.D. 1465, 10 July.
RICHARD CALLE TO JOHN PASTON.

[From Fenn, iv. 212.]

From what has been already said about the Duke of Suffolk's claim to the
manor of Hellesden, it is clear that this letter is of the year 1465.   Later it
cannot be, as John Paston was dead before July 1466.

To my mastre, John Paston, in hast.

PLESITH it youre maysterschip to witte of the
rwle and disposicion of the Master Philip and
the Balyf of Cossey, with others of my Lorde
of Suffolkes men.   On Monday last past, at aftre-
noon, [they] wer at Heylesdon, with the nombre of CCC.
men, for to have entred, notwithstandyng they seyde
they come not for to entre; but withoute dought, and
they had been strong inough for us, they wolde have
entred, and that we undrestonde nough, but we knowyng of ther comyng and purveyed so for hem, that we
wer strong j nough.   We had lx. men withinne the
place, and gonnes, and suche ordynauns, so that if

they had satte uppon us, they had be distroyed.   And
ther my mastres was withine, and my mastre, Sir John,
and hathe gate hym as grete worschip for that day as
any gentleman myght doo, and so is it reported of the
partye and in all Norwiche.   And my Lorde of Norwiche sent theder Master John Salett and Master John
Bulleman for to trete, and so they ded; and the Duc
men seide they had a warant for to attache John
Dawbeney, Wyks, Calle, Hunewrthe, and Bliclyng
and other, weche they wuld have; and my master, Sir
John, answerd them, and seide that they were not
withine, and though we had ben, they shuld not have
had hem ; and so they desired oon of our men.   And
so Naunton stede by my mastres and haxed hem whom
they wold have, and seyde if they wold have hem he
wold go with hem, and so he ded.   And on the next
day they caryed hym forthe to my Lord of Suffolk to
Claxton, through Norwich; and ther we had founde a
remedy for hym for to heve lette hym; and he wold
not, but nedys go forthe with hem; but like a jentelman
he was entreated amongs hem.   And Harleston desyred
at Heylesdon to speke with my mastre, Sir John, and
so he ded, and seyde to hym it were ryght weele don
that he rode to my Lord of Suffolk and desired
hym in any wice that he schulde do so, and seyde that
it was hes dwte so for to do, in asmoche as my Lorde
was come to contre, and that he wolde ryde with hym,
and brynge hym to my Lorde ; and he answerd and
seide to hym, whan that he undrestode that my Lord
were hes fathers goode Lord and hes, that thanne he
wolde se hes Lordship, and ell[es] he had non aronde to
hym; and so they departed.   And thanne appoyntement was taken that they shull sende home ther men,
and we schuld send home oure.   And nough my Lord
of Suffolks men come from Claxton to Norwich, and face
us and fray uppon us, this dayly.   Ther fylle uppon me
befor Sevayne dore xij. of hes men, viij. of them in
harneys, and ther they wold have myscheved me and
the Scheryf letted hem and other, and they make ther

awaunte were that I may be goten I schul dye; and
so they lye in a wayte for to myscheve me, Dawbeney,
and Wyks; and so I dare not ryde out alone withoute
a man with me.   And I undrestonde ther is comyn an
Heyre Determyner[1] to enquer of all ryots, and my Lord
of Suffolk and Yelverton be Comyscioners; and so they
sey as money of us as can be taken shal be endyted
and hanged forth with; and so the people here are
dysmayed with ther rwle.   Wherfore that it like you to
sende werd how my mastres schal do at Heylesdon,
and we in all other maters; and wether ye wol that
we feche a yene the flok of Heylesdon, for they are
nough dreven to Causton, and there go they on the
heyth; and my Lord of Suffolk wolbe at Drayton on
Lames Daye, and kepe the Coort ther; wherefor ye
must seke an remedy for it, or ell[es] it woll not do weele.

If my Lord of Norffolk wold come, he schulde make
all weele, for they feere hym above all thyngs, for it is
noyced here that my Lord of Norffolk hathe taken
partye in thes mater, and all the cuntre is cladde of it,
seyng that if he come they wooll hooly go with hym.

And me senethe it were wele don to meve my Lord
in it, though ye schuld geve hym the profyghts of
Heylesdon and Drayton for the kepyng, and som
money be side; for ye must seke som other remedy
than ye do, or ell[es] in my conseyte it schull go to the
Divell, and be distroyed, and that in ryght schorte
tyme.   And therfore at the reverence of God take som
appoyntement with Master Yelverton, suche as ye
thynke schuld most hurt.

I beseche you to pardon me of my writyng, for I
have pitte to se the trybulacion that my mastres hathe
here, and all youre frends, &c.

Almyghty Jesu preserve and kepe you.   Wreten the
Wednesday next Seint Thomas Daye.

Your pore servaunt and bedman,
RIC. CALLE.

---

[1] An Oyer and Terminer, or Special Commission.

513.

A.D. 1465, 12 July.
MARGARET PASTON TO JOHN PASTON.

[From Fenn, iv. 218].

It is needless to point out that this letter must have been written in the same year as the last.

To my right worschipfull husbond, John Paston, in hast.

RYGHT worshypful husbond, I recomaund me to yow, preyeng you hertyly that ye wyl seke a meen that yowr servauntys may be in pees, for they be dayly in fer of ther lyvys. The Duke Suffolks men thretyn dayly Dawbeney, Wykys, and Richard Calle, that wher so ever they may gete them they schold dye; and affrayes have ben made on Rychard Calle this weke, so that he was in gret jupperte at Norwych among them; and gret affrayes have ben made uppon me and my felashep her on Monday last passyd, of whych Rychard Calle tellyth me that he hath sent yow word of in wryghtyng, mor pleynly than I may doo at thys tyme, but I shal informe yow mor pleynly heraftyr.

I suppose ther shal be gret labor ageyn yow and yowr servaunts at the Assysis and Cescions her; wherfor me semyth, savyng your better advyce, it wer wele do that ye shold speke with the Justicys or they com her; and yf ye wol that I compleyn to them or to any other, if Good fortune me lyfe and helth, I wol do as ye advyse me to do, for in good feyth I have ben symply intretid among them; and what with syknesse, and troble that I have had, I am browte ryght lowe and weyke, but to my power I wyl do as I can or may in your maters.

The Duk of Suffolk and both the Duchessys shal com to Claxton thys day, as I an informyd, and thys next weke he shal be at Cossey; whether he wol com ferther hyddyr ward or not, I wot not yit. It is seyd that he schold com hyddyr, and yet hys men seyd her on Monday that he cleymyd no tytyl to thys place; they seyd ther comyng was but to take out such ryotus peple as was her within thys place, and suche as wer the Kyngys felonys, and indytyd and outlawyd men. Neverthe lesse they wold schew no warauntys wherby to take non such, thow ther had suche her; I suppose if they myght have com in pesably, they wold have made an other cause of ther comyng.

Whan alle was doo and they scholde departe, Harlyston and other desyryd me that I schold com and se myn olde Lady, and sewe to my Lorde, and if any thyng wer amysse it schold be amendyd. I said if I scholde sewe for any remedye, that I scholde sewe ferther, and lete the Kynge and alle the Lordys of thys lond to have knowlech what hathe be don to us, if so wer that the Deuk wolde meynten that hathe be don to us by hys servauntys, if ye wolde geve me leve.

I pray yow sende me worde if ye wyl that I make any compleynt to the Duke or the Duchesse; for as it is tolde me, they know not the pleynesse that hathe ben done in such thyngys as hathe ben don in her [their] namys.

I schold wryght muche mor to yow but for lak of leyser.

I comaundyd my Mayster Tom thys day to have com ageyn by me from Norwych, when he had spokyn with Rychard Calle, but he cam not. I wolde he wer qwyte of hys indytments, so that he wer qwyte of yowr servyce; for by my trowthe, I holde the place the mor ongracyous that he is in, for hys dysposycion in dyverce thyngys, the whych ye schal be informed of her after.

The Trynyte have yow in kepyng.   Wretyn the Fryday next after Seynt Thomas.

By yowr,   M. P.

514.

A.D. 1465, 13 July.
JOHN PASTON TO MARGARET PASTON.

[From Paston MSS., B.M.]

As this letter is dated on a Saturday, and refers to the Duke of Suffolk's attempt on Hellesden as having been made on the Monday preceding, here can be no difficulty in fixing the precise date, both of day and year.

To my cosyn, Margret Paston.

 Recummand me to yow, I thank of yow of yowr labour and besynes with the unruly felechep that cam befor yow on Monday last past, wherof I herd report be John Hobbis. And in god feyth ye aquyt yow rygth wel and discretly and hertyly to yowr wurchep and myn, and to the shame of your adversarijs, and I am wel content that ye avowid that ye kept possession at Drayton and so wold doo. Wherfor I pray yow, make yowr word god if ye may, and at the lest, let myn adversarijs not have it in pees if ye may. Jon Hobbys tellith me that ye be seekly, whech me lekith not to here ; praying yow hartyly that ye take what may do yowr eese and spar not, and in any wyse take no thowth no to moch labor for thes maters, ne set it not so to yowr hert that ye fare the wers for it. And as for the mater, so they overcome yow not with fors ne bosting, I shall have the maner sewrlyer to me and myn, than the Dewk shall have Cossey, dowt ye not. And in cas I come not home within thre wekis, I pray you come to me, and Wykes hath promisid to kepe the plase in yowr absens. Nevertheles whan ye come set it in sech rewle as ye seme best and most suer, bothe for Castre and Heylisdon if the werr hold. In cas ye have pees send me word.

As for that it is desyrid I shuld show my tytill and evydens to the Dewk, me thynkyth he had evyll cown-

cell to entre in opon me, trusting I shuld shew hym
evydens.   And [*if*] ye seme it may do yow god or eese,
lete my Lord of Norwich wet that the maner of Drayton
was a marchants of London callid Jon Heylisdon longe
er any of the Polis that the seyd Dewk comyth of wer
borne to any lond in Norfolk or Suffolk; and if they wer
at that tyme born to no lond, how may the seyd Dewk
klaym Drayton be that pedegre?   As for the seyd
John Heylisdon, he was a por man born, and from
hym the seyd maner dessended to Alice his dowtyr,
hos estat I have, and I soppose the seyd Dewk comyth not of hem.

Item, as for the pedegre of the seyd Dewk, he is
sone to William Pool, Dewk of Suffolk, sone to
Mychell Pool, Erl of Suffolk, sone to Mychel Pool, the
furst Erl of Suffolk of the Polis, mad be King Richard
seth my fader was born; and the seyd furst Mychell
was sone to on William Pool of Hull, whech was a
wurchepfull man grow be fortwne of the werld.   And
he was furst a marchant, and after a knygth, and after
he was mad baneret; and if any of thees hadde the
maner of Drayton I will los C*li.* so that any persone
for the Dewk will be bond in as moch to prove the
contrary; and I wot weel the seyd Dewkis Cowncell
wil not claym the seyd maner be the tytill of the fader
of the seyd William Pool.   And what the fader of the
seyd William was, as be the pedegre mad in the seyd
last Dewkis fadirs daijs I know rygt weell: wherof
I informyd Herry Boteler to tell my old Lady of
Suffolk, becawse he is of her cowncell; and more
will I not tell in thes mater, but if [*unless*] I be desyrid
or compellid.

Item, let my Lord of Norwich wete that it is not
profitabe ner the comen well of gentilmen that any
jentilman shuld be compellid be an entre of a lord to
shew his evidens or tytill to his lond, ner I wil not
begine that exsample ne thralldam of gentilmen ner of
other; it is god a lord take sad cowncell, or he begyne
any sech mater.

And as for the Pools that owth Drayton, if ther wer
C. of hern levyng, as ther is non, yet have they no
tytill to the seyd maner. God kepe yow. Wret the
Satirday, &c. Yowr Jon Paston.

I pray yow be as mery with yowr feluchep as ye kan.
Item, I send hom writt and prasens for yowr
servaunts and myn.
Item, I may sell you woll for xl*d.* the ston, redi
mony, as Arblaster can tell yow, and malt for iiij*s.*
the quarter at days xxj. for xx. delivered of Yermouth
mesur. If ye fayle mony ye most make it of yowr wole
or malt.
I send you hom writts of replevin for the shep and
the horses that wer take, and avise yow lete the writtis
be deliverd be fore my Lord of Norwich, and god
rekord; and if ye may make men with fors to take the
catell agey[n] be waran of replevyn, spar not rather
than fayle.

On the back of the letter is the following memorandum in a
different hand :—

Md. there lefte behynde of Heylesdon folde of my mastre schepe xlj.
modreschep. Item of lambes xxxiiij. Item of my mastres xij. modreschep.
Item of her lambes xij.

515.

A.D. 1465, [July?]
MARGARET PASTON TO JOHN PASTON.

[From Paston MSS., B.M.]

Margaret Paston, as will be seen by subsequent letters, was in London with
her husband in September 1465. This letter seems to have been written not
long before, when she first entertained the thought of going thither.

RIGHT worchepful hosbond, I recommand me
to yow, and pray you hertely at the reverence
of God that ye be of good comfort, and
trost veryly be the grase of God that ye shall
overcome your enemys and your trobelows maters

ryght welle, yf ye wolle be of good comfort, and not
take your maters to hevely that ye apeyr not your self,
and thynk veryly that ye be strong inowe for alle your
enemys be the grace of God.   My moder is your good
moder, and takyth your maters ryght hertely.   And zit
ye thynnk that I may do good in your maters yf I
come up to you, after I have knowlage of your entent
it shall not be longe or I be with you be the grace of
God.   And as for any othyr thyngs of sharge that be
in this contre, I hope I shall so ordeyn therfore that
it shall be safe.   I have delyveryd your older sonne
xx. mark that I have received of Ric. Calle, and I
kowd no more of hym syn ye departyd.   [And I send
yow another bage of mony that was in your square
cofyr.[1]]   And I pray God hertely send us good tydyngs
of yow, and send the victory of your enemys.   Wretyn
in hast on Saterday.   Your M. P.

Item, I take your sonne of your faders oode mony,
that was in the lytyll trussyng cofyr x. mark, for my
broder Clement seythe that xx. mark was to lytyll
for hym.

516.

A.D. 1465?

[MARGARET PASTON?] TO ————,

[From Paston MSS., B.M.]

The MS. of this letter seems to be a draft in a hand like that of James
Gresham. It is anonymous and without address. Even the writer is very
uncertain. But it may not unlikely be a draft letter from Margaret Paston
to some neighbour who, while the Duke of Suffolk was laying claim to
Hellesden and Drayton, was not too mindful of John Paston's rights.
Brandeston is about eleven miles from Norwich, eight miles beyond Drayton.
Thomas Hoop was parson of Brandeston from 1448 to 1475. He was pre-
sented to the living by Sir John Fastolf.

Cosyn, I recommaunde me to yow, letyng yow wete that I am
informid that the parson of Brandeston is take be yowr sowdiors
and led forth with hem, and they have ryfelid his godis, and
summe of myne husbondes also, and of his ballyes, weche were
left with the seyd parson to kepe.   Wherfore I avise yow, and

[1] This sentence is struck out.

praye that he maye be lete go agayn, and to have ower godes as were take fro hym ; for and yowr sowdioris be of sweche dis-posicion that they wyll take that they may gete it, shall no wurchip be to you, nor profite in tyme to come ; and therof wolde I be sory.   And if the seyd parson be othirwyse disposid thanne he owth to be, I wyll helpe that he shall be chaysteysid as conciens and lawe requerith.   I wolde ye shulde remembre that ye have bore blame for sweche thynges before this tyme that hath be do othirwise thanne lawe hath requerid.   And God have yow in His kepyng.   Wrete at Norwiche.

517.

A.D. 1465, 30 July.
JOHN WYKE TO SIR JOHN PASTON.

[From Paston MSS., B.M.]

The date of this letter is sufficiently apparent from the reference in the beginning to " the entry made at Hellesden in the Duke of Suffolk's name."

To my ryght wyrshypfull mayster, Sir John Paston, be thys letter delyveryd.

PLEASE it your maystershyp to wyte, uppon Satourday last, Mayster Wyll. Paston and I werre with my Lord the Byshoppe of York, and enformyd hys Lordshyp of the entre that was made at Haylesdon in the Duk of Suffolks name.   And my Lord asked of ous whether the C. marc wer payd or not, and we awnswered that it was payd many day a goon.   And than he sayd, " I dar swer uppon a boke that the Duchesse of Suffolk hath no knowlych therof."   And so he comaundyd ous to a wayte uppon hym, for he wold be at London a yen uppon Tewysday next; and soo we have non awnswer as yet.

Item, I have spoken with Mayster Robert Kent for your maters, and byddeth that ye shold not dowte therof; and as for the neglygens of your wytnes, Mayster Robert sayth it ys but a jape, and shall be no hurt.   And the copys therof wer deliveryd or than I cam hom from Parker ys hands, and that causyd me to spake no word to hym therof.

Item, the Lord Scales sayd at a soper where as he soped within thys iiij. nyztys that he wold ryde home and enter in ij. fayre maners in hys contray, and desyred Stanhope that shall wed Gernyngham ys suster to ryde with hym. I suppose it be to enter in to Caster and Cotton; wherfor maketh gode wache be tyme, for it ys mery to plede in possession, &c.

Item, I have send you an unce of myvers (?) by the beror of thys letter, and thay cost me iiijs. iiijd.

Item, your gesseren[1] and gaunteletts shall be send hom by the next caryours, for there be non hyre yete, &c. No more to you at thys tyme. The Holy Trynyte have you in Hys kypyng. Wryten at London uppon Tewysday next after Seynt Anne.

By youre servaunt, JOHN WYKE.

518.

A.D. 1465, 7 August.
MARGARET PASTON TO JOHN PASTON.

[From Paston MSS., B.M.]

This is another of the series of letters relating to Paston's dispute with the Duke of Suffolk about Drayton and Hellesden in 1465.

To my ryght worschipful husbond, John Paston, be this delyverd in hast.

RIGHT wurchepfull husbond, I recomaund me to you. Please it you to wete that I sent on Lammesse day[2] to Drayton, Thomas Bonde and Sir James Gloys to hold the court in your name, and to clayme your tytill; for I cowde gete none other body to kepe the court, ner that wuld go theder but the seide Thomas Bonde, be cause I suppose thei were a ferd of the pepill that shuld be there

[1] A sleeveless coat of mail.   [2] August 1.

of the Duke of Suffolks parte. The said Thomas and
James, as the Duke of Suffolks men, that is to sey,
Harlesdon, the parson of Salle, Mayster Phillip and
William Yelverton, the which was styward, with a lx.
persones or more be estymacion, and the tenauntes of
the same town, sum of hem havyng rusty pollexis and
byllys, comyn in to the maner yard to kepe the courte,
met with them, and told them that thei were comyn to
kepe the court in your name, and to clayme your titill.
Wherfore the seid Harlesdon, with ought any mor
words or occasion yovyn of your men, comytted the
seid Thomas Bonde to the kepyng of the new Baly
of Drayton, William Dokett, seyng that he shuld go
to my lord and do his herand hym self, notwithstandyng
that Sir James dede the erands to them, and had the
words ; wherfor thei toke the seid Thomas with ought
occasion. Thei wuld have mad the seid Thomas to have
had the words, and the seid James told hem that had
hem, because he was the more pesibill man, whan afterward thei bade avoyde, and sithen led forth Thomas
Bonde to Cossey, and bownde his armes be hynde
hym with whippe cord like a theffe, and shuld have
led hym forth to the Duke of Suffolk, ner had be that
I had spokyn with the juges in the morwyn or thei
yede to the shirehous and enformed hem of such ryottes
and assaugthis as thei had mad up on me and my
men ; the baly of Cossey and all the Duke of Suffolks
councell beyng ther present, and all the lerned men of
Norffolk, and William Jenney and my[che] pepill of the
contre ; the juge callyng the baly of Cossey befor them
all, and yaffe hym a gret rebuke, comaundyng the
shereffe to se what pepill thei had gadred at Drayton ;
which came after to Helesdon to se the pepill ther,
with weche [pe]pill he held hym wele content ; and
fro thens he rode to Drayton to se ther pepill, which
wer avoyded or he came. And ther he desired to
have delivered the seid Thom. Bonde to hym ; and
thei excusid hem and seid thei had send hym to the
Duke of Suffolk. Notwithstandyng, afterward thei

sent hym to Norwhich to hym, desiryng hym that he
shuld delivere hym not withought he mad a fyne, be
cause he trobilled the Kynges lete; for which thei
mad l . . . . to juges. But after that I under-
stod it, I sent Danyell of Mershlond and Thomas
Bonde [1] to enforme the juges how the seide
Thomas was intreted amonges hem; and so he ded.
And the juges were gretly . . . . . with the
Dukes men, and forwith comaunded the sheryf to
delyver the seide Bone withoute any fyne m[aking],
seyng that he out non to make. And in goode feythe
I founde the juges ryght gentell and forborable to me
in my matres, notwithstandyng the Duckes councell
had made her compleynt to them or I come in ther
werst wice, noysyng us of gret gatheryng of peopell and
many riotes thynges don be me and your men. And
after I enformed the juges of ther untrouthe and of
ther gidyng, and of our gidyng in like wice. And
after the juges undrestod the trouthe he gave the baly
of Cossey befor me and many other a passyng gret
rebuke, seyng without he amended hes condicion and
governaunce, thei wuld enforme the Kynge and helpe
that he schuld be punyschet. And wher as ye avyced
me . . . . . a felaschip to kepe the coorte at
Drayton with easy cost, it was thought be your coun·
cell it wer better otherwise, and not to gather no people,
for it was told me that the Dukes men had to the
nombre of v. C. men, and your councel avised me to
gete a felischip to kepe my place at Heylesdon, for it
was told me that they schuld come and pulle me out
of the place, weche cauced me to kepe the place the
strenger at that tyme. And as for kepyng of any
coort for you at Drayton, I can not wete how it cowde
be brought a boute withoute helpe of other but if there
schuld growe gret inconvenyence of it. And at the

---

[1] At this point the letter is continued in a different ink upon a new sheet
of paper, which was formerly stitched to the first sheet. A line which was
formerly covered by the sewing shows that Margaret Paston intended at first
to have written : "to the justice, and he . . . . . (*five words illegible,
the paper being cut*) thei toke the seid Thomas with ought warant, afftre
trobillyng of the lete."

ass[izes] . . . . made gret labor to endite your
men, notwithstandyng it was letted. And as for the
writtes of replevyn, they were delyverd openly be for
the juges to the scheryf, and also other writtes wech
Jamys Gresham brought; and aftre that Ric. Calle
spake with the high scheref for the servyng of hem.
And so he promysed to serve it and to send men of
hes owne to serve it; and so he sent ij. of his men
with Ric. Lynsted, and with ij. of Scheperdes to Cossey
for the schepe. And ther they wer answer that
Yelverton cleymeth the properte, and so wer they
answerd in all other places wher as any catell was.
And so they departed and come to the scheryf and
enformed hym; and I undrestande the scheryf taketh
it for an answere; nothwithstandyng I send hym word
withoute that Yelverton had ben ther in hes owne
persone he myte not cleyme the properte, and aviced
hym to be ware what retorne he made that he were
not hurte by it. And so he hathe made no retorne
yet. What he wul doo I wat ner. He is stylle in this
contre yet and schal be this iiij. or v. dayes, but your
councell thynketh it were well don that ye gete an
allias[1] and a *pluries* that it myght be sent don to the
scheryf and than he can mak non excuse but nedys
. . . . .[2] it well (?) to make a retorne as he wol
abide by. I can not wete how the catell woll be goten
ayen withoute other processe be had more than we
have yet.

   Item, on Tuesday next comyng schal the sescions
of the pees be at Wolsyngham. What schal be do
ther I wot not yet; for as for any indytementes that
we schuld labor a yenst them it is but wast werk;
for the scheryf ner the jurrours wol no thyng do ayenst
them.

   Item, wher as ye desire to knowe what gentelmen
wolde do for you at this tyme, in goode feythe I founde
Herry Greye, Lomnor, Alblastre, Wer . . . . (?),
Berney of Redham, Skyppewith, and Danyell of Merche-

lond, ryght weele disposed to you ward at this tyme
in helpyng and in zevyng ther goode avice to me for
suche maters as I had to doo. Ye schal have more
pleyne undrestondyng of all thynges her after than I
may write to you at this tyme.

Item, the *supersedias*[1] and the *supplicavit*[2] is delyverd
to Alblastre and to Wechyngham, and they have mad
out bothe warantes and *supersedias;*[1] nevertheles ther
is non servyd yet.

Item, I received the box with the writt and the
letter that Berney sent to me on Friday last and non
er [*no earlier*].

Item, as for the pris of malte it is fallen here sore,
for it is worthe but ij*s.* viij*d.* j. quarter at Yermoth.

Item, as for your wolle, I may selle a stoone for
xld., so that I wol geve halfe yere day of payment. I
prey you sende me word how I shal do in this matre
and in all other, &c. And God kepe you. Wreten in
haste the Wednesday next aftre Lammes daye.

Your M. PASTON.

519.

A.D. 1465, 7 Aug.
JOHN PASTON TO MARGARET PASTON.

[From Paston MSS., B.M.]

It is sufficiently clear from the reference to accounts of the 4th year of
Edward IV., that this letter cannot be earlier than 1465, which is the last
year of the writer's life.

To my cosyn, Margaret Paston, at Heylisdonn.

Recomaund me to you. And as for the letter
that I send yow touchyng John Russe, I will
that ye and your counsell see it openly; and
kepe this bille to your self or to some secret
frend of yours. And I pray yow remembir ij. thynges;

---

[1] So in MS.
[2] *Supersedeas* is a writ to stay certain proceedings ; *supplicavit* a writ for
taking surety of the peace when violence is threatened by any one.

on, if ye fynd hym in any maner wise disposed to leve
his bargeyn, take it at his offer, and take ayen the
writyng that he hath of that bargeyn, or a writyng of
his owne hand of relesyng his bargeyn to me; for
peraventure at this tyme he woll be glad to leve his
bargeyn, as I undirstand, and whanne he sethe that I
have peas he wolle calle theron ayen.   Wherfore I
pray yow werk wisely herin, for he may in no maner
wise aske the money of me and kepe his bargeyn, for
he hathe divers tymes desired me to have take of hym
more masse (?) therfore.   Another, as sone as ye may,
or ye breke this mater with John Russe, make due
serche with the fermours at Akthorp what mony Russe
hath reseyved ther in my tyme, that is to sey, for
Mighelmes the first, the ij., iij., iiij. yeres of Kyng E.,
of whech he hath reseyved ij. payments, that is xij*li.*
at the lest, or er the maner was trobelid by Jenney or
Yelverton.   And I deme that he hath reseyvid some
sithen, but that he kepith counsell.

Item, for as moch as Sir Thomas Howes gaderid
for the xxxix. yere of Kyng Herry, the seid John
Russe woll, under colour of that surmytte, that he
reseyvid in my tyme was therfore, wherfore ye must
make a serche what he hath reseyvid sith Sir John
Fastolff dyed, and what tyme; and therupon ye shall
undirstand what he hath reseyvid for me, and what
for hym; and in case he hathe reseyvid xii*li.*, and
Richard hath payd hym his dute as he promised,
thanne growyth nat to John Russe past iiij. or v*li.*;
notwithstandyng fare fayre with hym and resonabilly,
so that he leve his bargeyn, and lend hym the remnaunt
of the xx*li.* upon suerte for xx*li.*   He desireth to have
outher his dewte or borowyng at this tyme.

Item, he that shall speke with the fermours of
Akthorp, whos name is Langham, he must inquere
generally what mony he hath payd to all men sith Sir
John Fastolff dyed, and see his billes of payment, and
take therof a titelyng.   Ric. Calle hath a bille of
parcellis of every mannes ferme, and he can serche

this best, in case he be not to favorabill to John
Russe, wherfore I remitte this to your discrecion; but
I suppose John Russe woll telle yow what he hath
reseyvid for hand bifore this tyme wretyn by his
seying what he had reseyvid, and I suppose and he
remembird that he seid to me, he wold not aske his
mony in this forme; nevirthelesse it shall do good, so
he leve his bargeyn by this meane.

I merveyll that I here no tidyngges from yow hough
ye have do at the assises. The berer of this lettir is
a comon carier, and was at Norwich on Satirday, and
brought me lettirs from other men, but your servaunts
inquere nat diligently after the comyng of cariers and
other men. Wretyn at London the Wednesday next
after Lammes day.

Ye shall have lettirs of me this weke.

JOHN PASTON.

520.

A.D. 1465, 7 Aug.
JOHN PASTON TO MARGARET PASTON AND OTHERS.

[From Paston MSS., B.M.]

This is evidently the letter referred to in the beginning of the last.

*To my mastresse, Margret Paston, James Gresham
and Ric. Calle.*

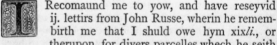

Recomaund me to yow, and have reseyvid
ij. lettirs from John Russe, wherin he remem-
birth me that I shuld owe hym xix*li.*, or
therupon, for divers parcelles whech he seith
he shuld have deliverid in to myn hows, wherof he
seith xiiij*li.* was deliverid in to myn howse ij. yere
g[oon], and that I had a bille deliverid me therof, and
the remnaunt sithen, and desireth of me payment of
the seid xix*li.* Wherfore I certi[fye] yow as I undirstand in the mater; ye may lete John Russe come to
yow and take such a direccion in the mater as reason

and trought woll. I lete yow wete that abought ij.
yer goo the seid John Russe deliverid me first a bille
of the seid xiiij. [*li.*], and I examined the parcelles;
and as I remembir xj*li.* was my dewte, wherof the
certeyn somme is writen in my blak book of foreyn
reseytes that yere, and the remnaunt was Ric. Calles
dewte, wherof he was allowed, savyng apart was Elys
dewte. And as for the seid xj*li.*, I offerid the seid
John Russe payment in hand at that tyme, and desired
hym he shuld no more send in to myn howse, and
warnyd yow and Richard that ye shuld no more stuffe
take in to myn hows without ye payd in hand, nowther
of hym ner of non other. And the seid John Russe
prayd me to remembir that I had grauntyd hym the
maner of Akthorp in Leystoft, at a certeyn prise, as it
apperyd by writyng undir my seall, and desired me
that I wold take the seid somme in party of payment.
And I told hym that as for such mony that shuld
come from hym for that lond, I wold take it of hym
and ley it up by the self, that I myght purchase other
lond therwith, bicause I wold lesse Fastolffs lyvelode
for the college, but I wold pay hym his dewte without
any stoppage. And he thanne desired me to take
that same xj*li.* and ley it up to the same use, seying to
me that it was as good to do so as I for to take it
hym, and he to take it me ayen. And thus he and I
agreed, and departed, and thanne he prayd me to take
more chafar of hym, whech I denyed. And nough I
merveyll what shuld cause hym to aske mony for
that dewte ; neverthelesse I deme he supposith that
he coud not opteyne his bargeyn by me, bicause
of the trobill that it standyth in ; and for that or
for some other cause he repentyth his bargeyn and
woll nomore of it. Wherfore send for hym, and take
James Gresham or some of your frends and Richard
Calle, and fele what he menyth ; and if ye can fynd hym
disposed to leve his bargeyn yet, though I myghte kepe
stille the seid mony I wold he shuld not lese therby.
Nevirthelesse if he woll refuse his bargeyn, thanne take

ayen the writyng that he hath of that bargeyn and a
writyng of his hand that he dischargyth me of the
graunt that I mad hym of that same bargeyn. And
thanne loke that ye enquere what mony he hath
reseyvid of the seid maner in my tyme, wherof the
ferme is vj*li.* yerly whech I suffird hym to occupie to
his owne use by fors of the seid bargeyn all my tyme ;
and aftir the parcellis cast what I have had of hym ;
abbate therof the mony that he hath reseyvid of the
seid maner, and also as moch of the xiiij*li.* as the seid
Ric. Calle and Elys owen, wher of he is alowid ; and
thanne see that the seid John Russe be content of the
remnaunt of his parcellis that is dew by me, but loke
ye pay non other mennes dewtes.

Also the seid John Russe writyth in his lettir that
rather thanne he shuld fayle this mony that I wold lend
hym asmoch to pay ayen at Cristemasse ; wherfore, if
he leve his bargeyn I woll ye lend hym asmoch mony
over his dewte as shall make up xx*li.*, takyng of hym
suerte to pay ayen at Cristemasse, as he writyth ; in
case be that he will kepe stille his bargeyn, thanne
ye may answere hym it is no reason that he shuld
aske me any part of that mony ayen, for he owyth
that and moch more.

Item, the seyd John Rus sent me heder a man for
this mater only with in thes ij. daijs. Wherfor let him
know an ansue letyng (?) for I fel well (?) he hath mad
agret bargen but late, wherfor he hath mor nede of
mony now, and I wol do for hym that I may resonably.
Nevertheles his wryting merveylith me that he askith
thes mony as dewte, wheche he toke me for parte of
my payment. I deme it comith not all of his owne
disposicion. Inquier ye that ye can what it menith.
God kepe yow. Wret the Wednisday nex Lammes.

Yowr JOHN PASTON.

In cas ye han Drayton in any quiete take sewertie
of yowr tenants for paiment as I have wret befor.

521.

A.D. 1465.—John Estgate to ————.

[From Paston MSS., B.M.]

The writer of this letter is reported to be dead in No. 523, which was written on the 18th August 1465. We have little doubt, however, that this belongs to the same year, as the names of Robert Ippeswell and John Salet occur in the correspondence more than once about this time.

SER, ze sent to me a letter conteynyng the substaunce of the processe off Mr. Robert Ippyswell for the mater off the codicill of Nicholas Pykeryng, &c. Me mervelyt gretly off the certificat off Mr. Robert in that be halve, for this is the truthe as forth forth as I kan remembre me. The codicill had nether day nor place lymyte, qwer or qwan it xuld a ben mad ; qwerfor to a reprovyd that that nether was qualifyid with day nor place it had be gret foly, &c. Therfor I askyd off the juge hys accounts, and specyally the deposicionys and attestacionys off the wytteness that wer swor in the seyd codicill, &c. ; by the qwyche it mowth appere clerly qwan and qwere this codicill xuld a be made and wrete. And this sen I mad protestacion to for the seyde Mr. Robert that I wolde impugne the mater as lawe requiryd. The qwych peticion I made diverse tyme to fore moche recorde, judicialy syttyng the seyde M. R.,[1] &c. The qwyche peticion he wold not her, but seyde expresse that nether Will. Pykeryng nor non other man xuld sen his accounts nor knowe qwat the deposicion wer in that parte this mater was comownyd to for Mr. John Selet and my mayster and yours diverse tymys, and ever he seyde we xuld not sen the seyde deposicions. And so qwat sum ever he hath certyfyid, this is the truthe, God to wetenesse and all Seynts, qwo preserve zow evermore.

And I pray zow to declare this to my mayster and zours ; and comende me hertly to hys good mayster-chep. And God sende hym victorye off all hys elmyes, and so pray all hys well wyllers at Norwich.

JOHN ESTGATE.

[1] Master of the Rolls.

522.

A.D. 1465.
WILL OF NICHOLAS PICKERING.

[From Paston MSS., B.M.]

From the contents of the preceding letter it is probable that this document was drawn up in 1465. Blomefield, indeed, states (vol. ii. p. 221) that Nicholas Pickering was buried in the steeple of Filby church in 1466. But the date may be an error, for he certainly seems to have been dead in or before 1465.

To alle trewe Cristen pepill the wiche these present letteres schall se or here, Roberd Banyngham, confessour to Nicholas Pekeryng of Filby, Alson the wyfe of the seide Nicholas, Roger Silveryn, John Herte of Cowteshall, Robarde Yoxsale, Richarde Hawe, Robarde Manufrac (?), John Case, servaunt of the forseid Nicholas, and Henry Becham, servaunt of the seide Nicholas, and Thomas Page of Beston, sende gretyng in oure Lorde. Where it is merytory nedefull to bere wytenesse of troughthe, alle ye mot knowe us that we herde the forseide Nicholas Pekeryng seyn, lying on his dede bedde, these wordes folwyng, as we willen answere before God, that whanne William Pekeryng, sone of the seide Nicholas rekenyd with his fadir for xx. quarteres barly that the seid William cleymed of his faderys yifte to his mariage; and for vij. dayes cariage of corne in hervest, and for als a thou- sande waltyle that his fadir had fro ye seide Williams wyfes place, the wiche reknyng greved the seide Nicholas his fadir, and seide, "Thou comyst in with many bak rekenyngges. Remembre the that thou hast be the costlyest childe that evere I hadde, and how that I yaf ye x. acres of fre londe, and [1] a place in mariage, and many othir thyngges that is muche better than all thi bak rekinyngges. And I have now yove ye other x. acres of fre londe aftir my discesse; and me thynketh be the thou heldest the not lowest, but woldest have all. But on thyng I shall sey to the; if thou trouble John, thy brother, or ony of myn executores, or cleyme ony more londes or goodys that evere were myne, I shal yeve ye Goddys curse and myn, for thou hast be ever frowarde to me." In witnesse and recorde herof we have sette oure sealys.

To alle trewe Cristen pepill the qwiche these presente letters shal see or here, John Herte of Couteshale, Roberd Yoxhale, Roger Silveryn, Thomas Dawes, and Thomas Drye, sende gretyng in oure Lorde. Where it is merytory, nedefull and nedefull to bere witnesse of trought, all ye mot knowe us, that

[1] *and* repeated in MS.

we herde William Pekeryng, sone of Nicholas Pekeryng, seyn
that his fadir wolde he shulde have but x. acres of fre londe aftir
his decesse be syde other x. acres of fre londe that he yaf hym in
maryage.   In wittenesse and recorde heer of we have setto oure
seales.

Endorsed : A Testymonyall.

523.

A.D. 1465, 18 Aug.

MARGARET PASTON TO JOHN PASTON.

[From Fenn, iii. 370.]

That this letter was written in the year 1465, appears clearly by the
reference to the Assizes held at Walsingham (*See* No. 518), and the intention
which the writer intimates of visiting her husband in London.   Moreover,
the first sentence of the letter, and also the postscript, are evidently written in
answer to her husband's complaint in No. 519, that she had not written to him
what she had done at the Assizes.

*To my ryght wyrshypfull mayster, John Paston, be thys
letter delyveryd in haste.*

RYGHT wyrshypfull husbond, I recomaund me
to you.   Please it you to wyte that the cause
that I wrote to you non er [*earlier*] than I
dyde after the sessyons was by cause that
Yelverton held sessyons at Dyrham and Walsyngham
the next wyke after the assyses, and to have knowlech
what labour that was made ther, and to have send yow
werd therof.   Ther was grete labours made by the
bayly of Coshay and other for to have endytyd your
men both at Dyrham and at Walsyngham, but I pur-
vayd a mene that her [*their*] purpose was lettyd at
thos ij. tymes.

Hugh a Fen ys in Flegge.   Richard Call spake with
hym thys wyke, and he sayd to Richard that he and
his wyff wold be with me here thys wyke toward a place
of hys that he hath purchasyd of Godehreds.   Yf he
come I shall make hym gode chyre, for it ys told me
of dyvers folks that have spoke with hym sythen he

II.   Q

com in to Norffolk as thay fele by hys sayng that he awyth you ryght gode wyle.

Item, as for my comyng to you, yf it please you that I come, y hope I shull purvey so for al thyngs or I com that it shull be sayff y nogh by the grace of God tyll I com ayen; but at the reverens of God, yf ye may purvey a mene that ye may com hom your sylf; for that shall be most profortabell to you, for men cut large thongs here of other mens lether. I shull wryte to you ayen as hastely as I may. God have you in Hys kypyng. Wryten in haste at Haylesdon, the Sonday next after the Assumpsyon of our Lady.

Item, my cosyn Elysabeth Clere ys at Ormesby and your moder purposyth to be at her place at Caster thys wyke, for the pestylens ys so fervent in Norwych that thay ther [*dare?*] no lenger abyde ther, so God help; me thynkyth by my moder that she wold ryght fayn that ye dyde well and that ye myght spyde ryght well in your mater. And me thynkyth by my cosyn Clere that she wold fayn have youre gode wyll, and that she hath sworyn ryght faythfully to me that ther shall no defaute be founde in her, nor noght hath be yf the trogh myght be understond, as she hopyth it shull be herafter. She sayth ther ys no man a lyff that she hath put her truste in so moch as she hath doon in you. She sayth she wote well such langage as hath be re-portyd to you of her other wyse then she hath deservyd causyth you to be other wyse to her then ye shuld be. She had to me thys langage wypyng, and told me of dyvers other thyngs the whych ye shall have knowlych of herafter.

As for the hygh shyrf [*sheriff*] he demenyd hym ryght well her to me, and he sayd to me, as for replevyns he wold aske counseyll of lernyd men what he mygt doo therin, and as largely as he mygt do ther in, or in any other mater touchyng you, savyng hymsylf harmlys, he wold doo for you and for yours that he mygt do.

Item, I have do layd in [*caused to be laid in*] the presentacyon of Drayton, and have presentyd Sir

Thomas Hakon, parson of Felthorp, the whych is hold
ryght a gode man and wel dysposyd, and the Duck of
Suffolk hath layd in a nother; and ther shall be take
an inquisicyon ther uppon, and Mr. Styven ys your a
voked [*your advocate*] therin.   Mr. John Estgade ys
passyd to God on Thursday last passyd, whos sawle
God assoyle !   Wherof in gode feyth I am ryght sory,
for I fynd hym ryght fayth full to you.   They deyy
ryght sore in Norwych.

John Rus sayth the profets that hath be take of the
maner of Caister syn Sir John Fastolf deyd hath be
take by Sir Thomas Howys and Jenney.

By yours, M. P.

I mervayll that ye had no tythyngs from me at that
tyme that your letter was wryten, for I send you a
letter by Chytockys son that ys prenteys in London,
and the seyd letter was of the demenyng at the assyes
at Norwych and of divers other maters.   I pray you
send me word yf ye have it.   As for the replevyns
Richard Calle sayth he hath send you a awnswere of
hem, and also the copys of them.

524.

Note.

In the Introduction to Volume I., p. xxi., will be found a
document entitled " A remembrance of the worshipful kin and
ancestry of Paston, born in Paston in Gemyngham Soken."   This
paper which was printed in the Preface to Vol. V. of the original
edition, p. xliv., appears to have been composed during the life-
time of John Paston by some one who owed the family no good
will, not unlikely by Sir William Yelverton.   The contents agree
very well with the imputation made on John Paston, for which he
was imprisoned in 1465, that he was a bondman to the King.
The original of this document I have not met with.

525.

A.D. 1465, Aug.—ABSTRACT.

[From Paston MSS., B.M.]

EXAMINATIONS TOUCHING FASTOLF'S WILL.

Among the Paston MSS. in the British Museum is a small volume (Addit. MS. 27,450) of 132 pages, with a contemporary parchment cover, consisting entirely of examinations of witnesses touching Sir John Fastolf's Will. It is in two parts, separated by a blank page, the first containing the depositions of John Paston, taken in 1465, and the second those of the witnesses brought forward by Yelverton and Worcester, which were taken in 1466. We give here the substance of Part I. only. An abstract of Part II. will be found under its proper date.

John Paston examined by a commission of Thomas, Archbishop of Canterbury, addressed to John Druell, LL.D., in the cause between Sir William Yelverton, Knight, and William Worcester, pretensed executors of Sir John Fastolf, and John Paston, Esq., and Thomas Howys, executors, as is said, dated 8 July 1465.

1. Whether Sir John Fastolf made his will, dated 14 June 1459, in English, and sealed by him with his seal of arms? Answer. He made a note of articles in his will, deponent thinks in Latin, probably on that day, but it was not then sealed, and no executor was named.

2. Whether before the will was fair copied an original note of it was made on paper, and corrected and interlined by Paston? And whether that note fair copied was the true will which was sealed by Fastolf?—There was such a note, which being made, Paston went to London and waited some time, when William Worcester informed him it had been fair copied in the beginning of July. Had seen an old will long before, in which some of the articles were the same, but Fastolf altered them from time to time in consultations held with this deponent. Does not know if he did interline, but the note will show, which was then in the keeping of William Worcester, Fastolf's clerk; nor does he know if the will was drawn up from it, as he was not present at the engrossing or sealing, but hears there were several things altered.

3. Where the will is, in whose custody, and whether he have power to execute it?—The parchment sealed by Fastolf, which Worcester says was his will, was kept some time after his death at Caister, and afterwards produced in audience of the Archbishop, and there remains.

28 Aug. Examined in the Fleet.—Said he was a prisoner, wished first to speak with his counsel, and desired another notary joined with Nicholas Parker, who was not indifferent.

10, 11, 12 Dec. Appeared before the commissary in the treasurer's house of St. Paul's Cathedral, London. Examination continued.

4. Whether the said will was kept in the tower called the treasury of Sir John Fastolf at Caister till his death, and whether Paston and Howys afterwards entered and took it, and what was then done with it? Whether, since Fastolf's death it was exemplified in Latin, and sealed with Fastolf's seal, and by whom? And whether the Latin contained more or less than the English? Who exhibited the English will in audience of Canterbury? Was it the true will, or was it written and sealed after Fastolf's death?—Soon after Fastolf's death the said parchment was exhibited to Paston by Howes and Worcester. It afterwards remained in the keeping of Howes and Paston, and has since been exhibited in the audience of Canterbury. It was not translated into Latin after Fastolf's death, nor sealed, to Paston's knowledge. Does not know any will, Latin or English, to have been sealed after Fastolf's death.

5. Whether Paston exhibited any English will sealed in the audience of Canterbury?—The note made in June contained an article relative to Fastolf's college, and lands in Norfolk and Suffolk granted conditionally on their being refused by Paston. When Paston went to London, and after a time Worcester came to him, Worcester told him this note was put in parchment and sealed, with the other articles, by advice of Master John Brakley, about the beginning of July. William Bukman, now Abbot of Wymondham, then Prior of Yarmouth, was present when it was sealed, and named as a witness. He and Thomas Ingham reported that Fastolf told them at the time it was his will that Paston should have those things he had granted at the time of the seisin of the said feoffment delivered, whatever was written in the parchment. The said parchment (English) remains in the court. As to the Latin, Fastolf made on paper a schedule of executors for the Latin parchment, and told Paston and Howys that he did not mean all the executors to have administration of his goods. He also told Paston, Bracley, and Clement Felmyngham, after Paston returned from London, that he was informed the Latin will gave equal powers to all the executors, which he never intended. Fastolf made his last will in November, not altogether the same.

6. Who kept Fastolf's seal of arms and signet after his death, how long did it remain whole, and how many writings did Paston seal with them?—At Fastolf's death his seal was in a purse sealed with his signet, and placed in a chest. The signet was on his finger at death, but was afterwards placed in the chest in presence of deponent and Thomas Howys, Master John Bracley, Master Clement Felmyngham, and three servants of Fastolf's chamber, and sealed with the seals of deponent, Howys, and others. The chest remained in Fastolf's chamber, sometimes in custody of his servants, and sometimes in that of Howys. Afterwards the seals were placed in a white box sealed in the presence

of divers men in the hall of the manor, which box was delivered along with certain rings to John Stokys, who opened the box, and after inspecting the seals and rings, sealed it up again and delivered it to Roger Malmesbury, in whose custody they now remain. This deponent sealed nothing with them.

7. Whether, after Fastolf's death, Paston or any other wrote on a schedule of paper a certain grant or bargain, viz., that Paston should have Fastolf's lands and tenements in Norfolk, Suffolk, and Norwich, for 4000 marks, and that Paston and Howys should have sole administration of his goods so long as Paston was alive ; and whether after Fastolf's death it was so recently written that Paston, to dry the writing, scattered ashes over it ? And if he say it was written during Fastolf's life, by whom was it written ? By himself, or John Russe, or Friar Brakley, or whom ? And how long before Fastolf's death, and in whose presence ? And whether that sum was specified in the schedule or a blank left for it ? And whether the contents of this schedule were extracted and put in a new one ? and by whom was that written ? Whether by J. Russe ? And what time elapsed between the two writings ? And whether the second schedule contained more than the first, and what the additional matter was, and by whom added ? And whether this asserted will of Fastolf, made, as Paston pretends, on Saturday, 3 Nov. 1459, was extracted or imagined from the contents of the said bills, or either of them ? And what was the matter in the said will added to the matters in the schedules ? And how long it was before the said pretended will could be formed to the satisfaction of John Paston ?

For two years before his death Fastolf had granted that Paston should have the above lands after his death, without any condition, but for the purpose that he should found a college at Caister of seven monks or priests, and pay 5000 marks to be distributed for the soul of Sir John Fastolf ; and about that time he enfeoffed Paston and others in the said lands, declaring that that enfeoffment was to the use of the said Sir John for life, and afterwards of Paston. After this, viz., in the said month of June, Fastolf made the said articles in certain paper notes in Latin and English. Master John Brakley kept copies, which he showed to Paston after his return to London. After that, viz., in September and October, Fastolf several times requested Paston to engross the agreements made between them about the college, saying he would remit to him 1000 marks of the said 5000 marks. And in October and November he recited in certain writings that in order that he might not be disquieted with worldly affairs he had bargained with this deponent that he should have the control of all his lands from which any profit might be derived in England, and of the households and foreign expenses belonging to him, so that he should put aside as much of his dues as he could spare for the college ; and that he should have all his lands in Norfolk, Suffolk, and Norwich, for 4000 marks, which he was to pay on certain stated days to Fastolf's executors for the benefit of his soul. Two paper writings were made of the premises, one by the hand of Paston and the other by Mr. John Brakley, which are severally remaining with them. This agreement Brakley, by Fastolf's order, got written out in parchment indented, and read to Fastolf, who sealed it in his presence as Brakley reported to Paston. Afterwards, another of the said writings was read to Fastolf in the presence of Paston, Brakley, Mr. Clement Felmyngham, and others, several times in October and November. Comments were made on the reading of it by Fastolf on one occasion, when he said a certain clause was not consistent with his intention, which was that Paston and Howys should be sole administrators of his goods, and that as to his lands in Norfolk, Suffolk, and Norwich, and the college to be founded, he would dispose of them according to his agreement with Paston,—the master to have a stipend of £10, and each of the fellows of 10 marks, and that seven poor men should be found with 40s. a year each, as stated in the will. Fastolf desired his will dated in June to be corrected in these particulars, and written anew by Walter Shipdam, for whom he frequently sent on this business. Meanwhile Brakley and Paston wrote another paper in English as a memorial of Fastolf's intention, of which deponent delivered a copy under his own hand in Court. The last two lines this deponent wrote and dried with ashes in presence of Thomas Howys. The will of 14 June and that exhibited by Paston and Howys differ little or nothing in effect, except in these articles touching the college, and the sole administration given to Paston and Howys.

As to new writings after Fastolf's death. Brakley translated those words about the sole administration from English into Latin, partly before his death and partly after. After Fastolf's death Paston, Howys, and Brakley caused the said Walter Shipdam to put into form (*fecerunt dictum W. S. formare*) the last will and testament of the said Fastolf, both of the said college and of the said single administration (*de dicta singulari administratione*), and of other things in the will of June not contrary to his last will and declaration, of which several writings were drawn by Shipdam, first in paper and afterwards in parchment. As to the writing of the agreements, Brakley kept it during Fastolf's whole life, and a year after, and a copy remained with this deponent after Fastolf's death ; at which time deponent and Howys were sitting in the hall of the manor of Caister at supper when William Worcester came into the hall, and Paston and Howys, rising from supper, had a talk with Clement Felmyngham, John Brakley, and William Worcester, immediately after Fastolf's death. At that time, by the advice

of Brakley, a copy of the agreement was delivered to William
Worcester, at his request, folded up and sealed that night by
Brakley, Clement Felmyngham, and Howys. It remained in
Worcester's keeping till he rode to London, and then he left it
with the said Master John Brakley, Clement Felmyngham, and
Thomas Howys. Its tenor was transcribed on parchment by
Shipdam shortly afterwards.

526.

A.D. 1465, 14 Sept.

JOHN PASTON THE YOUNGEST TO MARGARET PASTON.

[From Fenn, iv. 224.]

It appears by Letter 529 following that Margaret Paston was in London in
September 1465. This letter must therefore have been written in that year.

*To my mastras, Margaret Paston, be this deliveryd in
hast, at London.*

FTYR all humbyll and most dwe recomendacion, as lowly as I can, I beseche yow of
your blyssyng. Plesyt yow to wet that I
have sent to my fadyr to have an answer of
syche maters as I have sent to hym for in hast, of
whyche matyrs the grettest of substans is for the
maner of Cotton, besechyng yow to remembyr hym
of the same mater, that I may have an answer in the
most hasty wyse.

Also I pray yow that myn Ante Poonyngys[1] may
be desyiryd to send me an answer of syche materys
as sche wotyth of, by hym that schall brynge me an
answer of the mater of Cotton.

Also, modyr, I beseche yow that ther may be purveyd some meane that I myth have sent me home
by the same mesenger ij. peyir hose, j. peyir blak and
an othyr payir roset, whyche be redy made for me at

[1] Elizabeth Paston, now widow of Robert Poynings; afterwards married
to Sir George Brown of Betchworth Castle, Surrey.

the hosers with the crokyd bak, next to the Blak
Freyrs Gate, within Ludgate ; John Pampyng knowyth
hym well jnow I suppose.   And [*if*] the blak hose be
payid for he wyll send me the roset un payd for.   I
beseche yow that this ger be not forget, for I have not
an hole hose for to doon ; I trowe they schall cost
both payr viij*s*.

My brodyr[1] and my sustyr Anne[2], and all the
garyson of Heylysdon fare well, blyssyd be God, and
recomand hem to yow everychon.

I pray yow voysyt the Rood of Northedor[3] and
Seynt Savyour, at Barmonsey,[4] amonge whyll ye abyd
in London, and lat my sustyr Margery[5] goo with yow
to pray to them that sche may have a good hosbond
or sche com hom ayen ; and now I pray yow send us
some tydyngys as ye wer wonte to comand me ; and
the Holy Trinyte have yow in kepyng, and my fayir
mastras of the Fleet.   Wretyn at Norwyche on Holy
Rood Daye.

> Your sone and lowly servaunt,
> J. PASTON THE YOUNGEST.

527.

A.D. 1465, Sept. ?
ANONYMOUS TO MARGARET PASTON.

[From Paston MSS., B.M.]

This letter was probably written about or before the beginning of September
1465, as the proceedings of Salet and Ipyswell on the commission of inquiry
here referred to are alluded to in a letter of Margaret Paston to her husband
on the 27th of that month.

To my mestresse, Margaret Paston, by thys letter delivered.

---

[1] Sir John Paston.—F.
[2] Anne Paston, afterwards the wife of William Yelverton.—F.
[3] The Cross at the north door of St. Paul's.
[4] The Abbey of Saint Saviour at Bermondsey, in Surrey, was founded in
1081, 15th William the Conqueror, by Alwin Child of London ; it was surrendered in 1539, 31 H. VIII., when it was pulled down, and a Fair House
built on the site by Sir Thomas Pope, Knight.—F.
[5] Margery Paston ; she afterwards married Richard Calle.—F.

PLEASE your good mastreschep to have knowlage that as thys day was Master Stevyn of
Norwich at Caster, and ther he told me he
was yesterday at Hoxhon with the Byschop
of Norwych ; and ther he seythe that ther is gret labor
mad be Master Phylyp[1] and be the baly of Cossey;
in so moche ther is mad a comission on to Master
John Salet and Master Robert Ipyswell for an inquerry
that the parson[2] that my master[3] mad last at Drayton
ys deed, as they sey, and in so moche they purpose to
put in the parson of Felthorp, as he hard sey, for the
Duk of Suffolk.   And thes he thynkyth it were a gret
urt to my master tytyll.   And also another inquerry
howe [who] ys patorne of the seyd chyrche ; and thys
is leke to come in revelicion but yf [unless] ther be gret
labore mad to morowe be tymys and that ye have a
man at Hoxhon in all hast for a newe comicion; and in
that commysion Master Stevyn wold that ye shuld have
Master Jon Salet, Master Symond Thornaham, Master
Nicholl Stanton.   And that it be mad be the avice of
Master Jon Bulman; for he told Master Stevyn he wold
do for you that he may, in so moche Master Stevyn
hathe promyssyd hym a nobyll; and so the seyd Master
Stevyn wold ye shuld send hym a letter and late hym
have knolage that Master Stevyn shall reward hym
that he shall hold hym pleasyd.

Item, a told me that a sent a letter to Sir William
Maryys of all this mater yesterday, weder ye have er
not he can not sey, but in noo wyse that ye dyskure
not Master Stevyn, for he wold not for an *Cli.* that it
ware knowe that ye knewe ther of by hym, for he
seythe gold gothe gret plenty at Hoxhon on ther part.
And yf it be labord be tymys it may be remevyd to
Caunterbury.   Also yet it is good to send to Norwich
to the seyd Sir William for the letter ar the massanger
goth, &c.

[1] Doubtless Philip Lypgate.
[2] This must be John Flowerdew, presented by John Paston and Thomas
Howes in 1461.
[3] John Paston.

528.

A.D. 1465, [21] Sept.

JOHN PASTON TO MARGARET PASTON.

[From Fenn, iv. 90.]

From the mention of "this cold winter" at the beginning of this letter we might naturally suppose that the feast "of Sent Mathe," on or about which it was written, was that of St. Matthias. which occurs on the 24th of February. But we believe the day of St. Matthew to have been intended, so that the expression must have had reference to some unusually cold weather in September. It is clear from the contents of the letter that Margaret Paston had recently been with her husband in London, and had just left him in company with Richard Calle on her return towards Norfolk. Letters for her and Richard Calle had arrived from her two sons since they departed. Now the only time, so far as I can find, that Margaret Paston ever visited her husband in London,—at all events when her sons were grown up,—was in September 1465; and on that occasion Calle was with her, and everything else agrees. Indeed, no one can doubt that the latter portion of the letter immediately following was written in answer to this letter.

To my Cosyn Margret Paston.

YN owne dere sovereyn lady, I recomaund me to yow, and thank yow of the gret chere that ye mad me here to my gret cost and charge and labour. No more at thys tyme, but that I pray yow ye woll send me hedir ij. clue of worsted [1] for dobletts, to happe me thys cold wynter; and that ye inquere where William Paston bought his tepet of fyne worsted, whech is almost like silk, and if that be mech fyner thanne that he shuld bye me after vij. or viij.s., thanne by me a quarter and the nayle therof for colers, thow it be derer thanne the tother, for I wold make my doblet all worsted for worship of Norffolk, rather thanne like Gonnores doblet.

Item, as for the mater of the jx.^{xx}·*li.* askyd by my Lady of Bedford [2] for the maner of Westthirrok,

---

[1] Worsted is a small market-town in the most east part of the county of Norfolk, formerly famous for the manufacture of those stuffs which still bear its name, and of which, for the worship of Norfolk, J. Paston desired his doublet to be made.—F.

[2] Jaquetta, daughter of Peter of Luxembourg, Earl of Saint Pol, was the second wife of John, Duke of Bedford, the Regent of France during Henry VI.'s minority. She was married to him in 1433, and after his decease, in 1435, she became the wife of Sir Richard Wydvile, and died in 1472.

where as Sir Thomas Howes saith that he hath no
wrytyng therof, but that Sir John Fastolf purchased
the seid maner, and payd serteyn money in ernest,
and aftirward graunted his bargeyn to the Duc of
Bedford, and so the money that he toke was for the
mony that he had payd.   Peraventure Sir Thomas
hath writyng therof, and knowyth it not; for if ther be
any such mony payd upon any bargeyn he shall fynd
it in Kyrtlyngs bocks that was Sir John Fastolfs
reseyver, and it was abought such tyme as the Duc
of Bedford was last in Inglond, whech, as it is told
me, was the viij. yere of Kyng Herry the fift, or the
viij. yere of Kyng Herry the sext, and the somme
that he payd for the seid bargeyn was CCC. marks.
Also he shall fynd, the xxij. yere of Kyng Herry or
ther abought, in the acompts of on of Fastolfs Re-
seyvors at London, that ther was take of Sir Thomas
Tyrell, and of the Duchesse of Excestre,[1] that was wif
to Sir Lowes John, fermours of the seid maner, serteyn
mony for repayment of part of the seid CCC. marks.
Also he shall fynd in yeres after that, or in that yere,
or ther aboutes, that Sir John Fastolf reseyved mony
of my Lord Revers[2] that now is, by the name of
Richard Wydevile, for his owne dette dew to Sir John
Fastolf; wherfore, if Sir Thomas be trewe to his

[1] Anne, eldest daughter of John Montacute, third Earl of Salisbury,
married, 1st., Sir Richard Hankford, Knight ; 2dly, Sir Lewis John, Knight
(whose will was proved in 1442) ; and 3dly, John Holland, who was
created Duke of Exeter 6th January 1443, and died in 1446. Fenn erroneously supposed the lady to have been the widow of Thomas Beaufort, a
previous Duke of Exeter, who died in 1426. This Beaufort, Duke of Exeter,
married Margaret, daughter and heir of Sir Thomas Nevill, but his wife
did not survive him, as Fenn supposed, for at his death he was found to
have been tenant of her lands for life by the law of England. Fenn's note
on this passage is, however, so interesting that we must quote a part of it.
Beaufort, Duke of Exeter, was buried in the Abbey of Bury St Edmund's.
"On digging," he says, "amongst the ruins of this Abbey, the body of the
Duke was found, on the 20th of February 1772, wrapt in lead, and entire.
The face, hair, and every part were perfect, and the flesh solid, but being
exposed to the air, the body soon became offensive. . . . . . I procured
some of the hair, which was of a fine brown colour, and very flexible."

[2] Sir Richard Wydvile, in 1448, was created Baron Rivers of Grafton, in
Northamptonshire, and elected a Knight of the Garter. His daughter
Elizabeth afterwards became the Queen of Edward IV., who then advanced
her father to the dignity of Earl Rivers. He was seized by the Lancaster
mutineers, and beheaded at Banbury in 1469.—F.

master, lete hym do his devoir to make that Worseter,
whech is uphold be hym with the deds goods, to be
trewe to his master, or ellis it is tyme for Sir Thomas
to forsake hym, and helpe to punyssh hym, or men
mast sey that Sir Thomas is not trewe ; and more over
lete Sir Thomas examine what he can fynd in this
mater that I sent hym werd of, whech mater he shall
fynd in the seid Reseyvours bocks, if he list to seke it.

Item, on the day after your departyng, I reseyved
letters by Will. Ros from your sones to me, and to
yow, and to Ric. Calle, &c.

Item, I shall telle you a tale,
Pampyng and I have picked your male [1]
And taken out pesis [2] v.,
For upon trust of Calles promise, we may soon
onthryve ;
And, if Calle bryng us hedir xx*li.*,
Ye shall have your peses ayen, good and round ;
Or ellis, if he woll not pay yow the valew of the
peses, there
To the post do nayle his ere ;
Or ellis do hym some other wrongs,
For I will no more in his defaut borough ;
And but if the reseyvyng of my livelod be better
plyed
He shall Crists ours and mine clene tryed ; [3]
And loke ye be mery and take no thought,
For thys ryme is cunnyngly wrought.
My Lord Persy [4] and all this house
Recomaund them to yow, dogge, catte, and mowse,
And wysshe ye had be here stille,

---

[1] Male, or Mail, is a trunk or portmanteau. It is to be observed, that in
the original letter the verses do not finish the line but are written as
prose.—F.

[2] Pieces of money.

[3] I do not understand this line.—F.—Surely " ours " must be a misreading
of " curs " (curse)?

[4] Henry, Lord Percy, son and heir of Henry Percy, Earl of Northumberland, who was killed at the battle of Towton in 1461, by Eleanor, grand-
daughter and heir of Robert, Lord Poynings.

His father having been attainted, he continued to be called Lord Percy ;
but he was afterwards fully restored both in blood and title.

For the sey ye are a good gille.[1]
No more to you at this tyme,
But God hym save that mad this ryme.
Wret the   of Sent Mathe,[2]
By yowr trew and trustie husband, J. P.

529.

A.D. 1465, 27 Sept.
MARGARET PASTON TO JOHN PASTON.

[From Paston MSS., B.M.]

This letter is apostyled in the handwriting of John Paston, and numbered "IIII." at the head, showing that it is of the same sequence as the next, which is numbered "V." and dated on the very same day. In fact, the latter is clearly nothing but a postscript to this, and bears the address upon the back, which this does not.

RYGHT wourchipful husbonde, I recomaunde me to yow, dyssyryng hertely to here of yowr welfare, thankyng yow of yowr grett chere that ye made me, and of the coste that ye dede on me. Ye dede more cost thanne my wylle was that ye choulde do, but that it plesyd yow to do so, God gyf me grase to do that may plese yow. Plesyt yow to wet that on Fryday after myn departyng frome yow I was at Sudbury and spake with the schreve, and Ric. Calle toke hym the ij. writts, and he brake them, and Ric. hathe the copes of them; and he seyde he wolde send the writts to hys undre-schryf and a leter therwyth, chargyng hym that he schowlde do ther ine as largely as he owt to do. And I and Ric. informyd hym of the demenyng of hys undrchryf, how parciall he hade be with the other partye, bothe in that mater, and also for the accionnys beyng in the scher; and he was nothyng wel plesyd of the demenyng of hys undreschef, and he hat wretyn to hym that he choulde be indeferent for bothe

Vic. Norfolk pro ovibus.

Answer of the writts and of the replevyn.

---

[1] An agreeable companion.—F.
[2] St. Matthew's Day is the 21st September.

partyes acordyng to the lawe, bothe for that materys and for alle other. What the undreschryf wylle do therin I wot ner, for he is not yet spokyn with.

Item, as for Cotton, I entryd in to the plase as on Sunday last was, and ther I abode tyll un Wednysday last pasyd. I have left ther John Paston the yonger, Wykes, and other xij. men for to receive the profyttes of the maner; and ayenst the day of kepyng of the corte, I hope ther shall be more to streynkyth them, yf it nede. John Paston hath be with my lorde of Norfolk seyth [*since*] we entryd, and dyssyryd his good lorchyp to streynth hym with hys howsolde men and other yf nede be; and he hath promysyd he would do so. And I sent Ric. Calle on Tusday to Knevett, dysyryng hym that he woulde sende to hys baley and tenaunts at Mendlesham, that thei choulde be redy to come to John Paston whan he sent for them; and he sent a man of his forthwith, chargyng them in aney wyse that they choulde do so. And he sent me wourde be Ric. and hys sonne also, yf wee were not stronge inough, that owther he or hys sonne, or bothe yf nede were, would come with suche feleschipp as they coude gett abowt them, and that thei woulde do as feythfully as they kowde for yow, bothe in that mater and in alle other.

Item, on Saterday last was, Jenney ded warne a corte at Calcotte to be holde ther in hys name as on Tusday last was, and Debenham de[d] charge another court ther the Sunday next after to be holde ther the same Tusday in hys name. And Daubeney had knowleche ther of, and he dede send on Sunday at nyght to yowr elder sonne, for to have some men fro thens; and so he sent Wykes and Bernay to hym on Monday in the mornyng. And assone as thei were come to Castre thei sent for men ther in the contre, and so they gett them in to a iij.$^{xx.}$ men; and Daubeney and Wekes and Bernay rod to Calcott the same Munday at nyght with ther felechyp, and ther kept them prevye in the pl[a]se, so that non of alle the

margin notes:

Margareta Paston intravit manerium Cotton die Dominica proxima ante festum Michaelis.

I thank yow of your de- menyng at Cotton.

Remembir Nakton.

Mokenge of Jenney and Debenham at Calcotes the Tuisday next biiore Sen Migchell.

tenaunts kneue them ther, saf Rysyngs wyff and her
howsolde, tylle the Theusday at x. of the cloke.   And
than Sir Thomas Brews, Debunham the fadre,[1] and
the knyt hys sonne,[2] Jenney, Mykelfylde younger,
Jermyn, and younge Jernyngham, and the Baley of
Motforde, with other to the noumbre of a iij.ˣˣ· persones,
coum fro the sessionnys at Becklys, the whech thei
hade keppt ther on the day byfor, coume to Seynt
Olevys, and ther thei teryed and dynyd.   And whan
thei had dynyd, Sir Gylberde Debenham came to
Calcott with xx. hors for to wett what felechipp ther
was in the plase.   And than Wekes aspyed them commyng ; and he and Bernay and ij. with them rode owt
to a' spoke with them.   And whan Sir Gilberd aspyd
them comyng, he and his felechipp flede and rode
ayen to Seynt Olovys.   And than they sent young
Jernyngham and the Baley of Mottforde to yowr men
lettyng hem wete that the Justice of the Pese wer
coum doune with Debunham and Jenney, to se that
the pese choulde be kepte, and that thei choulde entre
and kepe the courte in pesible wyse.   And yowr
men answeryd and seyd that they knewe no man was
possessyd ther in, ner hade no ryght therin but ye,
and so in your name, and in your ryght they seyd
they woulde kepyt.   And so they yede ayen with thys
answer, and wer put fromme ther purp[o]se that day.
And all the tenaunts bestes wer put fro Calcalcott[3]
fee, and challe be tylle other remedy maye be hadde.
Yowr men woulde not kepe ther a cort that daye by
cause it was warnyd by the tother parte, but we wyl
do warne a corte and kepyt, I hope in hast.   Ye wyll
laugh for to here alle the processe of the demenyng
ther, wheche wer to longe to writt at thys tyme.
Bernay challe telle yow whane he come ; but he challe
not come to yow tylle after Seynt Feythesmesse,[4] that
he maye bryng yow answeres of other materys.   It is
tolde me the sessionys choulle be her at Norwiche

Marginal notes (left column):

Now your cost is doon, consideryng your frends be corayges and your enemyes discoraged, gadir up the profits in all goodly hast, and that I may see acompt for this trobill tyme.

Veneat[*sic*] Barney.

Cessiones Norwici

---

[1] Gilbert Debenham, Sen., Esq.
[2] Sir Gilbert Debenham.   [3] So in MS.   [4] Oct. 6th.

on Tusday next comyng, and in Suffolk the Sessionys et Dunwici Martis proximo post festum Michelis.
challe be the same Tusday owther at Dounwyche or at
Ypswyche.   I suppose ther challe be labowr ayenst
soume of our folks ther, but we cholle assay to lete
ther pourpose yf we maye.   It is tolde me yf ther De pruden-cia custo-diendi Heyles-don. Tenentes comitis Oxoniæ pro custodia Cotton.
hade no folks a' be left here in thys plase whyll I have
be owt, they choulde a' be neue masters her by thys
tyme ; therfor it is not good to leve it alone yett.

Item, Arblaster hathe sent a letter to myn Lorde of
Oxenefords tenaunts that be nerrest abowt Cotton to
help John Paston yf they be sent to, &c.

Item, I was thys daye with myn Lorde of Norwyche Episcopus Norwici pro ecclesia de Drayton.
at Thorppe, and informyd hym of the demenyng of
the mater for Drayton chyrche, and of alle the demenyng and parcialte of Master John Solatt and Ypswell;
and also I informyd what disposission that they were
of that were upon the quest.   And in good feyth me Lete yowr counsell comone with hym, but thei may sey they knowe not myn evidens nor titell, ner have no mor to do by my writynge that I sent yow thanne to avyse hough I shall take myn accion, and that in that accion I have as good titell as my Lord of Norwich hath to the chirch of Thorp.
thynkyth by hym that he is ryght ille plesyd that the
mater was so gydyt.   He seyde to me ryght pleynly
that the Jugis dede not therin as thei owght to do,
and he seyd thowe I hadde hade noo councell, the
he howght of ryght to have assyngyd me councell
suche as I hadde dyssyrid ; but he seyde he wyst well
he dede in that mater as he have do in other materys
byfor.   Me thynkyth by suche thynges I harde ther
that the seyd Master John ner the tother is not grettly
in conseyt at thys tyme ; and so tolde me Aschefylde
in councell.   What the cause was he myght have no
leyser to telle me.   I mevyd my lorde in the mater
acordyng to the intent of yowr wrytyng yf aney axcion
wer take ; and he seyd feythefully yf it myght prevayle
yow, he woulde with ryght good wylle that it choulde
be doo ; and ellys he woulde not in noo wyse that it
choulde be doo.   And he dyssyryde me to sende to
hym suche as be of yowr councell lernyd, that they
myght comune with hym therin, for he seyd he woulde
not ye choulde take non axcion therin withowt it
myght provayle.   He was well payed that I tolde hym
that ye woulde not do therin withowt hys knowleche

H.   R

and assent; and he seyd he woulde do therin as he
woulde do yf the mater wer hys owne.   Be avyse of
yowr councell, I purpose to sende Loumnowr and Playter to commone with hym therin.   He seyd he woulde
feyne that ye wer owt of troble ; and he seyd, yf he
myght doo owght to helppe yow forwarde in aney of
yowr materys, he swore by heys feythe he wode do hys

Episcopus
apud
London.

parte feythfully therin.   He purp[o]syd to be at London
thys terme, and thanne he seyd he woulde speke with
yow of maney thyngs ; he wycheyd herteley that he
myght have spoke with yow on owr.   He mevyd to

Cornwayle me of a mater of a jentyllman of Cornale.   He seyd
he woulde speke with yow therof her after ; yf it myght
be browt to, it myght do meche good in maney thyngis.
I harde yow onys speke of the same ; ye tolde me ye
hade be mevyd to therof by other.

Item, I received at letter frome yow yesterday,
wherof I thanke yow hertely, and I praye yow that I
maye be as ye writt.   And as for suche materys as Sir
Thomas Howys choulde be spoke to for [1] I sent Ric.
Calle this day to speke with hym, but he myght not
speke with hym ; but as hastely as I may I challe do
myn parte to spede the erands and other.   It is tolde

Ecclesia
de Mautby.

me that Sir Thomas wyll ressyng Mautby chyrche,
and yf it plesyd yow to geve it to on Sir Thomas
Lyndis, I truste verely that ye choulde leke hym
ryght well, for he is rit a prystly man and vertusly
dysposyd.   I have knowe hym this xx. yer and
mor ; he was brother to the goode parsone of
Seynt Michellys that ye lovyd ryght well; and yf he
myght havyt he woulde kepe an howsolde therupon
and bylde (?) well the plase (?); and therof have it
grete nede, for it is now rit evyll reparyd, and I wott
well he woll be rulyd and gydyt as ye wyll have hym.
I praye yow, yf it plese yow that he have it, that it

Wursted. lekyth yow to sende me an answer by the berrer herof.

Item, I have do spoke for yowr worstede [2] but ye
may not have it tylle Halowmesse ; and thane I am

_____
[1] See No. 528.   [2] See No. 528.

promysyd ye challe have as fyne as maye be made.
Ric. Calle challe bryng it up with hym.

Wretyn the Fryday next before Michelmas day.

530.

A.D. 1465, 27 Sept.

MARGARET PASTON TO JOHN PASTON.

[From Paston MSS., B.M.]

This letter is apostyled in the handwriting of John Paston, and numbered
"V" at the head. As it refers to Paston's dispute with the Duke of Suffolk
about the manors of Hellesden and Drayton, it must belong to the year 1465.
The reader will also perceive that it contains an allusion to John Paston's
imprisonment in the Fleet, and to my Lord Percy, who is mentioned in Letter
528, and who must have been a fellow prisoner of Paston's.

To my ryght worschipfull husbond, John Paston, in haste.

TEM, it was tolde me thys day that Master
John Salatt hathe made a serge in the regestre
this monethe aftre the wylles and testements
of suche as hought the maners of Heylesdon
and Drayton this c. yere, and be that hathe they founde
suche evidence as schal be gret strengthyng to the
Duks tittle, as it is seide. I undrestonde verely that
Mastre John Salet is all on that partye, and no thyng
with you.

To get a copy [of] that he hath . . hed; notwith-standyng [I] wote well thei have found non such evidens as ye wene.

Item, as for the bill that ye sent to Sir Thomas
Howys touchyng on Edmond Carvyll and on Fraunces,
I wote ner whether he had hem or nought, for he is
not spoken with yett in the maters. As wee spede owr
materys, we chall sende yow answers of them as hastely as we maye. At the reverense of God, spede ye
yowr materys that ye maye come owte of that loggyng
that ye ar in as hastely as ye maye, for I have non
fansey with some of the felechipp. I tolde yow, as
me thowth, I praye yow be ware, &c.

I praye yow yf it plese yow that I may be recom-
maundyd to my Lorde Percy, and to myn mastres, and

to my Lorde Abott. And I pray God bryng yow and
them owt of troble, and send yow good spede in alle
yowr materys. Wretyn in hast, the Fryday next afor
Michellmes.   Be yowr,   M. P.

Yf it plese yow to send aney thyng by the berer
herof, he is trusty inough.

531.

A.D. 1465, 3 Oct.
SIR JOHN PASTON TO JOHN PASTON.

[From Fenn, iv. 80.]

The signature of this letter, according to the fac-simile referred to by Fenn,
is that of Sir John Paston, the eldest son of the person addressed. The date
is undoubtedly 1465, as it will be seen by Letter 529 that Margaret Paston
entered Cotton on Sunday before Michaelmas in that year.

*To my ryth reverrend and worchepfull fadyr, John
Paston, be thys delyveryd.*

AFTYR all humbyll and most due recomendacion, as lowly as I can, I beseche yow of your
blyssyng. Plesyt yow to have knowlege that
as on Sonday next be for Myhelmas Day, as
my modyr came fro London ward, sche cam homward
by Cotton, and sche sent for me to Heylysdon to
come to hyr thedyr, and so I have ben in the plase
ever sethyn. And as sone as Myhelmas Day was past,
I begane to dystreyne the tenants, and gadryd some
syllvyr, as myche, I trowe, as wyll pay for our costs;
and yet I cepe here ryth a good felawschep, and
mor wer promysyd me, whyche that came not to me,
wherby I was ner deseyvyd. For when Debnam herd
sey how that I began to gadyr sylvyr, he reysyd many
men with in j. daye and an halfe, to the nombyr of
iij^c. men, as I was credebly assartaynyed by a yeman
of the chambyr of my Lordys [1] that owythe me good

---

[1] The Duke of Norfolk.

wyll, whech yeman, as sone as he had sene ther
felauschep, rod streyth to my Lord and informyd hym
of it ; and also he informyd my Lord how that I had
gadryd a nothyr gret felashschep, whyche felawschep
he namyd more then we wer by j^c. and an halfe and
yett more. And he seyd on to my Lord and my Lady,
and to their consell, that with owt that my Lord took
a dyrectyon in the mater, that ther wer leek to be do
gret harme on bothe oure pertyes, wheche wer a gret
dysworchep to my Lord, consederyng how that he
takyth us bothe for hys men, and so we be knowyn
well inow. Upon whyche informacion, and dysworchep to my Lord, that tweyn of hys men schold debat
so ner hym, contrary to the Kyngs pese, consedryd of
my Lord and my Lady and ther cownsell, my Lord
sent for me and Syr Gylberd Debnam to come to hym
to Framlyngham bothe, and as it fortunyd well my
modyr come to me to Cotton not half an owyr be for
that the mesenger came to me fro my Lord, wheche
was late upon Twysday last past at nyth; and the next
day on the mornyng I rod to my Lord to Framlyngham, and so ded Syr Gylberd also. And as sone as we
wer come, we wer sent for to come to my Lord, and
when we come to my Lord, he desiyryd of us bothe
that we schold neythyrthyr gadyr no felawschep, but
syche men as we had gadryd that we schold send hem
home a yen, and that the coort schold be contenuyd
in to the tyme that my Lord, or suche as he wold
asyngne, had spok bothe with yow and Yelverton and
Jenney, and that on indeferent man chosyn by us
bothe schold be assynyd to kepe the plase in to the
tyme that ye and they wer spook with.

And then I answed my Lord, and seyd how that at
that tyme I had my maistyr within the maner of Cotton,
whyche was my modyr, and in to the tyme that I had
spook with hyr I cowd geve none answer ; and so my
Lord sent Rychord Fulmerston, berer hereof, to my
modyr thys day for an answer, whyche answer he
schold bryng to my Lord to London, for my Lord rod

to Londons word as yesterday, and the soner be cause
he trustyd to have a good end of this mater and alle
othyr be twyx yow, whyche he takyth for a gret worchep to hym, and a gret avantage bothe, and he cowd
bryng this mater abowt, for then he wold trust to have
your servyse, alle whyche wer to hym gret tresour
and avantage.

And this was the answer that my modyr and I gave
hym, that at the instans of my Lord and my Ladye we
wold do thus myche as for to put the coort in con-
tenuans, and no more to receyve of the profyts of the
maner than we had, and had dystresid for tyll in to
the tym that sche and I had werd ayen fro my Lord
and yow, if so wer that they wold neythyr mak entreys
nor dystreyn the tenantys, nor chepe no coort mor then
we wold do.   And we told Rychord Fulmerston that
thys my modyr and I ded at the instans and gret
request of my Lord, be cause my Lord intendyd pes,
whyche resonably we wold not be ayenst, and yet we
seyd we knew well that we schold have no thank of
yow when ye knew of it, with owt it wer be cause we
ded it at my Lordys instans.   But be for thys answer
we had receyvyd as myche sylvyr full ner as Rychord
Calle sent us bokys of for to gadyryt bye ; and as for
the possessyon of the plase, we told hym that we wold
kepe it, and Syr Gylberd agreyd, so that Yelverton and
Jeney would do the same; for it was tyme for hym to
sey so, for my Lord told hym that he wold hym fast
by the feet ellys, to be suyr of hym, that he schold
make non insurreccions in to the tyme that my Lord
came ayen fro London.

I wene, and so dothe my modyr bothe, that thys
appoyntment was mad in good tyme; for I was deseyvyd of bettyr than an C. men and an halfe that I had
promyse of to have come to me when I sent for hem.
Thys promes had I befor that I sent to yow the last
lettyr the daye aftyr Seynt Myhell.   Jenney herd seye
that I cepyd Cotton, and he rod to Nacton, and ther
held a cort and receyvyd the profytys of the maner.

I beseche yow that I may have knowlage in hast fro yow how ye wyll that I be demenyd in thys mater and in al othyr, and I schal aplye me to fulfyll your intent in them to my power by the grace of God, whom I beseche have yow in guydyng, and sende yow yowyr herts desyir. Wretyn at Hemnalle Halle, in Cotton, the Thursday next befor Seynt Feythe.

My modyr recomandyth her to yow, and preyith yow to hold hyr excusyd that sche wrytyth not to yow at thys tyme, for sche may have no leyser. The berer her of schall informe yow whedyr Jeney wyll agre to thys appoyntment or not. I thynk he dar do non othyr wyse.

Your sone and lowly servaunt,
JOHN PASTON.

532.

A.D. 1465, 12 Oct.—THE DUKE OF NORFOLK TO JOHN PASTON, THE YOUNGEST.

[From Fenn, iv. 62.]

John Mowbray, third Duke of Norfolk, died on the 6th November 1461. It appears by the Inquisitions *post mortem*, 1 Edward IV., No. 46, that John, his son and successor in the title, was seventeen years old on St. Luke's Day (18th October) in that year. He must therefore have been born on the 18th October 1444, and would have been of full age on Friday, 18th October 1465. The John Paston, Esq., to whom this letter was addressed, must have been the youngest of that name, who, as we have seen already, had been serving in the Duke's household. His father was at this time a prisoner in the Fleet, so that the letter could not have been intended for him.

To owr trusty and enterly beloved servaunt, John Paston, Esquyr.

THE DEUKE OF NORFF.

RYGHT welbeloved servaunt, y grete yow hertly welle, sertefyng that we shulle be at fulle age on Fryday nexst comyng. Wherfor, wele consayled be the Lordes of owr Consayle and oder of owr Consayle, that ye, on of owr servaunts of howsholde, with oder, be with us at London on

Fryday or Saterday nexst comyng at the ffurdest, too
a companye us thann too owr worshyp, for we shull
have thann levery of owr landes and offyces; and that
ye ffayle us not, as ye woll have owr good Lordeshyp
in tyme comyng; and also that ye doo warne owr
ffeede men [1] and servaunts, suche as be nye too yow,
that they be ther thann in owr leverey.   Y wreton
the xij. day of October.   NORFF.

533.

A.D. 1465, 17 Oct.
MARGARET PASTON TO JOHN PASTON.

[From Paston MSS., B.M.]

This letter is not addressed, but seems undoubtedly to have been intended
for the writer's husband. The attack upon the lodge at Hellesden here
referred to was in 1465, as appears by the letter immediately following.

ON Tuesday in the morwyn whas John Botiller,
otherwyse callid John Palmer, and Davy
Arnald your cook, and William Malthows of
Aylsham, takyn at Heylesdon be the balyf of
Ey callid Bottisforth, and led for to Cossey, and ther
thei kepe hem yet with ought any warant or autoryte
of Justice of Peas.   And thei saye thei will carie hem
forth to Ey preson, and as many as thei may gete more
of your men and tenaunts, that thei may know that
owe yow good wyll or hath be to you ward, thei be
thret to be slayn or presoned.   The Duke came to
Norwich [2] on Tuesday at x. of clok with the nombre
of v. hundred men.   And he sent after the Meyr and
Alderman with the Sherefs desiryng hem in the Kyngs
name that thei shuld take an enqueraunce of the
constablys of every ward with in the cyte what men
shuld a go on your party to have holpyn or socowryd
your men at any tyme of thes gaderyngs, and if any

1 Those who held lands of the Duke as their superior.
2 "Norwich."—This word is interlined, tho writer having originally written "this town," and afterwards struck out the word "town."

thei cowde fynde, that thei shuld take and arest hym
and correct hym, and also certifie hym the names on
Wyndenesse day [*Wednesday*] be viij. of clok. Which
the Meyr dede, and wull do anythyng that he may for
hym and his. And her up on the Meyr hath arestid
on that was with me callid Roberd Lovegold, braser,
and threte hym that he shall be hanged be the nek;
wherfor I wuld that ther myght come down a writ to
remeve hym if ye thynk it be to do. He was not with
me not save that Harleston and other mad the assaught
up on me and Lammesse ; he is right good and feythfull on to you, and therfore I wuld he had help. I
have non man at this tyme to avayte upon me that
dare be avowyd but Litill John. William Nawton is
here with me, but he dare not ben avowyd, for he is
sore thret. It is told me the old Lady and the Duke
is set fervently ageyn us be the enformacion of
Harlesdon, the Bayly of Cossey and Andrewys and
Doget the balys sone, and suych other fals shrewys
the which wuld have thes mater born ought for ther
owyn pleser ; the which causith an[1] evyll noyse in this
contre and other places. And as for Sir John Hevenyngham, Sir John Wyndefeld and other wurchepfull
men ben mad but her doggeboldes ;[2] the whiche I
suppose wull turne hem to diswurchep here after. I
spake with Sir John Hevenyngham and enformed hym
with the trough of the mater, and of all owyr demenyng
at Drayton, and he seid he wuld that all thyng wer
wele, and that he wuld enforme my lord as I seid to
hym, but Harleston had all the words and the rewle
with the Duke here, and after his avyse and Doctor
Aleynes he was avysed here at this tyme.

The logge and the remenaunte of your place was
betyn down on Tuesday and Wednesday, and the
Duke rode on Wednysday to Drayton and so for to

---

[1] *an*—&, MS.
[2] The old word "dogbolt" seems to have meant a servile follower, or one
bound to wait the commands of another. Thus in Lilly's "Tragicall Comedie
of Alexander and Campaspe," where Manes complains that he serves a
master whose house is a tub, Granichus remarks "That Diogenes that dog
should have Manes that dogbolt it grieveth nature and spiteth art."

Cossey whille the logge at Heylesdon was in the betyng down. And this nyght at mydnyght Thomas Sleyforth, Grene Porter, and Joh. Botesforth the Baly of Eye, and other, had a cart and fetched awey fetherbeddes, and all the stuffe that was left at the parsones, and Thom Wateres hows to be kept of owrs. I shall send you billes er after, as ner as I may, what stuffe we have forborn. I pray you send me word how ye will that I be demened, wheder ye wull that [I][1] abide at Cayster or come to you to London. I have no leyser to write more. God have yow in His kepyng. Wretyn at Norwich on Sent Lukes Evyn.

M. P.

534.

A.D. 1465, 27 Oct.
MARGARET PASTON TO JOHN PASTON.

[From Fenn, iv. 226.]

The Eve of St. Simon and Jude is the 27th October. It fell on Sunday in the year 1465.

To my ryght wyrshypfull hosbond, John Paston, be thys delyveryd in hast.

RYGHT wyrshypfull hosbond, I recomand me to you. Please it you to wyte that I was at Haylesden uppon Thursday laste passyd, and sey the place ther, and in gode feyth ther wyll no cryatur thynke how fowle and orubelly it ys arayed but yf they sey it. Ther comyth moch pepyll dayly to wonder ther uppon, both of Norwych and of other placys, and they speke shamfully therof. The Duck had be beter then a m[l].*li.* that it had never be don ; and ye have the more gode wyll of the pepyll that it ys so foylle don. And they made youre ten-

1 Omitted in MS.

auntys of Haylesdon and Drayton, with other, to help
to breke down the wallys of the place and the logge
both,—God knowyth full evyll ayenst ther wyllys, but
that they derst no notherwysse don for ferre. I have
spoken with your tenauntys of Haylesdon and Drayton
both, and putte hem in comfort as well as I canne.
The Duck ys men rensackyd the church, and bare a
way all the gode that was lefte ther, both of ours and
of the tenaunts, and lefte not so moch but that they
stode uppon the hey awter, and ransackyd the images,
and toke a way such as they myght fynd, and put a
way the parson owte of the church till they had don,
and ransackyd every mans hous in the towne v. or vj.
tymys. And the chyff maysters of robbyng was the
Baylly of Ey, the Baylly of Stradbroke, Thomas Slyford, and Porter ; and Slyford was the chyff robber of
the cherch, and he hath most of the robbery next the
Baylly of Ey. And as for lede, bras, pewter, yren,
dorys, gatys, and other stuffe of the hous, men of
Coshay and Causton have it, and that thay myght not
cary, thay have hewen it a sonder in the most dys-
spytuose wyse. Yf it myght be, I wold som men of
wyrshop myght be send from the Kyng to see how it
ys both ther and at the logge, or than any snowys[1] com,
that they may make report of the troth, ellys it shall
not mo be seyn so playnly as it may now.

And at the reverens of God, spyde your maters
nowe, for it ys to orybell a cost and trobell that we
have now dayly, and most have tyll it be other wyse ;
and your men dar not goo abowte to geder uppe your
lyfflode, and we kype here dayly more than xxx. persons
for savacyon of us and the place, for, in very trowght,
and the place had not be kypyd strong, the Duck had
come hether. Arblaster thynketh verely that Hugh a

---

[1] Fenn remarks that if we may judge from the mention of snow in this
place, the winters began earlier in those days than they do now. But perhaps Margaret was only urging the necessity of timely action, taking into
consideration the ordinary delays of suitors. We have seen, however, from
Letter 528 that in the year 1465 there must have been unusually cold weather
even in the beginning of September.

Fen may do moch in your maters, and he thynkyth
that he wole do for you faythfully, yf ye wyll, &c.

At the reverens of God, yf any wyrshypfull and pro-
fetabile mene may be take yn your maters, for sake it
not in eschuyng of our trobell and gret costs and
charges that we have, and may growe here after.   It ys
thoght here that yf my Lord of Norffolk wolld take
uppon hym for you, and that he may have a comyssyon
for to enquer of such ryotts and robberyes as hath be
don to you and other in thys contray, that then all the
contray wyll a wayte uppon hym, and serve your
entent; for the pepyll lovyth and dredyth hym more
then any other lord except the Kyng and my Lord of
Warwyk, &c.

God have you in Hys kypyng, and send ous gode
tydyngs from you.   Wryten in haste, uppon the Sonday Seynt Symon and Jude ys Evyn.

By yours,   M. P.

535.

Message to Sir William Yelverton.

[From Paston MSS., B.M.]

This appears to be a message from the King rebuking Judge Yelverton for
partizanship in assisting the Duke of Suffolk against Paston in his entry into
the manor of Drayton. The date is therefore 1465. The MS., however, is
only a corrected draft, and it is not certain that such a message was actually
sent.

This is the Instruccion for the Messenger.

HAT ye grete well Sir William Yelverton,
letyng hym wete in our behalf we be informed
that certeyn persones, in the name of the
right worshipfull our cosyn the Duc of Suffolk,
have enterid in the manoir of Drayton that was Fastolffes, and have dreven from the seid manoir and other
xiij^{c.} shep and other bestes pastured upon the seid
manoir. Notwithstandyng, we merveyle gretly that the

seid Sir William, his sones and servauntes, as it is seid,
assiste and comfort the seid persones soo entryng and
withdrawyng the seid catell, seying that he is named
both feffe and executour.   And all be it so that there
is variaunce bithwene hym and our welbelovid John
Paston in our coort, consernyng as well the seid
manoirs as other goodes that were Sir John Fastolffes,
whom God assoyle, yit is may not acorde with worship
and consiens for the seid Sir William to assiste the
distruccion of the seid manoirs and goodes in the
meane tyme.   Wherfore we desire hym that he woll
do his devoir effectually to help to save the seid
manoirs from all such pretense of titell, and to cause
the seid catels to be restored to the manoirs aforeseid,
and not to be withdrawen and distroyed as they be;
and that he do his feithfull part in this behalf acordyng
to the trust that he was put in, as we may do for hym
in tyme to come.

536.

A.D. 1465 (?), 10 Nov.
JOHN WYMONDHAM TO JOHN PASTON.

[From Fenn, iv. 240.]

As to the date of this letter, we can only reproduce what is said of it by Sir
John Fenn:—" John Wymondham, Esq., the writer of this letter, married
Margery, the daughter of Sir Robert Clifton, Knight, of Denver, in Norfolk,
and widow of Sir Edward Hastings, of Elsing, Knight. He therefore calls
her ' My Lady.' He died in 1475.

" He purchased the manor and estate at Felbrigg, of the trustees of Sir
Simon Felbrigg, where he had resided ; but once in his absence Sir John
Felbrigg made a forcible entry, and dragging out his lady by the hair of her
head, who had locked herself up in a chamber to keep possession, got into
possession, and retained it till Wymondham obtained the King's order to
Thomas Montgomery, Esq., High Sheriff of the county, to put him again into
possession. The dispute was then settled with Sir John Felbrigg, and upon
Wymondham's paying to him 200 marks [£133 : 6 : 8] he released his claims,
&c.

" This letter seems to have been written during the time that he was dispossessed of Felbrigg, and which must have been either before the year 1461
or 1466, those being the years in which Sir Thomas Montgomery was Sheriff
of Norfolk, and as J. Paston at this time seems to have been under mis-
fortunes, it was probably near the latter year. I have therefore ventured,
though doubtfully, to date the letter in 1465."

To my worchipful cosyn, John Paston.

RYGTH worchipful cosyn, I comaunde me to yow. And forasmoch as ther was a child ded at Asteles, and on other lik to be ded in the same place, what tyme that I rode oute aboute my litil livelod, my lady and I bothe thoughte pite on my mastres your wif to se her abide ther, and desirid here to com to my pore hous on to soch tyme as ye shuld a be othirwise avised, wyche, if it plese yow, I am right wel apaied.

Sythen, I undirstande be my lady that ye desire to knowe whedyr that I shulde abide here stille or nowe [*or no*]. As to that, I have non other place that I wold abide at, and my lady seith how she is avised to ende hir lif here. Also she seith how ye desire to have a stabil with inne my plas; and as to that, afeith, sir, I have none, but that must nedis serve for my wode. As for a chambre, ye shall have on for your men al redy, and as touching a stabil, Sir John Sparham and I have gote yow on ther [*where*] your hors stode the last tyme ye were in this town, and an hows to ley inne hey and straw, and cost yow not but making of a rak and a mangeour, and more to your ease there than here; and yf ye wyl that it be made redy for yow, send werd be the bringer of this letter. And, cosyn, as towching to paiment, I can not sey how ye shal be pleasid with my pore fare, but aftir that ye arn com home, and arn aqweintid there with, we shal so acorde as shal be plesir to us bothe, with the grace of God, which have [you] in His blissid governaunce, and send yow your moderis blissing.

Wreten at Norwich, on Seint Martyn is Even.

Your poer cosyn and ffrend,

J. WYMONDHAM.

And how that ever ye do, hold up your manship.

537.

NOTE.

The letter of John Payn to John Paston (No. 99), which, on
account of the circumstances to which it refers, we have placed
in the year 1450, was written, as appears by the contents, fifteen
years later, *i.e.*, in 1465. We therefore call the reader's atten-
tion to it in this place.

538.

A.D. 1466 (?) [20] Jan.
SIR JOHN FELBRIGGE TO JOHN PASTON.

[From Fenn, iv. 242.]

The date of this letter cannot be ascertained with very great precision;
but as it belongs most probably to about the same period as Letter 536, which
we have referred to November 1465, we may assign this to the January
following.

To my Cosyn Paston, be thys letter delyverd yn haste.

RYGHT reverent and worshyppeful cosyn, y
comawnd me on to you, desyryng to her off
your welfare, the whyche Almyghty Jesu
preserve to Hys plesawns, and to your own
herts desyres. Forthermore and yff yt please your
gentylnesse to be my trusty frend, as my ful truste ys
yn you, as for swyche materys as the brynger off this
lettre shall enforme you, and beth effectualy my frend,
and brynge yt abowte, and by my trowthe y shall geve
you an C. marke for your labowr. For yn trowthe y
am aferde that Roberd Radclyff hathe deseyvyd me,
for he laboryd to me dayly by my Lords comawnde-
ment off Warwyk, and brought with hym Yllyngworthe
and oder off my Lords cownsel, and seen my evydens;
and so we stoden uppon apoyntement, and y for to
have had an unswere sent to Felbrygge Halle, and yff
ne had be for ffendyng off my Lords lordschyppe, y

myght have had my money for my ryght or y cam owt off London, as my man schall enforme you. For yn trowthe y muste now make an schiffte, for Wyndham hathe sold hys ryght, and rathere than yt schuld go that way to, y had lever my Lord had yt ij. C. marke with yn the pryse that y grawnt yt laste, and therfor y be scheche you to labowr to my Lord that y may have an unswer. And thies many townes longithe thereto, Felbrygge, Aylinton, Ronton, Colby, Bannyngham, Ingworthe, Styrston, besyde hamelets.

No mor to you at this tyme, but the Holy Trinyte have you yn His kepyng. Wryten at Felbrygg, the Monday affor Seynt Augnetes Day.[1]

By your cosyn,   JOHN FELBRYGGE.

539.

A.D. 1466, 17 Feb.

JOHN WYKES TO SIR JOHN PASTON.

[From Fenn, iv. 246.]

As this letter was written after Edward IV.'s marriage, and before the death of John Paston the father, the date must be either 1465 or 1466. Fenn assigns it to the latter year, and I think he is right, though he does not state his reasons. I find that John, Lord Lovel, died on the 9th January 1465, leaving his son and heir, Francis, only nine years old, so that even if we date this letter 1466, the young lad was married at the early age of ten. This was probably owing to his wardship having been obtained by Lord Fitzhugh, or some person interested; but as the inquisition on his father's death (*Inq. p. m.*, 4 Edw. IV., No. 27) was not taken till October 1465, there seems no ground for believing that he could have been forced into wedlock a month after he was left an orphan.

Un to the ryght wyrshypfull mayster, Sir John Paston, Knygt, be thys letter delyveryd.

YGHT wyrshypfull and my especyall gode mayster, I recomaund me unto your gode maystershyp, letyng you wyte that the berour

---

[1] The modern version in Fenn reads "the Monday *after* Saint Agnes's Day," and the date subjoined at the bottom of the page is in accordance with this reading. But it is more likely the text as printed in the old spelling is correct. St. Agnes' Day is the 21st January. The Monday before it would have been the 20th in 1466.

herof told me that ye had grete mervyll that I send to you no word ne letter of awnswer of the letters that ye had send to me to London. As for on letter ye send to me by Rychard Playtorys man, and therof I send you an awnswer in a letter by a man of the Prior of Bromholm; and as for other letters, ther com no more to me but that on.

Item, Mayster Flemmyng lokyth dayly for hys hors, and at every tyme that I mete with hym, he askyth of me when hys hors shuld com, and when I here any word from you. Wherfore I pray you send me word in a letter how he shall be awnswerd, and yf the hors shall com, lette me knowe when; for and he had not trustyd theruppon, he wold have purveyd hym in a nother place, &c.

Item, John Oter ys not yet payd, but as I suppose it shall not be long to tyll he have it, for he hath spoken to my mayster your fader a yer therfor; and as for Gylmyn, he hath not spoken to my mayster as yet, &c.

Item, I truste he wylbe your gode fader, for John Say hath told hym playnly of hys demenyng ayenst you, and told hym that he had the lasse favour for your sake, &c.

Item, the Erle of Arundell ys[1] son hath weddyd the Quyne ys suster.

Item, the Lord Lovell ys son[2] hath weddyd my Lady Fytzhugh ys doghter, &c.

Item, Jenney desyryth a trety with my mayster, and spake to my mayster therof hym sylf in Westminster Hall.

Item, all felaws in the Kyngs hows fareid well, and wold have you ther.

---

[1] Thomas Fitz Alan, Lord Maltravers, eldest son of William Fitz Alan, Earl of Arundel, married Margaret, second daughter of Richard Widville, Earl Rivers, and sister to Elizabeth, Queen of Edward IV. He succeeded his father as Earl of Arundel in 1487, 3 Hen. VII., and died in 1524, 16 Hen. VIII.—F.

[2] Francis Lovel, son and heir to John, Lord Lovel, married Anne, daughter of Henry, Lord Fitz Hugh. It is curious that she is here called "Lady Fitz Hugh's daughter," when her father was alive.

No more to you at thys tyme, but the Holy Trynyte
have you [in] kepyng.   Wryten at London, the Monday next after Seynt Volentyn.

Your servant,   JOHN WYKYS.

540.

A.D. 1466, 18 March.
CLEMENT PASTON TO JOHN PASTON.

[From Paston Letters, B.M.]

The reference to the dispute between Elizabeth Poynings and the Earl of
Kent, which is alluded to in a subsequent letter, proves this letter to have been
written in the year 1466. The earl in question was only so created on the 3d
of May 1465, and John Paston, to whom the letter is addressed, died in May
1466.

To hys rythe worchypfwll mayster, John Paston, Sqwyer.

RYTHE worchypfwll broder, I recomawnde me
to zow.   And as for zour letter to my Lorde
Chawnceler I have not delyveryd it; for I
askyd avysse there in, and I was aunsweryd
there in that sythen he was takyn to baylle, the Chawn-
celerer[1] cowde not compelle the swertes to bryng hym
in befor hys day.   Also me thowte zour letter was not
most plesauntly wrytyn to take to swyche a lorde.   And
as for the tresorer, hys name is Sir John Fooge, but he
is not in London nor wythe the Kyng, so I kan [not]
have the letter sent hym but if I hyeryd a man to bere
it.   And as for zour question of the patentes, Grenfeld
and Catesby and Sterkey holdyn it a good question, for
the statute is, *Patentes dez tenements dount null titill est
trouve pur le roy de recorde sount voydez,* anno xviij. H.
VI. ca. vj.   But I trowe in zour cas that be ther
opiniounis the Acte of the Parlement is a tytyll of
recorde.   It is said to the contrary intent, thow the
londs be forfetyd of record, yet ther is no certificacion
of recorde qwat londes they be, nor wer [*where*] nor in

1 So in MS.

qwat place they lye; but and thys clawse be in the patents, *Non obstante quod nulla inquisicio pro nobis inde est inventa,* by Grenfelde is consayle the patents xwld be clerly goode.   But me semythe that amendyt not the mater, for be for the makyng of the statute above sayde, patents graunttyd of londs be fore inquisicion were goode and effectuell and the statute is generall:—*Patents dount null tytill &c. sount voydez.* Thanne it folowyt well if the Acte of Parlement be no tytyll for the Kyng thann is ther no tytyll for the Kyng of recorde, for that clawse in the patente is no tytyll; than if ther [be] no tytyll, ergo the patents voyde.

My suster[1] standythe in the same casse with my Lord of Kent.

Broder, I pray zow send mor mony for my nevew John, for he mwst ellys com hom azen; for the Kyng gothe into Scotlonde, and he is nowther horsyd nor harneysyd, for his grett hors is lykly to dye; and if ze wyll sende it to me or to Christofyr Hanyngton it xall be save for hym.   I send zow a letter from hym closyde herin.   And I pray spek to my moder that my hors faylle not on Passyon Swnday,[2] for thann xall I be redy and thanne xall ower redyng be don.   Wrytyn on Twesday nexst after Seynt Gregory is Day.

Zowr broder,
CLEMENT PASTON.

On the back.—The man wold not tak my letter but I wass fayen to gyve hym ijd. for the beryng.

541.

A.D. 1466, 12 May.
FRIAR JOHN MOWTH TO JOHN PASTON.

[From Fenn, i. 256.]

Friar Brackley, who is here mentioned as dead, is spoken of in John Paston's deposition of December 1465, without any indication that he was

---

[1] Elizabeth, widow of Robert Poynings.
[2] March 23.

at that time deceased (See No. 525). We may presume, therefore, that he died between that time and May 1466, in which month and year died John Paston, to whom this letter is addressed.

To my worchepful mayster, John Paston the holdest, be this letter delyveryd in hast.

RYTH reverent and worchepful sire, I hartyly recomende me on to your reverens, thankyng yow for the gret cher and comfortabyll words that ye yovyn on to me wat tyme that I was last yn yowr presens ; desyryng ful specyaly of Almity God, owt of al your wordly tribulacyonys and adversyte, gracyowus delyverans, and yn al vertuows prosperite, good encres and contynuans. If yt like your maysterchep to know the cause of this wrytyng, it ys thys ; it is nowth unknow[1] on to yow that Mayster Brakle (Cryst rest hys sowle !), delyveryd to Wyllam Paston, your broder, certayn oblygacyonys, of the weche the dute xuld grow to my convent yn Norwyche. I have spoke on to Wyllam Paston her of, and he excuseth hym and seyth on this wyse ; that be the wyl of Mayster Brakle, wat tyme that Sire Tomas Todenham,[2] Knyth, xuld be put on to hys deth, he delyveryd hem on to hys confessor ; the weche, as he seth, xuld a be Grey fryer, hows name he knowyth nowt ; also he seyth that after the deth of the forseyd Knyt, he spake with the Fryer, confessor on to the Knyth, and hasked hym aftyr the forseyd oblygacyonys, and as he seyth, the Fryer seyd on to hym that he had delyveryd hem on to [the] Knyth Marchall. Werfor I beseche you, as specyaly as I may, that, now wyl your broder is at London, that ye of your grace wyl know the trowthe in this mater, for the comfort of the dede, and profyth of my convent. Nomor at this tyme, but that I be seche Almyty God in Trinyte conserve your, and kepe yow in all vertuows prosperite. Amen.

---

[1] *Nowth unknow.* I believe this to be the true reading of the original MS. Fenn prints it "nowth know."

[2] He was beheaded on Tower Hill in February 1462.

Wretyn at Heylysdon in gret hast, the xij. day of
May, in your maner aftyr mete.   The cause wy the
mayster delyveryd hem to hym mor than to yow, was,
as he seyd on to me, for as meche as ye had so many
maters yn hand for yowr self, and also for the dede,
that he durst not attempt yow with all; and al so be
cause he had lesse for to do hys hope was that he
xuld asped yt mor redyly.

Fr[e]re Willam Thorp dwellyng at Salisbury.

By yowr pore orator and bedman,

FRIER JAN MOWTH.

542.

Year uncertain.   Nov.
MARGARET PASTON TO JOHN PASTON.

[From Paston MSS., B.M.]

I find no very satisfactory evidence touching the date of this letter.
Allusion is made to John Paston having been at Lincoln.   The occasion
referred to might have been in 1458, when, as we know by No. 321, he went
into the North as far as Doncaster; or it may have been in the Spring of
1461.   (See Nos. 387 and 392.)   It is not probable, however, that this letter
was earlier than the latter date, as there is no appearance at that time of any
dispute having arisen between John Paston and his brother William.   On
the contrary, William Paston is in correspondence with his brother in April
1461 (No. 385).   On the other hand, if the occasion referred to when John
Paston was at Lincoln was in the Spring of 1461, this letter could hardly have
been written in the same year; for it cannot be supposed that he left books
at Caister on his return south, when Caister was in the possession of the
Duke of Norfolk.   The date, however, being so uncertain, I prefer to place
this letter at the end of John Paston's correspondence rather than assign it
doubtfully to any particular year.

*To my right wurchipfull husbond, John Paston, be this
deliverd in hast.*

RYTH worchepfull husbonde, I recomande me
to yow.   Plesyth yow to weet that Thomas
Grene was with me as on Saterday last paste,
and let me have knowlage that the scherre
schold be as thys day at the Gyld Hall in Norwyche,

and be desyiryd me that the swte that ye have ageyns
Thomas Jeryng and othyr myth be sesyd as for thys
schere; and I seyd that I durste do ryth not there in.
And he tolde me that Thomas Jeryng was with yow
in Flegge the laste tyme that ye wer ther, and ye seyd
to hym that he scholde not be hurte by the swte.
And Thomas Grene told me that if the seyd Jeryng
and othyrs in the same wryte mad not an end with
yow by the nexte schere, the whyche schall be thys day
monyth, that he the seyd Thomas Grene wole purchese
a new wryte of hys owne coste ayens that daye. I
woste not that the scher shuld be so sone when I wrote
to yow yowyr laste lettyr. And he remembyryd the
trobulus werd [*world*] that is nowe, and also that they
wer nowtye felawys that ye suyd, and ther fore he thowte
that it war best to let it be respyte at thys tyme, and so
they schall be respyth at thys tyme. I have sent to
Jaferay Spyrlyng for the bokys that ye sent to me fore,
and he seyth that he hathe none there of, for he seyth he
lefte hem with yow when he was with yow in the Northe
contre; for he seyth ye left hym behynd yow at Lynk-
colne. He supposyth they be at Kaster.

Item, my cosyn Crane recomandyth hyr to yow,
and prayith yow that ye wole wychesave to spek to
Jamys Gresham for to swe ferthe the mater betwyx
Dame Margaret Spurdans and hyr; and sche prayith
yow at the reverens of God that ye wole tendyr that
mater well, for all hyr troste is in yow.

Item, the tenauntys at Sweynysthorp prayid me for
to wryte to yow for to pray yow for Goddys sake that
ye wole help for to get hem a good baly of the
hundyryd that they be in; for they sey that they have
be gretly hurte by swyche offyserys as they have had
ther be fore tyme. Folk wold fayne in thys contre that
Heydon scholde be purveyd for, that he goo not so at
large as he dothe, for he is in thys towne nere every
wek, and hathe be ever syne ye yd hens. And also it
is seyd in thys towne that ye have be good maister
thys terme to Yatys, and many be ryth sory ther of,

and that he dothe so well as it [is] seyd here that he dothe.
It is seyd that he is scapyd all dangerys, and he hathe
tak new accionys ageyns hys neyborys, as it is seyd.
Othyr tydyngys have we none here but that ye have
more pleynly there.   And the Blyssyd Trinyte have
yow in Hys kepyng, and send yow good sped in all
yowyr materys.   Wretyn in haste at Norwyche the
Monday next be fore Seynt Edmunde the Kynge.

By yowyr,   M. P.

My modyr wold ryth fayne know how that ye and
my brodyr Wyllam wer acordyd, sche wold ryth fayne
that all wer well betwene yow.

543.

B. D. M. S. TO JOHN PASTON.

[From Fenn, iv. 262.]

There is no evidence of the date either of this or of the four following
letters beyond the fact that this and the two next are addressed to John
Paston, while the two last are addressed to Margaret Paston during her
husband's life.   None of them, therefore, can be later than 1466.

Be this delyvered to Mastyr John Paston.

RECOMAUNDE me unto you as unknowyn.
And as for the wryting I send unto you, the
cause why yt was nate endossed was, for the
berer ther of knew yow wel i now.   And as
for youre Cossyn Mary, she ys no longer with us, as a
pon Seynt Mathewys Evyn she departyd from me, and
went to Awdry Croxeston, and she told me that ye
wold pay for her borde ther.   But on thyng I let you
know ; she hathe demenyd her ful symply bothe for
youre worship and also for her awne.   Ther ys but
few within oure plasse but they know how yt is with
her, and al by her awne bessynes of her tunge.   And

I had knowyn as myche at the begynnyng as I have don sythe, I wold not have delt in the mater nat for xl. pound; for I wys she ys no thyng so sadde as I wold she wer.

No more to you at thys tyme, but the Holy Gost have you in His kepyng, and send you youre hertys esse. I pray you hertly that I may sp[e]ke with you.

B. D. M. S.

544.

ABSTRACT.

[From Paston MSS., B.M.]

RICHARD SUTHWELL TO JOHN PASTON, ESQUIRE.

Thanks him for speaking to the Mayor and Recorder for the appearance of certain persons at this last session, as he wrote from Walsingham. Thomas Wolvesby and Colyns make great labor for the poor men's undoing. Begs him to move the Mayor to have pity, considering their trouble at Walsingham, when they were prisoners.

Thetford, Shere-Thursday.

545.

ABSTRACT.

[From Paston MSS., B.M.]

JOHN PASTON, JUNIOR, TO HIS FATHER, JOHN PASTON.

Has spoken "with Warwyk and Stwkle" for the place and lands in Arleham. Declined their offer of 6d. an acre, they keeping the place in repair; but Stwkle has promised all the lands shall be purveyed for, as for this year. Warwyk this day offered my mother 7d. an acre for the lands in Arleham, but I counselled her to hold out for a longer term. Kook will no longer hold the place for 7d. or 8d. an acre, and will only give 6d., if he is to keep it in repair. Has spoken with Dame Alice Weche and Geoffrey Spyrlyng, who have agreed to set a tenant to occupy the lands in dispute till Paston comes home.

St. Martin's Even.

546.

ABSTRACT.

[From Paston MSS., B.M.]

THOMAS GNATYSHALE TO MRS PASTON.

I hope the young man I sent will please "my master and you."
I hope you will not receive him at this time, and when my master
comes home refuse him.   As for your lands at Sparham, there
are not many lands to let.   Has inquired at Salle.   Master
Edward [1] is clearly answered of £18 a year and 7s. or 8s. more.
Bryston, Thyrnyng, and Owleton are let, which belong to the
manor of Salle.   So he is clearly answered twice a year at London,
besides the fees, viz., of the receiver 26s. 8d., of the steward 20d.,
and of the bailliff 26s. 8d.

Sparham, Wednesday before Ascension.

547.

Date uncertain.—ABSTRACT.

[From Paston MSS., B.M.]

T. GNATYSHALE TO MRS PASTON.

James and Robert Radclef mean to take away my goods, and
I shall be taken if I be at Norwich at next shire.   Pray let my
master know.   I suppose it was by their commandment that my
two neat were taken on Saturday last at Lyng, "for one that is
under bailly of Richmond took hem."   John Everyton will tell
you more.   The receipts of the manor of Sparham with costs are
£10, 3s. 11½d.   If any man of yours come to Norwich please
send me your advice.   (Signed) "T. GNAT."

548.

ABSTRACT.

[From Paston MSS., B.M.]

JAMES ARBLASTER TO JOHN PASTON, [SQUIRE].[2]

John à Berney of Wychyngham wishes to disinherit him of his

---

[1] Probably Edward, son of Robert Mauteby.   He was Margaret Paston's
uncle.

[2] This designation is added on the address, but is struck out.

liberty of faldage in Colyette. Desires the help of one of Paston's
men. As for my Lady of Oxford, "I have get you a trusty man
against Tuesday or Wednesday next."

[There is no distinct evidence of the date of this letter, except that it is
probably not later that 1466, when John Paston died, though it may have
been addressed to his younger son John. Compare Nos. 192, 193, and 194].

549.

A.D. 1466.

JOHN PASTON'S FUNERAL.

[From Blomefield's Norfolk, vi. 483.[1]]

The original of this document was probably among the Paston MSS. when
Blomefield composed his History of Norfolk, but where it is at present cannot be ascertained. It is cited by Blomefield, or perhaps by his continuator, Mr.
Parkin, as "a very long but narrow roll," then in his possession. The text,
however, does not seem to be printed entire, as the Editor only professes to
give "several particulars therein."

*Expences paid by Gloys at Norwich the day the Cors
was ther and befor.*

YRSTE. The iiii. orders of fryers, viii*l.*
Item, almesse, ii*s.* vii*d.* Item, to xxiii.
susters of Normandys,[2] with the gardian
eche of them, iiii*d.*, and the gardian, viii*d.*—
viii*s.* Item, in offering on Pentecost Tuesday[3] for
my master, i*d.* ; for the herse, xl*s.* For xxiiii. yerdes
of brod wythtys for gowns, xxvii*s.* viii*d. ;* for dyeng of
the same, iiii*s.* For settyng on the tents, vi*d.* For
xxii. yerdes and iii. quarters of brod wythts, xxxiiii*s.*
iiii*d.* For grownedyng, iii*s.* iiii*d.* For dyeng, iiii*s.* To
xxxviii. prests at the dyryge at Norwyche, when the
cors lay ther, xii*s.* viii*d.* To xxxix. schyldern with
surplyces within the schurche and without, iii*s.* iiii*d.*
To xxvi. clerks with iiii. kepers of the torches, eche of
them ii*d.*, iii*s.* iiii*d.* To the clerks of St. Peters and
St. Stevens for the ryngers ageyn the cors, ii*s.* To the
iiii. orders of fryers that rede ageyn the cors——. To the
Prioress of Carow, vi*s.* viii*d.* To a maide that came

1 Folio edition, iii. 692.   2 At Norwich.   3 May 27th in 1466.

with her, xx*d*. To the ancors [*anchoress ?*] xl*d*. In almesse, xv*s*. To a woman that came from London with the cors to Norwyche, vi*s*. viii[*d*].

Payments be Gloys and Calle at Bromholme.

Fyrste. To the Prior, be my masters bequest, xl*s*. To ix. monks, eche of them vi*s*. viii*d*., iii*l*. To another monke, who was of the same place, xx*d*. For brinnyng of the Abbes with the torches, xx*d*. To the Priors boteler for bred, ii*s*. x*d*. For wasshyng of napry, xii*d*. To the boteler for hys reward, xx*d*. To the baker for cccx. eggs, xix*d*. To him for hys reward, iii*s*. iiii*d*. To xxviii. bedds with —— of clothys, and wasshyng of the same, v*s*. To ii. men that fyllyd the grave, viii*d*. To brueng of v. kome malte, xx*d*. For ix. pownd candyl, xi*d*. To the clerks of Bromholm, viii*d*. For viii. peces of peuter lost of the Priors, xx*d*. Geven among the men of the bakhouse, xx*d*. To the parisshe schyrche of Bromholm, x*s*. To xii. schyrchys, l*s*. viii*d*. To the prest that cam with the cors from London, iii*s*. iiii*d*. To servytors that awaytyd upon hym by the komawndment of W. Paston, xxi*d*. To Playters for hys offering, iiii*d*. To the vyker of Upton, ii*s*. To the sexton of Bromholm for xxii. crossys geven to Marget and Modeley, *per* John Paston, iiii*s*. vi*d*. To xiiii. rynggars, vii*s*. To xxiiii. servertors, eche of them iiii*d*., viii*s*. To lxx. servertors, eche of them iii*d*., xvii*s*. vi*d*. Paid to Dawbeny for servertors, vii*s*. For fyshh the day after the enterment, vi*s*. x*d*. For vi. barells bere, xii*s*. For a roundlet of red wine of xv. gallonys, &c., xii*s*. xi*d*. To a hors hyer for iii. days for Sir James, xii*d*. For a quarter malte, v*s*. For iiii. bushels wete, xxxii*d*. For a quarter of otys, ii*s*. viii*d*. For x. kombe malte brueng, xl*d*. For the boord of Rychard Hermer, wrythe, iii. days, and for hys hyer the sayde tyme, xiii*d*. *ob*. For William Yonge, barbor, v. days mete and drynke, and hys hyer the sayde tyme, xvi*d*. For vi. pownd candyl.

vii*d. ob.* To xii. pore men beryng torches from
London to Norfolk be vi. day, i*s*, takyng eche of them
on the day iiii*d*, and for iii. dayes in goyng homerward,
takynge every day vi*d.* Geven to Martyn Savage and
Denschers awaytyng upon my master at London be
vii. dayes before that he was caryed, ii*s. x*d.* For bred
bowthe, xxiiii*s.* For vii. barels bere, xvii*s.* vi*d.* For
a barel of the grettest assyse, iii*s.* iiii*d.* For iiii. barells
of alee, xiii*s.* iiii*d.* For bred and alee for xii. men
that bare torches, xiii*d. ob.* To a dole at Bromholm,
v*l.* xiii*s.* iiii*d.* To William Colens, one of the botelers
at Bromholm, xii*d.* To Wate Webster, another
boteler, xii*d.* To Greg. Worsteler, one of the porters
at Bromholm, iiii*d.* The parson at Mauteby,[1] and Sir
Thomas Lynes, to the prestes at the deryge at Bromholm, xliii*s.* In almesse, xlvii*s.* vi*d*; more, xx*s.* To
the glaser for takyn owte of ii. panys of the wyndons
of the schyrche for to late owte the reke of the torches
at the deryge, and sowderyng new of the same, xx*d.*
[This part of the roll, according to Blomefield, or his
continuator, seemed to be written by Gloys, above
mentioned, in an indifferent hand. The remainder is
in a very neat and curious old hand, which was supposed to be that of Margaret Paston.]

Vittelles bought by Richard Charles.

First. For xxvii. gees, xvii*s.* For xxvii. frankyd
gees, vi*s.* viii*d.* lxx caponnes, xvii*s.* vii*d*, For xxix.[2]
xvii. chekons, xvi*s.* vi*d.* For x. chekons, x*d.*
For xli. pygges, xiii*s.* x*d.* For xlix calvys, iiii*l.* xiii*s.*
iiii*d.* For xxxiiii. lambys, xxvii*s.* ii*d.* For xxii. shep,
xxxvii*s.* v*d.* x. nete, iiii*l.* xvi*s.* i*d.* For ii. napronnes
to Richard Lynstede, x*d.* For claretts and fawcetts,
vi*d.* MCCC. eggs, vi*s.* vi*d.* For xx. galons milk, xx*d.*
For viii. galons creme, ii*s.* viii*d.* For iiii. pints of
butter, iiii*d.* For i. quarter and ii. bushels of whete

---

[1] Robert Coteler, who was presented to the living by John Paston in 1465,
on the resignation of Thomas Howys.
[2] A short blank occurs in Blomefield after "xxix." and before "xvii."

mele, vii*s*. x*d*. To the parson of Crostweyt for i. quarter of whete, vi*s*. For xiiii. galons of ale, ii*s*. To a labourer for iii. days, xii*d*. To xxiiii. galons of ale, iiii*s*. For xiii. salt fysshe, iiii*s*. iiii*d*. For the purveying of bred, ale, and fysshe, iii*s*. iiii*d*. To William Reynolds for lodgyng of Master Prowet, the Prior of the White Freres, the parson of Mautby, Sir Thomas Lynds, and other, by ii. nyghtis, vi*d*. For bred, ale, and possets to the same persons, vi*d*. To Herman, fleyng bests by iii. days, ii*s*., and to John Foke, by iii. days, xx*d*. For purveying of all the velys, lambes, x. beefins, certain piggs and polaly [*poultry*], xl*d*.

Bill of the Prior of Bromholm.

Memorandum. The Prior toke to bord diverse persons laboryng abought the enterment, begynnyng the Thursday in Pentecost weke, the vi. yere of Kyng Edward the iiiith.

On Thursday I [1] find 3 persons who had xii*d*. for their board and hire ; on Friday 5 who had xv*d*. ; on Saturday 8 who had xxiii*d*. On Monday all were employed ; and on the day after 1 find 4 to be allowed for their board iiii*d*. *ob*., and for their hires v*d*.,—ix*d*. *ob*. Delivered by the Prior to Richard Charles :—Fyrst, v. quarters of otes, xiii*s*. iiii*d*. ; v. swyne, xii*s*. vi*d*. ; ii. bushel of mestlyn, xv*d*. ; v. pownd of candell, v*d*. ; xx. quarters of malte, xiii*s*. iiii*d*., and with gryndyng and brewyng, xviii*s*. For a cartfull of hey, iii*s*. iiii*d*. For ii. swyne, v*s*. For ii bushel otes, viii*d*. For a quarter of herryng, vi*d*. For half a quarter makerell, vii*d*. *ob*. To the parson of St. Peters for his fee of the wax abought the coors, beside ii. candels of i. *lb*. and i. hert candel of a pound, xx*d*. At my masters xxx. day for offeryng, i*d*. Geven to churches and in almes by Gresham, toward Bromholm, v. *marks*. To the clerk of St. Peters of Hungate [2] his felaship for

---

[1] Blomefield or his continuator here speaks in his own person.

[2] A church in Norwich, rebuilt by John Paston in 1460, the advowson having been acquired by him and Margaret, his wife, in 1458. The date of the rebuilding is engraved in stone on a buttress by the north door.

ryngyng when the coors was in the church, xii*d*. To
Dawbeney for bests and other stuffe for the enterment,
xx*l*. To him in gold for to chaunge into small mony for
the dole, xl*l*. To W. Pecok, in iii. bags to bere to Bromholm, in copper, the 20th day, xxvi. *marks*. To Medeley
for his reward, iiii. *marks*, and the same to Maryot. To
Maryot for costs he bare by the way to Bromholm, iii*l*.
xii*d*. More to Medeley for mony paid by him, xlis. x*d*.
To the keper of the inne where myne husband dyed,
for his reward. xx*s*. To Paston chirch, x*s*. To Bakton
chirch, vi*s*. viii*d*. To Gresham the London carrier, in
full payment for the Chaundeler of London, v*l*. xix*s*. iiii*d*.
More in almes mony, vi*s*. viii*d*. More for wyne and bere,
vii. *marks*. To the parson of St. Peters, vi*s*. viii*d*. For
wyne for the seingers when the coors was at Norwich, xx*s*.
To Skolehouse in part of his bille for torches and wax
made at Bromholm, for to brenne upon the grave, iiii.
marks. For x. yerds of narow blak for the viker of Dal-
lynge and Robert Gallawey, and for iii. yerds and quarter
of brod cloth for Illee, xx*s*. x*d*. To Freton chirch, vi*s*.
viii*d*. For a cope called a frogge of worsted for the
Prior of Bromholm, xxvi*s*. viii*d*. For bred at the enterment, ix*s*. In almes, viii*s*. iiii*d*. In wyne and spices, l*s*.
To Dom. John Loveday for cloth for a ridyng cope
for himself, xiiii*s*. ii*d*. To the makyng of Redham
Stepill, viii*s*. iiii*d*. To John Orford, wax chandeler,
for xii. torches and one candell of i. *lb*., lv*s*. ii*d*. *ob*.
To John Dewe for grey lynen cloth and sylk frenge
for the hers, vi*l*. xvi*s*. ii*d*. Given to the Austeners at
the chapter at the . . . . . . of Yarmouth,
lxxv*s*. To Daubeney for to kepe the yere day at
Bromholm the first yere after his dethe, viii*l*. ii*s*. iiii*d*.
Given at Castor to xxv. howsholders, every houshold
iiii*d*. the said tyme, vi*s*. iii*d*. To viii. pore men the
said tyme, xviii*d*. To the master of the College the
said tyme, vi*s*. viii*d*. To Master Clement Felmyngham the said tyme, vi*s*. viii*d*. To viii. prests at Castor
the said tyme, ii*s*. viii*d*. To childern in surplices and
other pore folk at the said tyme, xiiii*d*. To the

parson of Hungate, vi*s*. viii*d*. To the said parson for
a certeyn [1] unto Mighelmesse next after the said yere
day, viii*s*. viii*d*. To Skolous, wax chandeler, for
makyng of the hers at Bromholm, xxii*l*. ix*s*. viii*d*. To
Philip Curson, draper, for cloths, ix*l*. iii*s*. *ob*. To
Aubrey, draper, xxxiiii*s*. For a quarter of makerell,
xii*d*. To the Prior of Bromholm for malte spent at
the enterment, xl*s*. For light kept on the grave, x*s*.
Geven at Cristemasse next after the said yereday, to
eche of the iiii. orders of friers, x*s*.,—xl*s*. To the
vyker of Dallyng for bryngyng home of a pardon from
Rome, to pray for alle our frends sowles, viii*s*. iiii*d*.
For a black gowne to the said viker, viii*s*.

550.

A.D. 1466, May and June.—ABSTRACT.

[From Paston MSS., B.M.]

EXAMINATIONS TOUCHING SIR JOHN FASTOLF'S WILL.

The following examinations are contained in the same volume as the
depositions of John Paston of which an abstract will be found in No. 525.
They begin at page 21, immediately after Paston's depositions, a single blank
page intervening.

A.D. 1466. The following witnesses were examined secretly
and apart on behalf of Sir William Yelverton, "deceased," [2] in
the house of the treasurer of St. Paul's Cathedral by John Druell,
LL.D. :—

May 17. John Monke *alias* Smyth.
    19. John Dawson and John Gyrdyng.
    20. William Boswell, Robert Inglys, Ric. Horne, and
        Thos. Pykeryng.
    21. Henry Clerke, John Tovy, Thos. Hert, William
        Shawe, and Nich. Cherche.
    22. Thos. Newton, Th. Spycer, and Thos. Neve.
    23. John Rugge, John Clerke, and Rob. Bunche.
June 10. Stephen Scrope.
    11. Ric. Fastolf.

[1] *See* No. 39.
[2] By a singular mistake in the record, Sir William Yelverton is here spoken
of as deceased instead of John Paston :—"per partem venerabilis viri domini
Willelmi Yelverton militis defuncti contra testes Johannis Paston armigeri et
domini Thomæ Howys." Yelverton certainly lived for some years after this,
and was continued as judge by Henry VI. on his restoration (*see* Foss), but
John Paston died on the 26th May 1466.

I. John Monke, a smith of the parish of St. James, Pokethorpe, in Norwich, illiterate, of free condition, thirty-two years old and over, alleges bribery of witnesses by Paston and Howys, who offered to sell John Russe lands at Leystofte at little more than half their value. Howes made Russe a present of salt, barley, and malt to the value of £20, and promised him a full discharge of his account for goods of the testator in his custody to the value of £200 and over. He paid Robert Cutteler, vicar of Caster, "colore cujusdam ultimi *vale* dicti testatoris prius non debite" (*sic*), money and corn to the value of 20 marks, and promised to present him to the living of Mawdeby whenever Thomas Howse resigned it. They gave Felmyngham an annuity of 8 marks, and 40s. to a boy who is his servant. They gave Robert Boteler a fee (*feodum*) of 5 marks [a year] for life, and the farm of a close called Mawdeby close, besides some other gifts which are specified. Hence the said John Russe, Rob. Cutteler, Clement Felmyngham, and Rob. Butteler, falsely deposed in answer to the second interrogatory that on the Saturday before the testator's death they were present in a certain low room (*bassa camera*) in the manor of Caister, where the testator was principally between the hours of 8 and 11 a.m., and that with them were the said John Paston and John Brakley, and no others; for in reality there were present in the chamber with the testator on that day, and especially during those hours, the said Rob. Fitzrauf, Nich. Newman, and John Loer continually, and the said Dan John Davye, Dan Thomas Howys, Friar John Bernard, physician, and Henry Barbour, and several others [at intervals]. Moreover, Cutteler, Felmyngham, and Butteler, said Russe was present on that occasion, whereas both he and Cutteler were in other places. Moreover, bribes were given by Paston and Howes in various forms during the months of January, February, and March 1462[-3], and at other times in the parishes of Caister and Yarmouth, and in the city of London, to Ralph Lampet, brother William Bukenham, and the said Rob. Cutteler. Paston promised to promote Bukenham to the priory of Yarmouth, and also, as a reward for his testimony, to give him 13 acres of the testator's land in Scroudby and Caister called Isabell, to the use of the prior and convent of Norwich. Hence the testimony of these witnesses was false, that Fastolf, about the beginning of Autumn five years ago, had made to John Paston estate and feoffment and livery of seisin of his manor of Caister, and other lands in Cos. Norf. and Suff., and the city of Norwich, to the use of the said testator while he lived, and afterwards to that of the said John Paston and his heirs; for if any such thing was done (which is not admitted) it was on the 16th October 1457, in the 36th year of Henry VI., after the Autumn of the said year, and not to the use of Paston and his heirs, but to the use of Fastolf himself, and for the accomplishment of his will. Further, the testimony of Russe, Cutteler, Bukenham, Felmyngham, and Butteler, was untrue as to the alleged will of Fastolf that John Paston should obtain the King's license for the foundation of a college at Caister. It was in truth Fastolf's will that the executors should obtain the King's license to found a college there of seven Benedictine monks of the same profession as the monastery of St. Benet at Hulme, of whom one should be prior, and of seven poor men, and that they should be endowed out of his lands to the extent of 300 marks a year, all charges deducted, to pray for the soul of Lady Milicent, his wife, his parents and benefactors ; and if the executors were unable to obtain this license, they were to give the abbot and convent of St. Benet's lands and money for the maintenance of six new monks and seven poor men in that monastery with a like object. Further, it is not true as alleged that on Saturday before his death, viz., 3d Nov., between eight and eleven a.m., the testator openly declared his will with a clear voice in the hearing of by-standers, for he was so ill and weak from want of breath that he was unable to speak distinctly at any time that whole day, especially during the hours above mentioned.

Moreover, bribes were offered by Paston and Howes in May and June 1465, in the parishes of Caister and Yarmouth, and in the city of London, to Thomas Thorald, Robert Lawes, Will. Waterman, John Osbern, John Heydon, Will. Pykeryng, John Symmys, and John Shawe, for their testimony in this matter, viz., that they should have 20s. besides travelling expenses and divers other sums which were offered to them in Paston's name by Cutteler, vicar of Caister, and Ric. Calle ; and John Paston promised the said William Pykeryng that he should recover certain lands in the tenure of his brother John Pykeryng, in Fylby, to the value of 40s. Influenced by these bribes, Thos. Thorald deposed that on the Saturday before Fastolf's death, Bartholomew Elys and John Davy came to his house in Belton, two miles and more from Yarmouth, about eight a.m., when he was in his grange, and asked him to come with them to divers manors of the said Sir John, to receive certain grain from his farmers ; after which they drank in Thorald's house, and he went with them to Freton, and to the manor called Calcote hall, and other places in Lothynlond until midday. Robert Lawes also deposed that on Friday before Fastolf's death he went to Becclys, and next day, viz., Saturday, returning homeward (*rediens domorsum*), met on the way the said Bartholomew Elis, John Davy, and Thomas Thorald going to Freton, when Davy called him and bade him tell Thomas Howys or John Rus that on Monday or Tuesday next he would go to Caister and give an account of his steward-ship. Afterwards, about two p.m., Lawes came to Caister and told John Rus his business in the absence of Howys. But the said William Waterman, being bribed as aforesaid, falsely declares that on the Saturday before Fastolf's death Barth. Elys and John Davy came to his house at Gorlyston about seven a.m., and that he went with them to Thorald's house, and that they went and spoke with Thorald at the grange while he waited for them at the gate. Afterwards they all entered the hall of Thomas Thorald and drank beer together, and all four went together to Calcotehalle and waited there till ten a.m., when Watyrman left the other three and returned home. And about two p.m. Elys and Davy returned and drank beer at Watyrman's house. But the truth is that Elys and Davy were at Yarmouth that day from seven till past eleven a.m.

Further, John Osberne, Will. Pykerynge, and John Heydon were corrupt witnesses. John Osberne said that on Saturday before the Feast of St. Leonard, when Fastolf was ill of his last illness, the said Osberne, Pykerynge, and Heydon came to Caister to receive certain monies of John Rus for barley sold to him by Osberne ; that about eight a.m. they entered the hall of the manor and found Robert Hert and others, servants of Fastolf, sitting at breakfast ; and that John Russe immediately came to Osberne and talked to him about the payment. At last Russe took them into the *claustrum*, and leaving them, entered Fastolf's chamber ; then, after remaining two hours and more, returned into the *claustrum* and delivered the money to Osbern. This testimony was confirmed by Heydon and Pykeryng ; but the truth is that Russe that Saturday, from seven till near twelve o'clock (*a principio horæ septimæ usque ad finem horæ undecimæ*) and Robert Hert from seven to ten a.m., were at Yarmouth, three miles off.

Further, John Symmys and John Shawe were corrupt witnesses, the former saying that Robert Hert was present in the said manor house of Caister at eight a.m. on the said day, and even at nine o'clock at dinner time (*tempore prandii*), and that he saw the said Robert Hert sitting among Fastolf's other servants at breakfast (*jentaculum*) ; and that he (Symmys) and Henry Wynstall, Fastolf's barber, were occupied together in shoeing horses in the said manor from breakfast time aforesaid to dinner time, and that at dinner time Symmys saw the said Henry sitting in the hall with others ; and that on the said Saturday, about eight a.m., and even at noon, Symmys saw John Rus in the hall of the said manor. Also John Shawe deposed that on the Saturday before Fastolf's death he saw John Rus and Henry Wynstall in the hall of the said manor, both at eight a.m. at breakfast and at dinner at midday, and he also saw Robert Hert, porter at the gate of the manor, at those hours ; and that between breakfast and dinner Shawe and Wynstall were occupied along with John Symmys in shoeing Sir John's horses. But the truth is that both Rus and Hert were absent as above mentioned, and Wynstall was with Fastolf in his chamber from nine a.m. to half-past ten. Also Symmys, William Pykeryng, Heydon, Osberne, and Lawes were all absent the whole of that Saturday, and certainly between eight and eleven a.m. And notwithstanding that the contrary is alleged against them, John Davy, Barth. Elys, John Bokkyng, John Davy, chaplain, Thos. Upton, Nich. Newman, John Loer, Wm. Eton, Robert

Lynne, John Marshall, Wm. Lynne, Henry Wynstall, Robert Hert, and Robert Fitzrauff, gave honest testimony in behalf of Yelverton and Worceter, being men of good repute, sufficiently rich, and well worthy of credit.

Additional exceptions on the part of Yelverton and Worcester to the testimony of John Rus and Clement Felmyngham, showing that Paston had offered to let to the former a tenement in Yarmouth for less than its true value, and had promised the latter 100 marks for the Austin Friars at South-Town,[1] which was not bequeathed in Fastolf's will ; also that he had given Master Robert Popy, besides his expenses, 20 marks for his testimony, and remitted to him 10s. of the rent of a fishery which was five years in arrear, and that he had also released to him 40 marks of a penalty of 100 marks due by Popy upon a bond ; in consequence of which Popy deposed that on the 30th October three years previously,[2] John Paston had reported to him at Caister that he had made an agreement with Fastolf by which he was to have all Fastolf's lands in Norfolk, Suffolk, and the city of Norwich, after his death, paying for the same 4000 marks, and was to found a college in the manor, &c. ; on hearing which Popy returned to Fastolf, and related to him what Paston had said to him, and Sir John confirmed it, requesting him to show the same goodwill towards Paston, as he had done to himself. But in truth Fastolf never asserted or confirmed any such thing.

Answers to interrogatories by the same deponent, viz.—1. As to his knowledge of the parties and witnesses.

2. As to the alleged instances of bribery, and the absence of Rus on the day referred to. The latter fact deponent says he knows, because he and Rus lay together in the chamber of Thomas Howys, and on Friday before Fastolf's death Rus went to Yarmouth to buy victuals, and left with him the key of the chamber, Howys being then at Blowfeld ; and Rus remained at Yarmouth all that Friday and the Saturday following, and returned on Sunday.

4. As to the condition of Fastolf on the Saturday before his death. He was so weak for want of breath that he could not speak distinctly ; those about him could not hear what he said without inclining their ears to his mouth, and even then they could hardly understand him. And this deponent says he knows, because on Friday and Saturday before his death he was frequently in Sir John's chamber, and when people spoke to him to comfort him in his illness he only answered by sighs, so that deponent and others could not tell what he meant. Moreover, Sir John was accustomed when in health daily to say certain prayers with

---

[1] South-Town, Yarmouth, sometimes called Little Yarmouth.

[2] "Quod dictus Johannes Paston apud Castre penultimo die Octobris ultimo præterito ad tres annos proxime elapsos sibi retulit." It would seem by this that Popy's testimony must have been given within three years of Fastolf's death.

his chaplain, but on that day the chaplain said the service alone, while Fastolf lay on his bed and said nothing.

6. As to Russe and Hert being at Yarmouth, he says he heard Thomas Howys that Saturday morning order the latter to take horse and ride thither to get provisions for the household, and he saw him ride out of the manor accordingly about seven a.m., and also saw him return with the provisions about ten a.m. [In the margin here is written " Nititur deponere de absencia Hert, sed non probat."]

7. Knows that Henry Wynstall was absent from the hall of the manor from about nine to half-past ten, for he saw him enter the chamber with his instruments to shave Sir John, and wait there an hour and a half, and he could not have left without deponent seeing him. Moreover, John Symmys did not shoe horses in the manor that Saturday, for deponent had the custody of the forge and kept the keys.

Answers to another set of interrogatories proposed on behalf of Paston and Howes, and here quoted at length, to the following effect, viz. :—1. Where each witness has lived since he was born, and whether he be in the service of the party producing him? 2. As to his knowledge of the witnesses on the other side. 3. What particulars he can give as to any bribery he imputes to them, and what was its special object? 4. By what means he knew it, and by whom he has been asked to give testimony, and whether he has conferred with his fellow-witnesses; whether they have received instructions what to depose; how often he has come up to London to give evidence and returned without being called ; and how much he was promised for coming? 5. Each witness is to declare how he knows the facts, and to be charged not to reveal to the others on what subjects he was questioned.

The only point of interest in these replies is that deponent was asked by William Worcester in the city of Norwich on Sunday eight days to give his testimony in the cause. He denies all communication with his fellow-witnesses, &c.

Note.—The evidence of this first witness runs to five or six times the length of any other, and we have noted all the material points in it. Of the depositions of the others we shall not give any summary, but mention briefly any new statements that seem to be of interest :—

II. John Dawson, husbandman (*agricultor*), of Blowfeld, where he has been for four years, having formerly lived five years in the manor of Caister, and before that in Cambridge three years, *literatus, liberæ conditionis*, about thirty years old.

His testimony generally agrees with that of Monke, and he says the covenant of Akethorpe was made in the February before Fastolf's death. Between Christmas and Easter after his death deponent heard Howes in the manor of Caister say to Robert Cutteler the vicar that he should have 6 marks for his labour in giving evidence about Fastolf's will; and afterwards Howes in his chamber in the said manor paid him 6 marks. Paston also promised him a benefice worth 40 marks. He says, about a month before Fastolf's death, he heard Howes and Paston frequently repeat publicly in the household the tenor of Sir John Fastolf's will. About St. John Baptist's day last he was at Yarmouth, and heard John Symmys and John Shawe say they were hired by Paston and Howes to give evidence in the proving of Fastolf's will.

III. John Gyrdynge of Fretenham, where he has lived four years; before which time he lived with the Prior of St. Faith's two years, before that in the manor of Caster four years, before that with John Emeryngale of Wroxham two years, and before that in Norwich as an apprentice with Henry Toke five years; a cook, illiterate and of free condition, thirty-two years old and over.[1] Agrees with the evidence of corruption against Rus and others. Was present in Fastolf's room that Saturday forenoon, and saw the two chaplains celebrating mass. H. Wynstall the barber was present till ten a.m.

IV. William Boswell of Thetford, who was four years with Friar Bracley, &c., *literatus*, of free condition, thirty years old and more. Heard Howys, Paston, and Rus frequently confer at Caister about the sale of a house in Yarmouth, which Howys, at the request of Paston, at length granted to Rus at £20 less than its value, to the end that Rus might bear witness in their favour in the proving of Fastolf's will. [Here occurs a marginal note by another hand, "Male sonat. Quod alius consensit non probatur." At the head of this deposition also it is said that this witness has been proved corrupt.]

V. Robert Inglys of Lodon, gentleman, who has lived there two years, and before that in the parish of Hopton three years, before that with Henry None, Esq., for more than a year, before that with Sir John Fastolf two years, before that with the Abbot of Langley two years, and before that in Hopton with his father; illiterate, and of free condition, thirty years old and more.

VI. Richard Horne of Brundall, Norwich diocese, husbandman (*agricultor*), who has lived there four years, and before that with Thomas Howys six years, and before that in the parish of St. George, Southwark, three years; illiterate, of free condition, twenty-six years old.

VII. Thomas Pykeryng of Wroxham, Norwich diocese, who has been a schoolmaster at Norwich and Aylesham, and is now clerk to Robert Norwich, steward of the Abbot of St. Benet's, Hulme.

VIII. Henry Clerke of Blowfeld, husbandman (*agricultor*), once in the service of Sir John Fastolf, illiterate, twenty-eight years old, of free condition. Says that on the Saturday before Fas-

---

[1] The residences of every one of the witnesses are given from the time of his birth; but we have given these details only in one or two cases as specimens.

tolf's death Howys sent him and John Shawe to Yarmouth about
seven a.m., with a cart-load of malt to one named Chirche; that
they arrived about eight, and were spoken to by John Rus and
Robert Cutteler in the market-place; that they waited with their
cart till two p.m., when deponent took leave of Rus and Cutteler
in the street, having repeatedly seen them there in the interval.
Also that at eight and nine a.m. he saw Robert Hert in Yarmouth, who soon after his arrival delivered him a sack containing
meat, bought, as he said, by Rus for Fastolf's household.   He
says also that between eight and nine he spoke with the said John
Symmys, William Pykeryng, and John Osbern in Yarmouth.

Marginal notes are appended to the above statements, affirming
that bribery had been proved against this witness by four others,
and that he stood alone in his testimony.

XI. John Tovy of Caister, where he has lived ever since he was
born, *agricultor, literatus*, of free condition, twenty-four years
old and more; cannot depose of his own knowledge to the
bribery of John Rus and the others.   He says John Rus was not
present in the manor on the said Saturday, having to be at Yarmouth to provide victuals for the household.   About eight a.m.
witness conveyed to the said manor some linen, which his mother
had washed, for she was Sir John's washerwoman, and waited
there, sometimes in the hall and sometimes in Sir John's chamber,
till after mid-day, but did not see John Rus or any of the others
named, as he would have done if they had been present.

X. Thomas Hert of Caister, *agricultor*, who has lived there
from his birth, illiterate, of free condition, twenty-three years old.
Cannot depose to bribery except from hearsay.   Was sent to
Caister by his father on the Saturday before Fastolf's death with
capons to be sold to John Rus, purveyor of victuals for the household, but on inquiring for him, found he was absent, and delivered the capons to Sir Thomas Howes.   Waited till nine a.m.
and saw neither Rus, Cutteler, Boteler, nor Robert Hert, but
was told Rus was at Yarmouth, and Boteler sick in his chamber.
John Symmys had nothing to do with the shoeing of Sir John's
horses that day.   Was asked to bear witness in this cause a fortnight ago by Sir William Yelverton's servant at Caister.

XI. William Shave, roper of Yarmouth, illiterate, of free condition, fifty-eight years old.   On the Saturday before Fastolf's
death, was at the house of John Balle, at the sign of the Cock, in
Yarmouth, in a parlour near the public street, when Sir Thomas
Howes informed John Rus, there present, that he had been desired
by John Paston to remit to him £20 of the price of a house sold
to Rus by the said Thomas, and thereupon he remitted to him
the said £20 and 5 marks, in which he was bound to Sir John
Fastolf.   He also promised him the lands of Akethorp Hall for
40 marks less than any other, provided he would favour the
intention of Howes and Paston.   [It is remarked in the margin
that witness does not say what intention.]   William Lynde, a

servant of Sir John Fastolf, was present, besides others.   He saw
Rus and Cutteler that Saturday at Yarmouth, between nine and
twelve a.m., and spoke with them and drank in the house of
Thomas Lounde. As to Thomas Torald, witness was at Yarmouth one Saturday, when he heard Robert Cutteler and Torald
conversing; and the former told the latter that Sir Thomas
Howes loved him well, and that John Paston could do him much
good, and in the name of Paston and Howes he promised Torald
20s. for his labour, besides expenses, if he would depose for them.
Knows that on the Saturday before Fastolf's death Bartholomew
Elys was in Yarmouth from half-past eight to eleven a.m., for
he and witness bought fish called roches together, sold some, and
divided others in Elys's house. That day he saw John Rus in
Yarmouth several times every hour from seven to eleven a.m.,
for he was in the market-place all that time on his business, and
at vespers he saw John Rus in the parish church of the said town.
Next day, Sunday, he also saw him there at matins and at mass.

XII. Nicholas Chirche of Yarmouth, merchant, *literatus,* of free
condition, forty years old and more.   Testifies concerning a con-
versation held in John Balle's parlour at the Cock in Yarmouth
after the Christmas following Fastolf's death, with Sir Thomas
Howes, John Paston, John Rus, Friar Clement Felmyngham,
Dan Robert Cutteler, Robert Boteler, Thomas Neve, and others,
when Howes remitted to John Rus £20 of the price of a house
he had sold him, and 5 marks of the arrears of his accounts.
He also testifies to other acts of the same nature on that occasion,
and to the absence of Rus and Cutteler at Yarmouth on the
Saturday above referred to, &c.

[In the margin it is remarked that this witness has been proved
corrupt by three others.]

On the 22d May John Naseby, proctor for Yelverton and
Howes, produced as a witness one John Rugge in presence of
Master Robert Kent, Paston's proctor.

XIII. Thomas Newton of Burgh, *agricultor,* illiterate, of free
condition, fifty years old and more.

XIV. Thomas Spycer of Southtown, by Yarmouth, tailor, illiterate, of free condition, fifty years old and more.

XV. Thomas Neve of Jernemuth [*Yarmouth*], merchant,
literatus, of free condition, forty years old and more.

XVI. John Rugge, mariner, of Yarmouth, illiterate, of free
condition, fifty years old.

XVII. John Clerke of Gorlaston, *agricultor,* illiterate, of free
condition, fifty years old.   Heard Clement Felmyngham report
to him at the Austin Friars in Southtown that Paston and Howes
had given him a pension of 8 marks a year for life, and 40s. for
his servant, to say masses for the soul of Sir John Fastolf.   Cannot witness of bribery otherwise.   A little after Michaelmas,
two years before Fastolf's death, William Worceter in Fastolf's
name delivered possession of six of his manors in Lodylond, viz.,

Spytlyng in Gorlaston, Bradwell Hall in Bradwell, Hadlounde in Bradwell, Calcotes in Freton, Beytons in Belton, and Ake-thorpe in Leystoft, to Sir Thomas Howes and others, his co-feoffees named in a charter of enfeoffment, to the use of Sir John during his life, and to execute his will afterwards. This he knows, because he rode with Howes to the said manors when he took possession, and saw and heard Worceter deliver possession thereof. Thomas Torald reported to witness in Lent last that Paston and Howes had promised and paid him 20*s.*, besides his expenses, to give evidence in the proving of Fastolf's will, and had given each of his fellow-witnesses as much.

XVIII. Robert Bunche of Yarmouth, mariner, *literatus*, of free condition, fifty years old. Swears to having seen John Rus that Saturday at Yarmouth between seven and eight. [A marginal note says that being afterwards produced as a witness by Paston, he admitted having been suborned, and having deposed falsely.]

On the 22d July Yelverton's proctor, Naseby, produced in presence of Paston's proctor, Kent, two witnesses, viz.—Stephen Scrope, Esq., and Richard Fastolf.

XIX. Stephen Scrope, Esq., of free condition, seventy years old or about. Says he was several times with Sir John Fastolf in his manor of Caister within the two years before his 'death, when Sir John told him he had made his will, and had ordered his executors to erect a college of six or seven monks and seven poor men at Caister, and that they should have lands and goods to the value of 300 marks a year, if a license could be obtained from the King to that effect; otherwise that the number of monks at St. Benet's should be increased, and seven poor men supported in the monastery. [In the margin it is remarked that this wit-ness proves nothing against the accused witnesses, but only endeavours to depose concerning the will of the deceased.]

XX. Richard Fastolfe, of the parish of St. Mary Eldermary, in London, tailor, where he has lived for two years, and before that in the parish of St. Micha· , Crokydlane, London, for a quarter of a year, formerly with the Duke of York, *literatus*, of free con-dition, thirty-two years old. Went to Caister about the Feast of the Exaltation of the Holy Cross preceding Fastolf's death, along with one Thomas Plummer, *scriptor*, of London, now deceased. Found Sir John walking about his chamber led by two servants, when Plummer petitioned him to help deponent with goods that he might marry, as he was one of Sir John's relations. To this Sir John made answer that he had within a few [days] preceding made his will, which he would not alter, and that he had made mention of deponent therein. He also said to Plummer that if he had come in good time, he should have written his will.

[Throughout all the above depositions will be found marginal comments in another hand, a few of which we have noticed incidentally, tending to shew that the testimony given is insufficient to prove the bribery of Paston's wit-nesses, or to invalidate their statements.]

" Responsiones personaliter factæ per Johannem Paston, armi-
gerum, xxixº die mensis Julii anno Domini MºCCCClxvtº, Indictione xiijᵐᵃ, pontificatus sanctissimi in Christo patris et domini
nostri, domini Pauli Divina providencia Papæ Secundi anno
primo, in domo habitationis venerabilis mulieris Elisabethæ Venor
in le Flete vulgariter nuncupat' infra parochiam Sanctæ Brigidæ
Virginis in suburbeis civitatis London' situata, [et] x., xj., et xijᵐᵒ
diebus mensis Decembris anno Domini supradicto, Indictione
xiiijᵐᵃ, pontificatus dicti sanctissimi patris domini Pauli Papæ
Secundi anno secundo, in domo thesaurarii ecclesiæ Cathedralis
Sancti Pauli London' in parochia Sancti Gregorii civitatis
London' situata, coram venerabili viro Magistro Johanne Druell,
utriusque juris doctore, commissario et examinatore in hac
parte specialiter deputato, in præsentia mei, Nicholai Parker,
notarii publici, scribæ in ea parte assumpti et deputati, de et super
interrogatoriis per partem venerabilis viri domini Willelmi Yelverton militis et Willelmi Worceter, executorum testamenti
domini Johannis Fastolf militis ministratis, productum."

551.

NOTE.

EXTRACT FROM "AN INDEX TO DEEDS AND WRITINGS IN
THE TOWER, MAGDALEN COLLEGE, OXFORD."

" 34. The testimony of Th. Howes concerning the testament
of Sir John Fastolf, touching which controversies arose between
John Paston the elder, and Thos. Howes of the one party, and
William Yelverton, Knight, and William Worcetyr on the other."

552.

A.D. 1466, 17 July.

EDWARD IV. TO THE BAILIFFS OF YARMOUTH.

This letter is reprinted from the *Norfolk Archæology*, where it was first
published by Mr. Worship from a transcript made by Sandford in his MS.
Genealogy of the Paston family, compiled in 1674. Sandford states that
" the originall under the King's seale remaineth in the custody of Edward
Paston, Esq." The date is rendered certain by the warrant subjoined.

BY THE KINGE (Edward the Fourth).[1]

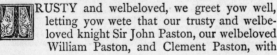RUSTY and welbeloved, we greet yow well,
letting yow wete that our trusty and welbe-
loved knight Sir John Paston, our welbeloved
William Paston, and Clement Paston, with

1 We have placed the words "Edward the Fourth" in parenthesis, though
they are not so printed by Mr. Worship, and are probably not so written in
Sandford's MS., because we suspect that they were not in the text of the
original document, but were added by Sandford by way of explanation.

other, have been before us and our councell worship-
fully declared of the surmise of great charge that was
laid on our behalfe unto John Paston deceased and
them, jointly and severally; so that we hold them and
every of them sufficiently declared in that matter, and
take and repute them as gentlemen descended lineally
of worshipfull blood sithen the Conquest hither; and
over that, have commanded that plenare restitution of
the mannor of Castor, and of all other lands and tenements, with goods and cattell, that the said John
Paston deceased had of the gift and purchase of Sir
John Fastolfe, Knight, shall wholly be restored unto
our said Knight Sir John Paston, like as the said John
Paston deceased had in any time of his daies. Wherefore, in as much as our said Knight intendeth to make
his abideing in Castor, we desire and pray yow that,
for our sake and contemplation, ye will be friendly and
neighbours unto him in his right, and such other things
as may be to his profitt and ease, wherein ye shall do
unto us full and good pleasure. Yeaven under our
signet in our Castle of Windsore the xvijth day of
July.

Subjoined to the above in Sandford's Genealogy is "the coppie of a
warrant sent from Kinge Edward the Fourth to restore Sir John Paston to
the lands and possessions which he purchased of Sir John Fastolfe, whereof
the originall remaineth in the custody of Edw. Paston, Esq." It is addressed
"To all tenaunts, fermors, or occupiers of all the lands and tenements, and
of every part of them, that late were John Paston's, Esq., now deceased, by
way of inheritance, or Agnes Paston, Margaret Paston, William Paston, and
Clement Paston, or any of them, and to all such persons what so they be, now
being in the mannor or place of Castor, or in any lifelode that was the said
John Paston, Esq., by way of gifte or purchase of late Sir John Fastolfe, or
of any other, within our counties of Norff., Suff., and Norwich, and to all the
tenants, fermors, baylies, or occupiers of the same, and of every part thereof;
and to all mayers, shreves, eschetors, bayliffs, and other our officers, as well
within franchise as without our counties aforesaid, hereing or seeing these our
letters." The King mentions in this warrant that "great part of the said
lands, tenements, and manors had been seized into our hands;" and the
tenants, farmers, bailiffs, and occupiers of the said lands are charged thence-
forth to pay the whole issues and profits thereof to Sir John Paston; and the
mayors, sheriffs, escheators, and others the King's officers are charged to be
"assisting, helping, and strengthening." The warrant is "Yeven under our
signet at Windsore, the xxvjth day of July, the sixth yeare of our reigne."

553.

A.D. 1466 (?) 20 July.—ABSTRACT.

[From Paston MSS., B.M.]

Latter clause of a writ of *supersedeas* to an escheator directing him not to make inquisition *post mortem* on the lands of John ————, until further notice.

Westminster, 20 July.

[From the time of year at which this writ is dated, it may have been issued after the death of John Paston, who died in May 1466, the inquisition on his lands not having been taken till October following. But it may possibly have applied to the lands of Sir John Fastolf, who died in November 1459, the inquisition after his death not having been taken till October 1460.]

554.

ANCESTRY OF THE PASTONS.

The following document is derived from a transcript made by Sandford in the Genealogy mentioned in No. 552, and some previous papers, and is likewise reprinted from Mr. Worship's article. Prefixed to it in Sandford's MS. are these words :—" The Briefe followinge was delivered to Edward Paston, Esq., amonge other evidence, by his uncle Clement Paston, and it is written in an old hand." It would appear, however, from the wording, not to be a " brief " or abstract, as Sandford considered it, but an extract from some certificate made in the King's name in behalf of Sir John Paston, setting forth what had been proved on examination as to the gentility of his ancestry.

THEY shewed divers great evidences and court rolles, how that they and their ancetors had been possessed of a court and seniory in the town of Paston, and of many and sundry bondmen, sithen the time that no mind is to the contrary ; and how that Agnes Paston, wife to the said William Paston, father to the said John, William, and Clement, in title of her dower, is in possession of bondholders, and also of bondmen, whose ancetors have been bondmen to the ancetors of the said John Paston sithen the time that no minde is to the contrary. And they shewed divers fines, some leavyed in the time of the begining of the reigne of our noble progenitor, Edward the First, son of Kinge Henry, son of King John, of liveloude whereof they and theire ancetors have been possessed ever since to this day.

Also they shewed divers inquests which is matters of record. Also they shewed divers deeds and grants before time of mind, how that their ancetors had licence to have a chaplen and have divine service within them. And that divers of their ancetors had given lyvelyhood to houses of religion to be prayed for, and confirmacions under the Great Seale of our noble ancestor Kinge Henry the Third, son of Kinge John, confirming the same grants.

Also they shewed divers old deeds, some without date, insealed under autenticke seales, of divers particular purchases in the town of Paston, reciting in the said deeds that the land was holden of the ancetors of the said . . . . . Paston, as of the chiefe lord of the fee, and by homage, and had ward, marriage and reliefe. Also they shewed how their ancestors were infeoffed in divers men's mannors and lands in trust. Also they shewed a great multitude of old deeds, without date and with date, wherein their ancetors were alwaies sett first in witness, and before all other gentlemen. Also they shewed how their ancetors had, in old time and of late time, married with worshipfull gentlemen ; and proved, by deeds of marriage and by other deeds, how their ancetors had indowed their wives, and by discents of livelyhood, and by testaments and wills of their ancestors under seale ; and made open by evident proofe, how they and their ancetors came lineally descended of right noble and worshipfull blood, and of great lords, some-time liveing in this our realme of Ingland. And also they made open proofe how they were nere of kin and blood to many of the worshipfullest of the country, and also nere to many and sundry great estates and lords of this realme, and was openly proved and affirmed, without contradiction or proofe to the contrary.

They shewed how they had kept pl'ce with divers

. . . . and with Plays that had wedded the Earle Warren's daughter, the third yeare of Edward the First. They shewed a lineall discent, how their first ancetor, Wulstan, came out of France, and Sir William Glanvile together, his kinsman, that after founded the pryory of Bromholme by the towne of Paston and the towne of Bentley; and how Wulstan had issue Wulstan, which bare armes gould flowret azure; and how he had issue, Raffe and Robert; which Raffe, senior, bare armes as his father, and Robert the younger bare silver flowret azure. And Robert had issue Edmund and Walter; which Edmumd the elder bare as his father; and his brother, because he married Glan-vile's daughter, a cheife indented gold, the field silver, flowret azure; and how their ancetors after bare with lesse number; and how Sir John Paston was heire to all those, for they died sans issue. And this was shewed by writinge of olde hand, and by old testaments and evidences.

555.

A.D. 1466, 16 Sept.
WILL OF AGNES PASTON.

[From Paston MSS., B.M.]

O all to whom this present writting xal come, I, Agnes Paston, late the wife of William Paston, Justice, send greting in God everlasting, lating hem know that I, the forseid Agnes, of goode and hole mende, the xvj. day of Septembre, the vj. yere of the reigne of Kyng E. the iiijth and the yere of our Lord a M^{l}CCCClxvj., make and ordeyne my last will in al the maners, londes, tenementes, rentes, ser-vices, mesuages, and places, that ony person or persones bene seased of to myn use and behof with in Norwiche, Norffolk, Suffolk, Essex, Hertfordshere, or in any other shere with in Englond, praying and desiring al the personez so feffed to myn use, after this my will, writtyn and incceled under my seale, be shewed unto them, that they wol make astate to the persones lemited in my seid will according.

And inasmoche as myn husbond, whos soule God assoile, dyverse tymes, and specialy among other the day of the moneth, rehersed to me that the lyvelod whiche he had assigned to his ij. yongest, William and Clement, by his will in writting, was so littill that they mizt not leve thereon withouzt they shuld hold the plowe to the tayle; and ferthermore, seying that he had dyvers oder maners, that is to say, the maner of Sporle, Sweynsthorp, and Bekham; which maner of Bekham he was purposed to chaunge with the maner of Pagrave; and if he myzt bring it abouzt, then xuld on of his ij. yongest sones have the seid maners of Sporle and Bekham, and no more, and the other yongest sone xuld have al the remenaunt. And he that had the maner of Sweynsthorp xuld be bound in a gret some to the prior of the Abbey of Norwiche, to paie dayly for ever to the monke that for that day singeth the masse of the Holy Goste in our Lady Chapell in Norwiche, where he purposed to leye his body, every day iiij*d.*, to sing and pray for his sowle and myn, and al the sowles that he and I have hade any goode of or be beholdyn to pray for. And after that the ——[1] day of ——————[1] next folowing my seid husbond lying seke in his bed, in the presens of John Paston, his sone and myn, John Bakton, John Dame, and of me, declared his will towching certein of his children and me, at whiche tyme he assigned to the seid John Paston the maner of Gressham in honde, and the revercion of suche lyvelode as he zave me after my decesse, askyng hym the question wheder he held hym not content so, seying to him in these termes, "Sir, and thow do not I doo, for I will not geve so mekyll to on that the remenaunt xal have to littill to leve on. At the whiche[2] . ."

---

[1] Blanks in MS.
[2] Here the fragment ends at the bottom of a leaf written only on one side.

556.

WILL OF AGNES PASTON.

[From Paston MSS.]

The following appear to be three separate fragments of an original draft of Agnes Paston's will, written on two sides of a small scrap of paper. Two of these fragments have the letters B and D prefixed to them, showing that they were intended as insertions in a part of the text now lost.

B.—And after that the —— day of the monethe my seyd husbond lyyng seke on hys bede sent for me, John Paston, Bakton, and John a Dame, to here hiis wyll rede ; and in owr presens all he began to reede hiis wylle, and spak fyst of me, and assynyid to me the maners of Paston, Latymer, and Schypden and Ropers, in Crowmer, for terme of my lyffe, and the manerys of Merlyngforthe, Stonsted, and Horwelbury, whyche wasse myn owne enherytans, and Oxned, whyche wasse my jontor, and [prayd me to hold me contente so, for][1] hadde do to lityll to ony it wasse to me, for somme he faryd the better, and so devedede (?) he ded for not of hem all, but he hadde more to care for, wyche myn as well as hys. And than he red John parte, and assynyd to hym and to hys wyffe the maner of Gressam, and after my desesse the maner of Oxned ; and he, thynkyng by John Pastons demenyng that he wasse not plesyd because . . . .

C.—Swynne of slowyth that hiis wyll wasse not made up, but wot swm ever cwm of me, Dame, I wyll ze know my wyll, and seyd that swyche lond as he hadde not wrytyn in hiis wyll wott xwlde he do with all, he wold his ij. yongest sonnys, Wyllam and Clement, xwlde have, and owte of Sweynthorpe to have hiis perpetuell masse. And of thys prayd me to reporte recorde and berre wyttnesse ; in qwyche disposicion and intent he continuyd in on to the day of hiis dethe, and I darre rytgh largely deposse that that same wasse hiis last wyll the tyme of hiis dethe ; qwyche wyll immediatly after my husbondes decesse I hopynd and declaryd to

[1] These words are struck through with the pen.

John Paston and al the other executores of my husbond, desyeryng hem to have performyd it. And the seyd John Paston wold in no wysse agree ther to, seyyng that by the lawe the seyd manerys xulde be hiis, in as moche as my husbonde made no wyll of hem in wrytyn, and gatte the dedis owte of my possession and estat of the feffees in the seyde manerys, myn un-knowyng.

And after that swyche tresowre of my husbons as wasse leyde in the Abbey of Norwyche by the seyd John Paston, John Bakton, John Dam, and me, to delyvere azen to us all, the seyde John Paston owte of the seyde Abbey unknowyn to the priour or ony oder person of the seyde Abbey, and withowte my wetyn[g] and assente, or ony of owre felawys, toke and bare awey all, and kepyng it styll azens my wyll and all the tother executores wyllys, nothere restoryng the seid Wyllam and Clement to the forseyd land, nother recompensyng them of my husbonds tresor, and ordeynyng for my husbonds sowle in havyng of hiis perpetuell masse acordyng to his wyll. Werfor, in as moche as I know and under-stonde verrely that it wasse my husbonds wyll the tyme of hys dethe, that the seyd Wyllam and Clement xwlde have the seyd manerys of Sporle, Sweynsthorp, and Bekham, and the annuyte for hys perpetuell masse to be going owte of the seyde maner of Sweynthorp, and that the possessioners of the seyd manerys at thys day wyll in no wysse by any fayer menez or spekyng tender my seyd husbonds sowle and myn, ner perform the wyll of my seyd husbond, I wyll have and xall by the gras[e] of swyche lyvelode as I have in my possession, that is for to sey, the maners of Stonsted, Marlyngforthe, and Horwellbury, that swm tym wasse my faders and my moders, and cwm on to me by them as myn enheritance. And after my decesse if I wolde soffer it to desend, xwld goo to the wronge posses-sioners of the seyd manerys of Sporle, Sweynsthorp, and Bekham, qwyche xall not be lettyd for me, but

if it be thorow her owne defaute, make, sta[b]lesse and
ordeyn myn husbonds perpetuell masse and myn, and
of the remenaunt, as swerly as can be made by the
lawe, I wyll the seyd Wyllam and Clement be recom-
pensyd to the valew of the seyde manerys of Sporle,
Sweynthorpe, and Bekkam, zerly [*yearly*], on to the tyme
that they be restoryd to the forseyd manerys of Sporle,
Sweynthorp, and Bekkam, in lik forme, and lyke astat
as xall be afterwards lymytyd in thys my last[1] [will;
chargyng and requiryng the seyd Wyllam and Clement
that after that they be restoryd to the manerys of Sporle,
Sweynsthorp, and Bekam, they restore myn heyres to
Marlyngforthe, Stons[ted], and Orwelbury.]

557.

NOTE.

In the Paston Genealogy drawn up by Sandford, to which we
have several times before alluded, occurs another extract from
the will of Agnes Paston, as follows :—

"Also I bequeath to the Whight Fryers of the said city of
Norwich, for I am there a suster, to helpe to pay hir [*their*] debts,
xx*li.*, which I will be gathered of the arrerage of my lyvelode.
Also I bequeath to the auter of Gracion of the said House,
whereas mine husband and I have a perpetuall masse, a vestment
which they have for a prist to judge in or [*of ?*] rede satern.   Also
to the mendinge of the chappell of our Ladie within the said place,
whereas Sir Thomas Gerbrege, my grandfather, and Dame Elizabeth his wife, and Sir Edmond Berrye my father, and Dame
Alice his wife, be buried, and Clement Paston my sonn."

558.

WILLIAM PASTON'S WILL.

[From Fenn, iii. 15.]

The following memorandum relative to the death of her husband was
written by Agnes Paston, probably about the time she made her will.

N the Thurseday at nyght before Our Ladys
Day the Assumpcion,[2] betwixt xj. and xij. of
the clokk, in the yer of Our Lord God
MCCCC. and xliiij., the Sondays lettre on

---

[1] The word "will" is omitted in the MS., and the words "my last"
repeated.   What follows is crossed out.
[2] The Assumption of Our Lady was the 15th August.

the D., died my husbond, God assoyle his sowle. And on the Fryday after I sent for John Paston, John Dam, &c. And on the Wedynysday after cam John Paston, &c. And on the Fryday John Paston, John Dam and I yede into the chambre, and they desyred of me to see the wyll. I lete them see it. And John Dam redde it; and when he had redde it, John Paston walkyd up and down in the chambere. John Dam and I knelyd at the beddys fete.

559.

ABSTRACT.

[Addit. Roll, 17,258, B.M.]

Roll of paper containing a draft in English of part of the inquisition on the death of John Paston, relating more especially to the foundation of Fastolf's college. In the latter part the jury find that John Paston died on the 22d May[1] last, and that Sir John Paston, Knight, is his son and next heir, and is of the age of 24 years and more.

*** Copies of the original inquisition, as returned into Chancery, and of that on the death of Sir John Fastolf, exist among the Paston MSS. in the Bodleian library.

560.

A.D. 1466, 29 Oct.

MARGARET PASTON TO SIR JOHN PASTON.

[From Fenn, iv. 272.]

The date of this letter is shown by the contents to be shortly after John Paston the father's death, probably in the same year.

To my ryght wyrshypfull mayster, Sir John Paston, Knyzt, be thys letter delyveryd in hast.

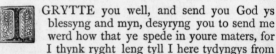 GRYTTE you well, and send you God ys blessyng and myn, desyryng you to send me werd how that ye spede in youre maters, for I thynk ryght leng tyll I here tydyngys from you; and in alwyse I avyse you for to be ware that ye kepe wysly your wrytyngys that ben of charge, that it com not in her [*their*] handys that may hurt you herafter. Your fader, wham God assole, in hys trobyll seson set

[1] The date in the inquisition returned into Chancery (6 Edw. IV., No. 44) is 21st May.

more by hys wrytyngys and evydens than he dede by any of hys moveabell godys. Remember that yf the wer had from you, ye kowd never gyte no moo such as the be for your parte, &c.

Item, I wold ye shold take hyde that yf any processe com owte a yenst me, or a yenst any of tho that wer endyted a fore the coroner, that I myght have know-lych therof, and to purvey a remedy therfor.

Item, as for your fader ys wyll, I wold ye shold take ryght gode counsell therin, as I am enformyd it may be prevyd, thogh no man take no charge thys twelf-month. Ye may have a letter of mynystracyon to such as ye wyll, and mynyster the godys and take no charge. I avyse you that ye in no wyse take no charge therof tyll ye know more than ye doo yet; for ye may verely knowe by that your unkell Will. seyd to you and to me, that thay wyll lay the charge uppon you and me for moo thyngys then ys exprest in your fader ys wyll, the whych shud be to grete for you or me to bere; but as for me, I will not be to hesty to take it uppon me, I ensure you.

And at the reverens of God, spede your maters so thys terme, that we may be in rest herafter, and lette not for no labour for the season, and remember the grete cost and charge that we have had hedyr toward, and thynk verely it may not lenge endur. Ye know what ye left when ye wer last at hom, and wyte it verely ther ys no mor in thys countray to bere owte no charge with. I awyse you enquer wysely yf ye canne gyte any more ther as ye be, for els by my feth I feer els it will not be well with ous; and send me word in hast hough ye doo, and whether ye have your laste dedys that ye fayled, for playnly they er not in thys contrey. It ys told me in consell that Ric. Calle hath nyer conqueryd your uncle Will. with fayre pro-myse twochyng hys lyflode and other thyngs, the whych shold prevayll hym gretly, as he sayth. Be ware of hym and of hys felowe be myn avyse. God sende you gode spede in all your maters.

Wryten at Caster, the moreu next after Symon and
Jude, wher as I wold not be at thys tyme but for your
sake, so mot I ches.   By your Moder.

561.

A.D. 1466 (?) 10 Nov.—ABSTRACT.

[From Paston MSS., B.M.]

SIR JAMES GLOYS to SIR JOHN PASTON.

Was at Snaylwell on Sunday, but could get no money.
Most of the tenants away at Canterbury or elsewhere. The
rest said when you were there last you had given them till
Candlemas, "so that thei myght malt ther corn and brynge it to
the best preffe." Warned them to be ready by Tuesday before
St. Edmond the King, when Richard Calle would visit them.
A thrifty man beside Bery is willing to take the farm; but
every one says the last farmer was undone by it. Advises
Paston not to overcharge his farms. I have seen Catelyn's
corn, and your tenants say it is sufficient to content you. Your
shepherd wishes to know if you will continue him, for no one
has spoken to him since my master your father died. Men of
Fordham have occupied your ground these two years that my
master has been in trouble. I think you should speak to my
Lord of Worcester, as he and Woodhous are lords of the town.
I have bid the farmers at Snaylwell sow some wheat land, and
have warned the tenants at Sporle, Pagrave, and Cressingham
to be ready to pay. Advises him to keep up his place at
Langham's. If "my master" had lived he would have exchanged
it for the parsonage. Supped on Monday night at a place of the
Duke of Suffolk's with the parson of Causton, a chaplain of the
Duchess, "and they talked sore of my Lady's bargain, and were
right sorry that she should forsake it." The parson asserted
that the feoffees had put her in possession of the manors. Talk
over this with your counsel; for if the feoffees be compelled to
release in Chancery it will be nought, because of the estate they
made before; so when you expect to be most quiet you will be
most troubled. There was also the parson of Brampston, and
he said W. Yelverton had sent a letter to the bailiff he has set at
Guton, but what it meant I could not find out. W. Yelverton
has put the parson of Heynford out of his farm. I did not speak
with your mother before writing this, as she was at Caister.

Norwich, St. Martin's Even.

From the mention of John Paston the father as dead, and the trouble he
had been in for two years, it would appear that this letter must have been
written in 1466, the year of his death. The letter is endorsed in a contemporary hand : "Literæ anno vj. et vij. Edwardi iiijti."

562.

A.D. 1466, 22 Dec.—ABSTRACT.

[From Paston MSS., B.M.]

THOMAS GRENE TO WILLIAM YELVERTON, ESQ.

Desires his favor for Frere John Chesteyn and John Russe of Yarmouth, who are suspected by Lord Scales of having treasures or jewels of my Master Paston's. He never trusted them with any, knowing they were familiar with William Jenney and Sir Thomas Howes. Is sure he put no treasure into any place in that town, religious or other, for he often said he wondered any thrifty man would live in it, "there were so much riotous people therein." Begs his favor for my mistress Paston, "which is now under your governance." Hopes to see her hereafter "as worshipful and well at ease as ever she was, and a great deal better when these troubles be passed; for I am sekir whan God woll that she be passed them she would not suffer them again for right great riches."

Norwich, morrow of St. Thomas Apostle.

[This letter has a great appearance of having been written shortly after John Paston's death. We place it therefore in the year in which he died.]

563.

Date uncertain.

SIR JOHN PASTON TO MARGARET PASTON.

[From Fenn, iv. 264.]

This and the two letters following are without any certain date, but they are all addressed to Margaret Paston, most probably after her husband's death.

To Mestresse Margrete Paston, be thys delyveryd.

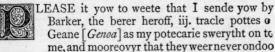PLEASE it yow to weete that I sende yow by Barker, the berer heroff, iij. tracle pottes o Geane [*Genoa*] as my potecarie swerytht on to me, and mooreovyr that they weer never ondoo syns that they come from Geane. Wheroff ye shalle take as many as pleasyth yow; neverthe lesse my brother John sente to me for ij., therfor I most beseche yow that he maye have at the lest on. Ther is on potte that is morkyn ondre the bottome ij. tymes with

thyes letteris M. P., whyche potte I have best truste
on too, and nexte hym to the wryghe potte; and I
mystruste moost the potte that hathe a krotte abovyn
in the toppe, lesse that he hathe ben ondoone. And
also the other ij. pottys be prentyd with that mar-
chauntys marke too tymes on the coveryng, and that
other pott is butt onys morkyn but with on prente,
notwithstondyng I hadde lyke othe and promyse for
on as well as for alle.[1]

564.

Date uncertain.—ABSTRACT.

[From Paston MSS., B.M.]

EDWARD MAWDBY to his Niece MARGARET PASTON.

Has a tenant, a widow in Sall, building a house on his ground.
She has been threatened with having it pulled down. Send for
Aleyn Roos, my receiver, and take his counsel what is to be done.

London, 24 Nov. Signed "By your nevew Edward Mawdby;"
although addressed "my most trusty and well beloved niece."

565.

Date uncertain.—ABSTRACT.

[From Paston MSS., B.M.]

E. CLERE[2] to MARGARET PASTON.

My little cousin your son[3] is a fair child. Wishes certain
evidences of Frethorp, which she delivered to Margaret Paston's
husband to make award between her and Rammesbury, a paper
book of the customs of Ormesby and a roll called "domysday,"
&c. Your father-in-law[4] was of counsel both wtth my mother[5] and
with my mother-in-law.[6] Supposes there may be other evidences,
as of Tacolneston, Therston, Reynthorp, Rusteynes in Wymondham, Kesewik, and Stratton. Sends back some rolls brought
by a man from Norwich, which belong to Margaret Paston and
not to the writer.

[1] The signature of this letter, Fenn says, is torn off the original MS.
[2] Elizabeth, widow of Robert Clere of Ormesby. She died in 1492.
[3] This must be one of the younger sons of John and Margaret Paston.
[4] Willam Paston, Justice.
[5] Margaret, wife of Thos. Owydale or Dovedale, of Tacolneston, daughter
and heir of William Reeves.
[6] Elizabeth, daughter of Sir Philip Branch, and wife of John Clere, Esq. of
Ormesby; after whose death she married again Sir John Rothenhale. *See*
No. 9.

566.

A.D. 1466?—SIR JOHN PASTON TO JOHN PASTON.

[From Paston MSS., B.M.]

The MS. from which this letter is printed is a draft in the handwriting of Sir John Paston There can be little doubt it was addressed to his brother John, and as it refers to the administration of their father's will, we place it in the year of his death.

TEM, Arb[l]aster must mak a proctyr by yowr advyce, and iff he lyst to make the seyd Master John Halfnothe he maye, elles he must sende uppe an other ; and he most also make a letter of waraunt to the seyde Master John Halfnothe undre hys selle by yowre advyce in thys forme :—

Master John, &c.   I recomande me, &c., letyng yow weet that I have made yow my proctor towchyng the testement off John Paston, Esquier ; wherffor I praye yow that ye on my behalve reffuce the admynystracion of hys seyde testamen, fur I woll nowt have ado ther with.   Wherffo[r] loke that ye on my behalve reffuce all admynestracion, entresse or besynesse, that I myght have there by.   And thys shewys yow my wyll here in, and shall be to yow a dyscharge att any tyme.   No moor, &c.
　　　　　　Yowr frend,
　　　　　　　　　　　　　JAMES ARBLASTER.

I wolde nat that myn oncle William scholde cawse hym to take on hym as hys felawe, for iff myn oncle William doo thus moche in the corte I suppose it may here afftre doo ease.   For as God helpe me I cannot sey verrely iff my fadre (God have hys sowle !) agreyd that he shold be one, but in my sowle he never thowt that he sholde be, for he never namyd no moor butt my modre and me, and afftre, yow, whan I rehessyd myn oncle Clement, yow and Arblaster, and than he chase yow, seyng he thoght that ye were good and trewe. Kepe thys secrett.   Iff myn oncle be noon executor, it maye happely brynge ageyn a trussyng coffre with CC. old peyse noblis, whyche he toke from me as executor.

567.

Between A.D. 1467-9.
J. STRANGE TO SIR JOHN PASTON.

[From Fenn, iv. 286.]

This letter being addressed to Sir John Paston touching a proposal of marriage for his sister, must have been after the death of his father in 1466, and,
of course, before the actual marriage of Margery Paston to Richard Call,
which seems to have taken place towards the close of 1469.

*To my rith worchipfull and good master, Ser John
Paston, Knyght.*

RYTH worchupful ser, after dewe recomendacion,
plesyt zow to understond the cause of my
wrytyng ys for a maryage for my Masterys
Nargery, zowr suster. For my nevyewe, John
Straunge, wold make her sur of xl*li.* joynture and CC.
marke be zer of inherytaunce ; and yf zee and zour
frendes wole agreve herto, I trost to God that xall take
a conclusion to the plesur of God, and worchup to both
partyes.

Moreover, and yt plesyth zow to wete, I am sore
troblyd with Bedston, as wele be the wcy of tache-
ments owte of the Chauncer as oderwyse. I must
beseche zow of zowr good mastershepe and help in
secrete maner as the Ser Thomas Lynes, the brynger
of thys, shall enforme zow. I xall be att London in
the begynnyng of thys terme, be the grace of God,
qwych preserve zowe.

Wretyn att Norwych in hast, the Monday after
Twelthe Day.

By yowr,   J. STRANGE.

568.

A.D. 1467 (?) 29 Jan.
T. DAVERSE TO SIR JOHN PASTON.

[From Fenn, iv. 172.]

The precise date of this letter is by no means certain. Fenn dates it merely between 1463 and 1469 ; but if it be "my Lady of Oxford," and not "my Lord," who is spoken of near the end (*see* page 298, foot-note 2), it may be many years later. The Earl of Oxford was committed to the Tower in the latter part of the year 1468. In 1470 he took part in the brief restoration of Henry VI., and on the return of Edward IV. he was obliged to quit the country. If the Earl, therefore, is alluded to as living in England, the date cannot well be later than 1468. Probably it is about the year 1467. In that year the 29th January fell on a Thursday, which would allow a reasonable time for the writer to suggest to Sir John Paston the expediency of his being in London on Monday or Tuesday following.

To my right good mayter, Sir John Paston, Knyght.

Y right especiall good mayster, I recomand me to yow, thankyng you right hertely of your gentell letter late send to me. And as to Pynchester mater, &c., I wulde I were youre nygh kynnesman, yef hit plesed God, and than shuld I know yef hit shuld greve your herte asmeche as hit dothe other of my kynne and frendes to see me thus cowardly hurte and maimed[1] by Pynchester, causeles ; and of myn entente in that mater, Wylliam Rabbes shall telle you more. All so I beseche yow to reco-mand me to my Lordes good grace, as to hym whom of erthely estates, next my dewte, I moste love and drede, and that shuld he well knowe and hit lay in my power, praying you hertely to declare his Lordship such mater as Wylliam Rabbes shall enfourme yow, and to send me my Lordes answere.

All so in asmoche as I understode by yow that money shuld cause you conclusion in your mater this next terme, and ye wull be at London on Monday at nyght or Tewsday by none, I truste that I have studyed such a mene that, up on surete as ye may make, to gete yow an *Cli.* or CC. mark to be lante un to yow for an halfe yere, with oute any chevysshaunce or losse of good by yow, as Wylliam Rabbes shall telle you more, &c.

And as to Ovyde " De Arte Amandi," I shall send hym you this next weke, for I have hyt not now redy ;

[1] The words "and maimed" are inserted from the right hand copy in Fenn. They are not in the left hand copy, having been overlooked, apparently, by the transcriber.

but me thenkeyth Ovide "De Remedio" were more mete
for yow, but yef [*unless*] ye purposid to falle hastely in
my Lady Anne P.[1] lappe, as white as whales bon, &c.
Ye be the best cheser of a gentell woman that I
knowe, &c. And I pray you to recomaunde me to
my Lord of Oxford,[2] and to my goods Maysters Nede-
ham, Richemond, Chyppenham, Stavely, Bloxham,
Stuard, and Ingulton in speciall, and all other good
masters and frendes in generall, &c. And, sir, Maystres Gaydade recomand me [? *her*] to yow and said
bessyng fare for charite, and she said me she wuld
fayne have a new felet, &c.

Wreten at London, this xxix. day in Janyver.

With herte and servyse your,

T. D.[3]

569.

A.D. 1467, 7 Feb.

JOHN PASTON TO SIR JOHN PASTON.

[From Fenn, iv. 276.]

This letter must have been written in February 1467. It was evidently
after Sir John Paston had succeeded to his father's estates, but before any
arrangement had been come to between him and Yelverton. It will be found
hereafter that on the 11th January 1468 Sir John Fastolf's executors, including Yelverton, released their rights in Caister and other manors to Sir John
Paston. On the back of this letter, Fenn says, is written in an ancient hand,
"Testes idonei ad negandum veritatem, ut patet infra."

YR, it is so that thys Saterday John Rus sent
me word by Robert Botler, that William
Yelverton hathe ben thys iij. dayis in Yermothe for to get new wytnessys up to London;
and, as it is thowt by the seid John Rus and Robert
Botler, ther wytnessyng is for to prove that it was Sir
John Fastolfs wyll that ther schold be morteysyd
iij.[c.] mark by yer to the colage, and also that syche
astat as my fadyr took her at Caster at Lames next

---

1 Who my Lady Anne P. was I cannot tell. The expression "as white as
whale's bone" is rather a strange one.

2 The modern version in Fenn reads "my Lady of Oxford."

3 Fenn says this subscription is explained by "T. Daverse" being written
under the direction, as he believes, in the hand of the receiver.

befor that Sir John Fastolf dyid, was delyveryd to my
fadyr to the intent for to perform the seyd wyll.

Bartholomew Elys, John Appylby, and John Clerk
ar the wytnessys; and as for Barthew Elys, he is owtlawyd, and also men say in Yermowthe that he is
bawde betwyx a clerk of Yermowthe and hys owne
wyfe; and as for John Appylby, he is half frentyk,
and so take in the towne, notwithstandyng he is an
attorny, as Barthew Elys is, in the Baylys Coort of
Yermowthe; and as for John Clerk of Gorleston, he
is owtlawyd at Sir John Fastolfys swte, and at dyvers
othyr menys, notwithstandyng he is thorow with Sir
T. Howys[1] for Sir John Fastolf, for thys cause, that the
seyd Clerk was on of Sir T. Howys[1] last wytnessys befor
thys.

I trow John Loer shall be ancthyr wyttnesse.   As
for Barthew Elys and John Appylby, they lye thys
nyht at Blyborowgh onward on her wey to London-
ward.   Make good weche on hem.

I pray yow send us some good tydyngs.   Wretyn
the Saterday, lat at nyght, next aftyr Kandylmas Day.

I pray yow remembyr John Grey and John Burgeys.
We have hom the most part of your barly, save fro
Wynterton, and that I trost to have this next wek, or
ellys we wyll strat [*distrain* ?] for it by the grace of
God, whom I beseche mak yow good.

I thynk ther comyng up is for to dysprove your
wyttnessys that he had in to the Chancery.

J. P.[2]

570.

A.D. 1467, March.
SIR JOHN PASTON TO JOHN PASTON.

[From Fenn, iv. 326.]

This letter is evidently of the same year as No. 573 following, and a little
earlier in point of date.

[1] Fenn has "Sir Thowys" in his left hand copy, which we cannot help
thinking a misreading of "Sir T. Howys."
[2] Fenn says this letter "has neither subscription nor date;" nevertheless
these initials stand at the foot of the text as he has printed it.

To my brother, John Paston.

RYGHT worschypful and verrely welbelovyd brother, I hertely comande me to yow, thankyng yow of yowr labor and dyligence that ye have in kepyng of my place at Castr so sewerly, both with yowr hert and mynde, to yowr gret bisynesse and troble; and I ageyn warde have hadde so lytell leyser that I have not spedde bot fewe of yowr erendys, ner kannot befor thys tyme.

As for my Lady Boleynes[1] dysposicion to yow werds, I kannot in no wyse fynde hyr a greable that ye scholde have her dowter, for all the prevy meanes that I kowde make, inso moche I hadde so lytell comfor by all the meanes that I kowde make, that I dysdeyned in myn own p[e]rson to comon with hyr ther in. Neverthelesse, I undrestande that sche seythe, "What if he and sche kan agre I wyll not lette it, but I will never advyse hyr therto in no wyse." And uppon Tewesday last past, sche rood hom in to Norfolke. Wherfor as ye thynke ye may fynde the meane to speke with hyr yowr selfe, for with owt that, in myn conceyt, it wyl not be.

And as for Crosseby, I undrestand not that ther is no maryage concluded betwen them, neverthelesse ther is gret langage that it is lyke to be. Ye be personable, and peraventure yowr beyng ones in the syght of the mayde, and a lytele descuveryng of your good wyl to her, byndyng hyr to kepe it secret, and that ye kan fynde in yowr hert, with som comfort of hyr, to fynde the meane to brynge suche a mater abowt as schall be hyr pleasur and yowrs, but that thys ye kannot do with owt som comfort of hyr in no wyse; and ber yor selfe as lowly to the moder as ye lyst, but to the mayde not to lowly, ner that ye be to gladde

---

[1] Anne, widow of Sir Geoffrey Boleyn. She was daughter of Thomas, Lord Hoo and Hastings. Sir Geoffrey had by her three daughters, of whom the youngest, Alice, is here referred to. This Alice was afterwards married to Sir John Fortescue.

to spede, ner to sory to fayle. And I alweys schall
be your herault bothe her, if sche com hydder, and at
home when I kome hom, whych I hope hastly with in
xl. dayes at the ferthest. My modre hathe a letter,
whych can tell you mor, and ye may lat Dawebeney
se it. JOHN PASTON, K.

I suppose and ye kall welle upon R. Calle, he
schall purvey yow mony. I have wretyn to hym inow.

571.

A.D. 1467, 3 April.
RICHARD CALLE TO SIR JOHN PASTON.

[From Paston MSS., B.M.]

This letter seems to relate to the summoning of witnesses to London for
the probate of Fastolf's will, and being addressed to Sir John Paston, we
may presume that it was written in the year after his father's death, and
before the final settlement of the dispute.

*To my ryght reverent and worschipfull mayster, Sir
John Paston, Knight.*

PLESITH it you to wete that I have spoken
with Henre Inglouse, and I fynde hym disposid weele; hough be it he hath be labored
to nough of late be divers, nevertheles he
woll not come withoute he have a suppena, and if he
come up be suppena, he can sey nor nought woll sey,
any thynge that schulde be prejudice or hurte to your
mater, and so he hathe tolde them that hath labored
to hym for it, weche hym thynkyth causith them to
have no grete hast to have hym up. He tellith me
that the Abbot of Langley schal come up and Wich-
yngham. Thes have her writtes of suppena delyverd
unto them. Also ther cometh up Doctor Vergraunt
and Frier Bernard. And as for Robert Inglouse, I
have spoken with hym, and I fynde hym no thyng so
weele disposid as his brother is; he hath be sore

labored be the meanes of my Lord of Norffolk and of
my Lord of Suffolk ; he seyth largely that he knoweth
moche of this mater, seyng to me that if he schulde be
examyned be for a juge, he wolde my master your
uncle[1] wer his juge, for he knoweth the mater as
weele as any man.   He seith if he be sworn be fore
my Lorde Chaunceler, he woll desire of my Lord that
Maister William schulde be sworn as weele as he ;
nevertheles I have so mevyd hym that withoute ther
come a suppena for hym he woll not come, as he seth
it is hard to truste hym.   It were weele doo if ther
were no suppena out for hym to cauce that ther schulde
non come, nouther to hym nor to hes brother, &c.   I can
not undrestonde of no moo that schulde come up yet,
but I schal enquere, and sende you word as hastely as
I can.   I have not spoken with John Maryot yet, but
I schall speke with hym within this iij. dayes and sende
you worde, &c.

Ferthermore, sir, like you to remembre the lees of
the maner of Sporle ; your fermours goth out at Michelmes next comyng.   Henry Halman wolde have it for
his sones, and if he schulde have it he wolde wete at
this tyme, be cauce he wolde somerlay[2] and tylle the
londe, otherwise then it is ; it were tyme to lete it, wo
so ever schulde have it.   Henry woll geve for it but
xx*li.*; wherfor, if ye wol that he have it, plese you to
sende word how we schal do with all, &c.   Almyghty
Godde spede you in all youre maters, and sende you
hastely a goode ende in hem.   Wreten at Castre on
Friday next after Esterne Day.

Your own Servaunt, Ric. C.

572.

A.D. 1467, April.
Sir John Paston to John Paston.

The following extract from a letter of Sir John Paston to his brother is

[1] William Paston.
[2] Halliwell gives the expression " to summerland a ground " which is used
in Suffolk, meaning to lay it fallow a year.   For this he refers to Ray.

quoted in Sandford's MS. Genealogy of the Paston family, and is here reprinted from Mr. Worship's article on that genealogy in the *Norfolk Archæology*. The original letter I have not been able to find. The tournament here referred to probably took place shortly after Easter. The next letter is evidently written in reply to this.

Y hand was hurte at the torney at Eltham upon Wednesday last. I would that you had been there and seen it, for it was the goodliest sight that was sene in Inglande this forty yeares of so fewe men. There was upon the one side, within, the Kinge, my Lord Scalles, myselfe, and Sellenger; and without, my Lord Chamberlyn, Sir John Woodvyle, Sir Thomas Mountgomery, and John Aparre, &c. By your brother,

JOHN PASTON, Mil.

573.

A.D. 1467, April.
JOHN PASTON TO SIR JOHN PASTON.

[From Fenn, iv. 330.]

This letter appears by the contents to have been written more than a week after Easter. The year must be 1467, as the dispute with Yelverton touching Sir John Fastolf's will seems to have come to an end before the January following (*see* No. 581).

YR, plesyth yow to weet that my modyr and I comonyd this day with Freyr Mowght to undyrstand what hys seying shall be in the coort when he cometh up to London, wheche is in this wyse:—He seyth at syche tyme as he had shrevyn Master Brakley, and howsyllyd hym bothe, he let hym wet that he was enformyd by dyvers personys that the seyd Master Braklèy owt for to be in gret consyens for syche thyngys as he had doone and seyd, and causyd my fadyr, whom God asoyle, for to do and seye also, in proving of Sir John Fastolfys wyll. To whom the seyd Mastyr Brakley answerd thus agayne : " I am ryght glad that it comyth to yow in mynd for to meve me with thys mater in dyschargyng of my

consyens ayenst God," seying ferther mor to the seyd
Freyr Mowght, be the wey that hys sowle shold to,
that the wyll that my fadyr put into the coort was as
veryly Syr John Fastolfys wyll as it was trew that he
shold onys deye. This was seyd on the Sonday when
the seyd Brakley wend to have deyid then. On the
Monday he revyvyd a yen, and was well amendyd tyll
on the Wednysday, and on the Wednysday he sekyned
a yen, supposyng to have dyeyd forthe with. And in
hys syknes he callyd Freyr Mowght, whyche was confessor on to hym, of hys owne mosyon, seyng on to
hym in thys wyse :—" Syr, wher as of your owne
mosyon ye mevyd me the last day to tell you aftyr my
consyens of Sir John Fastolfys wyll lyek wyse as I
knew, and now of myn owne mocyon, and in dischargyng of my sowle, for I know well that I may not
askape, but that I must dye in hast, wharfor I desyr
you that wyll report after my dethe, that I took it
upon my sowle at my dying that that wyll that John
Paston put in to be provyd was Syr John Fastolfys
wyll." And the seyd Brakley dyid the same Wed-
nesdaye.

And wher as ye wold have had Rychard Calle to
yow as on Sonday last past, it was thys Twyisday or I
had your lettyr; and wher as it plesyth yow for to
wyshe me at Eltam, at the tornay, for the good syth
that was ther, by trowththe I had lever se yow onys
in Caster Hall then to se as many Kyngs tornay as
myght be betwyx Eltam and London.

And, syr, whar as it lyekyth yow to desyir to have
knowlage how that I have don with the Lady Boleyn,[1]
by my feythe I have don nor spokyn nowght in that
mater, nor not wyll do tyll tyme that ye com hom, and
ye com not thys vij. yer. Not withstandyng, the Lady
Boleyn was in Norwyche in the week aftyr Estern, fro
the Saterday tyll the Wednysday, and Heydons wyfe[2]
and Mastras Alys[3] bothe, and I was at Caster, and

---

[1] *See* Note 1, p. 300.
[2] Anne, second daughter of Sir Geoffrey Boleyn.
[3] Third daughter of Sir Geoffrey Boleyn.

wyst not of it.   Hyr men seyd that she had non
othyr erend to the towne but for to sport hyr; bot
so God help me, I suppose that she wend I wold have
ben in Norwyche for to have sen hyr dowghter.   I
beseche yow with all my hart hye yow hom, thow ye
shold tery but a day; for I promyse yow your folk
thynk that ye have forgetyn hem, and the most part of
them must depart at Whytsontyd at the ferthest, they
wyll no lenger abyd.   And as for R. Calle, we can not
get half a quarter the mony that we pay for the bare
housold, besyd menys wagys.   Daube nor I may no
mor with owt coynage.

Your,   J. PASTON.

574.

A.D. 1467, 1 May.—ABSTRACT.

[From MS. Phillipps, 9735, No. 192].

" Bill indented " 1 May 7, Edw. IV., between Sir John Paston
and Thomas Lomnor, whereby the latter sells to the former an
ambling horse "upon this condition, that if the marriage betwixt
the Lord Charles, son and heir to the Duke of Burgon, and the
Lady Margaret, sister to our Sovereign Lord the King" take
effect within two years, Sir John agrees to pay 6 marks for the
horse on the day of the marriage; but if it do not take effect
within that period he will pay only 40 shillings.

[There is a modern copy of this document in the Heralds' College, in the
collection called Brooke's " Aspilogia," Vol. I., f. 47, where a drawing is given
of Sir John Paston's seal, which seems to have been attached to it when the
transcript was made.   It has been since removed at some time or other.]

575.

A.D. 1467 (?) 2 July.
JAMES GRESHAM TO SIMON DAMME.

[From Paston MSS., B.M.]

As this letter has reference to the disputes between the Duke of Suffolk and
the Paston family about Drayton, it might be supposed to have been written
about the year 1464, but that the entire absence of any mention of John
Paston the father makes it probable that the true date is after his death.   It
is therefore not unlikely to be of the same year as No. 576, in which Margaret
Paston mentions the probability of Hellesdon being taken again out of their

hands, and also desires an answer to a letter that she had sent to her son, Sir John, "by James Gresham's man."

To my worshipfull cosyn, Symond Damme, [at] Lyncoln Inne, at London, [be] this delyvered.

RIGHT worshipfull sir, and as in my trost my veray speciall good maister, I recomande me to you with al the servyce I can and may. Lyke it you to wytte that I have do my bysynes to enquere for suyche dedes as ye wrot for on to me, and, so God me helpe, I can not wytte where I shuld spede to have ony suyche dedes. I spak to a persone that is your good lover, the whiche tolde me that ther was a gret plee bytwene my Lord of Suffolk and Sir John Fastolf for the maner of Drayton, for whiche matier William Wysetre was sent to enquere for evydencez touchyng the Pooles lyvelond in suyche places as thei were lords of in their dayes. And the seid Wysetre fonde evydencez that touched a maner called Mundham maner, sum tyme longyng to the Pooles that were owenners of Drayton, the whiche evydences eased meche Sir John Fastolf; but the seid persone that enfourmed me of this can not telle the armes, ne what evydencez tho shuld be in certeyn, savyng he thynkyth indoubted that William Worcetre shuld not be unremembred of this. Wherfore it is thought to the same persone that enfourmed me of this and by me also, that it shuld be expedyent for you to comune of this matier by your wysdam with the same William Wysetre, now beyng at London, for he by lyklyhod can telle you a certeynte. And as touchyng my maister, Sir Thomas Mongomery, I trost veryly that he nothyr hath ne shall have cause of grudger by my defaut, for I can not understond ony cause of grudger; for ever whanne my cosyn Damme[1]

---

[1] As it appears by the postscript that this letter was hurriedly despatched, we may perhaps presume that it was intended in the first instance for Sir John Paston, but that as "my cousin Damme" required to be informed of the same particulars, it was afterwards addressed to him, with instructions to communicate the contents to Sir John.

hath spoken with my seid maisters attourne to have
knowelage by writyng of what thyng shuld be the
cause of callyng on you, he answerith that my maister,
W. Paston, hath a bille therof, but my cosyn can non
gete.   Wherfor I deme that the seid attourne meneth
not weel.   I entende noon other but in als meche as
in me is to se your indempnyte with the grace of
God, who ever mote be your guyde and protector.
Wretyn at Norwich the ij. day of Juylle.

> Your servaunt in that he can and may
> to his powar,
> > I, JAMES GRESHAM.

Cosyn, an noon after this was wretyn, had I knowelage of the massageris comyng to London berar of
this, and I had thought to have wretyn the letter above
wretyn newe, by cause of the foule wrytyng and inter-
lynyeng, but now I lakke leyser.   Wherfor I pray you
understond the pyth of my seid wrytyng, and enfourme
my seid maister Sir John P. of the same, for I wold
fayne do that shulde please hym, &c.   And the persone
that enfourmed me dar not be a knowe of his name,
ne he wold not it shuld be understond to them that
be of counsell ageyn my maister.   It was the parson
of Heylesdon, &c.   More over, as I have wretyn to
you of late, Palmer, undershireve of Norffolk, hath
sent his letter to his depute to acomplyssh our entent
for Chyldes matier as ye and I were accordet.   This
told Wykes me for verray certeyn, &c., the ij. day of Juylle.

On the back of this letter are some scribblings in another hand, viz. :—
First, a partial copy of the address ; second, the name " John Dode ;"
third, the following inscription, " Orate pro anima Johnnes (*sic*) de Boys
armenger de Londonn."

576.

A.D. 1467, 11 July.
MARGARET PASTON TO SIR JOHN PASTON.

[From Fenn, iv. 294.]

This letter must have been written some time after Sir John Paston had obtained possession of Caister by virtue of the King's warrant of the 17th July 1466 (No. 552), and before the Duke of Norfolk laid claim to it again in 1469. Thus the date is certainly either 1467 or 1468. But in the latter year Sir John Paston and his brother were both in Flanders at the marriage of the Princess Margaret to the Duke of Burgundy ; and Daubeney could not have been with them, as he was when this letter was written, for John Paston the younger says he had sent him five shillings by Calle's man. Thus 1467 appears to be the only year possible.

To Sir John Paston, Knyght, be this delivered in hast.

GRETE you wele, and send you Godds blissyng and myn, letyng you wete that Blykklyng of Heylesdon came fro London this weke, and he is right mery, and maketh his bost that with in this fourtnyght at Heylesdon shuld be bothe new lords and new officers. And also this day was brought me word fro Caystr that Rysyng of Freton shuld have herd seid in diverse places, ther as he was in Suffolk, that Fastolf of Coughawe maketh all the strenght that he may, and proposith hym to assaught Caystr, and to entre ther if he may, in samych that it is seyd that he hath a v. score men redy, and sendyth dayly aspies to understand what felesshep kepe the place. Be whos power, or favour, or supportacion that he wull do this, I knowe not ; but ye wote wele that I have ben affrayd ther befor this tyme, whan that I had other comfort than I have now, and I can not wele gide ner rewle sodyours, and also thei set nct be a woman as thei shuld set be a man. Therfor I wold ye shuld send home your brothers, or ell[es] Dawbenye, to have a rewle, and to takyn in such men as wer neces- sary for the saffegard of the place ; for if I wer ther withought I had the mor sadder or wurchepfull per- sones abought me, and ther comyn a meny of knavys, and prevaylled in ther entent, it shuld be to me but a vylney. And I have ben abought my liffelode to set a rewle ther in, as I have wretyn to you, which is not yet all performed after myn desyre, and I wuld not goo to Caystr till I had don. I wull no mor days make ther abowtyn if I may ; therfor in any wyse send sume body home to kepe the place, and whan that I

have do and performed that I have be gunne, I shall
purpose me thederward if I shuld do ther any good,
and ell[es] I had lever be thens.

I have sent to Nicholas, and such as kepe the place,
that thei shuld takyn in sume feles [*fellows*] to assiste
and strengh them till ye send hame sume other word, or
sume other man to governe them that ben therin, &c.

I marvayll gretly that ye send me no word how that
ye do, for your elmyse [*enemies*] begynne to wax right
bold, and that puttith your frends bothyn in grete fere
and dought. Therfor purvey that thei may have sume
comfort, that thei be no more discoraged ; for if we
lese our frends, it shall hard in this troubelous werd
[*world*] to kete them ageyn.

The blissid Trynyte spede you in your mater, and
send you the victory of your elmyse, to your herts eas
and ther confusyon. Wretyn at Norwich, the Saterday next befor Relyke Sonday,[1] in hast.

I pray you remembre wele the maters that I wrote
to you for in the letter that ye had be James Gres-
hames man, and send me an answer ther of be the
next man that comyth, &c.

Be your moder,   M. P.

577.

A.D. 1467, 28 Aug.—NOTE.

The following is an extract from "An Index to Deeds and
Writings in the Tower, Magdalen College, Oxford : "—

Documents relating to Norf. and Suffolk, No. 47.

" Thomas Archiep. Cant., Willielmus Episcopus Winton.,
et Johannes Beauchamp dominus de Beauchamp, juxta formam
barganiæ et effectum ultimæ voluntatis Johannis Fastolf in curia
Audientiæ, &c., concedunt Johanni Paston militi totum jus in
maneriis de Castre vocatis Vaux, Bosoms, et Redhams, Spensers
in Heringby, Reggisley, Reps, cum aliis terris in diversis villis ;
necnon in manerio de Guton cum advocatione ecclesiæ de Hein-

---

[1] Relick Sunday (the third Sunday after Midsummer Day) was the 12th
July in 1467.

ford in Saxthorp vocat. Loundhall, cum aliis terris in diversis villis, et in manerio de Caldecots et Akethorp, Spitlings, Habeland, &c., habit. ex feoffamento Rad. dom. de Sudley et aliorum.
    Aug. 28.   Edw. IV. 7.''

578.

A.D. 1467, 31 Aug.—ABSTRACT.

[From Paston MSS., B.M.]

A small slip of paper close written on both sides with accounts of wages. In the margin on one side is the name John Braham, with the memorandum, "Thys wrytynge, made the iiijth yere of Kynge Edward the iiijth, and in the monyth of Novembre, wytnessez of the wagez that my master payith to his men." A blank seems to have been left below this at first, but it was afterwards filled up in a different hand : "Memorandum that the v^e yer of Kyng Edward the iiij^e I rekenyd wyth my master at Stoke ; and on the v. day of Aprylle for the yerys that I have be wyth my mastyr, wheshe shal be at Hocke Monday next cumyng v^e yer and an halfe ; for the wheshe yerys I have reseyvyd at sondery tymeys vli. and iiij$s$., and thys seyd v. day I reseyvyd of my master v. marcs."

On the other side, in the first hand, is an account extending from the 11th April, 5 Edw. IV. (1465) to the last day of August 7 Edw. IV. (1467), of payments to a female named Rose,[1] for wages by "my master," Braham and Thorpe. These sums vary from 3s. 4d. to 8s. 4d., at a time ; but there are also two items for presents made to her, viz., for 4 ells of Holland cloth at 8½d. the ell, 2s. 10½d., and for a pair of hosen, 12d. On the 7th Oct. 6 Edw. IV. (1466) it is said "My master toke her for wages at Stoke, 5s."

579.

A.D. 1467, 2 Oct.—NOTE.

The following is another extract from the Index referred to in No. 577 :—

" 12. Concessio Joh. Paston militis Johanni Duci Norfolk et aliis manerii sui vocati Hemnales in Cotton in Com.' Suff., ac manerii sui de Haynford, et advocationis ecclesiæ ejusdem in Com.' Norff., habit' ex dono Th. Archiepisc. Cant. et Willielmi Episc. Wynton., cum littera attor. ad deliberandum scisinam. Oct. 2.   Edw. IV. 7.''

    [1] It appears by other letters that she was a servant "dwelling before Mrs. Paston's gate."

580.

A.D. 1467, or later.—ABSTRACT.

[From Paston MSS., B.M.]

PETITION OF JOHN HERLYNG OF BASYNGHAM TO "LADY" PASTON.

Requests "her Highness" to confirm some grants of her late husband to him of land at Basyngham. William Swan claims, and has taken from him 2 perches of ground in breadth near his (Swan's) gate, which has always been parcel of Herlyng's tenement of Greyve's during his and his father's time. John Pykerell, too, has made mean to the Abbot of St. Benet's to remove a boundary stone which has stood there sixty years. Pykerell also took the writer's horse and used it in his field without leave, on Friday before the Exaltation of the Holy Cross, 6 Edw. IV., which made the beast unserviceable till Fastegong next following. Pykerell has also done him other injuries.

[As this petition refers to the "Fastegong" or Shrovetide after Holy-Rood day 6 Edw. IV. as a past date, it cannot have been drawn up earlier than the year 1467. The manor of Basingham, in Norfolk, belonged to the Mauteby family, and came to John Paston by marriage. This paper, therefore, was addressed to his widow Margaret.]

581.

A.D. 1468, 11 Jan.—ABSTRACT.

[MS. in Bodleian Library.]

Release by William Bishop of Winchester, John, Lord Beauchamp, Sir John Howard, Sir William Yelverton, Justice of the King's Bench, Thomas Lytelton, Justice of the Common Pleas, William Jenney, Serjeant-at-Law, William Paston, Esq., Thomas Howys, clerk, and William Grene, to Sir John Paston, Knight, of the manors of Castre, in Flegge, called Vaux and Bosoms, and the lands in Castre called Redham, the manors or tenements in Heryngby called Spensers and Fennes, a third part of the manor of Runham, the manor of Wynterton, called Begvyles, with a windmill, the manor of Reppes in Bastewyk, and messuages, &c., in Yarmouth; the lands called Billes in Stokesby and Cattes in Heryngby, &c.; the manors of Guton in Brandeston, Heynford, the manor of Saxthorp, called Loundhalle, with a watermill, the manor of Lincolnhalle, in Boyton, &c., in Norfolk; and the manor called Caldecotes in Freton, Suff.; the manors of Akethorp in Lowestoft and Spitlyngges in Gorleston, and lands called Haveloune in Bradwell, &c.; also in the manor

of Tichewell, &c., in the hundred of Smethedon, Norf.; and
the manor of Hempnales in Cotton, and Burnevyles in Naketon,
Suff.; all which the said Bishop and the others had, *inter alia*,
of the gift of Ralph, Lord Sudeley, Sir William Oldhall, Richard
Waller, Esq., Thomas West, Esq., William Wangford, and
Nicholas Girlyngton.

Dated 11th Jan. 7 Edw. IV.

582.

A.D. 1468?

WILLIAM WORCESTER TO MARGARET PASTON.

[From Fenn, iv. 280.]

It seems probable that this letter was written about the beginning of the
year 1468. As to the time of year, we may judge by one expression that it
was not very long after Christmas; and as the writer congratulates Margaret
Paston that Caister is to be at her command, we may with great probability
suppose the date to be about the same as that of the preceding document.

*To my ryght worshypfull maistras, Margyt Paston,
wedowe.*

RYGHT worchypfull maistras, aftyr dew recomendacion, please your gode maistrasshyp
to wete that I comyned late wyth your entier
welbelovyd son, Sir John Paston, of the fundacion of my Maister Fastolf Collage myght ben at
Cambrygge, yn case hyt shall nat bee at Castre, nether
at Seynt Benetts, because that Universyte lyeth neere
the cuntree of Norffolk and Suffolk; for albe it my
Lord of Wynchestr ys disposed to found a Collage yn
Oxford for my seyd maister to be prayd for, yhyt wyth
moch lesse cost he myght make som othyr memorialle
also yn Cambrygge, and yt weere of ij. clerkys, iij. or
iiij. scolers, founded at leest wyth the value of gode
benefices and ryche parsonages, that myght be purs-
chased the advowsons, wyth moch lesse goodes then
lordshyppes or maners may; and I fonde your son
well disposed to meofe and excyte my seyd Lord.
Also now the Cristmasse weke next before the feest
att London, my Lord Wynchester called me to hym

yn presence of Sir John, and desyrid hym effectually
to be my gode wyller; and maister wold hafe no
wordes rehersed on my behalf, and he seyd full welle.
Wold Jesu, Maistras, that my gode maister that was
som tyme your husbond, yn my seyd Maister Fastolf
lyfe dayes, as he shewed to me, their coude hafe
founded yn hys hert to hafe trusted and lovyd me as
my Maister Fastolf dyd, and that he wold not hafe
geven credence to the malyciouse contryved talys that
Frere Brakley, W. Barker, and othyrs ymagyned
ontruly, sayvng your reverence, of me. And now ye
may opynly ondrestand the sothe, and your son Sir
John also; and yhyt for all that I put nevyr my
Maister Fastolf lyfelode yn trouble, for alle the
unkyndnesse and covetuse that was shewed me, as I
hafe declared to the berer heroff, that I know ye trust
welle, to whom yn thys ye may gefe credence at thys
tyme.

God amend J. Russe. I wold he had ben at Irland
for one day ys sake.

Your,   W. W.

And I thank you hertly for my pore woman, she
shuld com to you at your commaundment late or
rathe, but for gelosye and mysdemyng of peple that
hafe me yn greete awayt; and ye know welle, maistras,
better ys afrende unknow then knowen; the world ys
to mysdemyng and redy to make dyvysyon and debate
that comyth of an envyouse disposicion. And I am
ryght glad that Castr ys and shall be at your comaund-
ment, and yowres yn especialle. A ryche juelle yt ys
at neede for all the cuntre yn tyme of werre; and
my Maister F. wold rather he had nevyr bylded yt
then hyt shuld be yn the gouvernaunce of eny sovereyn that wole oppresse the cuntree. And I fynde
the relygyoux of Seynt Benetts full unkynde toke away
a chambre, the elder Abbot had put me yn possessyon
for my solace, when I myzt com thedr and desport
me, and toke that chambre to Maister John Smyth,

that Sir Thomas Howys seyd to me, was none holsom counceller yn the reformacion of the last testament made but ij. executors to hafe the rule allone. I wold he had nevyr medled of yt, that councell made moch trouble. I pray you kepe thys letter close to your sylf, as I trust you and Sir Jamys, and also yn R. Toly that I undrestand hym close and just.

I had no tyme to speke withyn now late, when I was but one day at Norwych. W. Barker sclaundred me yn certeyn maters of gode to the some of v$^{c.}$ mark that Reynold Harneys shuld kepe and take me half. Wold Jesu B[a]rker had seyd true, hyt myzt hafe do me moch gode ! And, Maistras, as I dar desyre you, I pray you recomaund me to my best maistras, your moder Agnes, for she favorued me and dyd me grete cherytee, to be the better disposed to hyr son, Maister John, and by my soule yt made me the hertyer to safe the lyfelode fro trouble or from claymes, as I support me to alle the world, I put nevyr maner ne lyfelode of my Maister Fastolf yn trouble, ne entitled no crettur to na place, and ye may speke wyth hyr herof when ye be allone.

583.

A.D. 1468 [12 April].
HUGH FENN TO SIR JOHN PASTON.

[From Fenn, iv. 290.]

This letter was written on the Tuesday before Easter, probably in the year 1468, *i.e.*, after the other executors of Fastolf had released to Sir John Paston. The date could hardly be later than 1469 when Sir John was driven out of Caister by the Duke of Norfolk ; and in 1469 he does not seem to have been residing there about Easter.

To the right worchepfull Sir John Paston, Knyght.

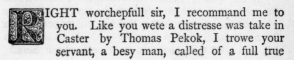

IGHT worchepfull sir, I recommand me to you. Like you wete a distresse was take in Caster by Thomas Pekok, I trowe your servant, a besy man, called of a full true

sowle, John Hadynet of Haryngby, a pore man, his
plow hath loyn ever sith, he seith ; I understonde it
is for Catts landes. I sent my clerk to my mastresse,
your moder, and the seid John with hym therfor;
and my mastresse wold hym come ageyn a nother
day, for Pecok was not thanne at home ; so he ded,
and can not have it, as he seith, but that ye wold I
shuld speke with you at Castr therof, and of other
maters he tolde me this day. And by cause of my
moders yereday holden this day, God have hir sowle,
and to morwe shal be a good day, I wol by Goddes
grace dispose me to His mercy ageyns Thursday, as I
have used; therfor I pray you pardon my comyng. In
the weke after Ester, I entend to se you and my seid
mastresse certeynly ; it is loong seth I sy hir, me
semeth. And if ye be not thanne at Castr, I pray you
send me worde that I may come soner to you to
comon with you in this mater, and in all other what ye
wil, and sone departe to London fro thens; and therfor I wil abide with you a good while.

Sir, as to Catts ye be remembred what I seid to
you at London at ij. tymes. I am the same man; I
have sith I cam geten th'evidences in to myn handes,
and I am redy to shewe them what lerned man her
that ye wol assigne. The mater is cler to my thynkyng.
Titleshale that solde it to Sir J. Fastolf myght as wele
a solde hym your lande or myn; and if the sale be
lawfull, I shal leve my hands at the first as I said at
London. The distresse to be kept for that, I wisse it
nede not, and it was unlawfully taken. Like it you to
do delyvere the pore man his goods ageyn, I am redy
to answer you for elde and new as right wol. I shal
breke no day to be assigned, for to leve all other
thyngs.

By the blissed Lady I beleve that ye wol dispose
you wele, and so I pray God ye do, and have you in
His blissed governaunce. Wretyn at the hede town of
Norffolk this Tuysday.

Your owen,   H. atte FENNE.

584.

A.D. 1468, 18 April.

EDWARD IV. TO SIR JOHN PASTON.

This letter is reprinted from Mr. Worship's article on Sandford's Genen-
logy of the Paston family in the *Norfolk Archæology*. The original was
transcribed by Sandford, but is not now to be found. Margaret, sister of
Edward IV., was married to Charles the Bold, Duke of Burgundy, at Bruges,
on the 3d July 1468.

To our trusty and welbeloved Sir John Paston, Knight.

BY THE KING.

TRUSTY and welbeloved, we greet yow well.
And where it is accorded betwixt us and our
cozen the Duke of Burgundye that he shall
wedde our derrest sister, Margaret, and that
in shorte while we intende to sende her into the parts
of Flanders for the accomplishment and solempniza-
cion of the marriage so concluded; at the which time
it behoveth her to be accompanied with great nobility
of this realme, for the honour thereof, of us and our
said sister : We therefore, wele understanding and
remembering the good affection ye bere towards us
all, our pleasure is, and our said sister, whereupon we
greatly trust, desire and pray yow right effectuously
that, every excuse or delaye laide aparte, ye will dispose yourselfe to the saide intent and purpose against
the first day of June next cominge, according to your
honour and degree, and that ye faile not so to doe, as
we singularly trust yow, and as ye intende to do us
justys, pleas.[1] Yeven under our signet at our mannor
of Greenwich, the xviij. day of Aprill.

[1] So, as printed in the Norfolk Archæology.

585.

A.D. 1468, 8 July.

John Paston the Younger to Margaret Paston.

[From Fenn, ii. 2.]

As this letter gives an account of the marriage of the Princess Margaret to Charles, Duke of Burgundy, there is no doubt of the year in which it was written.

To my ryght reverend and worchepfull modyr, Margaret Paston, dwellyng at Caster, be thys delyveryed in hast.

RYTH reverend and worchepfull modyr, I re-comaund me on to you as humbylly as I can thynk, desyryng most hertly to her of your welfare and herts ese, whyche I pray God send yow as hastyly as my hert can thynk. Ples yt yow to wete, that at the makyng of thys byll, my brodyr and I, and all our felawshep, wer in good helle, blyssyd be God. As for the gydyng her in thys contre, it is as worchepfull as all the world can devyse it, and ther wer never Englyshe men had so good cher owt of Inglong that ever I herd of.

As for tydyngs her, but if it be of the fest, I can non send yow ; savyng my Lady Margaret[1] was maryd on Sonday[2] last past, at a towne that is callyd the Dame, iij. myle owt of Brugys, at v. of the clok in the mornyng ; and sche was browt the same day to Bruggys to hyr dener ; and ther sche was receyvyd as worchepfully as all the world cowd devyse, as with presession with ladys and lordys, best beseyn of eny pepyll, that ever I sye or herd of. Many pagentys wer pleyed in hyr wey in Bryggys to hyr welcomyng, the best that ever I sye. And the same Sonday my Lord the Bastard,[3] took upon hym to answere xxiiij. knyts and gentylmen, with in viij. dayes at jostys of pese ;

[1] Margaret, sister of King Edward IV.   [2] July 3.
[3] Anthony, Count de la Roche, commonly called the Bastard of Burgundy, a natural son of Duke Philip the Good.

and when that they wer answeryd, they xxiiij. and hym selve schold torney with othyr xxv. the next day aftyr, whyche is on Monday next comyng; and they that have jostyd with hym into thys day, have ben as rychely beseyn, and hymselve also, as clothe of gold, and sylk and sylvyr, and goldsmyths werk, myght mak hem; for of syche ger, and gold, and perle, and stanys, they of the Dwkys coort, neythyr gentylmen nor gentylwomen, they want non; for with owt that they have it by wyshys, by my trowthe, I herd nevyr of so gret plente as ther is.

Thys day my Lord Scalys[1] justyd with a Lord of thys contre, but not with the Bastard; for they mad promyse at London that non of them bothe shold never dele with othyr in armys; but the Bastard was one of the Lords that browt the Lord Scalys in to the feld, and of mysfortwne an horse strake my Lord Bastard on the lege, and hathe hurt hym so sore, that I can thynk he shalbe of no power to acomplyshe up hys armys; and that is gret pete, for by my trowthe I trow God mad never a mor worchepfull knyt.

And as for the Dwkys coort, as of lords, ladys and gentylwomen, knyts, sqwyers, and gentylmen, I hert never of non lyek to it, save Kyng Artourys cort. And by my trowthe, I have no wyt nor remembrans to wryte to yow, half the worchep that is her; but that lakyth, as it comyth to mynd I shall tell yow when I come home, whyche I tryst to God shal not be long to; for we depart owt of Brygys homward on Twysday next comyng, and all folk that cam with my Lady of Burgoyn owt of Inglond, except syche as shall abyd her styll with hyr, whyche I wot well shall be but fewe.

We depart the soner, for the Dwk[2] hathe word that the Frenshe Kyng[3] is purposyd to mak wer upon hym hastyly, and that he is with in iiij. or v. dayis jorney of Brugys, and the Dwk rydyth on Twysday next comyng, forward to met with hym; God geve hym

1 Anthony Woodville, Lord Scales, afterwards Earl Rivers.
2 Charles the Bold, Duke of Burgundy.   3 Lewis XI.

good sped, and all hys; for by my trowthe they are the goodlyest felawshep the ever I cam among, and best can behave them, and most lyek gentylmen.

Othyr tydyngs have we non her, but that the Dwke of Somerset,[1] and all hys bands depertyd welbeseyn owt of Brugys a day befor that my Lady the Dwches cam thedyr, and they sey her, that he is to Qwen Margaret that was, and shal no more come her ayen, nor be holpyn by the Dwk. No more; but I beseche yow of your blyssyng as lowly as I can, whyche I beseche yow forget not to geve me ever day onys. And, modyr, I beseche yow that ye wolbe good mastras to my lytyll man, and to se that he go to scole.

I sent my cosyn Dawbeney vs. by Callys man, for to bye for hym syche ger as he nedyth; and, modyr, I pray yow thys byll may recomend me to my sustyrs bothe, and to the mastyr, my cosyn Dawbeney, Syr Jamys,[2] Syr John Stylle, and to pray hym to be good mastyr to lytyll Jak, and to lerne hym well; and I pray yow that thys byll may recomand me to all your folkys, and my wellwyllers. And I pray God send yow your herts desyr.

Wretyn at Bruggys the Fryday next aftyr Seynt Thomas.

Your sone and humbyll servaunt,
J. PASTON, the yonger.

586.

A.D. 1468, 16 July.—ABSTRACT.

[From Add. Charter 17,248, B.M.]

General pardon to William Paston, son of the judge, for offences committed before the 15th April last. The grantee is described by different *aliases*, as William Paston of London, of Caster, of Norwich, and of Wymondham, gentleman. Westminster, 16th July, 8 Edw. IV. *Great Seal attached.*

---

[1] Edmund Beaufort, Duke of Somerset.
[2] Sir James Gloys, a priest.

587.

A.D. 1468 (?) 18 July.
THE EARL OF OXFORD TO SIR JOHN PASTON.

[From Fenn, ii. 26].

The writer of this letter was committed to the Tower in November 1468, and though afterwards released, it was not long before he became a declared enemy of Edward IV.; so that, after the brief restoration of Henry VI. in 1470 he was obliged to leave the kingdom. The date of this letter, therefore, is not likely to be later than the present year, but it may be a year or two earlier.

To Sir John Paston, Knyght.

RIGHT worshipfull, and my especiall true hertid frende, I commaunde me un to you, preying you to ordeyne me iij. horsse harneys as godely as ye and Genyn kan devyse, as it were for yourselfe; and that I may have thyme in all hast, ordere. Also Skerne saith ye wolde ordeyne ij. standarde stavys; this I pray you to remembre, and my wife shalle deliver you silver,—and yit she most borowed it; vj. or vij*li.* I wold be stowe on a horsse harneys, and so Skerne tolde me I might have. The Lord Hastings had for the same price, but I wolde not myne were lik his; and I trust to God we shalle do right welle, who preserve you. Wreten at Canterbury in hast, the xviij. day of Juyll.

OXYNFORD.

588.

A.D. 1468, 22 July.

Sir John Paston to Mrs Anne.

[From Fenn, ii. 294.]

The Mrs Anne to whom this letter was addressed seems to have been a Mrs Anne Haute, to whom Sir John was for a long time engaged. That it was written before the year 1469 will appear probable on referring to Margaret Paston's letter written on Easter Monday (3d April) in that year, in which she wishes to know for certain if he be engaged ; and we have therefore little difficulty in referring it to the year 1468, when Sir John was over in Flanders at the marriage of the Princess Margaret to Charles of Burgundy. Mrs Anne appears to have been a lady of English extraction, who was either born abroad or had passed most of her life on the Continent. She was, moreover, related to Lord Scales, and is therefore not unlikely to have been the daughter of one William Haute of Kent, who married at Calais, in 1429, the daughter of a certain Richard Wydeville.—(See *Excerpta Historica*, p. 249.) But she could speak and even read English ; and Sir John, who was now returning homewards to England, designed in this letter to open a correspondence with her. He appears, however, not to have despatched it, as the original remained among the papers of the Paston family ; or else, perhaps, it was returned to him on the breaking off of the engagement.

To Mastresse Annes.

RYTHE it is so that I may not, as oft as I wold, be ther as [*i.e.* where] I might do my message myselff, myn owne fayir Mastresse Annes, I prey yow to accept thys byll for my messanger to recomand me to yow in my most feythfull wyse, as he that faynest of all other desyreth to knowe of yowr welfare, whyche I prey God encresse to your most plesure.

And, mastresse, thow so be that I as yet have govyn yow bot easy [*i.e.* little] cause to remembyr me for leke of aqweyntacion, yet I beseche yow, let me not be forgotyn when ye rekyn up all yowr servaunts, to be sett in the nombyr with other.

And I prey yow, Mastresse Annes, for that servyse that I owe yow, that in as short tyme as ye goodly may that I myght be assarteynyd of yowr entent and of your best frends in syche maters as I have brokyn to yow of, whyche bothe your and myn ryght trusty frends John Lee, or ellys my mastresse hys wyff, promysyd befor yow and me at our fyrst and last being togedyr,

that as sone as they or eyther of theym knewe your
entent and your frendys that they shold send me woord.
And if they so do, I tryst sone aftyr to se yow.

And now farewell, myn owne fayir lady, and God
geve yow good rest, for in feythe I trow ye be in bed.

Wretyn in my wey homward on Mary Maudeleyn
Day at mydnyght.

Your owne,
JOHN PASTON.

Mastresse Annes, I am prowd that ye can reed
Inglyshe; wherfor I prey yow aqweynt yow with thys
my lewd [*uncouth*] hand, for my purpose is that ye shalbe more aqweyntyd with it, or ellys it shalbe ayenst
my wyll; but yet, and when ye have red thys byll, I
prey yow brenne it or kepe it secret to yoursylff, as
my feythefull trust is in yow.

589.

A.D. 1468, 10 Oct.

THOMAS HOWES TO CARDINAL BOURCHIER.

[From Fenn, iv. 298.]

*To my moste honorabyl Lord Cadenall, and Archibushop
of Caunterbury.*

MOSTE reverent and my ryght good Lord, I
recomaund me to your gracyous Lordshyp
yn my moste humble wyse. Please your
Lordshyp to wete that my Lord Norffolk
councell hath now late mevyd Sir Wylliam Yelverton,
Knyght, and me to be preferryd for to purchasse the
maner of Castre, and certeyn other lordshypps that
wer my Maystyr Fastolf, whom God pardon, owt
excepted the maner of Gunton that yowr Lordshyp
desyryth to purchasse, and othyr certeyn maners that
my Mastyr Fastolf frendys hafe desyred to be pre-

ferryd. And be cause the pretens bargayn that John
Paston yn hys lyffe surmytted, bye colour of which he
entended to hafe all my Mastyr Fastolf londes in
Norffolk and Suffolk for nought, savyng the hygh
reverence of your astate, was not juste ne trew; and
be cause that I wyth othyr of my Master Fastolf
executors may have wher of to dyspospose yn cheryte
full dedys to do for hys sowle; I have condescended
the rather that my seide Lord of Norffolk shall be
preferryd to the purchasse of the seyde maner of
Castre, and othyr maners that may be sparyd to th'encresse of hys lyfelode yn thys land; and thys covenantys
to be engroced upp wythynne shorth tyme, as by all
Halowaunce, in case yowr Lordshyp be agreed and
plesyd wyth all; wher uppon I wold beseche yowr
nobyll Lordshyp to lete me wete your good plesur
and avice yn thys behalfe.

And be cause my seyd Lord Norffolk ys so nere
of blode to yowr hyghnesse knyghted, that meevyd me
to be the more wyllyng to condescend to the forseyd
purchasse, and so trustyng your Lordshyp wold be
ryght well pleased wyth alle. Wretyn at Norwich the
x. day of Octobyr, anno viij. R. E. iiij^{ti.}

Yowr pore chapleyn,

T. Howys.

590.

Abstract.

[From a MS. in Magdalen College, Oxford.]

The following Abstract is derived from Mr. Macray's Report on the Muniments of Magdalen College, printed in the Fourth Report of the Historical
MSS. Commission.

[*Circa* 1468.] Long declaration in English (on a paper roll)
by Thomas Howes, "for the discharge of his conscience,"
impugning the authenticity of the will nuncupative, said to have
been made by Sir J. Fastolf on the day of his death, and propounded by John Paston and the said Thomas in opposition

to an earlier will propounded by Sir W. Yelverton and W.
Worcetyr; containing details intended to prove that the alleged
will was fabricated by Paston. Amongst other things, Howes
says that at Paston's desire he did, a year before Fastolf's death,
move Fastolf that Paston might buy three of his manors and live
in his college, "and the seyd Fastolf, mevyd and passyoned
gretely in his soule, seyd and swar by Cryst ys sides, 'And I
knewe that Paston woolde by ony of my londes or my godes he
shulde nevyr be my feffe, nother myn executor.' Albeit he seyde
that he wolde suffer that the said Paston for terme of hys lyf
shall have a loggyng yn a convenyent place yn the seyd maner
of Castre withoute denyance of ony havyng intrest yn the seyd
maner."

591.

A.D. 1468, 28 Oct.

ANONYMOUS TO SIR JOHN PASTON.

[From Paston MSS., B.M.]

The reference to the Earl of Pembroke, who was only so created in 1468,
and who was beheaded in July 1469, fixes the date of this letter to the former
year.

*To Maistyr Syr John Paston, Knyght, at London, with
my Lorde the Archebisshop of Yorke, be this letter
delyverid.*

Recommand me unto you. It is tolde me
that the man that ye wote of cam ridyng by
my Lady Suthfolk and by Cotton, which is
in gret decay; and Barnay tolde him that
Edward Dale tolde hem he durst no lenger serve him
of ale, for it was warnid hym that my Lady Suffolk[1]
wolde entyr, and whan she shulde enter few men
shulde knowe, it shulde be do so sodenly. She taryeth
but of tythynges fro London. He spak nat with hyr.
I pray you speke to my Lorde of Zorke[2] for the subpena in the Chanceri ayen William Paston that he
take noon hurte. He desyrith to write to yow for it.
My Lorde of Northfolk men have warnid the tenantis

---

[1] Alice, widow of William de la Pole, Duke of Suffolk.
[2] George Nevill, Archbishop of York.

to pay you no mony, and thai speke alle in the Kynges
name.   Ye may tell my Lorde of Yorke that it is open
in every mannys mouth in this contre the language
that my Lorde of Yorke and my Lord of Warwik had
to my Lorde of Norfolk in the Kings chambre, and
that my Lorde of Yorke saide, rathir than the londe
shulde go so, he wolde com dwell ther hym sliff.   Ye
wolde mervaile what harts my Lords hath goten, and
how this language put peeple in comforte.   My Lorde
of Norffolk answerde that he wolde speke to my Lady
his wiff, and entret hir.   And your adversarys reherce
that my Lorde shall never be Chanceleer til this mateer
be spede,[1] for ther bargans ar made condicionall, to
holde and nat holde as afftir my Lorde be Chaunceler
and nat.   Sothwell is all the doar, and he hath saide
that my Lorde of Zorke licensid hym to labour in the
mateer.   My Lorde of Norwich shuld by xl. marke of
.he same lond.   Thai entende to have a man of my
Lady of Suthfolks sheryve, and specially Harcort.   My
Lorde coude nat bileve it but if [*i.e.* unless] he harde
it, how it is rejoysshid in som place that he is nat
Chaunceleer.   Ther cam oo man into the contre with
a newe patent, saying that my Lorde was Chanceler, and
at that was the first patent that was sealid sithen he
was officeer.   The tythandes did goode *pro tempore.*
Ther are witnes labourid, as it is said, to witnes and
swere ageyn you of men of *cli.* a yeer, and many oder
men, som that knew never of the mateer nor never
harde Sir John Faskolff speke ; ye know what jure is
in this contre in maters that ar favoured by them
that ar now ageyn you.   It is harde whan a mateer
restid by jure in this contre, som of the same quest
that founde you bondeman shall witnesse ayens you.
Syr Thomas Howys comyth to London, and if my
Lorde of Zorke wolde entret frendely my Lorde of
Ely,[2] and get feithfully his promyse that my Lorde of

---

[1] The Great Seal was taken from Archbishop Nevill on the 8th June 1467.
Apparently in 1468 he was hoping to be made Chancellor again.
[2] William Grey, Bishop of Ely.

Ely sende for Hawys, he shulde make Hawys to go
home ageyn and leve all his fellowis post allon; and
that my Lorde wolde entret my Lorde Tresaurer, my
Lord Penbrok,[1] my Lady Bedford,[2] and remembre the
bargan is not yit made, it may be better lettid affor
than afftyr; and if the mateer spede my Lorde getith
gret worshipp and gret thanke. I doute not he undir-
stondyth it, for it is well undirstonde what he hath
saide. And pray his Lordeshipp to remembre a shereve
this yeer, for ther is mych to be undirstonde in the
shereve. And sende me worde if my Lorde Penbrok be
go, and if my Lorde be Chaunceler. Et memorandum,
Sir William Terell your testimoniall. Et memorandum,
my Lord Cardynall to sende answer to Sir Thomas
Howys; and though my Lorde Cardynall be nat ther
now, yit lat Townysende make it redy ageyns my
Lords commyng. If Sir Thomas Howys wer handelyd
by Maister Tressam and made byleve and put in hope
of the moone shone in the water and I wot nat what,
that such labor wer made that eythir he shulde be a
pope or els in dyspeyr to be depryved *de omni beneficio
ecclesiastico* for symony, lechory, perjory, and doubble
variable pevyshnesse, and for admynystryng without
auctoryte; and how he promisid bi his feith to my
Lord t'obey his rewle and brak it, and what he hath
saide to my lords in this mateer; and if ye recur in
the courte, he shall be undo, and this mateer tolde
hym by my Lorde of Ely and Maister Tresham, halff
in game and halff in ernest, it shulde make hym to
departe, for Yelvyrton and he ar halff at variance now.
And entret my Lords servaunts to speke in your maters
to all such persones as nede is. And I shall be hastyly
with you by the grace of God, whom have yow in
kepyng. Writen on Seynt Simonde Day and Jude.

                                    By your owne.

---

1 William Herbert, Earl of Pembroke.
2 *See* page 234, Note 2.

592.

A.D. 1468, 9 Nov.
SIR JOHN PASTON TO JOHN PASTON.

[From Fenn, iv. 302.]

The original of this letter, Fenn informs us, was written upon a whole sheet of paper, of which a quarter was cut away before the letter was finished, so that the bottom part of it was only half the width of the upper. Roger Ree was made Sheriff of Norfolk in 1468, which fixes the date.

To my ryght welbelovyd brother, John Paston, Esqer, beyng at Caster, or to John Dawbeney there, be this letter delyvered.

RYGHT welbelovyd brother, I comand me to yow, letyng yow wete that I have wagyd for to helpe yow and Dawbeney to kepe the place at Castr, iiij. wel assuryd and trew men to do al maner of thyng what that they be desyryd to do, in save gard or enforcyng of the seyd place ; and mor ovyr they be provyd men, and connyng in the werr, and in fetys of armys, and they kan wele schote bothe gonnys and crossebowes. and amende and strynge them, and devyse bolwerkys, or any thyngs that scholde be a strenkthe to the place; and they wol, as nede is, kepe wecche and warde. They be sadde and wel advysed men, savyng on of them, whyche is ballyd, and callyd Wylliam Peny, whyche is as goode a man as gothe on the erthe, sav-yng a lytyll he wol, as I understand, be a lytel copschotyn [*high-crested*], but yit he is no brawler, but ful of cortesye, meche uppon James Halman ; the other iij. be named Peryn Sale, John Chapman, Robert Jakys Son, savyng that as yit they have non harneyse comyn, but when it komyth it schall be sent to yow, and in the meane whyle I pray yow and Dawbeney to purvey them some.

Also a cople of beddys they most nedys have, whyche I pray yow by the help of my modre to

purvey for them, tyl that I com home to yow. Ye
schall fynde them gentylmanly, comfortable felawes,
and that they wol and dare abyde be ther takelyng;
and if ye undrestond that any assawte schold be
towardys, I sende yow thes men, becawse that men of
the contre ther about yow scholde be frayed for fer of
losse of ther goods; wherfor if ther wer any suche
thyng towards, I wolde ye take of men of the contre
but few, and that they wer well assuryd men, for ellys
they myght discorage alle the remenant.

And asfor any wryghtyng fro the Kyng, he hathe
promysyd that there schall come non; and if ther do
his unwarys [*without his knowledge*], yowr answer may
be thys, how the Kyng hathe seyd, and so to delay
them tyll I may have worde, and I schall sone purvey
a remedy.

I understond that ye have ben with my Lorde of
Norfolke now of late.   What ze have done I wete not;
we se that he shal be her ageyn thys daye.   Mor ovyr,
I trow John Alforde schall not longe abyde with my
Lorde; I schall sende yow tydyng of other thyngys in
haste, with the grace of God, who, &c.   Wretyn on
Wednysday nexte befor Seynt Martyn.

JOHN PASTON.

I fer that Dawbeney is not alther best storyd to
contenew howsold longe; lete hym send me worde in
hast, and I wyll releve hym to my power, and or longe
to I hope to be with yow.

Roger Ree is scheryff of Norfolke, and he schall be
good jnow.   Th'excheter I am not yit assertaynyd of.

Also, that thes men be at the begynnyng entretyd
as corteysly as ye can.

Also, I pray yow to sende me my flowr [1] be the
next massanger that comyth.

Also, as for my Lorde Fytz Waters oblygacion, I
know non suche in myn adward as yit.

Also, the obligacion of the Bisshop of Norwychys

[1] This may mean flour for household use ; or it may signify his flower, his
device or cognizance.—F.

oblygacion, I never sye it that I remembre ; wherfor I
wolde and prey my modre to loke it up.

Also, as for the Byble [1] that the master hath, I wend
the uttermost pryse had not passyd v. mark, and so I
trowe he wyl geve it : wet, I pray yow.

Also, as for Syr Wylliam Barber and Syr Wylliam
Falyate, I wolde, if they kan purvey for them selfe,
folfayne be dyschargyd of them.

593.

About A.D. 1468, 15 Dec.

ELIZABETH POYNINGS TO SIR JOHN PASTON.

[From Fenn, iv. 266.]

Elizabeth Paston, as we have seen (No 322), had married Robert Poynings
by the beginning of January 1459. We must, however, correct a slight in-
accuracy in the preliminary note to that letter, where it is said that by the
year 1470 they must have been married several years. Their union, in fact,
lasted little more than two years ; for Robert Poynings was slain at the
second battle of St. Alban's on the 17th February 1461. The inquisition *post
mortem* taken some years afterwards (9 and 10 Edw. IV., No. 49) gives that
day as the date of his death. His son and heir, Edward, named in this letter
(who was afterwards Lord-Deputy of Ireland in the reign of Henry VII.), was
probably born towards the close of the year 1459, for he is mentioned at the
date of the inquisition (31 Jan. 49 and 1 Hen. VI., *i.e.* 1471) as eleven years
old and over. Elizabeth Poynings must have remained a widow some years ;
but before 1472 she had married Sir George Browne of Betchworth, Surrey.
This letter is certainly of later date than No. 540, for the lands which she
was then endeavouring to recover from the Earl of Kent were now occupied
by the Earl of Essex. It may perhaps have been a year or two after 1466,
but it was probably not later than 1469, as in 1470 Henry VI. was restored,
and Essex, being a Yorkist, would not have been so powerful. The year 1468
must be a tolerable approximation to the true date.

*To the worshipful Sir John Paston, Knyght, be thys
delveryd in hast.*

ORSHIPFULL and with all myn hert interly
wilbeloved nevoue, I recomaunde me to
yow, desyryng to here of your prosperite
and wilefayr, which I pray All mighti God
maynteyn and encres to His plesour and your herts

---

[1] This must mean some MS. copy, for at this time there was only one
printed edition of the Bible, which would have sold even then for a much
greater sum than is here mentioned. I mean "Biblia Latina Mogunt. per J.
Fust et P. Schoiffer, 1462."—F.

desir, thankyng God of your amendyng and helth;
forthermore, certefying yow that Sir Robert Fenys
hath doon grete hurte in the lyvelode whiche per-
teyned to my husbond and me in the Shire of Kent,
wherein William Kene and other persones arn enfeffid,
and gretly troubleth hit, and receyveth the issuez and
profitez of gret part of theym. And as of my seid
husbonds lyvelode, aswell in the same shire as in other
shirez, besyde myn jounter, my seid husbond, whan he
departyd towarde the feld of Saint Albons, made and
ordeyned his wille, that I shuld have the rewell of
all his lyvelode, and of Edwarde his soon and myn,
and to take the issuez and profitez of the seid lyvelode,
to the fyndyng of his and myn seid son, to paie his
dettez, and to kepe the right and title of the same
lyvelode, which I myght nat accordyng occupie for
Sir Edwarde Ponyngs, myn seid husbonds brother;
and so sith myn seid husbonds departyng, I assigned
that the seid Sir Edwarde for certeyn yereez shuld
have and take the revenuez of the maners of Westwode,
Estwell, Levelond, Horsmonden, Totyndon, Eccles,
Staundon, and Conbesdon, parcell of the seid lyvelode,
which arn clerely yerely worth lxxvj*li.* xiij*s.* iiij*d.*, to
the entent that the seid Sir Edwarde shuld paye myn
husbonds dettez, for he wold not suffer me to be in
rest without that he myght have a rewell in the lyvelode; and after the seid assignement made, the seid
Robert Fenes, contrary to trowth, and withoute cause
of right, interupted me and the seid Sir Edwarde, aswell of and in the seid maners as of other maners undir-
wretyn; wher uppon the same Sir Edwarde suet unto
the Kyngs Highnesse, and hade the Kyngez honorable
lettres undir his signet, directed to the said Sir Robert
Fenys, the tenour wherof I send unto yow herin
inclosid; and as for residue of the lyvelode of myn
seid husbonds and myn, within the same shire of
Kent, wherin the said William Kene and other arn
enfeffed, that is to say, the maner of Tyrlyngham,
Wolverton, Halton, Newyngton, Bastram, Rokesley,

and Northcray, with th'appurtenauncez, I of them, by myn seid husbonds wille, shuld have residue, and take the issuez and profitez of theym, contrarye to right and conciens, takyng away my ryght, and brekyng my said husbonds wille, the seid Robert Fenys hath doon gret wast and hurte ther, and long tym hath take upe the revenuez and profitez of the same, wher thorough I have not my ryght, and the seid wille may not be performed.

Wherfor I hertely pray yow that ze will labour unto the Kynges Highnes, at yt lyketh hym addres his honorable lettres to be directed to the seid Robert Fenys, dischargyng hym utterly of the menuraunce, occupacion, and receyt of the revenuez of the said maners of Tyrlyngham and other, accordyng to the tenour of the lettres labored by Sir Edwarde, for the maners assigned to hym from the Kyngs Highnes, directyd to the same Robert Fynes, or strayter if hit may be, and that I and myn assignez may peasseble rejoie theym ; and if eny person wold attempt to do the contrarye, that a comaundement, yf it ples the Kyngs Hignes, by hym myght be yevyn to my Lorde Chaunceller to seall writtyngs sufficiaunt with his gret seall, in eydyng and assisting me and myn assignez in this same.

And as for the maners of Esthall, Faukham, Asslie, and Chelsfeld, with th'appurtenauntez in the seid schire of Kent, whereof my hysbond at his departur was seassed, and my son sethens, unto the tyme that the Erle of Kent[1] without eny inquission or title of right for the Kyng, by colour of the Kynges lettres patentes, entret into theym, and hym therof put owte, and now my Lorde of Essex[2] occupieth them in lyke maner and forme ; yf eny remedy therin wilbe hade, I pray yow attempt hit.

Also, forther more, I hertely pray yow that if eny

---

[1] Edmund Grey, Lord Grey of Ruthin, and Baron Hastings, who was created Earl of Kent in 1465.

[2] Henry, Viscount Bourchier, created Earl of Essex in 1461.

generall pardon be grauntyd, that I may have on for
John Dane my servaunt, whom the said Robert Fenys
of gret malice hath endyted of felonye, and that ze
secretly labour this, and send me an aunswer in
writtyng in as godly hast as ze may.   As soon as that
may ples yow to send me passels of costes and
expences ze bere and pay for the said causez, I will
truely content yow hit of the same, and over that
rewarde yow to your plessour by the grace of Jesu,
quo have yow in His blessed keping.   Wrettyn in
Suthwerk the xv^th daie of Decembyr.

By your awnt,   ELIZABETH PONYNGS.

594.

About A.D. 1468.—ABSTRACT.

[From Paston MSS., B.M.]

THE KING TO SIR ROBERT FYNYS.

Commanding him not to levy the rents of Westwode, Estwell,
Levelond, Horsmonden, Totyngdon, Eccles, Stondon, and
Comebesdane in Kent.

[This was evidently the copy of the writ obtained by Sir Edward Poynings
referred to in the preceding letter. Below is written, "The copie of the
lettre myssyve endossid by the Kynges awn handes."]

595.

Date uncertain.
SIR GEORGE BROWNE TO JOHN PASTON.

[From Fenn, iv. 100.]

The writer of this brief and enigmatical letter was the second husband of
Elizabeth Paston, as mentioned in the preliminary note to No. 593 preceding.
If the John Paston, Esquire, to whom it is addressed be the first of that name,
that is to say, Elizabeth Paston's brother, the date is not later than 1466 ; but
as it was certainly some years later before the writer became connected with
the Pastons by marriage, the person addressed is more probably John Paston
the youngest, brother of Sir John.   The date of this communication, however,
is unimportant.   Its purport, of which Fenn has suggested rather a compli-
cated explanation, appears to me simply a promise of secrecy on some subject: "*Loyauté, aimé* (*i.e.*, Honour bright, my dear friend). It shall never
come out for me."

*To my trusty and welbelowyd cosyn, Jhon Paston,
Esquyer, in haste.*

Loyawlte Ayme.

Be zowr howne

G. BROWNE.

Hyt schal newyr cum howt for me.

596.

A.D. 1469?

WILLIAM EBESHAM TO SIR JOHN PASTON.

[From Fenn, ii. 10.]

By the date of one item in the account subjoined to this letter, it must have
been written after the year 1468, probably in the year following.

*To my moost worshupfull maister, Sir John Paston,
Knyght.*

Y moost woorshupfull and moost speciall
maister, with all my servyce moost lowly I
recomande unto your gode maistirship, besechyng you most tendirly to see me sumwhat
rewardid for my labour in the Grete Booke[1] which I
wright unto your seide gode maistirship.   I have often
tymes wrytyn to Pampyng accordyng to your desire, to
enforme you hou I have labourd in wrytyngs for you;
and I see wele he speke not to your maistership of
hit.   And God knowith I ly in seint warye [*sanctuary*]
at grete costs, and amongs right unresonable askers.
I movid this mater to Sir Thomas[2] late, and he tolde
me he wolde move your maistirship therein, which Sir
Thomas desirid me to remembir wele what I have had
in money at soondry tymes of hym.[3]

.   .   .   .   .   .

And in especiall I beseche you to sende me for
almes oon of your olde gownes, which will countirvale

[1] This "great book" is now Volume 285 among the Lansdowne MSS.
[2] Sir Thomas Lewis, a priest.
[3] Here (according to Fenn) follows the account as stated more at large in
the subjoined Bill.

much of the premysses I wote wele; and I shall be yours while I lyve, and at your comandement; I have grete myst of it, God knows, whom I beseche preserve you from all adversite. I am sumwhat acqueyntid with it. Your verry man,　　　　W. EBSHAM.

Folowyng apperith, parcelly, dyvers and soondry maner of writyngs, which I William Ebesham have wreetyn for my gode and woorshupfull maistir, Sir John Paston, and what money I have resceyvid, and what is unpaide.

First, I did write to his maistership a litill booke of Pheesyk,
for which I had paide by Sir
Thomas Leevys[1] in Westminster,　　　　　　xx*d*.

Item, I had for the wrytyng
of half the prevy seale of Pampyng - - - - - - - -　　　　　　viij*d*.

Item, for the wrytynge of the
seid hole prevy seale of Sir
Thomas - - - - - - -　　　　　　ij*s*.

Item, I wrote viij. of the Witnessis in parchement, but aftir
xiiij*d*. a peece, for which I was
paide of Sir Thomas - - - -　　　　　　x*s*.

Item, while my seide maister was
over the see in Midsomerterme.

Calle sett me a warke to
wryte two tymes the prevy seale
in papir, and then after cleerely
in parchement - - - - -　　　　　　iiij*s*. viij*d*.

And also wrote the same tyme
oon mo of the lengist witnessis,
and other dyvers and necessary
wrytyngs, for which he promisid
me x*s*. whereof I had of Calle
but iiij*s*. viij*d*. car. v*s*. iiij*d* - -　　　　　　v*s*. iiij*d*.

---

[1] Fenn's modern transcript reads Lewis. Is "Leevys" in the other a misprint for "Lewys?"

I resceyvid of Sir Thomas at Westminster, penultimo die Oct., anno viij. - - - - - -   iij*s.* iiij*d.*

Item, I did write to quairs of papir of witnessis, every quair conteynyng xiiij. leves after ij*d.* a leff - - - - - - - - -   iiij*s.* viij*d.*

Item, as to the Grete Booke —First, for wrytyng of the Coronacion, and other tretys of Knyghthode, in that quaire which conteyneth a xiij. levis and more, ij*d.* a lef - - - - - - - -   ij*s.* ii*d.*

Item, for the tretys of Werre in iiij. books, which conteyneth lx. levis aftir ij*d.* a leaff - - -   x*s.*

Item, for *Othea*[1] pistill, which conteyneth xliij. leves - - -   vii*s.* ij*d.*

Item, for the Chalengs, and the Acts of Armes which is xxviij*ti* less - - - - - - -   iiij*s.* viij*d.*

Item, for *De Regimine Principum*, which conteyneth xlv*ti* leves, aftir a peny a leef, which is right wele worth - - - -   iij*s.* ix*d.*

Item, for Rubrissheyng of all the booke - - - - - - -   iii*s.* iiij*d.*

Summa rest' - - - - - -   xxij*s.* iiij*d.*

Summa non solut' - - - -   xlj*s.* j*d.*, unde pro magno[2] libro scripto xxvij. cum diu'chal.[3]

Summa Totalis - - - - -   iij*li.* iij*s.* v*d.*

WILLIAM EBESHAM.

---

[1] *Othea* means a treatise on Wisdom.—F. The name is derived from the Greek 'Ω θεὰ, but was used in the Middle Ages as a proper name. See a poem beginning

      "Othea of prudence named godesse,"

mentioned in the Third Report of the Historical MSS. Commission, p. 188.

[2] *magno.* "m°" in Fenn.

[3] So in Fenn. Qu. *cum diurnali challengiorum?* Fenn omits the whole of this clause, *unde* . . . . *chal'*, but notices its occurrence in a footnote.

In further illustration of the payments made in that age for writing, &c., Sir John Fenn gives the following extracts from an original quarto MS. then in his possession, containing—

The various expences of Sir John Howard, Knight, of Stoke, by Neyland, in Suffolk (afterwards Duke of Norfolk), page 136.

Item, the vij^th yere of Kynge Edward the iiij^th, and the xxviij. day of July (1467). My master rekened with Thomas Lympnour of Bury, and my master peid hym—

For viij. hole vynets . . . prise the vynett, xii*d.*,	viij*s.*		
Item, for xxj. demi vynets . . . prise the demi vynett, iiij*d.* - - - - -	vij*s.*		
Item, for Psalmes lettres xv^c. and di' . . . the prise of C., iiij*d.* - - - - -		v*s.*	ij*d.*
Item, for p'ms letters lxiij^c. . . . prise of a C., j*d.*		v.	iij*d.*
Item, for wrytynge of a quare and demi . . . prise the quayr, xx*d.* - - - -		ij*s.*	vj*d.*
Item, for wrytenge of a calender, - -			xij*d.*
Item, for iij. quayres of velym, prise the quayr, xx*d.*		v*s.*	
Item, for notynge of v. quayres and ij. leves, prise of the quayr, viij[*d.*]		iij*s.*	vj*d.*
Item, for capital drawynge iij^c. and di', the prise,			iij*d.*
Item, for floryshynge of capytallis, v^c. - -			v*d.*
Item, for byndynge of the boke, - - -	xij*s.*		
		c*s.*	ij*d.*

The wyche parcellis my master paid hym this day, and he is content.

This is an account of a limner or illuminator of manuscripts, who resided at Bury.

597.

A.D. 1469 (?) 7 Jan.

THE EARL OF OXFORD TO SIR JOHN PASTON.

[From Paston MSS., B.M.]

It will be seen by No. 591, that in October 1468, the Duchess of Suffolk had a design of suddenly entering the manor of Cotton and dispossessing Sir John Paston. This letter in which it is said she proposes to hold a court there was probably written in the beginning of the following year.

To the worshipfull, and with alle myn hert right entierly bilovyd Sir John Paston, Knyght, this lettre be delivered.

Th'Erle of Oxinford.

RIGHT hertly welbilovyd, I grete you wele. And
where I am for trowth enformyd that the
Duchesse of Suffolk wolle hold a court on
Monday next commyng at Coton, to th'entent
that she wolle fynde the maner of Thempnals holde of
hir by knyghts service and they that ben possessioners
of the same shulde payle certeine of the Parke of
Weverston; and by cause this is nat performyd nor
don, thoo that ben possessioners shall at the said court
be amersid. And it is agreed that Sir William Yelverton, Sir Thomas Hoo, shalle be at the said court and
wolle pay the amercyment, and to delyver the said
Duchesse possession of the said service and palyng,
and so by this meane to be come tenauntes to the said
Duchesse. And what wolle be falle more herof I kan
nat sey. Wherfor me thinkith it were welle don ye
were at the said court with your councell, and to do
therin as they wolle avise you. Also as ye come to
the said court take your wey by the said Duchesse to
th'entent that ye come to se hir welfare, &c. Do herin
as your councell wolle avyse you. I wolde ye dud welle.
And to my power I wolle help you. And our Lorde kepe
yow. Writyn at Tatyngston the vij. day of Januer.

Endorsed : Th'Erle off Oxenfford.

598.

A.D. 1469, 9 Jan.—Abstract.

[From Paston MSS., B.M.]

W. Coting to John Cook, draper of Norwich, "and that he
deliver or send this bill to Richard Kalle in all goodly haste, for
the matter is of substance."

This day in the grey morning three men of my Lord of Norfolk with long spears carried off three good horses from John
Poleyn, "one of your farmers at Tichewell," telling him to treat
with my Lord of Norfolk. Wishes to know what to do, "for
such an open wrong unremedied knew I never." Saturday
after Epiphany.

"Anno viijᵒ" is written below.

[The signature of this letter is written in an abbreviated form, "W. Cot." According to Blomefield, W. Cotyng was rector of Titchwell from 1450 to 1457, and he had been previously rector of Swainsthorp, to which he was presented by Judge Paston in 1444. This letter is twelve years later than the date at which his incumbency of Titchwell is said to have terminated; but doubtless he is the writer. He is referred to as living even in the year 1485, in a letter written by Dame Elizabeth Browne, who says that he and James Gresham were clerks to her father Judge Paston].

599.

A.D. 1469, 18 Jan.
EDWARD IV. TO SIR JOHN PASTON.

This letter is reprinted from the Paston Genealogy in the *Norfolk Archæology*, to which we have already several times referred (*See* Nos. 417, 552, 554, &c.) Edward IV. was at Salisbury in January 1469, one of his privy seals being dated there on the 16th of the month.

To our trusty and welbeloved Sir John Paston, Knight.

BY THE KINGE.

RUSTY and welbeloved, we grete yow well. And how be it that we late addressed unto yow our letters, and commanded yow by the same, for the consideracions in them conteined, to have ceased of makinge any assemblye of our people for the matter of variance dependinge betwixt yow on that one partie, and our right trustie and right entirely beloved cosin the Duke of Norffolk on that other, and to have appeared before the Lords of our Councell at our Palleys of Westminster at a certeine day in our said letters specified; yett nevertheless we understonde not as yet if ye have conformed yow to the performinge of our said commandement or not. We therefore eftsones write unto yow, willing and straitly charging yow to cease of the said ryotts and assemblies; and that incontinent upon the sight of these our letters that ye dispose yow personally to appear afore the said Lords of our Councell at our said Pallis, there to answere to such thinges as in that behalfe by them shall be laid and objected against

yow, not failinge hereof, all excuses laid aparte, as ye
will avoide our displeasure. Yeven under our signet
at our citye of Salesbury, the xviij. day of January.

600.

A.D. 1469, 17 March.

SIR JOHN PASTON TO JOHN PASTON.

[From Fenn, iv. 308.]

Sir Thomas Howes appears to have died in the latter part of the year 1468.
Before the end of that year his living of Pulham was vacant, and his death is
alluded to in a letter of Margaret Paston's, written on the 30th September
1469, as having occurred "within this twelvemonth." It would appear by
the following extract, quoted by Fenn, from the Institution Books of the Bishop
of Norwich, that Sir John's presentation referred to in this letter was not
allowed, or was not made out in time, and that the Bishop presented by a
lapse :—

"Cantaria in Cayster-hall.

"Lib. xi. p. 170, 21 Mar. 1468. Mr. Joh'es Yetton, S.T.P. ad col. Ep'i.
per laps'."

To myght' well belovyd brother, John Paston, or to John
Dawbeney, in his absence.

RYGHT worschypful and well belovyd brother,
I comand me to yow, letyng yow wete that
Sir Thomas Howes hadde a free chapell at
Castr, wher of the gyfte longyth to me, whyche
chapell, as I understande, scholde be in the olde tyme,
er the place at Caster wer bylte, with in the motte,
wherfor I ame but the better pleased ; and soo it is
now that at the speciall request of the Qwen and
other especiall good Lordes of myn, I have gevyn it
to the berer her of, callyd Master John Yotton, a
chapleyn of the Qwenys. Neverthelle[ss] in tyme passyd
I proposyd that the master of the colegg scholde have
hadd it, and so er longe to I hope he schall, wherfor
I thynke he most take possession, and that is the
cawse of hys comyng. Wherfor I pray yow make hym
good cher. He is informyd that it scholde be worthe
C*s*. be yer, whyche I belyve not ; I thynke it der jnow
xl*s*. by yeer. He most have it as it was hadde befor.

Item, thys daye I understonde that ther be comen

letteris from my moder and yow, and Dawbeney, wherin I schall sende yow answer when I have seyn them.

No mor at this tyme, for within this iij. dayes I shall lette yow have kneleche of other maters.

Wretyn the xviij. day of Marche.

Whether he nedyth indoccion, or institucion, or non, I wot not; if it nede, brother, ye may seale any suche thynge as well as I.   Master Stevyn kan tell all suche thynges.   JOHN PASTON, K.

601.

A.D. 1469, 3 April.
MARGARET PASTON TO SIR JOHN PASTON.

[From Fenn, iv. 312.]

Allusion is made in this and the next letter to the expected visit of Edward IV. to Norfolk in 1469. Owing to the proposed marriage of Sir John Paston with his kinswoman, Anne Haute, Lord Scales appears at this time to have interested himself in Sir John's behalf. On the back of this letter, Fenn tells us, is a note, but whether in a contemporaneous hand he does not say: "The L. Scales is now frend to Sr. J. Paston."

To Sir John Paston.

GRETE you wele, and send you Godds blissyng and myn, thankyng you for my seall that ye sent me; but I am right sory that ye dede so grete cost ther up on, for on of xl*d.* should have served me right wele.   Send me ward what it cost you, and I shall send you money therfor. I send you a letter be a man of Yarmoth; send me word if ye have it, for I marveyll ye sent me non answer ther of be Juddy.

I have non very knowleche of your ensuraunce [*engage-ment*], but if ye be ensured I pray God send you joy and wurchep to geder, and so I trost ye shull have, if it be as it is reported of her; [1] and a nemps God, ye arn as gretly bownd to her as ye were maried, and therfor I charge you up on my blissyng, that ye be as trew to her as she wer maried on to you in all degrees, and ye shall have the mor grace and the better spede in all other thyngs.

[1] The lady here referred to is Anne Haute.

Also, I wuld that ye shuld not be to hasty to be maried till ye wer more suer of your lyvelode, for ye must remembr what charge ye shall have, and if ye have not to mayntene it, it wull be gret rebuke ; and therfor labour that ye may have releses of the londs, and be in more suerte of your lond, or than ye be maried.

The Duchesse of Suffolk [1] is at Ewhelm, in Oxford shir, and it is thought be your frends her that it is do that she myght be ferr and ought of the wey, and the rather feyne excuse be cause of age or sikenesse, and if that the Kyng wuld send for her for your maters.

Your elmyse [*enemies*] be as bold her as thei wer befor, wherfor I can not thynk but that thei have sume comfort. I sent to Cayster that thei shuld be war in kepyng of the place, as ye dede wright to me. Hast you to spede your maters as spedily ye can, that ye may have lesse felesshep at Cayster, for the expences and costs be grete, and ye have no nede therof and [*if*] ye remembre you wele what charges ye have beside, and how your liffe-lode is dispoyled and wasted by your adversaries.

Also I wuld ye shuld purvey for your suster [2] to be with my Lady of Oxford,[3] or with my Lady of Bedford,[4] or in sume other wurchepfull place, wher as ye thynk best, and I wull help to her fyndyng, for we be eyther of us werye of other. I shall tell you more whan I speke with you. I pray you do your devyr her in as ye wull my comfort and welefar, and your wurchep, for diverse causes which ye shall understand afterward, &c.

I spake with the Lord Skales at Norwich, and thanked hym for the good lordshep that he had shewed to you, and desired his Lordship to be your contynuall good lord ; and he swore be his trought he wold do that he myght do for you ; and he told me that Yelverton the Justice had spoke to hym in your maters,

---

[1] Alice, widow of William de la Pole, Duke of Suffolk.

[2] This was most probably Margery Paston, with whom the whole family were, very soon after the writing of this letter, so much displeased for having without their consent contracted herself in marriage to Richard Calle.—F.

[3] Elizabeth, the daughter of Sir John Howard. Knight, and widow of John de Vere, Earl of Oxford, who was beheaded in 1461-2.—F.

[4] *See* page 235, Note 2.

but he told me not what; but I trow, and ye desired hym to telle you, he wuld. Ye ar be holdyng to my Lord of his good report of you in this contre, for he reported better of you than I trow ye deserve. I felt be hym that ther hath be profered hym large proferes on your adversaries parte ageyn you.

Send me word as hastly as ye may after the begynnyng of the terme, how ye have sped in all your maters, for I shall thynk right long till I her sume good tidyngs.

Item, I pray you recomaund me to the good mayster[1] that ye gaffe to the chapell of Cayster, and thank hym for the gret cost that he dede on me at Norwych; and if I wer a grette lady he shuld understand that he shuld far the better for me, for me semyth be his demenyng he shuld be right a good man.

Item, I send you the nowche[2] with the dyamaunch, be the berer herof. I pray yow forgate not to send me a kersche[3] of Cr'melle for nekkerchys for your syster Anne, for I am schente of the good lady that sche is with, be cawse she hathe non, and I can non gette in all thys towne.

I xuld wrythe mor to yow but for lakke of leyser. God have yow in Hys kepyng, and send yow good spede in alle your maters. Wryten in haste on Eestern Munday.   Be your Moder.

602.

A.D. 1469, 7 April.
JOHN PASTON TO SIR JOHN PASTON.

[From Fenn, iv. 318.]

For the date of this letter see preliminary note to the last.

[1] Dr. John Yotton. *See* No. 600.
[2] An ouch is a collar of gold, formerly worn by women; a gold button, set with some jewel, is likewise so called, and that most probably was the ornament here mentioned to be sent to Sir John by his mother; we may suppose it was intended as a present to his betrothed bride.—F.
[3] A kersche of Cr'melle, perhaps means a kerchief of Cremell, crewel or worsted, to be made into neck-handkerchiefs for her daughter Anne, who appears to have been for education and board with some lady of consequence.—F,

To Master Syr John Paston.

YR, I pray yow recomand me to my Lord Scalys good lordshep, and to let hym weet that, in lyek wyse as hys Lordshep gave me in comandement, I have enqweryd what the gentyllmanys answer was that my Lord of Norffolk sent to to awayte up on hym at the Kyngs comyng in to thys contre. Hys answer was to my Lord of Norfolks messenger, that he had promysyd my Lord Scalys to awayte up on hym at the same seson, and in as myche as he had promysyd my Lord Scalys, he wold not false hys promesse for no man on lyve. I fond the menys that the seyd gentylemanys wyfe mevyd hyr husbend with the same mater as thow she had axyd hym of hyr awne hed, and he told hyr that he had gevyn thys answer. Thys gentylman is Sir William Calthorp;[1] but I pray yow tell my Lord Scalys that ye undyrstand not who it is, for he preyid me to be secret ther in.

I pray with all my hart, hye yow hom in hast, for we thynk longe tyll ye coome. And I pray yow send me woord whedyr ye shall be mad a Crysten man or ye com home, or nowt; and if so be that ye send eny man hom hastely, I pray yow send me an hat and a bonet by the same man, and let hym bryng the hat upon hys hid for mysfacyonyng of it. I have ned to bothe, for I may not ryd nor goo owt at the doorys with non that I have, they be so lewde [*shabby*]. A murry bonet, and a blak or a tawny hat. And God send yow your desyr. Wretyn at Caster, the viij. day of Apryll.

Your J. PASTON.

603.

A.D. 1469, 10 April.
LORD SCALES TO THE COUNCIL OF THE DUKE OF NORFOLK.

[From Fenn, iv. 322.]

---

[1] Sir William Calthorpe, Knight, had been High Sheriff of Norfolk and Suffolk, both in this and the preceding reign, and died very old in 1494. His second wife was Elizabeth, daughter and co-heir of Sir Miles Stapleton, Knight, of Ingham.—F.

This and the following letter were printed by Fenn from contemporaneous copies, written on the same paper without signature or address. On the back, however, was the following memorandum :—"Copea litērz Dn̄i de Scales ad Conciliū Duc' Norff' et aliis (*sic*) in favore J. Paston mil. eo quod maritaret cognatā suam Annā Hawte." The date is clearly in the year 1469, when the Duke of Norfolk laid claim to Caister.

Ih's.

WYRSHYPFULL and my ryght gode frend, I comaund me to you. And where as I am enformed that my Lorde of Norffolk pretendeth title to serteyn londys of Sir John Pastons whych were late of Sir John Fastolf, it is sayd that by the comaundement and supportacyon of my sayd Lord, sertayn hys servaunts felleth wode, maketh grete wast, and destrayned the tenants of the seyd lands, to the grete damage of the seyd Sir John Paston and hys sayd tenants ; and also that my sayd Lord entendyth to entre sertayn places of the same. And for asmoch as maryage ys fully concluded by twyx the seyd Sir John Paston and on of my nerrest kynneswomen, I dout not that your reason wele cenceyveth that nature must compelle me the rather to shewe my gode wylle, assystens, and favour unto the seyd Sir John in such thyngs as concerne hys enherytans. And because I am on of my said Lordys councayll, and must and will tendre hys honour, I hertely pray you that it may lyke you to advertyse and avyse my sayd Lord and yourys, that all such entres, fellyng of wode, destraynyngs of tenants, and all such maters lyke touchyng the sayd londes or any part of them, be cessyd unto such tyme as a resonabell meane may be founde by my sayd Lords counsayll, my Lord my faders[1] and other cousyns and frendes of my seyd kynneswoman thys next terme, as may be to my sayd Lordys honour, and to the savyng of the ryght tytle of the seyd Sir John Paston.

Over thys I•pray you that ye wille enforme my gode frend James Hobard of the premysses, that he may advertyse my seyd Lord in lyke wyse ; and that ye will

[1] Richard Woodville, Earl Rivers.

yeve credens unto William Paston, and I shal be wel-
willed to do that may be to your plesur, with Godds
mercy.

Fro Westmynstre, the x. day of Apryll.

604.

A.D. 1469, 10 April.

LORD SCALES TO ——————.

[From Fenn, iv. 324.]

See preliminary note to the last letter.

RYGHT trusty and welbelovyd, I grete you well.
And for asmoch as a maryage ys fully concluded bytwyx Sir John Paston and my ryght
nere kynneswoman Hawte, I will that ye and
all other my servaunts and tenants understand that my
Lord, my fader,[1] and I must of nature and reason shewe
unto hym our gode assystens and favour in such maters
as he shall have a doo. Wherfor I pray you hertely that
ye will take the labour to come to Norwych, to comen
with William Paston, and to yeve credens unto hym in
such maters as he shall enforme you of myne entent,
and of sertayn persones with whom ye shall comen by
th'avyse of the seyd William Paston, of such maters as
touch the sayd Sir John Paston; prayng you to tendre
thys mater as ye wolde do myne owne.

Fro Westmynstre, the x. day of Aprill.

605.

A.D. 1469, 5 May.—ABSTRACT.

[Add. Charter, 18,249, B.M.]

Citation by Thomas, Cardinal Archbishop of Canterbury, to William [Waynflete], Bishop of Winchester, and John Beauchamp,
Knight, Lord Beauchamp, to appear before the Archbishop in

[1] *See* page 344, Note 1.

fifteen days after being summoned, and take upon them the charge of the execution of Sir John Fastolf's will, if they so will to do.

Lambeth, 5th May 1469, in the 15th year of the Archbishop's translation.

[The MS. belongs to the Castle Combe collection.]

606.

A.D. 1469(?) 7 May.
ARCHBISHOP NEVILL TO SIR JOHN PASTON.

[From Fenn, ii. 34.]

This letter was almost certainly written between the years 1467 and 1469, and is not unlikely to be of the latter year, before the Nevills and the Archbishop had come to be regarded as open enemies of Edward IV.

To my right trusty and welbeloved Sir John Paston.

Ih's.

RIGHT trusty and welbeloved, I grete you hertely well, and sende you by Thomas your childe xx.ˡⁱ, prayng you to spare me as for eny more at this tyme, and to hold you content with thessame, as my singlr truste is in you; and I shalle within bref tyme ordeigne and purveye for you such as shalbe unto your pleasir, with the grace of Almightty God, who have you in His proteccion and keping.

Writen in the manoir of the Mor[1] the vij^th daye of Maye.   G. EBORAC.

607.

A.D. 1469, [May].
JOHN PASTON TO SIR JOHN PASTON.

[From Fenn, iv. 344.]

This letter appears by the contents to have been written a little before Whitsuntide after the death of Sir Thomas Howes, and when the Duke of

[1] The Moor in Hertfordshire, a seat of the Archbishops of York.

Norfolk was preparing to make good a claim to the manor of Caister, which, as we shall see, he regularly besieged and took in September 1469. The date is therefore certain.

SYR, plesyth it to undyrstand, that I conceyve, by your lettyr whyche that ye sent me by Jwde, that ye have herd of R. C.[1] labor whyche he makyth by our ungracyous sustyrs [2] assent ; but wher as they wryet that they have my good wyll ther in, savyng your reverence, they falsly lye of it, for they never spake to me of that mater, ner non othyr body in ther name.   Lovell axyd me onys a qwestyon whedyr that I undyrstood how it was betwyx R. C. and my suster.   I can thynk that it was by Callys menys, for when I axyd hym whedyr C. desyird hym to meve me that qwestyon or not, he wold have gotyn it aweye by humys and by hays, but I wold not so be answeryd ; wherfor at the lest he told me that hys oldest sone desyird hym to spere [*inquire*] whedyr that R. C. wes swyr of hyr or nowt, for he seyd that he knew a good maryage for hyr, but I wot he lyeyd, for he is hole with R. Cale in that mater.   Wherfor to the entent that he nor they sholl pyck no comfort of me, I answerd hym, that and my fadyr, whom God asoyle, wer a lyve, and had consentyd ther to, and my modyr, and ye bothe, he shold never have my good wyll for to make my sustyr to selle kandyll and mustard in Framlyngham ; and thus, wythe mor whyche wer to longe to wryet to you, we departyd.

And wher as it plesythe you in your lettyr to crye me mercy for that ye sent me not syche ger as I sent yow mony for, I crye yow mercy that I was so lewde [*bold*] to encomber yow with eny so sympyll a mater, consyderyng the grette maters and weyghty that ye have to doo ; but need compellyd me, for in thys contre is no syche stuffe as I sent to yow for.

Also, wher as it plesyth yow to send to Rychard Calle to delyver me monye, so God help me, I wyll

---

[1] Richard Calle's.   [2] Margery Paston.

non axe hym for my sylfe, nor non had I of hym, nor of
non othyr man but of myne owne, syne ye depertyd;
but that lytyll that I myght forbere of myne owne, I
have delyveryd to Dawbeney for howsold, and pay it
for yow in menys wagys; and ther for who ever sendys
yow word that I have spent yow eny mony syne ye
went hens, they must geve yow an othyr reknyng,
savyng in met and drynk, for I eete lyek an horse, of
purpose to eete yow owte at the dorys. But that nedythe
not, for ye com not within them; wherfor, so God help
me, the felaushep her thynkys that ye have forgetyn us
alle. Wherfor and eny thyng be ille rewlyd when ye
come home, wyet it [*impute it to*] your selfe for defawt
of oversyght.

Also, I undyrstand for verry se[r]teyn, and it is sent me
so woord owt of my Lordys howse, that thys Pentcost is
my Lordys consell at Framlyngham, and they purpose
thys week and the next to hold coortys her at Caster,
and at all othyr maners that wer Sir John F.,[1] and
purchasyd of Yelverton and of Syr T. H.,[2] whom
God asoyle, and how that my demenyng sholbe,
it is to late to send to yow for avyse; wherfor, and I
do well I axe no thank, and if I do ille, I pray yow
leythe the defawt on over lytyll wyte, but I purpose to
use the fyrst poynt of hawkyng, to hold fast and I maye;
but so God help me, and they myght pulle downe the
howse on our hedys, I wyet [*blame*] hem not, whyche I
trust to God to help hem from; for by God that bowght
me, the best Erle in Inglond wold not dele so with my
Lord and my Lady as ye do, withowt makyng of some
menys to them; so God help me, whoso ever avyse yow
to do so, he is not your frend. And I may, I trust to
God to se yow abowght Mydsomer or befor, for in good
feythe I wene ye purpose yow that it shall be Estern
er ye come hom, for all your servants her wen [*here
ween*] that ye purpose ne more to dele with them, but
to leve hem her [*here*] in ostage to my Lord of Norfolk.

Also, syr, I pray yow purvey what Ine that my

---

[1] Fastolf's.   [2] Sir Thomas Howes.

brodyr Edmund shall be in, for he losythe sore hys tyme her, I promyse yow ; I pray yow send me word by the next messenger that comyth, and I shall eythyr send hym or bryng hym up with me to London.

Also, syr, we pore *sanz deners* of Castr have brook iij. or iiij. stelle bowys ; wherfor we beseche yow, and ther be eny maker of steele bowys in London whyche is very kunnyng, that ye wyll send me woord, and I shall send yow the bowys that be broken, whyche be your owne greet bowe, and Roberd Jacksonys bowe, and Johon Pampyngs bowe ; thes iij. have kast so many calvys, that they shall never cast qwarellys[1] tyll they be new mad.

I praye yow fynd the menys that my Lord have some resonable meane profyrd, so that he and my Lady may undyrstand that ye desyr to have hys good lordshep. I promyse yow it shall do yow ease and your tenaunts bothe, and God preserve.   J. P.

608.

A.D. 1469, 22 May.—ABSTRACT.
RICHARD CALLE TO SIR JOHN PASTON.

[From Paston MSS., B.M.]

I would have been with you on Sunday before Ascension Day, nad I received any command to that effect. Henry Wheler told me my day of the surety of peace was *quindena Trinitatis,* "and thereof he made me a bill. He is foully to blame to serve me so." I am much bound to you, nevertheless, for the safeguard of my sureties. Gives an account of monies disbursed since parting with Sir John at London. Repaid "my mistress" 66s. 8d., part of 100s. she lent for Mariot's matter. Paid Dawbeney for household since Midlent, 30s. Received from the farmer of the dairy, £11, 11s. 4d. Delivered "to the master of the college onward for his hire," 50s. Has received of Paston's "lifelode" since he came from London but £18, 10s. Has spent £12, 10s. more than he received, and has borrowed of John Wellys and others. Could borrow nothing of Mr. William. "And of all this twelvemonth I have not had one penny for my wages. There is none of them that hath purveyed nor chevised have so

[1] *See* Vol. I., page 82, Note 4.

much as I have done.   Here is no man paid of their wages, but all spent in household."   Cannot get a penny in all Suffolk or Flegge, of Paston's "lifelode," nor in Boyton nor Heyneford. Can get money only at Gughton, which I must gather myself, for the bailiff will not come there.   Much malt made, which had better be sold to pay the men's wages, who complain grievously, "and the master of the college and Sir John Stille both."   Will obtain for Dawbeney in ten days 6 or 7 marks more, which should keep the household for the next seven or eight weeks. The price of malt is but 20*d.* a quarter, but it would be better to sell some than that the men should be unpaid.   Wonders he has no word from him about letting Spoorle.   Cannot give Mariot an estate in Bekham as Paston directs, for Paston has the deed which James Andrewes sealed, but will talk with him and see how he is disposed; for it would be well that Paston were through with him.   He is not trusty, but seeks pretexts for delay. Jekson's crossbow is broken.   Shall he send it to London to be mended?

Caster, Monday in Pentecost week.

[The mention of Jekson's crossbow being broken proves this letter to be of the year 1469.   Compare last letter.]

609.

A.D. 1469.
RICHARD CALLE TO MARGERY PASTON.

[From Fenn, iv. 350.]

This letter was evidently written about the same period as No. 607.   The original appears to have had no address, although Fenn prints one in the right hand copy; but on the back was the following memorandum, evidently not quite contemporary, "Litera Ric'i Calle Margeriæ Paston filiæ Joh'is Paston ar'i quam postea duxit in uxorem."

MYN owne lady and mastres, and be for God very trewe wyff, I with herte full sorowefull recomaunde me unto you, as he that can not be mery, nor nought shalbe tyll it be othe-wise with us then it is yet, for thys lyf that we lede nough is nowther plesur to Godde nor to the worlde, consederyng the gret bonde of matrymonye that is made be twix us, and also the greete love that hath be, and as I truste yet is be twix us, and as on my parte never gretter; wherfor I beseche Almyghty Godde comfort us as sone as it plesyth Hym, for we that ought of very ryght to be moost to gether ar moost asondre; me semyth it is a m^{ll.} [*thousand*] yere a goo son that I speke with you. I had lever thenne all the goode in the worlde I myght be with you. Alas, alas ! goode lady, full litell remembre they what they doo that kepe us thus asunder; iiij. tymes in the yere ar they a cursid that lette matry- monye; it causith many men to deme in hem they have large consyence in other maters as wele as herin. But what lady suffre as ye have do ; and make you as mery as ye can, for I wys, lady, at the longe wey Godde woll of Hys ryght wysnes helpe Hys servants that meane truly, and wolde leve accordyng to Hes lawys, &c.

I undrestende, lady, ye have hadde as moche sorwe for me as any gentelwoman hath hadde in the worlde, as wolde Godd all that sorwe that ye have hadde had rested upon me, so that ye hadde be discharged of it, for I wis, lady, it is to me a deethe to her that ye be entreted other wise thene ye ought to be. This is a peyneful lyfe that we lede. I can not leve thus withoute it be a gret displesure to Godde.

Also like you to wete that I had sent you a letter be my ladde from London, and he tolde me he myght not speeke with you, ther was made so gret awayte upon hym and upon you boothe. He told me John Threscher come to hym in your name, and seide that ye sent hym to my ladde for a letter or a token, weche I shulde have sent you, but he truste hym not ; he wold not delyver hym noon. After that he brought hym a rynge, seyng that ye sent it hym, comaundyng hym that he schulde delyver the letter or token to hym, weche I conceyve sethen be my ladde it was not be your sendyng, it was be my mastres and Sir Jamys[1] a vys. Alas, what meane they ? I suppose they deeme we be not ensuryd to gether, and if they so doo I merveyll, for thene they ar not wele avised, remembryng the pleynes that I breke to my mastres at the begynnyng, and I suppose be you bothe, and ye dede as ye ought to do of very ryght; and if ye have do the contrare, as I have be enformed ye

---

[1] Sir James Gloys, a priest.

have do, ye dede nouther concyensly nor to the plesure
of Godde, withoute ye dede it for feere, and for the
tyme to please suche as were at that tyme a boute you ;
and if ye so dede it for this service it was a resonable
cause, consederyng the grete and importable callyng
upon that ye hadde, and many an on trewe tale was made
to you of me, weche God knowt I was never gylty of.

My ladde tolde me that my mastres your modre axyd
hym if he hadde brought any letter to you, and many
other thyngs she bare hym on hande,[1] and a monge all
other at the last she seide to hym that I wolde not
make her prevy to the begynnyng, but she supposyd I
wolde at the endyng ; and as to that, God knowt sche
knewe furst of me and non other.   I wott not what her
mastreschip meneth, for be my trowthe ther is no
gentylwoman on lyve that my herte tendreth more then
it dothe her, nor is lother to displese, savyng only your
person, weche of very ryght I ought to tendre and love
beste, for I am bounde therto be the lawe of Godde,
and so wol do whyle that I leve, what so ever falle of
it.   I supose, and ye telle hem sadly the trouthe, they
wold not dampne ther soules for us ; though I telle hem
the trouthe they woll not be leve me as weele as they
woll do you ; and ther for, goode lady, at the reverence
of Godde be pleyne to hem and telle the trouthe, and
if they woll in no wise agree therto, betwix God, the
Deelf, and them be it, and that perell that we schuld
be in, I beseche Godde it may lye upon them and not
upon us.   I am hevy and sory to remembre ther disposicion, God sende them grace to gyde all thyngs
weele, as wele I wolde they dede ; Godde be ther gide,
and sende them peas and reste, &c.

I mervell moche that they schulde take this mater so
heedely as I undrestonde they doo, remembryng it is
in suche case as it can not be remedyed, and my desert
upon every be halfe it is for to be thought ther shulde
be non obstacle a yenst it ; and also the worchipfull
that is in them, is not in your mariage, it is in ther

[1] *See* Vol. I., page 90, Note 1.

owne mariage, weche I beseche Godde sende hem
suche as may be to ther worschip and plesur to Godde,
and to ther herts ease, for ell[es] were it gret pety.
Mastres, I am aferde to write to you, for I undrestonde
ye have schewyd my letters that I have sent you be for
this tyme ; but I prey you lete no creatur se this letter.
As sone as ye have redde it lete it be brent, for I wolde
no man schulde se it in no wise ; ye had no wrytyng
from me this ij. yere, nor I wolle not sende you no mor,
therfor I remytte all this matre to your wysdom.
Almyghty Jesu preserve, kepe, and [give] you your
hertys desire, weche I wotte weele schulde be to
Goods plesur, &c.

Thys letter was wreten with as greete peyne as ever
wrote I thynge in my lyfe, for in goode feyth I have
be ryght seke, and yet am not veryly weele at ease
God amend it, &c.

610.

A.D. 1469, 22 May.
JAMES HAWTE TO SIR JOHN PASTON.

[From Fenn, ii. 16.]

The King's visit to Norfolk and the creation of Lord Stafford as Earl of
Devonshire both fix the date of this letter as 1469. The writer seems to be
the brother of Anne Hawte, to whom Sir John Paston was engaged, and he
accordingly calls him his brother.

*To my worchypfull brother, Sir John Paston, be thys
byll delyvered in hast.*

RYGTH worchipfull brother, I recomaund me
onto you, lettyng you to wytte, that my
Lorde Stafford[1] was made Erle of Devene-
schere apon Sonday ; and as for the Kyng,
as I understond, he departyt [*departeth*] to Walsyng-

---

[1] Humphrey Stafford, Lord Stafford of Southwick, was created Earl of
Devonshire on Sunday, 7th May 1469 ; so that the writer ought to have said,
not "upon Sunday," but "upon Sunday fortnight."

game apon Fryday com vij. nygth, and the Quene also, yf God send hyr good hele.

And as for the Kyng [he] was apoyntyd to goo to Calys, and now hyt ys pute of. And also as for the goyng to the see, my Lord of Warwyke schyppys gothe to the see, as I understond. None other tydynggys I can none wryte unto you, but Jesu have you in Hys kepyng.

Wretyn at Wyndysore on Monday after Whytsonday, in hast, &c.

By your brother,

JAMES HAWTE.

611.

A.D. 1469, June.
SIR JOHN PASTON TO JOHN PASTON.

[From Fenn, ii. 22.]

This letter must have been written in the beginning of June 1469. Edward IV., as appears by the dates of his privy seals, was at Windsor on the 29th May and at Norwich on the 19th June in that year. Fenn says he was also in Norfolk in the year 1474, but I can find no evidence of the fact.

To my Modr, and to my brother, John Paston.

BROTHER, it is so that the Kyng schall come in to Norffolk in hast, and I wot nat whethyr that I may come with hym or nowt; if I come I most do make a livere of xxⁱ gownes, whyche I most pyke owt by your advyse; and as for clothe for suche persones as be in that contre, if it myght be had ther at Norwyche, or not, I wot not; and what persones I am not remembryd.

If my modre be at Caster, as ther schall be no dowt for the kepyng of the place whyl the Kynge is in that contre, that I may have the most parte at Caster; and whether ye woll offre your selfe to wayte uppon the Lorde of Norfolk or not, I wolde ye dyde that best wer to do; I wolde do my Lorde plesur and servyse,

and so I wolde ye dyde, if I wyst to be sur of hys
gode lordeschyp in tyme to kome. He schall have
CC. in a lyverye blewe and tawny, and blew on the
leffte syde, and bothe darke colors.

I pray yow sende me worde, and your advyse by
Judd of what men and what horse I cowde be purveyd off, if so be that I most nedys kome, and of your
advyse in all thyngs be wryghtyng, and I schall send
yow hastely other tydyngs. Late Sorell be well kept.

JOHN PASTON, Kt.

612.

A.D. 1469, June.
JOHN PASTON TO SIR JOHN PASTON.

[From Fenn, iv. 334.]

Edward IV. arrived at Norwich in the middle of the month of June 1469.
There are privy seals dated at Bury on the 15th and 16th of the month, at
Norwich on the 19th and 21st, at Walsingham on the 21st and 22d, at Lynn
on the 26th, and at Stamford on the 5th July. Edward did not return with
the Queen as he intended, but she visited Norwich without him a little later.
See a paper on the subject of her visit by Mr. Harrod, in the *Norfolk Archæology*, Vol. v., p. 32.

O begyn, God yeld yow for my hatys. The
Kyng hathe ben in this contre, and worchepfully receyvyd in to Norwyche, and had ryght
good cher and gret gyftys in thys contre,
wherwythe he holdyth hym so well content that he wyll
hastyly be her agayn, and the Qwen allso, with whom,
by my power avyse, ye shall com, if so be that the terme
be do by that tym that she com in to this contre. And
as for yowr maters her, so God help me, I have don as
myche as in me was, in laboryng of theym, as well to my
Lord Revers [1] as to my Lord Scalys,[2] Syr John Wydwyll,[3] Thomas Wyngfeld, and othyr abowt the Kyng.

---

[1] Richard Woodville, Earl Rivers, father to the Queen, Lord Treasurer
and Constable of England.
[2] Anthony Woodville, Lord Scales, eldest son of the Earl Rivers.
[3] A younger son of Earl Rivers.

And as for the Lord Revers, he seyd to myn oncyll William, Fayrfax, and me, that he shold meve the Kyng to spek to the two Dukys of Norffolk and Suffolk, that they shold leve of ther tytyls of syche lond as wer Syr John Fastolfs. And if so be that they wold do nowt at the Kyngs reqwest, that then the Kyng shold comand theym to do no wasts, nor mak non assawtys nor frayis upon your tenants nor plasys, tyll syche tym as the lawe hathe determynd with yow or ayenst yow; this was seyd by hym the sam day in the mornyng that he depertyd at noon. Whedyr he meved the Kyng with it or nowt I can not sey, myn oncyll Wyllyam thynkys naye. And the same aftyr none folowyng I told my Lord Scalys that I had spokyn with my Lord hys fadyr, in lyek forme as I have rehersyd, and axyd hym whedyr that my Lord hys fadyr had spokyn to the Kyng or nowt, and he gave me thys answer, that whedyr he had spokyn to the Kyng or nowt, that the mater shold do well inow.

Thomas Wygfeld told me, and swore on to me, that when Brandon meuvyd the Kyng, and besowght hym to shew my Lord favour in hys maters ayenst yow, that the Kyng seyd on to hym ayen, "Brandon, thow thou can begyll the Dwk of Norffolk, and bryng hym abow the thombe as thow lyst, I let the wet thow shalt not do me so; for I undyrstand thy fals delyng well inow." And he seyd on to hym, more over, that if my Lord of Norffolk left not of hys hold of that mater, that Brandon shold repent itt, every vayn in hys hert, for he told hym that he knew well inow that he myght reauyll [*rule*] my Lord of Norffolk as he wold; and if my Lord dyd eny thyng that wer contrary to hys lawys, the Kyng told hym he knew well inow that it was by no bodys menys but by hys; and thus he depertyd fro the Kyng.

Item, as by wordys, the Lord Scalys and Syr John Wydwyll tok tendyr your maters mor then the Lord Revers.

Item, Syr John Wydvyll told me, when he was on horsbak at the Kyngs depertyng, that the Kyng had

comandyd Brandon of purpose to ryd forthe fro Norwych to Lyne, for to tak a conclusyon in your mater
for yow ; and he bad me that I shold cast no dowghtys
but that ye shold have your entent, and so dyd the
Lord Scalys also ; and when that I preyd them at eny
tyme to shew ther favor to your mater, they answered
that it was ther mater as well as yours, consyderyng
the alyans [1] betwyx yow.   Comon with Jakys Hawt,
and he shall tell yow what langage was spekyn betwen
the Duk of Suffolks consell, and hym, and me ; it is
to long to wryght, but I promyse yow ye ar be held
to Jakys, for he sparyd not to spek.

Item, the Kyng rod thorow Heylysdon Waren towads
Walsyngham, and Thomas Wyngfeld promysyd me that
he wold fynd the menys that my Lord of Glowsestyr [2]
and hym sylf bothe shold shew the Kyng the loge
that was breke down, and also that they wold tell hym
of the brekyng down of the plase.   Contrary to thys
maters, and all the comfort that I had of my Lord
Scalys, Sir John Wydvyll, and Thomas Wyngfeld, myn
oncyll Wylliam sethe that the Kyng told hym hys
owne mowthe, when he had redyn for by the loge in
Heylysdon Waren, that he supposyd as well that it
myght fall downe by the self as be plukyd downe, for
if it had be plukyd down, he seyd that we myght have
put in our byllys of it, wehn hys jugys sat on the *oyeer
determyner* in Norwyche, he beyng ther.   And then
myn oncyll seythe how that he answered the Kyng,
that ye trustyd to hys good grace that he shold set yow
thorow with both the Dwkys, by mene of trete ; and
he seythe that the Kyng answerd hym that he wold
neythyr tret nor spek for yow, but for to let the lawe
proced, and so he seyth that they depertyd.   And by
my trowthe, and my Lord Tresorer encorage you not
more than he dyd us her, ye shall have but esy [*indifferent*] help as on that party.   Wherfor labor your

---

[1] This refers to the contract between Sir John Paston and Anne Hawte.
—F.

[2] Richard, Duke of Gloucester, afterwards King Richard III.—F.

maters effectually; for by my trowthe it is nedy[s], for, for all ther wordys of plesur, I cannot undyrstand what ther labor in thys contre hathe don good; wherfor be not ovyr swyft tyll ye be swyr of your lond, but labor sore the lawe, for by my trowthe tyll that be passyd with yow, ye get but esy help as I can undyrstand.

I had with me on day at dener in my modyrs plase, she beyng owt, the Lord Scalys, Sir John Wydvyll, Sir John Haward, Nicolas Haward, John of Par, Thomas Garnet, Festux Cheyny, Trussell, the Knyghts son, Thomas Boleyn, *qua propter*, Brampton, Barnard, and Brom, Perse, Howse, W. Tonstale, Lewes Debretayll, and othyr, and mad hem good cher, so as they held them content.

Item, my Lord of Norffolk gave Bernard, Broom, nor me no gownys at thys seson, wherfor I awaytyd not on hym; notwithstandyng I ofyrd my servyse for that seson to my Lady, but it was refusyd, I wot by avyse; wherfor I purpose no more to do so. As for Bernard, Barney, Broom, and W. Calthorp, ar sworn my Lord of Glowsetyrs men, but I stand yet at large; not withstandyng my Lord Scalys spok to me to be with the Kyng, but I mad no promes so to be, for I told hym that I was not woorthe a groote withowt yow, and therfor I wold mak no promes to nobody tyll they had your good wyll fyrst; and so we depertyd.

It was told me that ther was owt a preve seall for yow to attend upon the Kyng northeward; and if it be so, I thynk veryly it is do to have yow fro London be craft, that ye shold not labor your maters to a con-clusyon thys terme, but put them [in] delaye. I pray yow purvey yow on it to be at hom as sone as the terme is doone, for be God I take gret hurt for myn absence in dyvers plasys, and the most part of your men at Caster wyll deperte withowt abod, and ye be not at hom within thys fortnyght. I pray yow bryng hom poynts and lasys of sylk for yow and me.   J. P.

613.

A.D. 1469, 3 July.—Abstract.

[From Paston MSS., B.M.]

Richard Calle to Sir John Paston.

Has arranged with Mariot's debtors at Bekham, and discharged him of the debt of £16. Has thus taken an open estate in the manor, as Paston desired. Had much trouble to bring Mariot, and especially his wife, [to reason], but with fair words and money got her out of the house. Lord Scales has sent to-day to Mr Roos and others for men to come to Middleton on Wednesday,—short warning enough ; and we were in doubt " what purveyance ye had made at London." I believe my mistress and my master your brother have sent you word of the demeaning of the King and the Lords here.

Norwich, Monday after St. Peter's day.

[The reference to the King's being in Norfolk fixes th date of this letter to the year 1469].

614.

A.D. 1469, 9 July.

John Aubry[1] to Sir Henry Spelman.

[From Fenn, ii. 18.]

To the right reverent Sir Henry Spelman, Recordor oj the Cite of Norwich, be this Letter delivered.

RIGHT reverent sir, I recomaunde me to you. Plese it you to knowe, this same day com to me the Shirreve of Norffolk[2] hymself, and tolde me that the Quene shall be at Norwich up on Tuysday[3] cometh sevenyght suyrly. And I desired to have knowe of hym, by cause this shuld be hir first comyng hedir, how we shuld be rulyd, as well in hir resseyvyng, as in hir abidyng here. And he seide, he wold nat ocupie hym ther wyth, but he

---

[1] Mayor of Norwich in 1469.
[2] Roger Ree was Sheriff of Norfolk this year.   [3] July 18th.

councelid us to wryte to you to London, to knowe of hem that ben of counsell of that cite, or wyth other wurshepfull men of the same cite, that ben knowyng in that behalf, and we to be ruled ther aftir, as were acordyng for us; for he lete me to wete that she woll desire to ben resseyved and attendid as wurshepfully as evir was Quene a forn hir. Wherefore, sir, I, be the assent of my Bretheren Aldermen, &c., prey you hertily to have this labour for this cite. And that it plese you, if it may be, that at that day ye be here in propre persone; and I trust in God, that outher in rewards, or ellys in thankynges, both of the Kyngs comyng, and in this, ye shall ben plesid as worthy is.

Wrete in hast at Norwich the vj. day of Juyll Anno ixᵒ Regis E. quarti. By your weelwyller,

JOHN AUBRY, &c.

615.

A.D. 1469, 9 July.
EDWARD IV. TO THE DUKE OF CLARENCE, &C.

[From Fenn, ii. 40.]

The dates of Edward the Fourth's privy seals show that he was at Nottingham in July 1469. He was not there in 1470, the year to which Fenn assigns these letters; and both Clarence and Warwick were then in France. It would appear, therefore, that these letters were written at the time of Robin of Redesdale's rebellion, which the King was going Northwards to suppress.

These iij. letteres undirwreten, the Kyng of his own hand wrote unto my Lords Clarence, Warrewyke, and Archbishop of York. The credence wherof in substaunce was, that every of them shulde in suech pesibil wise, as thei have be accustumed to ryde, come unto his Highness.

R. E. *To our Brother of Clarence.*

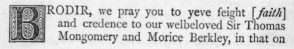

RODIR, we pray you to yeve feight [*faith*] and credence to our welbeloved Sir Thomas Mongomery and Morice Berkley, in that on

our behalf thei shal declare to you. And we truste
ye wole dispose you accordyng to our pleser and
comaundement. And ye shal be to us right welcome.
At Notyngham the ix. day of Jull.

To our Cosyn Th'erl of Warr'.

COSYN, we grete you well, and pray you to yeve
feight and credence to Sir Thomas Mongomery and Morice Berkley, &c. And we
ne trust that ye shulde be of any suech
disposicion towards us, as the rumour here renneth,
consederyng the trust and affeccion we bere in yow.
At Notyngham the ix. day of Jull. And, cosyn, ne
thynk but ye shalbe to us welcome.

To our Cosyn Th'archbyshop of Yorke.

COSYN, we pray you that ye wul, accordyng to
the promyse ye made us, to come to us as
sone as ye goodely may. And that [ye] yeve
credence to Sir Thomas Mongomery and
Morice Berkley, in that un our behalve thei shal sey to
you; and ye shalbe to us welcome. At Notyngham
the ix. day of Jul.

616.

A.D. 1469, 31 Aug.

MARGARET PASTON TO SIR JOHN PASTON.

[From Fenn, iv. 366.]

This letter was written after the Duke of Norfolk had begun to besiee
Caister, which he did in the year 1469.

To Sir John Paston, be this delivered in hast.

I GRETE you wele, and send you Godds
blyssyng and myn, letyng you wete that Sir
John Hevenyngham was at Norwich this day,

and spake with me at my moders, but he wuld not that
it shuld be understand, for my Lord hath mad hym on
of the capteynes at Caystre of the pepill that shuld
kepe the wetche abaught the place, that no mann shuld
socour them, if my Lord departed.   I desired hym to
favour them, if any man shuld come to them fro me or
you, and he wuld not graunte it, but he desired me to
write to you to understand if that my Lord myght be
mevyd to fynde suerte to recompense you all wrongs,
and ye wuld suffre hym to entre pesibilly, and the lawe
after his entre wuld deme it you.   Be ye avysed what
answer ye wuld yeve.

Item, sith that that I spake with hym, and the same
day a feythfull frende of owrs came on to me and
mevyd me if that my Lord myght be entreted to suffre
endifferent men to kepe the place, and take the profites
for bothe parties till the right be determyned be the
lawe; and my Lord for his parte, and ye for your parte,
to fynde sufficient suerte that you nowther shuld vex,
lette, ner trobilled the seid endifferent men to kepe
pesibiley the possession of the seid place, and to take
the profights on to the tyme to be determyned be the
lawe, to his behowe that the lawe demeth it.   And the
seid persones that so endifferently kepe possession
befor ther entre into the seid place, to fynde also
sufficient suerte to answer the parte that the lawe
demeth it to, of the profits duryng ther possession, and
to suffre hym pessibilly to entre, or any in his name,
whan so ever thei be required be the parte to whom
the right is demyd of all thes premyses.   Send werd
how ye will be demened be as good advyse as ye can
gete, and make no longer delay, for thei must neds have
hasty socour that be in the place, for thei be sore hurt,
and have non help.   And if thei have hasty help it
shall be the grettest wurchip that ever ye had, and if
thei be not holpen it shall be to you a gret diswurchep;
and loke never to have favour of your neybors and
frends but if this spede wele; therfor pretend it in
your mend, and purvey therfor in hast.   How so ever ye

do, God kepe you, and send yow the vittory of your
elmyse, and geve yow and us al grace to leve in peas.
Wretyn on Sent Gyles Evyn,[1] at ix. of the belle at
nyght.

Robyn came home yester evyn, and he brought me
nowther writyng from you, ner good answer of this
mater, which grevyth me right ill that I have sent you
so many messangers, and have so febill answers ageyn.

Be your Moder.

617.

A.D. 1469.

MARGARET PASTON TO SIR JOHN PASTON.

[From Fenn, iv. 358.]

This letter has reference to the contract of marriage between Richard
Calle and Margery Paston in 1469. See No. 607, preceding. The last paragraph seems to have reference to the propositions mentioned in the preceding
letter.

I GRETE zow wel, and send zow Godds
blyssyng and myn, letyng zow wete that on
Thurysday last was my moder and I wer
with my Lord of Norwych,[2] and desyerd hym
that he woold no mor do in the mater towscheyng
zowr syster, tyl that ze and my brother and other that
wern executors to zowr fader mythe beyn her to geder,
for they had the rule of her as weel as I ; and he sayde
playnly that he had be requeryd so oftyn for to
exameyn her, that he mythe not nor woold no longar
delay yt, and schargyd me, in peyn of cursyng, that sche
schuld not be deferred, but that she xuld a per beforn
hym the nexte day ; and I sayd pleynly that I woold
nowder bryng her nor send her ; and than he sayd that
he woold send for her hym sylfe, and schargyd that
she schuld be at her lyberte to cume wan he sent for
her ; and he seyd be hys trowthe that he woold be as
sory for her and [*if*] sche ded not welle, as he wold be

---

[1] St. Giles' Day is the 1st September ; St. Giles' Eve the 31st August.
[2] Walter Lyhert.

and sche wer ryth ner of hys kyn, bothe for my moder ys
sake and myn, and other of her frendds, for he woost
welle that her demenyng had stekyd soor at our harts.

My moder and I in formyd hym that we kowd never
onderstond be her sayyng, be no language that ever
sche had to hym, that neyther of hem wer bownd to
other, but that they myth schese bothe.   Than he seyd
that he woold sey to her as wele as he kowde, before
that he exameynd her ; and so that was told me be
dyverse persones that he ded as welle and as pleynly
as sche had be rythe ner to hym, wych wer to long to
wrythe at thys tyme : her aftyr ye xalle wete, and hoo
wer laberers ther in.   The schanseler[1] was not so gylty
her in as I wend he had ben.

On Fryday the Bysschope he sent for her be Assche-
feld and other that arn ryth sory of her demenyng.
And the Bysschop seyd to her ryth pleynly, and put
her in rememberawns how she was born, wat kyn and
frendds that sche had, and xuld have mo yf sche wer
rulyd and gydyd aftyr hem ; and yf she ded not, wat
rebuke, and schame, and los yt xuld be to her, yf sche
wer not gydyd be them, and cause of forsakyng of her
for any good, or helpe, or kownfort that sche xuld have
of hem ; and seyd that he had hard sey, that sche loved
schecheon [*such one*] that her frend[es] wer not plesyd
with that sche xuld have, and therfor he had her be ryth
weel avysyd how sche ded, and seyd that he woold undyrstand the woords that sche had seyd to hym, wheyther
that mad matrimony or not.   And sche rehersyd wat sche
had seyd, and seyd, yf thoo wordds mad yt not suher, she
seyd boldly that sche wold make that suerher or than
sche went thens, for sche seyd sche thowgthe in her
conschens sche was bownd, wat so ever the wordds
wern.   Thes leud wordds greveth me and her grandam
as myche as alle the remnawnte.   And than the

---

[1] Fenn thinks this was Dr. John Saresson, otherwise Wigenhale, who, he
tells us, was Chancellor to the Bishop from 1435 to 1471, and had other church
preferment in the Diocese.   But I am a little doubtful whether he lived so
long, as it does not appear that he kept any other of his preferments to so late
a date.   We know that Dr. William Pykenham was Chançellor in 1471.

Bysschop and the Schawnseler bothe seyd that ther was neyther I ner no frend of hers wold reseyve [her].

And than Calle was exameynd aparte be hym sylfe, that her wordds and hys acordyd, and the tyme, and wher yt xuld a be don. And than the Bysschop sayd that he supposyd that ther xuld be fownd other thynggs ageyns hym that mythe cause the lettyng ther of; and ther for he say he wold not be to hasty to geve sentens ther upon, and sayd that he wold geve overe day tyl the Wednsday or Thursday aftyr Mykylmes, and so yt tys delayyd. They woold an had her wyl performyd in haste, but the Bysschope seyd he woold non other wyse than he had seyd.

I was with my moder at her plase whan sche was exameynd, and wan I hard sey what her demenyng was, I schargyd my servaunts that sche xuld not be reseyved in my hows. I had zeve hir warnyng, sche mythe a be war a for, yf sche had a be grasyows; and I sent to on or ij. mor that they xuld not reseyve her yf sche cam; sche was browthe a geyn to my place for to a be reseyved, and Sir Jamys[1] tolde them that browthe her that I had schargyd hem alle and sche xuld not be reseyved; and soo my Lord of Norwych hath set her at Roger Bests, to be ther tyle the day befor sayd, God knowyth fule evel ageyn hys wyle and hys wyvys, yf they durst do other wyse. I am sory that they arn a cumyrd with her, but zet I am better payed that sche isther for the whyle, that sche had ben in other place be cause of the sadnes and good dysposysion of hys sylfe and hys wyfe, for sche xal not be sou'd [*suffered* ?] ther to pleye the brethele.[2] I pray zow and requer zow that ye take yt not pensyly, for I wot wele yt gothe ryth ner zowr hart, and so doth yt to myn and to other; but remembyr zow, and so do I, that we have lost of her but a brethele,[2] and set yt the les to hart, for and sche had be good, wherso ever sche had be, yt xuld not aben as it is, for and he wer ded at thys owyr, she xuld never

---

[1] Sir James Gloys.
[2] *Brethele* or *brethelyng* signified a worthless person.

be at myn hart as sche was.   As for the devors [*divorce*]
that ze write to me of, I supose wat ze ment, but I scharge
zow upon my blyssyng that ze do not, ner cause non
other to do, that xuld offend God and zour conschens,
for and ze do, or cause for to be do, God wul take ven-
gawns ther upon, [and] ye xuld put zour sylfe and other
in gret joparte ; for wettyt wele, sche xal ful sor repent
her leudnes her aftyr, and I pray God sche mute soo.
I pray zow for myn hard ys hese [*heart's ease*], be ze
of a good cownfort in alle thynggs ; I trust God xal
helpe ryth wele, and I pray God so do in alle our maters.
I wuld ze toke hed yf ther weher any labor mad in
the kort of Cawntrybery for the leud mater forsayd.

But yf [*i.e.* unless] the Duke[1] be purveyd for, he and
hys wyse kow[n]sel xalle lefe thys cuntre ; yt is told me
that he seythe that he wul not spar to do that he is purposyd, for no Duke in Ynglond.   God helpe at nede.

618.

A.D. 1469 [Sept.]
SIR JOHN PASTON TO MASTER WRITTILL.

[Fom Fenn, iv. 370.]

Master Writtill, to whom this and the next letter are addressed, is mentioned
later as a servant of the Duke of Clarence, by whose means Sir John was
endeavouring to arrange a suspension of hostilities with the Duke of Norfolk,
who was now besieging Caister.

To Mastyr Wryttyll.

ASTER WRYTTYLL, I recomande me to yow,
besechyng yow hertely, as myn holl trust is in
yow, that ye doo yowr devoyr to contynew
trews tyll Fryday or Saturday in the mornyng,
by whych tyme I hope the massanger shall come, and
that ye be not dryven to take an appoyntment if ye kan
undrestand by any lyklyed that itt be able to be abydyn
and recystyd, and that ye fele my brotherys dysposycion
therin, as my trust is in yow, prayng yow to remembre

[1] The Duke of Norfolk.

that it restythe, as God helpe me, on all my well. For as God helpe me, I hadd levyr the place wer brennyd, my brother and servants savyd, than the best appoynt-ment that evyr ye and I comonyd of scholde be my goode wyll be takyn, if this massage from the Kynge may reskwe it. And if it be so, that my Lorde be remevyd by the Kynges comandement, whyche restythe with hys honour, I may in tyme to kome do hym servyse, as schall recompence any grodge or dysplesur that he evyr had, or hathe to me or myn; and ye, if it the rather by your wysdam and polesye the moene above wryten may be hadd, schall be as sewr of the servyce of my trewe brother and servantys, and me, as ye kan devyse by my trowthe; for in goode feythe thys mater stykyth mor nyghe myn hart and me than I kan wryght on to yow, and to my brother and servaunts mor ner than as God knowyth they wot off. Wherfor, Master Wryttyll, all owre welfare restyth in yow, besechyng yow to remembre it. For thys mater is to all usse eyther makyng or marryng.

Item, asfor Arblaster or Lovell, I kan not thynke that they or any of them may be with yow. Wherfor in yow is all, and God have yow in kepyng.

Wretyn at London, the day next affor yowr depart-yng. I schall sende yow mor knowleche to morrow, with Godds grace. Yowrs,

JOHN PASTON, K.

619.

A.D. 1469, 10 Sept.

SIR JOHN PASTON TO MASTER WRITTILL.

[From Fenn, iv. 372.]

See preliminary note to last letter. We have adopted a different punctua-tion from that of Fenn in some parts of this letter.

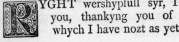YGHT wershypfull syr, I recomaund me to you, thankyng you of your grete labour whych I have nozt as yet, but I shall deserve

to my power; and ferthermore lyke yow to wyte that I have thoght ryght long after you; nevyrthelesse I remember well that ye delt wythe ryght delayous peple. My Lord Archbyshop and other of my Lords, and I, dempte by cawse of your long tarryng, that by youre sad dyscrescyon all hadde ben sett thorow.   Never-thelesse I understend by your wrytyng that my Lord of Norffolks concell thynketh that hys entent, whych ye sertefyed me by your wrytyng, sholde be more to hys wyrshep than the appoyntements and rewll made by the Lords of the Kyngs concell whych be to my seyd Lord of Norffolk ner kyne [*near kin*]; whych ap-poyntements sythen yourr departyng hath be largely remembryd amongs the seyd Lords here, thynkyng it in hem self so honorabyll to my Lord of Norffolk, that ther shuld non of my Lords concell well avysed mevyd to the contrary.

Jamys Hobard[1] was sent fro my [Lord] of Norffolk heder, and spake with my Lord Archbyshop,[2] and answer he had of my seyd Lord; and howe my Lord tendryd the mater yet and wyll I trowe he have told you, and yf he have not, the brynger her of schall informe you; and he broght thys same appoyntement from my Lord, that my Lord was well agryed that I shulde ocupye.   For my parte, iff I shud take no other apoyntement but acordyng to your letter, it wer hard for me and for my tytell to putte my Lord in that possessyon; for ther ys thyngs in erthe [*uneath, i.e.* scarcely] to myn esse in your letter, gode for me in that appoyntement, savyng the suerty of my brothers lyffe and my servants, whych ye thynke dowtefull yf so be that thay lakke stuff, shotte, and vytayll; mervaylyng sore, and thynk it impossybell in thys shorte season, or in iiij. tyme the season heder towards, that thay shuld lakk other [*either*], with owte it soo be that my Lords men have enterd owght the place, and so had ther stuffe from hem, whych I cannot thynk.   Also, sir,

---

[1] This most probably was James Hobart, who, in 1478, was Lent-Reader at Lincoln's Inn, and in 1487 Attorney-General.—F.
[2] George Neville, Archbishop of York.

for [*fore*] the tyme of your comyng to my Lord of Norffolk, servaunts of [my Lords wer with][1] my moder at Norwych, mevyng to send to my brother hyr sone, to delyver
the place under such a forme as youre lettere specefyeth,
and so I cannot understand what regard my Lords
concell takyth to my Lords letter, and to your labour
in thys behalf, but that they offeryd as largely afore.
Ze wryteth in your letter that ye durst not passe your
credens; please you to remember that seyd your credens
affore the Lords was ryght large, and as large as myght
well be in thys mater, both to my Lords concell of
Norffolk to withdrawe the seege, with moor other mater
as ye knowe ; and to the Justice of the Peas and to the
Shyryff and hys offycers, your awtoryte was grete inow
to iche of them.

Wherfor, Mayster Wretell, I never for this, nere zet
wyll, take appoyntement in thys mater, but as my Lords
wyll and my Lord Archbyshop, whych, as well as I
my self, have holy putte our tryst to youre dyscrete
dyreccyon ; and my seyd Lord sythen youre departer,
zour zoyng,[2] thynkyng you alls mete a man in executyng
ther comaundement as cowde be chosyn. Neverthelesse
for awnswer to you at thys season, my Lord Archbyshop
ys north wards towards the Kyng; how be it, it ys seyd,
uppon a metyng with my Lord of Clarens, my Lord
shuld retourne a yen ; and as zester evyn he send a
servaunt of hys to me, wenyng to hys Lordship that
Sir Humfray[3] and ye wer in Caster as was appoynted,
and ye shuld send to hys Lordshyp answer of the
gydyng ther by wrytyng, comaundyng me that yff any
such wrytyngs cam from you, yf hys Lordshyp wer not
past xx. myle fr[om Lond]on,[1] to com to hys Lordshyp
with the same. Understandyng for sertayn that he ys
nott yet so ferr, wherfor I will in althe hast possybell
ryde nygt and day till I see hys Lordshyp, and after
comunicacyon had with hys Lordshyp, as sone as ys

---

1 The original MS. was indistinct in these places.
2 The words " zour zoyng " (your going) seem to be redundant.
3 Sir Humphrey Talbot was a Captain at this siege, under the Duke of
Norfolk.—F.

possybell that a man may go be twext, ye shall have
an answer of hys dysposicyon; for hys intres is such
that, as I have wryten, I shall never do therin withoute
hym, as my cosyn, brynger herof, more playnly shall
enforme you; for I canne thynke ryght well, that as ze
wryteth to me, my broder wyll not delyver the place
to non erthly person, but yf he see wrytyng fro my
Lord.

It semyt be yowr wrytyng that my Lord of Norffolk
conseyll intende not that my Lord Archbyshop shuld
dele in thys mater, for he ys not named in your letter,
wherof I mervayle; for it was movyd to you at your
departyng hens, the Kyngs concell shuld have take
dyreccyon in thys mater, or els my Lord Cardenall,[1]
my Lord of Clarens, my Lord Archbyshop, and my
Lord of Essex,[2] &c.   Neverthelesse, Mayster Wryttyll,
all profytht, maner, or lyflod, leyd apart, if it be so
that thorow reklesnese my brother and servaunts be in
such joperte as ye have wryten to me (whych shold be
half impossybell in my mynd that thay shold myssuse
so mech stuff in iiij. tymes the space), and that ye have
evident knowlych by my seyd brother hym self therof,
I woll praye yow to se hym and them in suerte of ther
lyffys, what so ever shold fall of the lyfflode; how be
it I wold not that my brother and servaunts shold
gyft upp the place not for a m*li.*, yf thay myght in any
wyse kepe it and save ther lyves.   And therfor, at the
reverens of God, sycht it ys so, that my Lord Archbyshop and my Lords all, and I, have putte our trust
in you, that ye wyll do your devoyer to have the
verrey knowlech of my brother hymself, and not of
my Lords men, wheder he stante in such jopertye as
your letter specefyeth or net, for I dowte not uppon
the syzth of thys letter, and of the letter that ye had
before, that my brother will put no mystrust in you,
consyderyng that he knowyth that ye com from my
Lords, and my Lord Archbyshop, and have my wryt-

---

[1] Thomas Bourchier, Archbishop of Canterbury, and Lord Cardinal.
Henry Bourchier, Earl of Essex.

yng; and as for my Lord Archbyshop wrytyng and
aunswere, such as it shalbe, ye shall have it in all the
haste possybell. But I thynke veryly that my Lord
eschewyth to telle you any thyng without that he
myght speke with you allone, and me thynketh veryly
that thay ought not to lette [*hinder*] you to speke with hym
allone, consyderyng that ye have auctoryte and wrytyng from the Lords so to do. And as for the justifica-
cyon of entryng the place, and sege layng to [the same],[1]
and the comaundement of the Justice of the Pease and
the Sherewe to assyste my Lord in thys gydyng, I wote
ye understond that the Lords knowe all that mater,
and ye herd it comened, and how thay toke it in ther
consayts.

Ther ys no more, Mayster Wryttell, but I commyth
all thys wrytyng unto your dyscrescyon; and as ye
thynk best acordyng to such menys desyre as have
entretyd you therin, and for my moyst avayle, I pray
you, sir, soo doo, and I shall se un to your besynes
and labour, that ye shall have cause to do for me in
tyme comyng, and as the brynger herof shall tell you.
And I pray God have you in Hys kepyng.

Wryten at London, the x. day of Septembr.

By your frend for ever,

JOHN PASTON, K.

620.

A.D. 1469, 12 Sept.
MARGARET PASTON TO SIR JOHN PASTON.

[From Fenn, iv. 382.]

This and the other letters relating to the siege of Caister are all rendered
certain in point of date by the documents touching its surrender on the 26th
September.

I GRETE you wele, letyng you wete that your
brother and his felesshep stand in grete
joperte at Cayster, and lakke vetayll; and

1 Here the original MS. was indistinct

Dawbeney[1] and Berney[2] be dedde, and diverse other
gretly hurt; and they fayll gunnepowder and arrowes,
and the place sore brokyn with gonnes of the toder
parte, so that, but thei have hasty help, thei be like to
lese bothe ther lyfes and the place, to the grettest
rebuke to you that ever came to any jentilman, for
every man in this countre marvaylleth gretly that ye
suffre them to be so longe in so gret joperte with
ought help or other remedy.

The Duke hathe be more fervently set therup on,
and more cruell, sith that Wretyll, my Lord of Clar-
aunce man, was ther, than he was befor, and he hath
sent for all his tenaunts from every place, and other,
to be ther at Cayster at Thorysday next comyng, that
ther is than like to be the grettest multitude of pepill
that came ther yet.   And thei purpose them to make
a gret assaught—for thei have sent for gannes [*guns*] to
Lynne and other place be the seeys syde—that, with
ther gret multitude of gannes, with other shoot and
ordynaunce, ther shall no man dar appere in the place.
Thei shall hold them so besy with ther gret pepill,
that it shall not lye in their pore within to hold it
ageyn them with ought God help them, or have hasty
socour from you.

Therfor, as ye wull have my blyssyng, I charge you
and require you that ye se your brother be holpyn in
hast.   And if ye can have nonmeane, rather desire
writyng fro my Lord of Clarens, if he be at London, or
ell[es] of my Lord Archebusshop of York, to the Duke of
Norffolk, that he wull graunte them that be in the place
her lyfes and ther goodes; and in eschewyng of insurreccions with other in convenyens that be like to growe
within the shire of Norffolk, this trobelows werd [*world*],
be cause of such conventicles and gaderyngs within

---

[1] John Dawbeney, Esq.

[2] Osbert Berney, the other person here mentioned as dead, was not killed
at the siege.   He survived, and died without issue some years after, when he
was buried in Bradeston Church in Norfolk, there being a brass plate in the
chancel having the following inscription to his memory:—" *Hic jacet
Osbertus filius Joh. Berney, Armig. de Redeham Dni. et de Brayston.*"
He was the son of John Berney, Esq., by Catherine, daughter of Osbert
Mundeford of Hockwell, Esq.—F.

the seid shire for cause of the seid place, thei shall
suffre hym to entre up on such appoyntment, or other
like takyn be the advyse of your councell ther at
London, if ye thynk this be not good, till the law
hath determyned otherwyse ; and lete hym write a
nother letter to your brother to deliver the place up
on the same appoyntment.   And if ye think, as I can
suppose, that the Duke of Norffolk wull not aggre to
this, be cause he graunted this aforn, and thei in the
place wuld not aceept it, than I wuld the seid massanger
shuld with the seid letters bryng fro the seid Lord of
Clarence, or ell[es] my Lord Archebusshop, to my Lord
of Oxenford, other letters to rescue them forth with,
thowghe the seid Erle of Oxenford shuld have the
place duryng his lyfe for his labour.   Spare not this to
be don in hast, if ye wull have ther lyves, and be sett
by in Norffolk, though ye shuld leys the best maner
of all for the rescuse.   I had lever ye last the lyffelode
than ther lyfes.   Ye must gete a massanger of the
Lords or sume other notabill man to bryng ther letters.

Do your devoir now, and lete me send you no mor
massangers for this maters ; but send me be the berer
her of more certeyn comfort than ye have do be all
other that I have sent be for.   In any wyse, lete the
letters that shall come to the Erle of Oxenford comyn
with the letters that shall comyn to the Duke of
Norffolk, that if he wull not aggree to the ton, that ye
may have redy your rescuse that it nede no mor to
send therfor.   God kepe you.

Wretyn the Tuesday next befor Holy Rood Day,
in hast.   Be your Moder.

621.

A.D. 1469, 15 Sept.

SIR JOHN PASTON TO MARGARET PASTON.

[From Fenn, iv. 386.]

This letter was clearly written in reply to the last

OODR, uppon Saterday last was, Dawbeney and Bernay wer on lyve and mery, and I suppose ther com no man owt of the place to yow syn that tyme that cowde have asserteynyd to yow of ther dethys. And as towchyng the fyrsenesse of the Duke or of hys peple schewyd syn that tyme that Wryttel departyd, I trowe it was concludyd that trews and abstynence of werre scholde be hadd er he departyd, whych shalle dewr tyl Monday next comyng; and by that tyme I trow that trews shall be takyn tyll that day vij. nyght aftr, by whych tyme I hope of a goode dyreccion schall be hadde.

And wher as ye wryght to me that I scholde sewe for letteris from my Lordys of Clarans and Yorke, they be not her, and if they wrot to hym as they have don ij. tymes, I trow it wolde nat advayle; and as for to labor thois letteris and the rescu to gedre, they ben ij. sendry thyngys, for when the rescu is redy, that the cost ther of is don. For if I be drevyn therto to rescu it er they com ther that scholde do it, it shall cost a m^l. escuys, and as meche after, whyh wey wer harde for me to take, whyll that I maye do it otherwise; but as to sey that they schall be rescuyd if all the lands that I have in Ingelond and frendys maye do it, they shall, and God be frendly, and that as schertly as it may goodlely and wele be brout abut. And the grettest defawt erthly is mony and som frendys and neyborys to helpe; wherfor I beseche yow to sende me comfort with what money ye coude fynde the menys to get or chevysche uppon suerte sufficient, er uppon lyflod to be inmorgage er yit solde, and what peple by lyklyed yowr frendys and myn kowde make uppon a schort warnyng, and to send me worde in all the hast as it is needfull. But, moodre, I fele by yowr wryghtyng that ye deme in me I scholde not do my devyr withowt ye wrot to me som hevye tydyngs; and, modre, if I had nede to be qwykynyd with a letter in thys nede, I wer of my selfe to slawe [*too slow*] a felaw; but, moodre, I ensur yow that I have herde x. tymes

werse tydyngs syn the assege by gan than any letter
that ye wrot to me, and somtyme I have herde ryght
goode tydyngs both.   But thys I ensure yow that they
that be within have no werse reste than I have, ner
castyth mor jupperte; but whethyr I had goode
tydyngys er ill, I take Gode to wittnesse that I have
don my devoyr as I wolde be don for in case lyke,
and schall doo tyll ther be an ende of it.

I have sent to the Kynge to Yorke, and to the
Lordys, and hope to have answwer from them by
Wednysday at the ferthest, and after that answer shall
I be rewlyd, and than send yow word, for tyll that
tyme kan I take non dyreccion.   And to encomfort
yow, dy[s]peyre yow not for lak of vytayle ner of gonne
powder, ner be natt to hevy ner to mery therfor; for
and hevynesse or sorow wolde have be the remedy
ther of, I knew nevyr mater in my lyfe that I kowde
have ben so hevy or sory for, and with Goddys grace
it schall be remedyed well inow; for by my trowthe
I hadde lever lose the maner of Caister than the
symplest mannys lyfe therin, if that may be hys savea-
cion.   Wherfor I beseche yow to sende me worde wat
mony and men ye thynke that I am lyke to get in that
contre; for the hasty purchace of mony and men
schall be the getyng and rescu of it, and the sauevacion
of most mennys lyfys, if we take that weye.

Also thys daye I porpose to sende to Yorke to the
Kyng for a thyng, whych same only maye be lyklyod
be the savacion of all.   Ye must remembre that the
rescue of it is the last remedy of all, and how it is nat
easy to get; and also ye sende me worde that I
scholde nat kome hom withowt that I kome stronke.
But if I had hadd on other stronge place in Norfolke
to have comen to, thowe I have browt ryght fewe with
me, I scholde, with Godds grace, have rescued it by
thys tyme, er ellys he scholde have ben fayne to have
besegyd bothe placys or yit, and the Duke had not
kept Yarmoth owthe.   But, mother, I beseche yow
sende me som mony, for by my trowth I have but *xs.*

I [1] wot not wher to have mor, and moreovyr I have ben x. tymes in lyke case or werse within thys x. wekys. I sent to Rychard Call for mony, but he sendyth me non.

I beseche yow to gyde the evydence that Pekok can tell yow of, and to se it saffe; for it is tolde me that Richard Call hath hadd right large langage of them. I wolde nat they com in hys fyngrys. I have no worde from yow of them, ner whether ye have yit in yowr kepyng the evydence of Est Bekham owt of hys handys, ner whethyr ye have sent to my manerys that they schold not paye hym no mor mony or not. Also that it like yow to geve credence to Robyn in other thyngs.

Wret the Fryday next after Holy Roode Day.

JOHN PASTON, K.

622.

A.D. 1469 [Sept.]

WRITTILL TO THE BESIEGERS OF CAISTER.

[From Fenn, iv. 404.]

This letter is anonymous, but was evidently written by Writtill during his negotiations for a suspension of hostilities.

Sir John Hevyngham,[2] *Th. Wyngfeld,*[3] *Gilbert Deben-ham,*[4] *Wil. Brandon,*[5] *and to everych of them severally in otheris absence.*

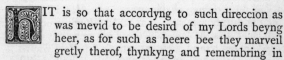IT is so that accordyng to such direccion as was mevid to be desird of my Lords beyng heer, as for such as heere bee they marveil gretly therof, thynkyng and remembring in

[1] *I.* The right hand copy in modern spelling reads "and."

[2] Sir John Heveningham, Knight and Banneret, was a descendant of an ancient family situated at the town of Heveningham, in Suffolk. His son Thomas became owner of the estate at Ketteringham, in Norfolk, where this family continued for several generations.—F.

[3] Sir Thomas Wingfield was a younger son either of Sir Robert or Sir John Wingfield of Letheringham, in Suffolk.—F.

[4] Sir Gilbert Debenham, Knight, was descended of an ancient and knightly family in the county of Suffolk.—F.

[5] Sir William Brandon married Elizabeth, daughter of Sir Robert Wingfield, and was ancestor to Charles Brandon, afterwards Duke of Suffolk.—F.

themself that such offre as was made by my credence to
my Lorde,[1] and to fore you reported, shuld have sownyd
more to his pleasure and honour than this his desire.
Nevirthelesse my Lords thenke where as they wrote
and desirid joyntly that such credence as ye remembre
myght be observyd and taken, and by you refusid,
nowe yif they shuld assent to the desire of this direccion,
hit is thought in them not so to doo; for it is so fortuned that dyvers of my Lords, from whome I brought
both wrytyng and credence, be at the Kyngs high
commaundement hastely departed unto his Highnesse,
trustyng in God to have heeryng in brief tyme of their
hasty ayen comyng, atte which tyme my Lords that
heere be, and they that shal come ayen, shal comon
and speke to gyder of this desire and direccion, and
such answere as they geve and make shall be sent
unto you than with haste possible. Ovir this, me
thenkith for your excuse of burden and charge such
as I hier will be leid unto you concernyng the grete
werks that dailly be and ar at the maner of Castre,
yif ye thenk that God shuld have pleasir, and also the
Kyng oure sovereign Lorde, and that my seide Lords
shuld thenk in you gode avise or sad, and that ye
entendid to avoide the sheddyng of Cristyn blode and
the destruccion of the Kyngs liege people, that at your
politik labour and wisedome ye myght bryng my Lord
to th'abstynence of warre, and a trieux to be had and
contynued unto tyme of the retourn of my seid Lords,
or els knowlege of their entent; certifieng you for
trouth that ther be messengers sent unto my seid
Lords with lettrez of such answere as I had of you to
your desire to gyder, knowyng certeinly that ther shal
be hasty relacion of ther entents in the premisis, which
answers ye shall have atte ferthist by Monday cometh
sevenyght. Ferthirmore lettyng you wit that I understond for certein that my Lords that be heere eschewe,
for such inconveniense that myght fall, to conclude
any answere by them self, consideryng that my

---

[1] The Duke of Norfolk.

credence was geven by all the Lords ; prayng you, as shal be doon to the continuaunce of this trieux aforesaid, that I may be acerteyned, or yif at this houre ye coude yit thenk my credence resonable and honourable to be accepted and taken, sendith me woorde in wrytyng from you by my servant, brynger of this, al delaies leid aparte. For I acertein you, as he that owe you service, I was and yit am gretly blamed for my long tarying with you, for dyvers of my Lords taried heere for me, by th'assent of al my Lords, lenger than they wold have don, to know myn answere and guydyng from you.

And ovir this I certyfie you that ye cannot make my Lords heere to thenk that yif ther be inconvenient or myshief, murdre, or manslauter had or done, but and your wills and entents were to the contrarye, my Lord is notid so well disposid that, with oute your grete abettement, he neither will doo nor assent to non such thyng ; prayng you therfor, as your frende, to remembre wele your self, and so to rule you, as my Lords may have in tyme to come knowlege of your more sadd disposicion than as yit I feele they thenk in you. And how that my Lords note sum of you, James Hobert, beyng of my Lords counsel, can enforme you ; wherefor for Godds sake remembr you, and delyver my servant, and yif ye thenk my first credence or this advertisement shal be taken to effect, than I pray you that my servaunt, brynger hereof, may have sure condyte to speke with John Paston, and to report to hym these direccions, and upon that to delyver hym a bill certifyng the same.

623.

A.D. 1469, [Sept.]
WRITTILL TO THOMAS WINGFIELD.

[From Paston MSS., B.M.]

This and the letter following are corrected drafts upon the same paper, and both evidently written at the same time, and by the same writer, as the last letter.

R. WYNGFELD, I recomande me to you. Please you to wit I have sent a lettre joyntly to you and to al my Lordes [1] counsel; nevirtheles, for the special favor and service that I bere and owe to you, I write to you aparte, praying you to put your hasty devoir to the delyverans of my servaunt, with th'answere of the same; and ovir that for Goddis sake remember you hou that ye stond my Lordes nygh kynnesman, and by whom my Lordes wulle gretly be steerid, that ye eschewe and avoide to be non of those that my Lordes here thenk shuld set or cause my Lord to do thynges otherwise than accordith to the pleasir of my Lordes; for it is so that there be dyvers of my Lordes counsel stond in hevy report of my Lordes, of which I wold ye were non; certifieng you that I know so ferre that yif ye any thyng doo in this mater to the pleasir of my Lordes, it will neither be unremembrid ne unrecompensid, not doutyng but that hereafter to have a large thonk of you for this my counsel; praying you ferthermor to move Sir John Hevyngham, and such as ye knowe wele disposid, to assist you in this; and that this bille be kept secrete, as my trust is in you. Wreten at London.

624.

WRITTILL TO JOHN PASTON.

[From Paston MSS., B.M.]

See preliminary note to last letter.

R. PASTON, it is so that sith tyme I spake with you I sent you a bill which concludith an abstinence of werre to be had unto Fryday last was, trustyng in that season that by the menes of my Lordes heere a conclusion shal be taken; lettyng you wit that before my comyng hider certein of my Lordes were departid hens towards the Kyng northwards. And for asmich as I cannot in this

[1] The Duke of Norfolk's.

season have no hasty answere of such lettrez as were
sent unto them concernyng this mater, I have wretyn
by the meanes of my Lordes heere I have wretyn a
lettre to my Lordes counsell a lettre,[1] and amonges
other thynges movid them in the seid lettre to advertise
my Lord for abstynence of werre til Monday come
sevenyght ; and yif my Lordes and his counsell so agree,
I have comaundid my servaunt, brynger hereof, to
geve you knowlege of the same, avisyng you that con-
tenuyng the seid seson to absteyne you from werre
gevyng outward in like wise ; and by that season I
hope to have knowlege of my Lordes ententes.

625.

A.D. 1469, 18 Sept.
SIR JOHN PASTON TO JOHN PASTON.

[From Fenn, iv. 394.]

See preliminary note to No. 620.

To John Paston, and to non othyr.

 Recomand me to yow, and promyse yow
that I have and schall labore and fynde the
meane that ye schall have honor of yowr delyng
as ye have hyddr towards, as all Ingelond and
every man reportythe ; and moreover I am in weye for
it by many dyverse weys, wherof ther schall be one
exicutyd by thys day xiiij. nyght at the ferthest, and
peraventur within vij. dayes.   And iff ye maye kepe it
so longe, I wold be gladde, and aftr that iff ye have
nott from me other wryghtyng, that than ye do ther in
for yowr saffgarde and yowr felaschep only, and to yowr
worschypys ; and as for the place, no force therfor.
Ye knowe thys hande, therfor nedythe no mencion from
whem it comythe ; and more ovyr, they that be abut
yow be in obloquy of all men, and mor ovyr they have

---

[1] So in the MS., the redundant words being left uncancelled.

ben wretyn to by alse speciall wryghtyng as myght be, after the worlde that now is, and promyse yow that the Dukes concell wolde that they had nevyr be gon it; and more ovyr they be chargyd in payne of ther lyvys, that thow they gate the place, they scholde not hurt on of yow. Ther is nowther ye ner none with yow, but and he knewe what is generally reportyd of hym, he or ye, and God fortewne yow wele, may thynke hym iiij. tymes better in reputacion of all folk than evyr he was. Be war whom ye make a concell to thys mater.

Also I lete yow wete that I am in moche mor comfort of yow than I maye wryght, and they that be about yow have cawse to be mor ferde than ye have; and also bewar of spendyng of yowr stuffe of qwarellys, powdr, and stone, so that if they assaut yow er we come, that ye have stuffe to dyffende yow of over, and than of my lyfe ye get no mor, and that your felaschyp be evyr ocopyed in renewyng of your stuffe.

Wretyn the Mondaye next aftr Holy Roode Daye.

I trow, thow ye be not prevy ther to, ther is taken a trews new tyl thys day vij. nygh.

626.

A.D. 1469, 26 Sept.
Passport to the Besieged on Surrender of Caister.

[From Fenn, ii. 24].

The Duc of Norffolk.

WHERE John Paston, esquier, and other divers persones have, ageyn the peas, kepte the manoir of Caster with force, ageyne the wille and entent of us the Duc of Norffolk, to oure grete displeaser; whiche notwithstanding, at the contemplacion of the writing of the

moost worshipfull and reverent Fader in God the
Cardenall of England, and our moost trusty and
entierly beloved Unkel the Archbisshop of Canterbury,
the right noble Prince my Lord of Clarence, and other
Lords of oure blood, and also at the grete labour and
enstaunce of our moost dere and singler belovid wiffe,
we be agreed that the seid John Paston and his seid
fellaship, beyng in the seid maneur, shall depart and
goo out of the seid maneur without delay, and make
therof deliveraunce to suche persones as we will
assigne, the seid fellaship havyng their lyves and
goods, horsse, and harneys, and other goods beyng in
the kepyng of the seid John Paston; except gonnes,
crossebows, and quarells, and alle other hostelments, to
the seid maneur annexed and belonginge. And to
have xv. dayes respyte aftir their seid departing out,
to goo in to what place shall like theim, without any
accions or quarell to be taken or made by us, in our
name to theim, or any of theim, within our fraunchise
or without, duryng the seid tyme.

Yoven under our signet at Yermouth the xxvj. day
of Septembr the ix^te yere of King Edward the iiij^th.

NORFF'. (LS)

627.

A.D. 1469, 26 Sept.

JOHN PASTON AND THE SURRENDER OF CAISTER.

[From a MS. in the College of Arms.]

The original of this document, signed and sealed by the Duke of Norfolk
is inserted in the MS. Volume called Brooke's *Aspilogia*, Vol. I., p. 35.

The Duc of Norff'.

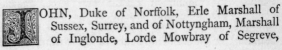OHN, Duke of Norffolk, Erle Marshall of
Sussex, Surrey, and of Nottyngham, Marshall
of Inglonde, Lorde Mowbray of Segreve,

Bromfelde, and Yalle, to al our frendes, servauntes, and othir Crystyne people, gretyng. Wher John Paston, esquier, and othre diverse persones forseble hath kepte the manoir of Castre, contrary to our will and pleaser, and aftirwarde by his lowly labour and gret meanese to us maade, the seide John Paston hathe maade deliveraunce of the seide manoir to such persons as we have assignede, and he and his seide felouship by our lycence to departe out of the same. Wherefore we pray, wil, and charge you and everysche of you, that ye ne vexce, trouble, manase, ne greve the forseid persones, nor eny of them, for the kepyng of the seide manere contrary to the Kynge our Sover-eynge Lordes lawyes, for we have takyne them in our safe garde. Yevin undir our signet and signmanuell the xxvj^{ti} day of Septembre, the ixth yere of Kynge Edward iiij^{t}.   NORFF'.   (LS)

628.

A.D. 1469, [Sept.]
JOHN PASTON TO SIR JOHN PASTON.

[From Fenn, iv. 410.]

Caystr yelded.—J. P.

RYGHT werchepfull sir, I recomand me on to yow. And as for the serteynte of the de-lyverance of Caster, John Chapman can tell yow how that we wer enforsyd therto, as well as mysylf. As for John Chapman and his iij. felaws, I have purveyd that they be payid ache of them xl$s$., with the mony that they had of yow and Dawbeney; and that is inow for the seson that they have don yow servys. I pray yow geve them ther thank, for by my trowthe they have as well deservyd it as eny men that ever bare lyve; but as for mony, ye

ned not to geve hem with owt ye wyll, for they be
plesyd with ther wagys. Wryttyll promysyd me to
send yow the serteynte of the apoyntment. We wer
sor[1] lak of vetayl, gonepowdyr, menys herts, lak of
suerte of rescwe, drevyn therto to take apoyntement.

If ye wyll that I come to yow, send me woord, and
I shall pervey me for to tery with yow a ij. or iij. dayis.
By my trowthe, the rewardyng of syche folkys as hathe
ben with me dwryng the sege hathe putt me in gret
danger for the monye. God preserve yow, and I pray
yow be of good cher tyll I spek with yow, and I trust
to God to ese your hert in some thynggys.

J. PASTON.

629.

A.D. 1469, 22-30 Sept.
MARGARET PASTON TO SIR JOHN PASTON.

[From Fenn, iv. 396.]

This is written, as will be seen, in reply to No. 621.

To Sir John Paston, in hast.   A matre.

 GRETE zow wele, and send zow Godds blyssyng and myn, letyng zow wete that me
thynke be the letter that ze sent me be
Robeyn, that ze thynke that I xuld wryte to
zow fabyls and ymagynacyons ; but I do not soo.   I
have wrytyn as yt have be enformed me, and wulle do.
It was told me that bothe Daubeney and Berney wer
dedee, but for serten Daubeney is dede, God asoyle
hys sowle ; wher of I am rythe sery, and yt had plesyd
God that yt mythe abe other wysse.

Remembyr zow, ze have had ij. gret lossys withyne
thys towylemonth, of hym and of Sir Thomas.[2]   God
wysyth [*visiteth*] zow as yt plesythe Hym in sundery wyses ;
He woole ze xuld know Hym, and serve Hym better than

---

[1] *sor.* So the word stands in Fenn, and "sore" in the copy in modern
spelling ; but I suspect a misreading of "for."   [2] Sir Thomas Howes.

ze have do be for thys tyme, and than He wull send zow the mor grace to do wele in ale other thynggs. And for Godds love, remembyr yt rythe welle, and take yt pacyentely, and thanke God of Hys vysitacyon ; and yf ony thyng have be a mysse ony other wyse than yt howte to have ben befor thys, owther in pryde or in laves expences, or in eny other thyng that have offendyd God, amend yt, and pray Hym of Hys grace and helpe, and entende welle to God, and to zour neybors ; and thow zour poor heraftyr be to aquyte hem of her maleys, zet be mersyfulle to hem, and God xale send zow the mor grace to have your entente in other thynggs.

I remembyr thys clawsys, be cause of the last letter that ze sent me. I have sent to Hary Halman of Sporylle to helpe to gete as ze desyerd me, and he canne not gette passyd v. or viij. at the most, and zet yt wule not be but yf [*unless*] he cume that ze trust upon that xuld cume, for they long a parte to hym. And Rys-chard Sharman hathe asayed on hys parte, and he cane not gette passyd v. ; for thoo that long to us, thei long also to our adversarys, and they have be desyerd be them, and they woold nowte do for hem, and ther for they thynke to have magery of the toder parte.

As for the jantylman that ye desyerd me to speke with, I spake with hys wyfe, and sche told me he was not in thys cuntre, ner nowte woost wan he xuld be her ; and as for the toder man, he hath bowthe [*bought*] hym a livery in Bromeholme Pryery, and have geve upe the woord [*world*], &c.

Item, as for mony, I kowde getee but x*li.* upon pledges, and that is spent for zour maters her, for payeng of zour men that wern at Caster, and other thynggs, and I woot not wer to gette non, nowther for suerte ner for pleggs ; and as for myn owyn lyvelod, I am so sympely payed ther of that I fer me I xale be fayn to borow for my sylfe, or ell[es] to breke up howsold or bothe.

As for the zeddyng [*yielding*] of the place at Caster, I trowe Wretyll hathe told of the pawntements [*appointments*] how ytts delyvered. I woold that [it] had be so her [*ere*] thys tyme, and zan [*then*] ther xuld not a ben do so mykyle herte as ther is in dyverse weyes; for many of our welewyllers arn putte to loosse for our saks, and I fer me that [it] xale be long her yt be recumpensyd ageyn, and that xale cause other to do the lesse for vus her aftyr.

I woold ze xuld [send] zour brother woord, and sum other that ze truste, to see to zour owyn lyelod to sette yt in a rule, and to gader ther of that may be had in haste, and also of Sir John Fastolf lyoeld that may be gadyrd in pesybyle wyse. For as for Ryschard Calle, he wulle no mor gadyr yt but yf ze comaund hym, and he woold fayn make hys . . acowntte, and have zour good maystyr schepe, as ytts told me, and delyvere the evydens of Bekkeham, and alle other thynggs that longyth to zow, that he trustythe that ze wylle be hys good mayster heraftyr. And he sethe he wylle not take non newe master tyle ze refuse hys servyse.

Remembyr that zowr lyvelod may be set in soche a rule that ye may knowe how ytts, and wat is owyn to zow; for be my feythe I have holpyn as mysche as I may and mor, savyng my sylfe, and therfor take hede er yt be weers.

Thys letter was begune on Fryday was vij. nythe, and enddyd thys day nexte afftyr Mychylmes Day. God kepe zow, and yeve zow grace to do as wele as I woold ze dede; and I scharge zow be war that ze sette no lond to morgage, for if eny avyse zow ther to, they arn not zowr frendds. Be war be tymes myn avyse, &c. I trow yowr brother wyll geve zow tydyngs in haste.

630.

NOTE.

[MS. Phillipps, 9735, No. 201.]

Inventory of household goods (including guns) left at Caister by Sir John Paston at the entry of my Lord of Norfolk.

631.

A.D. 1469, 5 Oct.
JOHN PASTON TO SIR JOHN PASTON.

[From Fenn, iv. 412.]

This is a letter desiring instructions about the garrison of Caister after its surrender.

To my master, Sir John Paston, in Flett-Stret.

RYGHT worchepfull sir, I recomand on to you, praying yow that ye wyll in all hast send me word how that ye wyll that Sir John Style, John Pampyng, W. Mylsent, Nycolas Mondonet, T. Tomson shall be rwlyd, and whedyr that they shall sek hem newe servysys or not; and Mathewe Bedford also, for he hathe be with me this seson, and is fro my modyr. And if so be that ye wyll have thes to abyde with yow, or eny of them, send word whyche that they be; for betwyx thys and Halowmas my modyr is agreyd that they shall have met and drynk of hyr for syche a serteyn wekly as my modyr and yu and I can acord when we met. Notwithstandyng, if ye kowd get Barney or eny of thes seyd folkys, whyche that ye wyll not kepe, eny servyse in the mene seson, it wer more worchep for yow then to put them from yow lyek masterles hondys [*hounds*]; for by my trowthe they ar as good menys bodys as eny leve, and specyally Sir John Stylle and John Pampyng. And I wer of power to kepe them and all thes befor rehersyd, by trowthe they shold never depert fro me whyll I leveyd.

If ye send me word that I shall come to yow to London for to comon with yow of eny mater, so God help me, I have neythyr mony to com up with, nor for to tery with yow when I am ther but if [*unless*] ye send me some; for by my trowthe thes werkys have causyd me to ley owt for yow bettyr then x. or xij*li.*, besyd that money that I had of my modyr, whyche is abowt on viij*li.* God amend defowts; but this I warant yow, with out that it be Mathew, whyche ye sent woord by John Thressher that ye wold have to awayt on yow, ther is no man that was hyryd for the tyme of thys sege that wyll axe yow a peny.

Also I pray yow send downe a comandment to Stut-vylle, or to some awdyter, to take acomptys of Dawb-neys byllys; for hys executors ar sore callyd upon for to admynyster by the Byshop, or ellys he seythe that he wyle seqwester. Dawbeney set in hys dett that ye owt hym xij*li.* and x*s.* Whedyr it be so or nowt, hys byllys of hys owne hand wyll not lye, for he mad hys byllys clere or then the sege com abowt us.

As for the evydence of Bekham, my modyr sent to Calle for hem; and he sent hyr woord that he wold make hys acomptys, and delyver the evydence and all to gedyr. My modyr hathe sent to hym ayen for hem thys day. If she sped, they shall be sent to yow in all hast, or ellys, and ye send for me, I shall bryng hem with me. Send my modyr and me word who ye wyll that have the rwyll of your lyvelod her in thys contre, and in what forme that it shall be delt with. I wyll not make me mastyrfast with my Lord of Norff., nor with non othyr, tyle I spek with yow; and ye thynk it be to be don, get me a mastyr.

Dell corteysly with the Qwen and that felawshep, and with Mastras Anne Hawte for Wappys,[1] tyll I spek with zow. Wretyn on Seynt Feythys Evyn.

J. PASTON.

By Sent George, I and my felawshep stand in fer of my Lord of Norff. men, for we be thret sore, not with-standyng the save gardys[2] that my felawshep have. As for me, I have non, nor non of your howsold men, nor non wyll have; it wer shame to take it.

---

[1] This expression "for wappys" I do not understand.—F. Perhaps it may be a proper name.

[2] *Save gardys.* This is printed "same gardys" in Fenn, but is evidently a misreading; in the right hand copy the word is "safeguards."

632.

A.D. 1469, [Oct.]
SIR JOHN PASTON TO MARGARET PASTON.

[From Fenn, i. 292.]

The allusion in an unprinted passage in this letter to the approaching marriage of Richard Calle with Margery Paston proves it to be of the year 1469. In that year it appears by the dates of the privy seals that Edward IV. remained during the whole of September in Yorkshire, having been detained by Warwick at Middleham as a prisoner during the month of August; but he was in London as early as the 13th October.

To Mestresse Margret Paston, be thys delyveryd.

RYGHT worchypfull Moodre, I comand me to yow, and beseche yow of yowr blyssyng and Gods. Thanke yow for yowr tendrenesse and helpe bothe to me, my brother, and servants.[1]

.   .   .   .   .   .

The Kynge is comyn to London, and ther came with hym, and roode ageyn hym, the Duke of Glowcestr, the Duke of Suffolke, the Erle of Aroundell, the Erle of Northumbreland, the Erle of Essex, the Lordes Harry and John of Bokyngham, the Lord Dakres, the Lorde Chambreleyn, the Lorde Montjoye, and many other Knyghtys and Sqwyers, the Meyr of London, xxij. Aldremen, in skarlett, and of the Crafftys men of the town to the nombre of CC., all in blewe. The Kynge come thorow Chepe, thowe it wer owt of hys weye, be cawse he wold not be seyn, and he was accompanyed in all peple with m[l.] horsse, som harneysyd and som nat. My Lorde Archebysshop[2] com with hym from Yorke, and is at the Moor,[3] and my Lorde of Oxenfford roode to have mett the Kyng, and he is with my Lorde Archebysshop at the Moor, and come nat to town with the Kynge; some sey that they wer

---

[1] Here, according to Fenn, follow passages touching "an account of monies, debts, &c., a dispute with his uncle William, and a desire to defer his sister Margery's marriage with Richard Calle till Christmas."

[2] George Nevill, Archbishop of York.   [3] *See* page 346, Note 1.

yesterdaye iij. myle to the Kyng wards from the
Moor, and that the Kyng sent them a massangr that
they scholde com when that he sent for them. I
wot not what to suppose therin; the Kyng hymselffe
hathe good langage of the Lords of Clarance, of
Warwyk, and of my Lords of York [and] of Oxenford,
seyng they be hys best frendys; but hys howselde
men have other langage, so that what schall hastely
falle I cannot seye.

My Lorde of Norffolke schall be her thys nyght.
I schall sende yow mor when I knowe mor.

Item, iff Ebysham come not home with myn oncle
W., that than ye sende me the ij. Frenshe bookys
that he scholde have wretyn, that he may wryght
them her,   JOHN PASTON, Kt.

633.

A.D. 1469.—ABSTRACT.

[From Paston MSS., B.M.]

[JOHN PASTON] TO [SIR JOHN PASTON].

Has reckoned with Maryot. Accounts of Bekham. Has not
spoken with W. Bakton, but will before returning to Norwich.
Means to visit Bekham on his way thither. Sends copy of the
condition wherein ye be bound to John Maryot. As for Sir T.
Mongomere's man, &c.

Richard Calle says he has delivered to me all writings he had
of you except an endenture for letting Saxthorp, which is but a
jape. All but a rental of Snaylwell are but accounts, &c. He
has delivered me four or five court rolls of Sir J. Fastolff's lands,
of his own hand. He has done reasonably well about showing
me the arrears of your lifelode. "As for his abiding, it is in
Blakborow nunnery, a little fro Lynn, and our unhappy sister's
also. And as for his service, there shall have no man have it
before you, and ye will. I hear not speak of none other service,
of no lord's that he shall be in." Has not yet spoken with
Daubney's executors, but will on his way homewards. Sends
copy of the inventory[1] he (John Paston) made on leaving Caister.
Means to be at Sporle to-morrow or Thursday, to see what may

1 See No. 630.

be made of the wood, and who will give most for it. . . . .
(*MS. mutilated at the bottom.*)

[This letter is in the handwriting of John Paston, but the signature
is lost. It is quite certain that it was written in 1469 after the surrender
of Caister. Allusion is also made to the unpleasant subject of the engage-
ment of Richard Calle and Margery Paston, who seem to have retired to
Blackborough nunnery prior to their marriage.]

634.

A.D. 1469, 6 Nov.—ABSTRACT.

[Add. Charter, 14,526, B.M.]

Indenture between Sir John Paston, of the one part, and Roger
Townsende, gent., of the other part, containing covenants for
the sale of the manor of Est Beckham, and of all Paston's other
lands in Est Bekham, West Bekham, Bodham, Sherryngham,
Beeston near the Sea, Runeton, Shipden, Felbrigg, Aylmerton,
Sustede, and Gresham, which the said Sir John had of the gift
of John Mariet the elder of Est Bekham, for 100 marks, of which
he has received already £54, leaving £12, 13s. 4d. to be paid by
the said Roger at the Feast of St. Luke next coming. Dated
6th Nov. 9 Edw. IV.

Seal, with inscription, " Si Dieu vuet."

635.

ABSTRACT.

The following abstract is taken from Mr. Macray's Report on the MSS. in
Magdalen College, Oxford.

1469, 25 Nov., 9 Edw. IV. " In the priory of Saynt Marye
Overy in Suthwarke." Acknowledgment (in English) by Will.
Yelverton, Knt., Just. of K. B., of the receipt from Bishop
Waynflete of £87, in full satisfaction of all claims on Sir J.
Fastolf by Jaquet, Duchess of Bedford ; solemnly promising
also that he will not hereafter receive any sums, great or small,
on account of Fastolf's goods, debts, or possessions, without the
assent of the Bishop, that he will at all times be ready to seal
such grants, &c., as the Bishop may require to be sealed, and
that he will not himself make or seal any grant, &c., without the
Bishop's will and agreement.

636.

A.D. 1469, Dec.
JOHN PASTON TO SIR JOHN PASTON.

[From Fenn, iv. 416.]

It appears by the contents that this letter was written about Christmas after the siege of Caister. An appeal of murder was a process sued by the nearest relative of a person killed. It was quite independent of any prosecution for murder by the Crown, and no royal pardon was of any avail against it; but the appeal had to be brought within a year and a day of the fact.

To Master Syr John Paston, Knyght.

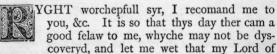RYGHT worchepfull syr, I recomand me to you, &c. It is so that thys day ther cam a good felaw to me, whyche may not be dyscoveryd, and let me wet that my Lord of Norff. consayll hathe this Crystmas gotyn the two wydows, whows husbands wer slayn at the sege of Caster, and have hem bowndyn in a gret some that they shall swe a peel ayenst me and syche as wer ther with me within the plase, and they be bownd also that they shall relese no man within the apell namyd tyll syche tyme as my Lord of Norff. wyll lycence them.

Item, the cawse is thys, as it is told me by dyvers, that ye meke no more swte to my Lord for yourself then ye do, and therfor they do the wors to me for your sake.

Item, as for my comyng up to London, so God help me, and I may chese, I com not ther, for *argent me fawlt*, without apell or an inkyr [*inquiry*?] of som specyall mater of your cawse it. Item, I pray yow remembyr Caleys, for I am put out of wagys in thys contre.

Item, I pray yow send me some tydyngs how the world gothe *ad confortandum stomacum.*

Item, ye must purvey anewe atorny in thys contre. As for me, for our maters and clamore is to gret, and our purse and wytte to slendyr, but I wyle rubbe on as long as I maye bothe with myn owne, and other menys that wyle do for me tyll better pese be.

Wretyn thys Saturdaye, at Norwcyche.   J. P.

637.

A.D. 1470, March.
Sir John Paston to John Paston.

[From Fenn, ii. 28.]

From the reference to the King's being about to go into Lincolnshire, and what is said of the Earl of Warwick, it may be clearly inferred that this letter was written on the outbreak of the insurrection of Sir Robert Welles in the beginning of March 1470.

To John Paston, Esquier, beyng at Norwyche, be thys letter delyveryd.

Comande me to yow, letyng yow wete, &c.[1]

. . . . .

Item, as for Mestresse Kateryn Dudle, I have many tymes recomandyd yow to hyr, and she is noo thynge displeasyd with itt. She rekkythe not howe many gentylmen love hyr; she is full of love. I have betyn the mater for yow, your onknowleche, as I told hyr. She answerythe me, that sche woll noon thys ij. yer, and I beleve hyr; for I thynke sche hathe the lyffe that sche can holde hyr content with; I trowe she woll be a sore laboryng woman this ij. yer for mede of hyr sowle.

And Mestresse Gryseacresse is sure to Selenger, with my Lady of Exestre, a fowle losse.

Item, I praye yow speke with Harcort off the Abbeye, for a lytell clokke, whyche I sent hym by James Gressham to amend, and that ye woll get it off hym, and it be redy, and sende it me; and as for mony for hys labor, he hathe another cloke off myne, whyche Sir Thomas Lyndes, God have hys sowle! gave me; he may kepe that tyll I paye hym. Thys klok is my Lordys Archebysshopis, but late not hym wete off it, and that itt [be] easely caryed hyddre by yowr advyse.

[1] Here (according to Fenn) follows an account of bills and receipts, &c.

Also as for orenges, I schall sende yow a serteyn by the next caryer. And as for tydynge the berer hereoff schall infforme yow; ye most geve credence to hym.

As for my goode spede, I hope well. I am offryd yit to have Mestresse Anne Haulte, and I schall have help i nowe, as some say.[1]

⁕ ⁕ ⁕ ⁕ ⁕

Item, it is soo that I am halffe in purpose to com home with in a monythe her afftr, or abowt Med Lente, or beffor Esterne, ondyr yowr coreccon, iff so be that ye deme that [my] modre wolde helpe me to my costys, x. mark or ther abowt; I praye feele hyr dysposicion and sende me worde.

Item, I cannot tell yow what woll falle off the worlde, for the Kyng verrely is dysposyd to goo in to Lyncoln schyr, and men wot not what wyll falle ther off, ner ther afftre; they wene my Lorde off Norffolke shall[2] brynke x.ᵐˡ· men.

Item, ther is comen a newe litell Torke, whyche is a wele vysagyd felawe, off the age off xl. yere; and he is lower than Manuell by a hanffull, and lower then my lytell Tom by the schorderys, and mor lytell above hys pappe; and he hathe, as he seyde to the Kynge hymselffe, iij. or iiij. sonys, chyldre, iche one off hem as hyghe and asse lykly as the Kynge hym-selffe; and he is leggyd ryght i now, and it is reportyd that hys pyntell is as long as hys legge.

Item, I praye yow schewe, or rede to my moodre suche thynges as ye thynke is for her to know, afftre yowr dyscression; and to late hyr undrestond off the article off the trete between Syr Wylliam Yelverton and me.

Item, my Lorde of Warwyk, as it is supposyd, schall goo with the Kynge in to Lyncolne schyre; some

---

[1] Here (according to Fenn) follows an account of some disputes between Sir William Yelverton and Sir John Paston, his uncle William, &c., of no consequence.

[2] *shall.* This word is not in Fenn's left hand or literal transcript, but is given as part of the text in the right hand copy.

men seye that hys goyng shall doo goode, and som
seye that it dothe harme.

I praye yow evyr have an eyghe to Caster, to knowe
the rewle ther, and sende me worde, and whyther my
wyse Lorde and my Lady be yit as sottyt [? *besotted*]
uppon it as they were; and whether my seyd Lorde
resortythe thyddre as offte as he dyd or nott; and off
the dysposycion off the Contre. J. P., K.

638.

A.D. 1470, 27 March.
ANONYMOUS TO JOHN PASTON.

[From Fenn, ii. 36.]

This letter gives an account of the suppression of the rebellion in Lincolnshire in 1470.

To my Cosyn, J. Paston.

THE King camme to Grantham, and ther taried
Thoresday all day; and ther was headed
Sir Thomas Dalalaunde, and on John Neille,
a greate capteyn; and upon the Monday
next after that at Dancastr, and ther was headed Sir
Robert Wellys, and a nothr greate capteyn; and than
the King hadde warde that the Duk of Clarence and
the Erle of Warwick was att Esterfeld [*Chesterfield*],
xx. mile from Dancastre.

And upon the Tewesday att ix. of the bell, the
King toke the feld, and mustered his people; and itt
was seid that wer never seyn in Inglond so many
goodly men, and so well arreiyed in a feld. And my
Lord was whorsshupfully accompanyed, no lord ther
so well; wherfor the King gaffe my Lord a greate
thanke.

And than the Duk of Clarence and the Erle of
Warwik harde that the King was comyng to them
warde, in contynent they departed and wente to

Manchestre in Lancasshire, hopyng to have hadde
helpe and socour of the Lord Stanley, butt in conclucion ther they hadde litill favor, as itt was enformed
the King, and so men sayn they wente westward, and
sommen demen to London.   And whan the King
harde they wer departed and gon, he went to York,
and came theder the Thoresday next aftr, and ther
camme in to hym all the gentilmen of the shire; and
uppon our Lady Day [he] made Percy Erle of Northumberland, and he that was Erle affore Markeys
Muntakew.   And [so][1] the King is purposed to come
southwarde, God send hym god spede.

Writen the xxvij. day of March.

FOR TROWYTH.

639.

A.D. 1470.—ABSTRACT.

[From MS. Titchwell, 120, in Magdalen College, Oxford.]

WILLIAM WORCESTER TO ———

From internal evidence it would seem that this letter must have been
written shortly before that which follows it. The abstracts of these two
letters have been kindly supplied to me by Mr. Macray.

Letter in English, on paper (signed W. W., but unaddressed),
desiring some one to propose to "my Lord" [the Bishop of Winchester?] the obtaining of a letter from Sir John Paston to the
tenants of Titchwell that he will not claim any rents from them,
and another from "my Lord," to the same effect, on behalf of
Sir William Yelverton; and the sending a warrant to expend
4 or 6 marks upon making up the sea banks before the
Titchwell pastures, because at Spring the sea breaks in upon
them. Desires to know whether Sir W. Yelverton's advice shall
be taken upon business matters.   "Frere" Geffrey Westvale is
going to be created Doctor in Theology at Cambridge, at the
Feast of St. John, who twenty years past, when at Yarmouth
convent, belonged to "my Maister Fastolf;" and Sir Thomas
Howys, a month before his decease, promised to help him on
Mr. Fastolf's order.   He would have come now to "my Lord"
to ask his alms had not the writer letted him.   Desires to be informed whether "my Lord" will help him.   "Maister Briston

[1] This word is not in the text of Fenn's literal transcript, but it is given
without brackets in the transcript in modern spelling.

yn lykewyse Maister Spicer, and Maister Stevyns, trustyn appon me and dyvers others to speke to my Lord for a relyeve," and Thomas Fastolf and Milcent Fastolf, and many others, "that make me noyed and werye."

640.

A.D. 1470, 17 May.—Abstract.

[From MS. Titchwell, 199, in Magdalen College, Oxford.]

Letter in English from W. Wyrcestre to Bishop Wayneflete.— Has been at Tychewell to endeavour to let the manor and farm, but none of the farmers there will take it without guarantees from Sir John Paston and Sir William Yelverton in writing against any distraint. . . . . the younger, who owes £9, will come to the Bishop about the letting. The writer represents his own poor condition. Has been at charges ten years in London, and in riding on the infinite process of "my Maister Fastolf's testament yn the court of audience." Is now obliged to retire from London to Cambridge in order to live cheaply. Had been promised 25 marks on Paston's behalf, 20 marks for ever of Fastolf's lands, 5 marks of fee for his life, and £15 worth of land for ever. Has not had clearly 8 marks.

641.

A.D. 1470, 22 June.
John Paston to Sir John Paston.

[From Fenn, iv. 428.]

As this letter refers to an incident in the siege of Caister as having taken place "in August last," there can be no doubt about the date.

To Syr John Paston, Knyght, or to Thomas Stompys, to delyver to the seyd Syr John.

RYGHT worchepfull syr, and my specyall good brodyr, I recomand me to yow; and for as myche as I can not send yow good tydyngs, ye shall have syche as I knowe.

It is so that on Wednysday last past ye and I,

Pampyng, and Edmund Broom were endyttyd of
felonye at the Sessyons her in Norwyche for shotyng
of a gonne at Caster in August last past, whyche goone
slowghe two men, I, Pampyng and Broom as pryncy-
pall, and ye as accessary; notwithstandyng Townysend[1] and Lomner held an oppynyon that the verdytt
is voyd, for ther wer ij. of th'enqwest that wold not
agre to th'endyttment.   And in as myche as they ij.
wer agreyd in othyr maters, and not in that, and that
they two wer not dyschargyd fro the remnant at syche
tym as that verdyth of yowyr endytment was govyn,
ther oppynyon is that all the vordyght is voyde, as
well of all othyr maters as of yowyr.   Whedyr ther
opynyon be good or not, I can not determyne, nor
them sylf neythyr.

I pray yow let not thys mater be slept, for I can
thynk that my Lord of Norff. consaylle wyll cawse the
wedows to tak an apell, and to remeve it up in to the
Kyngs Benche at the begynyng of thys term.   Townysend hathe promysyd me that he shall be at London
on Twysday next comyng, and then ye may comon
with hym in that mater, and take hys avyse.

Item, Townysend and Lomner thynk that and ye
have good consayll, ye may justyfye the kepyng of the
plase for the pesybyll possessyon that ye have had in
it mor then iij. yeer; but in conclusyon, all thys is doo
for nowght ellys but for to enforse yow to take a
dyreccyon with my Lord of Norff.

I undyrstood by R. Sothewell—for he and I comonyd in thys mater ryght largely betwyx hem and me—
in so myche he tellyth me that and I be at London in
the wek next aftyr Seynt Petyr, at whych tyme he shall
be ther hym sylf, he seyth that my Lady hathe promysyd me hyr good ladyshep, and sent me woord by
hym, in as myche as he spak for me to hyr, that she
wold remembyr myn old servyse, and for get the gret
dysplesyr in syche wyse that I shall undyrstand that
the swtte that I have mad to my Lord hyr husbond

_____
[1] Probably Roger Townsend, afterwards Justice of the Common Pleas.

and hyr shall torne to your avantage and myn, more
then we weene as yett or shall undyrstand tyll syche
tyme as I have spokyn with hyr good grace. And
upon thys promesse I have promysyd Sothewell to
meet with hym at London that same weeke next aftyr
Seynt Petyr; wherfor I wold passyngly fayne that ye
wer in London at that season, or nye abowght London,
so that I myght undyrstand at your plase wher that I
myght spek with yow or then I spek with my Lady.

I propose to go to Canterbery[1] on foot thys next
week, with Godds grace, and so to com to London
fro thense. I pray yow se that I be safe for Parker
and Herry Coletts mater.

Sothewell[2] told me thys, that if so be that ye wyll
your sylf, ye shall have bothe goode lordshep and
ladyshep, and mony or lond, or both, and all your
maters set cler. What that he menyth, I can not sey.
As for all othyr maters in thys contre, I shall do as
well as I may for fawt of monye tyll I spek with yow.
I have many collars on, as I shall tell yow when I
come.

No more, but God preserve yow and yours. Wretyn
at Norwyche, Fryday next aftyr Corpus Christi Daye.

J. P.

I ded as myche as I kowd to have lettyd th'endyttment, but it wold not be, as I shall enform you; and
Townysend knowyth the same.

642.

A.D. 1470, 25 June.
JOHN PASTON TO SIR JOHN PASTON.

[From Fenn, iv. 434.]

This letter, it will be seen, refers in the beginning to the same matter
the preceding.

1 On pilgrimage to the shrine of Saint Thomas Becket, I suppose.—F.
2 Richard Southwell, Esq. of Wood-Rising. He acquired this estate by
marrying Amy, daughter and co-heir of Sir Edmund Wichingnam, Knight.
—F.

To Syr John Paston, Knyght, or to Thomas Stomppys,
to delyver to the seyd Syr John.

S I sent yow woord by a lettyr that John Wymondham browght to London, J. Pampyng is endyghtyd of felony, and Edmund Broon as princypallys, and ye as axcessary, for schotyng of agonne in Awgust last past, whyche gonne kyllyd ij. men; and I trowe that my Lord of Norff. consayll wyll make on of the wedows, or bothe, to swe an apell up on the same endyghtment thys terme. Wherfor I pray yow se well to thys mater, that when it is sertyfyid in to the Kyngys Benche, Broom and Pampyng may have warnyng that they may purvey for hem self, if ther com eny *capyas* owght for hem. Townysend can tell yow all the mater.

Also ye must in eny wyse be ware, for my grauntdam[1] and myn Lady Anne[2] and myn Oncyll Wyllam shall be at London within thes viij. or x. dayis, and I wot well it is for nowght ellys but to make myn Oncyll Wyllam swyr of hyr lond, notwithstandyng she hath reryd affyn of it be for Goodreed,[3] the Justyse, in my grauntfadyrs dayis, and my modyr tellyth me that ye have the copye of the same fyne; I wold avyse yow to have it redy, what so evyr betyd. I trow they wyll be the more besy abowght the same mater, because they thynk that ye dar not com in London, nor at Westmenstyr to lett [*stop*] them; but if so be that ye have not the copy of the same fynne, look that ye spare for no cost to do serche for itt, for it wyll stand yow on hand, I feell by the werkyng.

Thys day sevennyght I trust to God to be forward to Caunterbery at the ferthest, and upon Saterday com sevennygh I tryst to God to be in London;

---

[1] Agnes Paston, widow of William Paston, the Judge.
[2] Anne, daughter of Edmund Beaufort, Duke of Somerset, married William Paston, the uncle of Sir John Paston.—F.
[3] William Goodrede was created a Serjeant-at-Law in 1425. In 1431 he was appointed King's Serjeant, and in 1434 became a Justice of the King's Bench.—F.

wherfor I pray yow leve woord at yowr plase in Fleet
Strett wher I shall fynd yow, for I purpose not to be
seyn in London tyll I have spook with yow.

I pray yow remembyr thes maters, for all is doon to
make yow to drawe to an ende with thes Lordys that
have your lond fro yow. No more, but I pray God
send yow your herttys desyir in thees maters and in
all othyr.

Wretyn at Norwyche, the Monday next aftyr Seynt
John Baptyst.   J. P.

643.

A.D. 1470, 3 July.—ABSTRACT.

[From Paston MSS.]

Indenture between Sir John Paston and Edmund Shaa, goldsmith, London, concerning 20 dishes and a saucer of silver
pledged to the latter, 3d July 10 Edw. IV.

644.

A.D. 1470, 8 July.—ABSTRACT.

[From Add. Charter, 17,249, B.M.]

Indenture, dated London, 8th July 10 Edw. IV., whereby Sir
John Paston places in pawn to Stephen Kelke, goldsmith, of
London, 16 pottingers, weighing 22 lb. 10½ oz. Troy weight, for
£40, till Whitsuntide following.

645.

A.D. 1470, 14 July.—ABSTRACTS.

FASTOLF'S LANDS.

The following entries are taken from the old index of deeds and writings
relating to Norfolk and Suffolk, preserved in the tower of Magdalen College,
Oxford.

" 11. A triparted indenture betweene William Bishop of Winton and John Paston, Knight, and others, touching the intent of
two feoffmentes of the Bishop of Wynton, the one of the mannors
of Drayton and Tolthorp, in the county of Norfolk and the city of
Norwich, which were somtymes Sir John Falstofs ; the other of

the mannors of Wynterton, cald Bregmiles (?), of Reppys in Bastwyke, the third part of the mannor of Rowneham, londes and tenementes cald Cutts in Haringby, and lands cald Buley in Stokesby, to Guy Fairfax, John Paston, Squier, et aliis. July 14, Edw. IV. 10."

" 17. Relaxatio Johannis Paston, Georgii Arch. Cant. et aliorum Willielmo Waynflet totius juris de et in omnibus maneriis, terris &c. quæ fuerunt Johannis Falstolf in comit' Norf., exceptis manerio de Castre et Spensers in Haringby, ac terris vocat' Vaux, Redham, et Bosoms, et maner' de Hayleydon, Drayton, et Tolthorp. Julii 14, Edw. IV. 10."

" 28. An indenture contayning mutuall releases of the Bishop of Wynton to John Paston, Knight, et cᵃ. July 14, Edw. IV. 10."

" 29 and 61. An indenture containing the agreement betweene Wylliam Wainflet, Bishop of Wynton, and Sir John Paston, concerning Sir John Fastolfes landes and goods. July 14, Edw. IV. 10."

This last document, of which there is another copy or draft, numbered 36 in the Index, is more fully described, as follows, by Mr. Macray, in the Fourth Report of the Historical MSS. Commission :—

1470, 14 July, 10 Edw. IV.   Indenture tripartite (very long, in English) between Bishop Wayneflete and Sir John Paston, Knight, containing an agreement for the termination of disputes between the executors of the will of Sir John Fastolf, whereby the property of the latter has been much wasted ; dividing the manors between the Bishop and Paston, and providing for the foundation of seven priests and seven poor scholars in Magdalene College ; Paston to deliver up all deeds and muniments to the Priory of St. Mary Overy, in Southwark, to be put in a chest, locked with two locks and two keys, of which the Bishop to have one and Paston the other, and the Bishop to bring thither also all his deeds ; one part of this indenture to remain with each of the parties, and the third with the Prior of St. Mary Overy.

646.

A.D. 1470, 15 July.

PAMPYNG TO SIR JOHN PASTON.

[From Paston MSS., B.M.]

Reference is made in this letter to the appeal which the two widows were to sue against Sir John Paston. *See* Nos. 641, 642.

To my most reverent and worshipfull master, Sir John Paston, Knyght.

RIGHT worshipfull sir and my good master, I recomaund me unto yow in my moost lowly wise. And please yow to wete I have with the mony ye sent me by Judy rewardid my felaship as ye comaundid, wretyn in a bille closid herin; and as for William Milsent I lete hym wete hough ye undirstood he was disposed to goo hoom to his fadere, wherof ye were pleasid and wold he shuld do so. He said he intendid not to be with his fadir, ner it was not in his power so to do; nevirthelesse he is home to his fadir and ther abidith, but what he purposith to do I wote not. Davy is at home and takyth heed to his lond. Homeworth is content and gooth to his labour. As for Stompis, I have be with the Abbot of Sen Benetts for hym as ye comaundid. And he recomaundith hym to yow, and said to me he was right glad that ye wold send to hym for any servaunt ye had, saying that if he coud do any thyng for yow, and for any servaunt of yours, he wold do it feithfully. And also he said he wold not fayle yow whill he levid in that he coud and myght do, trustyng heraftir to have your help and favour in that he shall have a do. And he told me and Stompis bothe, whanne so evir he come he shuld be welcome, and that he wold do as welle to hym as to fewe servauntes he had for yowr sake, and that he wold kepe hym for yow. As for my self my mastres saith she woll geve me mete and drynk for a season; nevirthelesse I am warnyd to be ware, for it is told me that ther is processe out upon the appele ayens me and other; wherfore I beseche yow that that mater may be take heed to as ye may, that we myght have knowlech of any processe ther be, that we may be ware, for I thynk verely, and I or any other come in ther hands this world, we shuld not escape without shame at the leest.

Item, as for the remnaunt of the mony biside

this bille, ye owe to the parson of Sent Edmondes
Caster for iiij. combe malt, and ij. combe whete, xs.
whiche I promysid hym to pay; and Rob. Newton
lymebrenner for lyme, xiijs. iiij*d*., calling upon me for
it; and Robert Bery for shoyng, xs.; and if it please
yow that I make payment herof there shall remayne
in my handes xxiijs. iiij*d*. And what ye woll I do
herin, I beseche yow to send me word. Judy hath
be with Thom Fastolff, he can telle yow answer in
that mater. As for the rewle at Caster, they selle
and make mony of such stuffe as they fond there, and
kepe other rewle that the contre is full sory and irk of,
and of my lordes men resortyng to hem, and riden
about the contry onknowen, and by berynges on hand [1]
take large bribys. I pray God be your spede and
send yow some good meane for your wele and ease to
them that owe yow servise. Wretyn at Norwich the
Monday next aftir Relik Sonday,

Your pore servaunt,

Pampyng.

647.

A.D. 1470, 15 July.
MARGARET PASTON TO SIR JOHN PASTON.

[From Paston MSS., B.M.]

This letter, although subscribed "By your mother," is neither signed nor
addressed. It is, however, undoubtedly from Margaret Paston to her son
Sir John. It is written in Pampyng's hand. and seems to be of the same year
as his own letter immediately preceding, which is dated on the same day.

GRETE yow well and send yow Goddes
blissyng and myne, letyng yow wete that
your fermours have brought me a gret bille
of reparacion, the which I send yow, with
lxs. in mony. I wold have had the residue of the
mony of them, and they said it was your agrement

[1] See Vol. I., page 90, Note 1.

that this reparacion shuld be do and alowed now at this payment, and so I coud get no more mony of them. And they say that the parson[1] was prevy to the reparacion. If ye were thus agreed and woll have the reparacion examined ye may send word; but I wold ye shuld purvey for your self as hastely as ye may, and come home and take heed to your owne and to myn therto, otherwise thanne ye have do bifore this, bothe for my profite and for yours, or ellis I shall purvey for my self otherwise in hast, so that I trust shall be more ease and avayle for me and non ease nor profite to yow in tyme to come. I have litell help nor comfort of non of yow yet, God geve me grase to have heraftir. I wold ye shuld assay whedir it be more profitable for yow to serve me thanne for to serve such masters as ye have servid afore this, and that ye fynde mooste profitable theraftir do in tyme to come. Ye have assayed the werld resonabilly, ye shall knowe your self the bettir heraftir. I pray God we may be in quyete and in rest with oure own from hens forth. My power is nat so good as I wold it were for your sake and other; and if it were, we shuld not longe be in daungere. God brynge us oute of it; who have yow in His kepynge. Wretyn with onhertes ease the Monday next aftir Relike Sonday.

> By your Modir.

648.

A.D. 1470, 5 Aug.

SIR JOHN PASTON TO JOHN PASTON.

[From Fenn, ii. 46.]

This letter, as it will be seen from the contents, was written at the period just before the restoration of Henry VI.

---

[1] Sir Thomas Howes.

. . . . . *Paston, &c.*

BROTHER, I comand me to yow, &c. . . .[1]
Also telle John Pampyng that the mayde at
the Bulle at Cludeys at Westminster sent me
on a tyme by hym to the Moor a rynge of
goolde to a tookne, whyche I hadde not off hym.
Wherffor I wolle he scholde sende it hyedre, ffor sche
most have itt ageyn, or ellys vs., ffor it was not hyrrys.
Item, I praye yow be redye ; the mater qwykennythe
bothe ffor yowe and yowres as well as ffor us and
howrys.

As ffor tydynges, my Lorde Erchebysshop[2] is at the
Moor, but ther is beleffte with hym dyverse off the
Kynges servantes, and as I understond he hathe
lysence to tarry ther tyll he be sente ffor. Ther be
many ffolkes uppe in the northe, soo that Percy[3] is
not able to recyst them; and soo the Kynge hathe
sente ffor hys ffeeodmen to koom to hym, for he woll
goo to putt them downe. And soom seye that the
Kynge sholde come ageyn to London, and that in
haste, and as it is sayde Cortenayes be londyd in
Devenschyr, and ther rewle.

Item, that the Lordes Clarance and Warwyk woll
assaye to londe in Inglonde evyrye daye, as ffolkes
ffeer.

I praye yow late not John Mylsent be longe ffrom
me, with as moche as can be gaderyd : and also that
ye wryght to me off all thynges that I have wretyn to
yow ffor, so that I may have answer off every thynge.
Other thynges Bacheler Walter, berer heroff, schall
informe yow.

---

1 Here follows an order about searching for some writings, &c.—F.
2 This must mean George Neville, Archbishop of York, and brother to the
Earl of Warwick, who seems to have been suspected by the King, and left at
the Moor as a kind of state prisoner.—F.
3 Henry Percy, who was restored to the Earldom of Northumberland this
year on its surrender by John Nevill, Lord Montague. *See* No. 638.

Wretyn at London, the Sondaye nexte beffor Seynt Lawrence Daye.[1]

Also my brother Edmonde is not yet remembryd. He hathe not to lyff with, thynk on hym, &c.

JOHN PASTON, KT.

649.

A.D. 1470, 7 Aug.—ABSTRACT.

[From Add. Charter, 17,250, B.M.]

Indenture, dated London, 7th Aug. 10 Edw. IV., whereby Sir John Paston puts in pawn to Ric. Rawlyn of London, grocer, 2 chargers and 4 potengers, weighing 11 lb. 1¾ oz. silver, for £20, till Whitsunday following.

650.

ABSTRACT.

The following abstract, like some others peceding, is taken from Mr. Macray's Report to the Historical MSS. Commission on the Records of Magdalen College, Oxford.

1470, 10 Aug. 10 Edw. IV., at Eshher.   Undertaking in English by John Paston, Esq., son of John Paston, Esq., who was one of the feoffees and executors of Sir John Fastolf, that whereas Bishop Waynflete, also one of the feoffees, and now sole executor, has taken upon him to perform the will of the said Sir John, so far forth as it may be performed (it being in most substance not yet performed, and his property wasted and devoured), out of his manors and lands in Essex, Surrey, Norfolk, Suffolk, and the city of Norwich, he (the said John Paston) will do true and faithful service to the said Bishop, and will be aiding and assisting to him and Magdalen College, in order that the lands may be let to their greatest profit, he being rewarded by the Bishop, to show his very good will to the due performing of Fastolf's will ; and that before the Feast of All Saints next he will deliver up to the said Bishop all charters, deeds, evidences, rentals, accounts, &c., pertaining to any of the said manors, excepting such as concern solely the manor of Castre, which by covenant of the said Bishop with Sir John Paston, Knight, brother of the said John Paston, Squire, must remain with the same Sir John.

---

[1] St. Laurence's day is the 10th of August.

651.

A.D. 1470.—ABSTRACTS.

[From Paston MSS., B.M.]

PAINTER'S WORK.

1. Account of payments to Robert Spery, servant of Vyol, and others, for working at the Frerys[1] in June and July; also for varnish, lead, earthen pans, yellow ochre, oil, bristles to make brushes, &c., for painter's work.

Endorsed: "Vialles byll comprisid in the iij. rolles of stuff and werkmanship to A. P.[2] place and the Freris, which, as Clargynet understondith, is paid to Viall."

"Memorandum : j. copy of this bill remayneth amonges the billes of werkmanship at the White Freres and Baretts place, and a noder among the billes of plate and Vialles plegis."

2. "Bill indented," 15th Aug. 10 Edw. IV., between William Paston, Esq., and Thomas Vyall of Norwich, painter, relative to the pledging of certain coral beads and plate to the former, for £5.

3. Account of sums owing to one Vyall for certain persons "at the Freris," during August, September, and October. Total, 32s. 10d.

Endorsed: "Viall's reckoning written in the roll of the Freris werke not paid, and must be allowed of the £5 that was lent to Viall not yet content again.

"Memorandum : one copy of this bill remaineth amongs the bills of workmanship at the White Freris and Baretts place, and another bill amongs the bills of plate and pledges."

652.

A.D. 1470, 27 Aug.

FASTOLF'S COLLEGE.

The following entry is from the same old index of deeds in Magdalen College, Oxford, referred to in previous Nos.

"4. John Paston, Squier, bindes himself to doe true and faith-full service to the Bishop of Winton, and to be ayding to his college and other his officers and tenants, for the landes of Sir John Falstolf, and to deliver to him all deedes, evidences, &c., except such as concerne the manor of Castre. Aug. 27, Edw. IV. 10."

---

[1] Apparently the White Friars at Norwich.　　　[2] Agnes Paston's ?

653.

A.D. 1470, 7 Sept.—Edward IV. to William Swan.

[From Fenn, iv. 438.]

This letter does not properly belong to the Paston correspondence. It was copied by Fenn from an original in the library of Brigg Price Fountaine, Esq. of Narford, in Norfolk, nephew and heir of the celebrated antiquary, Sir Andrew Fountaine. The MS. was contained in a volume of State Papers, some of them originals, and some copies, of various dates, which had belonged to Sir Edward Coke.

The date of the document is undoubtedly in September 1470, when Edward was at York, anticipating the invasion of Clarence and the Earl of Warwick. aided by the King of France.

To oure welbelovid William Swan, Gentilman.

R. E.   By the King.

TRUSTY and welbeloved, we grete you well. And for soo muche as we be credibly acertayned that our auncient ennemyes of Fraunce and our outward rebells and traitors be drawe to gadre in acorde, and entende hastily to lande in our countre of Kent, or in the parties therof ner adjonyng, with grete might and power of Frenshemen, utterly to destroie us and our true subgietts, and to subverte the comon wele of the same our royalme : We straitly charge and commaunde you, upon the feyth and liegeaunce that ye bare unto us, that ye arredie you with alle the felaship ye can make, and as sone as ye may undrestonde that thay lande in our said countie or nerbye, that you draw thider, as we have comaunded othere our subgietts to doo, and put you in uttremost devoir with thaim to resiste the malice of our said ennemyes and traitours ; and if thai and ye be not of power soo to doo, that thanne ye drawe you to our citie of London, by which tyme we trust to be there in our owne personne or nerby; and if we be not that, that thanne ye do farther all ye shal bee commaunded by our Counsail there, upon the payne above said.

Yeven undre oure signet at oure citie of York, the vij. day of Septembr.

THE PASTON LETTERS.

Henry VI. Restored.

654.

A.D. 1470, 12 Oct.
JOHN PASTON TO MARGARET PASTON.

[From Fenn, ii. 50.]

The contents of this letter clearly refer to the state of matters on the restoration of Henry VI.

To my ryght worchipfull Modyr, Margaret Paston, be thys delyuered.

FTYR humbyll and most dew recommenda-cyon, as lowly as I can, I besche yow of yowr blyssyng. Plesyt yow to wet that, blyssyd be God, my brodyr and I be in good hele; and I tryst that we shall do ryght well in all owyr maters hastyly; ffor my Lady of Norff.[1] hathe promyssyd to be rewlyd by my Lord of Oxynforthe[2] in all syche maters as belonge to my brodyr and to me; and as for my Lord of Oxynforthe, he is bettyr Lord to me, by my trowthe, than I can wyshe hym in many

---

[1] Elizabeth, daughter of John Talbot, first Earl of Shrewsbury, was the wife of John Mowbray, fifth Duke of Norfolk.
[2] John de Vere, a staunch Lancastrian.

maters; for he sente to my Lady of Norff. by John
Bernard only for my mater, and for non othyr cause,
my onwetyng [*i.e.* without my knowledge], or wythout
eny preyer of me, for when he sente to hyr I was at
London, and he at Colchestyr, and that is a lyeklyod
he remembyrthe me.

The Dwk and the Dwchess swe to hym as humbylly
as evyr I dyd to them; in so myche that my Lord of
Oxynforth shall have the rwyll of them and thers, by
ther owne desyirs and gret meanys.

As for the ofyces that ye wrot to my brodyr for and
to me, they be for no poore men; but I tryst we shall
sped of othyr ofyseys metly for us, for my Mastyr
the Erle of Oxynforthe bydeth me axe and have.   I
trow my brodyr Syr John shall have the Constabyllshep
of Norwyche Castyll, with xx*li.* of ffee; all the Lordys
be agreyd to it.

Tydyngs, the Erle of Wyrcestyr[1] is lyek to dye this
day, or to morow at the ferthest.   John Pylkyngton,
Mr. W. att Clyff, and Fowler ar takyn, and in the
Castyll of Pomfrett, and ar lyek to dye hastyly, with
owte they be dead.   Sir T. Mongomere and Joudone
be takyn; what shall falle of hem I can not sey.

The Qwen[2] that was, and the Dwchess of Bedford,[3]
be in seyntuary at Westmestyr; the Bysheop of Ely[4]
with othyr Bysheopys ar in Seynt Martyns.   When I
here more, I shall send yow more.   I prey God send
yow all your desyrs.   Wretyn at London on Seynt
Edwards Evyn.

Your sone and humbyll servant,

J. P.

Modyr, I beseche yow that Brome may be spoken
to, to gadyr up my syllvyr at Gwton in all hast pos-

---

[1] John Tiptoft, Lord Treasurer and Chief-Constable of England.   He was
beheaded on a charge of cruelty, 18th October 1470.
[2] Elizabeth Woodville, Queen of Edward IV.
[3] Jaquetta of Luxemburg, Duchess-Dowager of Bedford, widow of Sir
Richard Woodville, the mother of Edward's queen.
[4] William Gray.

sybyll, for I have no mony. Also that it lyek yow that John Mylsent may be spoken to, to kep well my grey horse, and he be alyve, and that he spare no met on hym, and that he have konnyng lechys to look to hym. As for my comyng hom, I knowe no serteynte, for I terry tyll my Lady of Norff. com to go thorow with the maters, and she shall not be here tyll Sonday.

655.

A.D. 1470, 22 Oct.—The Duke of Suffolk's Men.

[From Fenn, iv. 448.]

The battle here referred to as "Lincoln Field" is what is commonly called the battle of Stamford, in which the insurrection of Sir Robert Welles in Lincolnshire was completely defeated in March 1470. Just before the date of this document, Edward IV. had left the kingdom, and Henry VI. had been restored ; but perhaps Suffolk was not aware of the situation, or did not recognise it.

To the Baillies, Constables, and Chamberleyns of our Burgh of Eye, and to everch of them.

The Duke of Suff.

FOR asmuche as Edmond Lee and John Barker, which were waged for your town to awaite upon us in the Kings service to Lincolne Feld, and from thens to Excestre and ayen, and for that season, as we be enformed, thei ar not yet fully contented and paied of their wages ; wherfore upon the sighte herof we woll and charge that ye, with oute any lenger delay, paie them their hooll duties acording the covenants that ye made with them, and ye faille not herof as ye entende our pleaser.

Wreten at Wyngefeld, the xxij^{th} day of Octobr.

SUFFOLK.

656.

A.D. 1470, 15 Nov.
SIR JOHN PASTON TO JOHN PASTON.

[From Fenn, iv. 450.]

From what is said in this letter about the Earl of Oxford, it is impossible it could have been written at any other time than during the brief restoration of Henry VI., which only lasted from October 1470 till April following.

To John Paston, Esquyere, in haste.

BROTHER, I comand me to yow, praying yow that thys be yow guydyng, if other folkys wy[ll] agree to the same, that Mr. Roos, olde Knevett, ye, and the worshypfullest that wyll do for owr sake, as Arblaster, John Gyneye, Wodhows, and al other gentelmen that at the daye wyll be in Norwyche, that ye all holl as on bodye come to geder, that my Lorde of Oxenforde maye ondrestande that som strenkethethe restyth ther by, whyche if it be well handely[d] and prove in the handely[ng], I trow Heydonnes parte woll be but an easy comparyson. Neverthelesse ye than most ye bewar of on [*one*] payn, and that is thys : Heydon wyll of crafte sende amonge yow for [1] case vj. or mor with harneyse for to sclandre yowr felawschep, with seyng that they be ryotous peple, and natt of substance. Requer the gentelmen above wretyn that if any men be in Norwyche of the contre that ber any suche harneyse, to do them leve it or any glysteryng byll.

The Meyr and siteseynes of Nowyche wher wonte to have asertayne [2] in harneyse of men of the town to the nombr of ij. or iij. or v.c, whyche if they now do in lyke case, those wole owe better wyll to Mr. Roos and yow than to other folkys ; and if it be so that the thowt nat to have non suche at thys tyme, I thynke the Meyr woll do it at the request of Mr. Roos and yow, if lak of tyme cawse it not.

---

[1] *for.* The copy in modern spelling reads *per.*
[2] *A certain, i.e.* a number.

Item, be well war of Clopton, for he hathe avysed my Lorde to be all to gydre rewled by Heydon, in so moche he hathe reportyd that all thyng and all materys of my Lordes, and in all the contre, scholde guydyd by Heydon. If Clopton or Hygham or Lowes John be besy, prese in to my Lorde byfor them, for the be no Suff.[1] materys, and tell the raylyng; prayng them not to cawse my Lorde to owe hys favor for the pleser to som folkys ther present. For if my Lorde favoryd or theye owther, by lykelyed my Lorde and they myght lose vj. tyme as many frendes as he scholde wynn by ther meanes. Also if ye cowde fynde the meanes, Mr. R. and ye, to cawse [the] Meyr in my Lordes ere to telle hym, thow he scholde bynde my Lorde to concell, that the love of the contre and syte restyth on owr syde, and that other folkys be not belovyd, ner nevyr wer, thys wolde do nonn harme, if it be soo that that all thynge go olyver currant (?); with mor to remembre that ther is owt of that contre that be nat at Norw. besyde me, that be ryght worshypfull, and as worshypfull as few be lengyng to Norff., that woll and schall do my Lorde servyse the rather for my sake and Master Rossys, and the rather if my Lorde semyth nat moche thynge to Heydon guydyng.

Also, the godely menes wherby ye best can entrete my cosyn Sir W. Calthorpe at the seyde day, wse them to cawe hym, if itt wyll be, to come, ye in hys companye, and he in yow in cheff at yow cheff schew, and Mr. Roos and he in company, latyng my seyde cosyn wete that I tolde hym ones that I scholde meve hym of a thyng I trostyn scholde be encressyng bothe to hys honor and well.

I sende yow a lettyr, com to Norwyche by lyklyed to yow on Monday last past. It come some what the lattre, for I wende have dyed nat longe by foer it. Also I receyved on from yow by Mr. Blomvyle yister

---

[1] I retain this word in the abbreviated form in which it is printed in Fenn's literal transcript; the copy in modern spelling reads *sufficient*.

evyn. Tell my cosyn W. Yelverton that he may not
appyr of a whylle in no wyse. I trow my cosyn hys
fadr schall sende hym worde of the same. Do that ye
can secretly that my Lorde be nat hevy Lorde on to
hym. It is undrestande that itt is doon by the craffte
of Heydon. He gate hym in to that offyce to have to
be ageyn me, and nowe he sethe that he hathe don all
that he can ageyn me, and now may doo no mor;
nowe he wolde remeve hym. The daye is comen that
he fastyd the evyn for, as an holye yonge monke fastyd
mor than all the covent, aftr that for hys holynesse
and fastyng hopyd to be abbott, whyche afterwarde
was abbott; than lefte he hys abstynens, seyng, "The
daye was come that he fast the evyn for."

Brother, I pray yow recomand me to my Lord of
Oxford gode Lordshyp. And wher as I told my Lord
that I shuld have awayted uppon hys Lordsyp in
Norff., I wold that I myght soo have don lever then a
hundred *li.*; but in godefeth thos maters that I told
my Lord trewed shold lette me war not fynyshed tyl
yesterday. Wherfor yf that cause, and also syn Halow-
masse every other day myst not hold uppe myn heed,
nor yet may, in semech that sythen the seyd day, in
Westminster Halle and in other place, I have goon
with a staffe as a goste, as men sayd, more lyke that I
rose owte of the erth then owte of a fayr laydys bedd;
and yet am in lyke case, savyng I am in gode hope
to amende. Wherfor I beshyche hys Lordshyp to
pardon me, and at a nother tyme I shall make dobell
amends; for by my trouth a man cowyd not have
hyred me for v. mark with so gode will to have ryden
in to Norff. as to have at thys season ther to have
awaytyd in hys Lordshyp, and also I wold have ben
glad for my Lord shold have knowyn what servys that
I myght have don hys Lordshyp in that contray.

Item, your geer ys send to you, as Thomas Stampes
sayth, savyng Mylsents geer and the shafeson,[1] whych
I cannot entrete Thomas Stampes to goo therfor thys

---

[1] *Chevron.* a covering for a horse's head, made of iron and leather.

iij. or iiij. days, wherfor I knokkyd hym on the crowne, &c.

Item, loke that ye take hyde that the letter wer not broken or that it com to your hands, &c. Wryten at London, on Thursday next after Seynt Erkenwolds Day, &c.   JOHN PASTON, K.

657.

A.D. 1470, 6 Dec.—ABSTRACT.

The following abstract is taken from Mr. Macray's Report on the Documents in Magdalen College, Oxford, already referred to.

[1470] 6 Dec., on paper. Notice in English from the Duke of Norfolk to Philippe Cosard, William Dux, and other of his servants and tenants in the counties of Norfolk and Suffolk, to depart out of the manor of Castre, and all other manors and lands which he bought of Sir W. Yelverton and other executors of Sir J. Fastolf, as soon as they can conveniently remove all his stuff and their own which is therein, he having consented, at the desire of the Archbishop of Canterbury, the Chancellor of England, and the Bishop of Winchester, to give up the said manor, &c. Signed by the Duke, "Norff." Small seal of arms, three lions passant, in chief, a label of three points, a straw round the seal.

658.

A.D. 1470, 11 Dec.—ABSTRACT.

This abstract is also taken from Mr. Macray's Report on the Documents in Magdalen College.

1470, 11 Dec., 49 Hen. VI., "and of the readepcion of his roiall power 1." Release (in English) from John, Duke of Norfolk, to Bishop Wayneflete,,of the manors of Castre, Wyntertone, Baytone, Bastwik, and Tolthorpe, in Norfolk, and of Caldecote, Burneviles or Burnegyles, in Suffolk, which had been sold to him by Nicholas, Abbot of Langle, Will. Yelverton, Knight, Justice, Thomas Howes, clerk, and Will. Worcetre, and of which the said Yelverton, Howes, and Will. Jenney, as feoffees, with others, for Sir J. Fastolf, of the said manors, enfeoffed the said Duke and others by deed, dated 1st Oct., 8 Edw. IV. [1468], the said Duke being informed by the Archbishops of York and Canterbury, and by the said Bishop of Winchester, that the said bargain was made contrary to the will of the said Sir John Fastolf. Covenants also to deliver up all evidences concerning the same, specially the said deed of feoffment and two papers,

II.   2 E

one with four seals specifying the said bargain, and another with
three seals specifying a license to enter on all Fastolf's manors
till the bargain be performed. And for this reconveyance the
said Bishop pays to the said Duke 500 marks.

659.

A.D. 1470, 24 Dec.—ABSTRACT.

This abstract is from the same report as the two last.

1470, 24 Dec., 49 Hen. VI., "and of the readepcione of his
royall power, the first." Acknowledgment by "the highe and
myghti Prynce, John, Duke of Norff.," of the receipt of 100 marks
from the Bishop of Winchester, being part of 250 marks which
the said Bishop has promised to pay upon knowledge of the
delivery of the manor of Castre, and other lordships specified in
a writing between the said parties, unto the feoffees of the said
Bishop.

660.

A.D. 1470 (?) [28] Dec.
MARGARET PASTON TO JOHN PASTON.

[From Fenn, iv. 288.]

This letter was probably written in or about the year 1470. Anne Paston,
the sister of John Paston, here mentioned, was married to William Yelverton,
a grandson of the Judge, in 1474 (Itin. W. Wyrc. 369), and the match had
been already determined (as will appear in a future letter) before June 1472.
At the date of this letter she was still staying in Calthorpe's household, into
which, after the manner of the times, she had been sent for her education;
and Calthorpe desiring to reduce his establishment, suggested, somewhat
earlier than her mother anticipated, that it was time to provide a husband
for her.

To John Paston the yonger, be this delivered in hast.

 GRETE you wele, and send you Godds blyssyng and myn, latyng you wete that sith ye
departed my Cosyn Calthorp sent me a
letter, compleyning in his wrytyng that for
asmych as he can not be payd of his tenaunts as he
hat be befor this tyme, he purposith to lesse his hows-

hold, and to leve the streytlyer. Wharfor he desireth
me to purvey for your suster Anne; he seth she
waxeth hygh, and it wer tyme to purvey her a mariage.

I marveyll what causeth hym to write so now; outher
she hath displeased hym, or ell[es] he hath takyn her
with diffaught. Therfor I pray you comune with my
Cosyn Clere at London, and wete how he is dysposyd to
her ward, and send me word, for I shall be fayn to send
for her, and with me she shall but lese her tyme, and
with ought she wull be the better occupied she shall
oftyn tymes meve me, and put me in gret inquiete-
nesse. Remembr what labour I had with your suster,
therfor do your parte to help her forth, that may be to
your wurchiep and myn.

Item, remembr the bill that I spake to you of, to
gete of your brother of such money as he hath receyvid
of me sith your faders disseas. Se your Unkyll
Mautby, if ye may, and send me sume tydyngs as
sonee as ye may. God kepe you.

Wretyn the Fryday next befor Sent Thomas of
Caunterbury, in hast.

By your Moder.

661.

A.D. 1471, 12 Feb.—ABSTRACT.

[From MS. Index in Magd. Coll., Oxford.]

Norfolk and Suffolk Deeds, No. 50. "John Paston, Knight,
binds himself to performe all appoyntments made betweene him
and W. Wanflet, Byshop of Winton, concerning certayne landes
which were Sir John Fastolfes. Feb. 12, Hen VI. 49."

662.

A.D. 1471, 14 Feb.—ABSTRACT.

[From a MS. in the Bodleian Library.]

Release by John Beauchamp, Knight, Lord Beauchamp, to
John Paston and Roger Townesend, Esqs., of his interest in the

manors of Castre called Redhams, Vaus, and Bosoms ; and in the
manors of Begviles in Wyntirton, Spensers in Heryngby, Reppes
in Bastwyk, and a third part of the manor of Runham ; and in
all lands called Billes in Stokesby, Cattes in Haringby, a mes-
suage called Dengayns in Yarmouth, and all lands and tenements
in the hundreds of East Flegge and West Flegge in Norfolk ;
which premises Lord Beauchamp lately had in conjunction with
Thomas Archbishop of Canterbury, William Yelverton, Justice,
William Jenney, Serjeant-at-law, and William Paston, now sur-
viving, and John Radclyff of Attylburgh, John Paston, Hen.
Fylongley, Esqs.. Thomas Howes, clerk, and Thomas Grene,
now deceased, of the gift and feoffment of Ralph Boteler, Knight,
Lord Sudeley, Ric. Waller, Esq., Sir William Oldhall, Esq., Thos.
West, Esq., William Wangford, and Nich. Girlyngton.

Dated 14th Feb., 49 and 1 Hen. VI.

663.

A.D. 1471, 14 March.
THE EARL OF OXFORD TO THOMAS VERE.

[From Fenn, ii. 54.]

It is sufficiently apparent from the contents that this was written during
the restoration of Henry VI., and in anticipation of the attempt by King
Edward, which was very soon afterwards successful, to recover his throne.
Edward in fact landed at Ravenspur the very day this letter was written.

To my right dere and welbeloved brother, Thomas Veer.

RIGHT dere and welbeloved brother, I command me hertly unto you ; certyfying you that
I have receyved your writing, directed now
laste unto me, by my servant William Cooke,
by which I understande the faithfull gwydyng and disposicion of the cuntre, to my gret cumfote and pleaser ;
which I dowbte not shall redunde to the grethest presyng
and worship that ever dide till eny cuntre ; certyfying
you ferdermore that by Nicheson of your other tydyngs
laste send unto me ; also thes by Robt. Porter.   I
have disposed me with all the power that I can make
in Essex and Suffolk, Cambrygeshire, and other places,
to be on Monday next comyng at Bury, which purpose
I intende to observe, with Godds grace, towards you

in to Norffolk, to the assistence of you and the cuntre, in case Edwarde with his companye had aryved ther, and yete I shall do the same noughtwithstandyng; for if he aryve northwarde, like as ye wete by likelyhode he shulde, I caste to folow and porsew hym. And where ye desire that I shulde send you woorde what disposicion shalbe take in the cuntre wher ye be, I desire you that ye, by theadvyse of the gentilmen which ben there, chese iij. or iiij., and send theym to me at Bury on Monday next; and than I and they, with my Counceyle, shall take a direccion for the suretie of all that cuntre, by Godds grace; by whome I shall send than to you relacion, wheder ye shall remayne still ther your selff, or resorte to me with all thos that be accompanyed with you. And Jhesu preserve you. At Hithingham [*Hedingham*], the xiiij. day of Marche.

> By your lovyng brothyr,
> OXYNFORD.

664.

A.D. 1471, 19 March.
THE EARL OF OXFORD TO HENRY SPILMAN AND OTHERS.

[From Fenn, ii. 58.]

This letter was evidently written five days after the last.

To my right trusty and welbelovyd Henry Spilman, Thos. Seyve, John Seyve, James Radclif, John Brampton the older, and to eche of them.

TRUSTY and welbeloved, I comende me to you, lettyng you witte that I have credible tydyngs that the Kyngs gret enemys and rebellis, acompanyed with enemys estraungers, be nowe aryved, and landyd in the north parties of this his land, to the utter destruction of his roiall persone, and subversion of all his realm, if they myght atayne; whom to encountre and resiste the Kings Highnesse hath comaunded and assigned me, under his seall, sufficient power and auctorite to call, reyse, gader, and assemble, fro tyme to tyme, all his liege people of the shire of Norff., and other places, to assiste, ayde, and strenght me in the same entent.

Wherfor, in the Kyngs name, and by auctorite aforesaid, I straitly charge and command you, and in my owne byhalf hertly desire and pray you, that, all excuses leid apart, ye, and eche of you in your owne persones defensibly araied, with asmony men as ye may goodly make, be on Fryday next comyng at Lynne, and so forth to Newark, where, with the leve of God, I shall not faile to be at that tyme; entendyng fro thence to goo foorth with the help of God, you, and my fryndes, to the recountr of the said enemyes; and that ye faill not hereof, as ye tendre the weele of our said sovereygne Lord, and all this his realme.   Written at Bury, the xix^{th} day of Marche.   OXYNFORD.

665.

A.D. 1471.
JAMES GRESHAM TO SIR JOHN PASTON.

[From Fenn, ii. 60.]

The political news in this letter show that it was written after the landing of Edward IV. in Yorkshire.

To the right worshipfull and speciall singler maister,
Sir John Paston, Knyght, be this delyvered.

FTER due recomendacion hadde with all my service, &c. . . . . . .[1]
As for tydyngs, here in this cuntre be many tales, and non accorth with other.   It

---

[1] "Here," according to Fenn, "follow copies of indictments and appeals procured against Sir John Paston and his servants; and likewise other law business." The indictments and appeals in question are doubtless those referred to in the next No.

is tolde me by the Undirshireve that my Lord of
Clarence is goon to his brother, late Kyng; in so
moche that his men have the Gorget[1] on their breests,
and the Rose over it. And it is seid that the Lord
Howard hath proclamed Kyng E. Kyng of Inglond
in Suff., &c.

Yours, and at your comandement,
JAMES GRESHAM.

666.

ABSTRACT.

[From Paston MSS., B.M.]

A Register of Writs, &c., which was probably sent with the
preceding letter. It is addressed on the back, "To Sir John
Paston," and endorsed "James Gresham."

Distringas against Sir John Paston, late of Castre, for his
appearance in the King's Bench, Easter, 8 Edw. IV. "Per
Contr. de Anno viijo E. iiijti Ro. xxviij.[2] Vynter."

Distringas against Sir John Paston and Ric. Calle, late of
Castre, with *capias* against William Wykes, late of Castre;
Edmund Brome, late of Redeham ; and John Dawebeney, late
of Castre ; Thurstan Cokesson, *alias* Starky, late of Castre; John
Pampyng, late of Castre ; and Henry Swete, late of Castre,
yeoman, for their appearance in the King's Bench in Easter to
answer for offences against the statute *de ingressibus manu forti.*
"Per Contr' de Anno viijo E. iiijti Ro. xxviij. Vynter."

"Of these ij. writtes ar *supersedeas* delyvered to the Undir-
shirreve."

Writ of exigent against John Pampyng, late of Castre, gent.,
and Edmund Brome of Castre, gent., "Oct' Joh'is," appealed by
Cecilia, widow of John Colman, as principals in the death of
her husband. Ro. 67. "Breve istud deliberatur de recordo,
Hill. xlix. Sonde."

Another writ of exigent against Pampyng and Brome at the
King's suit for divers felonies and murders. "Ro. xvj. Per
Contr' de Anno xo E. iiijti Ro. xijo Vynter.

Distringas against Sir John Paston and Ric. Calle for their
appearance in the King's Bench in Easter term, on an indictment
for forcible entry. "Per Contr' de Anno viijo E. iiijti Ro.
xxix."

---

[1] A collar worn round the neck.—F.

[2] The Controlment Roll 8 Edw. IV. is now missing.

Distringas against Sir John Paston and Ric. Calle, with *capias* against John Wykes, late of Castre, Edmund Brome, John Dawebeney, and Thurstan Cokesson, *alias* Starky, late of Castre, for their appearance in the King's Bench in Easter term, on an indictment of forcible entry. "Per Contr' de Anno viij. E. iiijti. Ro. xxviij. Vynter."

Distringas against Sir John Paston and Ric. Calle, with *capias* against John Wykes, Edmund Brome, John Dawebeney, and Thurstan, &c., for Easter. "Per Contr. de Anno viij. Ro. xxviij. Vynter."

Capias against John Pampyng, late of Castre, Edmund Brome, late of Redeham, William Bedford, and Edmond Mason, late of Bychamwelle, laborer, and Alex. Cok of Norwich, yeoman, "xv. Pasch.," appealed by Christiana, widow of Thos. Mylys, in Easter term, as principals in the death of her husband. Also *capias* against William Paston of Norwich and Ralph Lovell of Bychamwelle, gent., appealed as accessaries. Ro. lxix. Registrum Sonde."

*** All the above writs are for the county of Norfolk.

667.

A.D. 1471, 10 April.—ABSTRACT.

The following is another entry from the old index of deeds in Magdalen College, Oxford. There is probably some slight error in the date, as Edward IV. was not acknowledged as king on the 10th April, in what would otherwise have been the eleventh year of his reign. He was so acknowledged a few days later—*i.e.*, after the battle of Barnet, which was fought on the 14th April—so that if the date had been, say, April 20, instead of April 10, it would have been quite consistent. It is impossible, however, to say where the error lies, so we place the document under the date actually expressed in it.

"30. Relaxatio Johannis Paston facta episc. Winton. et aliis totius juris in maneriis vocat. Akethorp in Leyestoft, Spitlings in Gorleston, Habland in Bradwell, &c., quæ quondam fuerunt Johannis Fastolf.—April 10, Edw. IV. 11."

END OF VOLUME II.